T0114288

<small>Thomas Bernhard</small>

Gathering Evidence
and
My Prizes

Thomas Bernhard was born in Holland in 1931 and grew up in Austria. He studied music at the Universität Mozarteum in Salzburg. In 1957 he began a second career, as a playwright, poet, and novelist. The winner of the three most distinguished and coveted literary prizes awarded in Germany, he has become one of the most widely translated and admired writers of his generation. He published nine novels, an autobiography, one volume of poetry, four collections of short stories, and six volumes of plays. Thomas Bernhard died in Austria in 1989.

INTERNATIONAL

ALSO BY THOMAS BERNHARD

Gathering Evidence

A Memoir

Translated from the German by David McLintock

and

My Prizes

An Accounting

Translated from the German by Carol Brown Janeway

THOMAS BERNHARD

VINTAGE INTERNATIONAL
Vintage Books
A Division of Random House, Inc.
New York

SECOND VINTAGE INTERNATIONAL EDITION, NOVEMBER 2011

Gathering Evidence translation copyright © 1985 by Alfred A. Knopf, Inc.
My Prizes translation copyright © 2010 by Carol Brown Janeway

The Cataloging-in-Publication Data is available at the Library of Congress.

Vintage ISBN: 978-1-4000-7762-5

www.vintagebooks.com

CONTENTS

TRANSLATOR'S NOTE

Thomas Bernhard published his autobiography in five separate volumes in 1975, 1976, 1978, 1981 and 1982. The first four deal with his boyhood between the ages of thirteen and nineteen; the fifth, which is here placed first, completes the cycle with a record of his early childhood.

Bernhard once told an interviewer (Jean-Louis de Rambures of *Le Monde*): "I never wanted to write an autobiographical work, being averse to anything autobiographical. The fact is that at a certain moment in my life I conceived a curiosity about my childhood. I said to myself, 'I haven't much longer to live, so why not try and record my life down to the age of nineteen? Not as it really was—there's no such thing as objectivity—but as I see it today.' I set to work, intending to write a small volume. This was followed by a second. Then by a third . . . until I reached the point where I began to get bored. After all childhood always remains childhood. After the fifth volume I decided to call it a day."

Readers already acquainted with Bernhard's fiction may be surprised by this professed aversion to autobiography when they find familiar motifs and attitudes recurring in the present work. Bernhard has never gone in for straightforward narration, and even here he prefers to describe isolated or recurrent incidents, states of affairs and states of mind, filtered through the consciousness of the writer in his middle to late forties. There is a shifting perspective: at times he views his youth from the standpoint of the present, at others from some intermediate point; sometimes he seems to succeed in recapturing the sensations and attitudes of his former self.

At one point in the autobiography Bernhard expatiates on the impossibility of being objective, insisting that while we may always wish to tell the truth we succeed only in telling lies. Considering that the autobiography was written over a period of years (during which Bernhard was chiefly engaged in writing for the theatre), the reader will not be surprised to discover certain minor or major contradictions. The most striking of these is perhaps the discrepancy between his two accounts of his mother's aborted career as a ballerina. Throughout the work his chief concern is to discover how his personality was shaped by his ancestry, the surroundings in which he grew up, and the conditions he had to endure during his adolescence. If we are to believe him, this search for evidence began during his isolation in the sanatorium of Grafenhof at the age of nineteen, when he became desperately aware of the dissolution of his family and obsessed by how little he knew of his antecedents, especially the sinister father he never met.

Bernhard insists that his style is characteristically Austrian and could never have been produced by a German, since it is coloured by Austrian pronunciation and speech melody. These of course cannot be conveyed in translation. However, Bernhard's style is sufficiently idiosyncratic for the translator to hope that he has captured some of the syntactical and rhythmical characteristics of the original German text and so done at least partial justice to an author who considers the content of what he writes less important than the manner in which it is written.

David McLintock

A
CHILD

No one has found or will ever find.

VOLTAIRE

1

AT THE AGE OF EIGHT I rode my first few yards on a bicycle in the street below our apartment in the Taubenmarkt in Traunstein. It was midday, and the streets of the self-important little provincial town were empty. The bicycle, made by the firm of Steyr-Waffen, belonged to my guardian, who was serving in the German army in Poland and would later march into Russia. At once acquiring a taste for what was to me an entirely novel discipline, I rode out of the Taubenmarkt and along the Schaumburgerstrasse into the town square, where, having made two or three circuits of the parish church and believing myself to be in perfect control of the bicycle, I made the bold and, as it proved only hours later, fateful decision to visit my Auntie Fanny in Salzburg, some twenty-two miles away. Auntie Fanny lived in a house surrounded by a flower garden, which she tended with all the loving care of which a small householder is capable, and on Sundays she cooked her famous veal cutlets. I judged this the most appropriate destination for my first outing and intended, having arrived at my aunt's house and been received by her with predictably lengthy expressions of her boundless admiration for this remarkable feat of mine, to eat my fill and sleep off my fatigue. From my first conscious moments, when I had first become curious about the world around me, I had looked up to cyclists as a kind of élite, and to this élite I myself now belonged. No one had taught me the art, which I had so long admired in vain: I had pushed my guardian's precious Steyr-Waffen bicycle out of the hall, without asking permission, though not without a twinge of compunction; and, not reflecting for a moment on how it was done, I had hoisted myself onto the pedals and ridden off. In these first few moments, since I did not at once fall off, I felt like a conquering hero. It would have been quite contrary to my nature to dismount after simply riding round a few times; in this venture, as in everything else I undertook, I persevered to the very limit. Without a word to anyone who might have had a say in the matter, I left the town square riding high on my mount and made my way through the area called Au and out into the open country, heading for Salzburg. Though I was still too small to reach the pedals and at the same time sit on the saddle—like all undersized beginners I had to stand on them—I got up a fair speed, and the fact that the road went downhill afforded me additional delight. If only my people knew what I've achieved already by my surprise decision, I thought; if only they could see me and at the same time admire me—for they would not be able to do otherwise! I pictured their amazement, their utter astonishment. I did not doubt for a second that my skill was such as to cancel out any offence, indeed any crime, I might have committed. Who, apart from myself, would be capable of getting on a bicycle for the very first time and simply riding off—with the supreme ambition, moreover, of reaching Salzburg? They would have to realise that I always succeeded in whatever I set my mind to, despite any constraint and opposition, and emerged as victor! Above all, I wished, as I pressed down on the pedals, having already reached the ravines below Surberg, that I could be seen by my grandfather, the person I loved more than anyone else in the world. But since they were not there to see me and knew nothing of my adventure (which was by now well advanced), I had to perform my feat without witnesses. When we are riding high, there is nothing we long for so much as an admiring observer; but there was none present. I had to make do with observing and admiring myself. The harder the air blew in my face and the nearer I got to my destination, my Auntie Fanny's house, the greater was the distance between myself and the scene of my enormity. When I came to a straight stretch of road and closed my eyes for a moment, I felt the thrill of triumph. Secretly I was at one with my grandfather, for on this day I had made the greatest discovery of my life so far; I had given my existence a new turn, possibly the decisive turn, by learning the art of movement on wheels. This was how the cyclist met the world—from above! He raced along, his feet not touching the ground. He was a cyclist, which was as much as to say, I am the ruler of the world. In a state of unparalleled elation I reached Teisendorf, famous for its brewery. Immediately afterwards I had to dismount and push the bicycle, the property of my guardian, who had vanished almost completely from our lives by joining the army. Now I got to know the unpleasant side of cycling. The road became very long, and I began to count first the stones lining the edge of the road, then the cracks in the asphalt. Only now did I notice that the stocking on my right leg was covered with oil from the chain and hanging down in ribbons. I felt dejected at the sight of my torn stocking and my oil-covered leg, which had already begun to bleed. Was this the first stage in a developing tragedy? Before me lay Strass. I knew the countryside and the villages from a number of train journeys I had made to visit my Auntie Fanny, who was married to my mother's brother. It all looked quite different now. Would my lungs last out as far as Salzburg? I jumped onto the bicycle and pedalled away, adopting the well-known racing posture, more out of despair and ambition than out of exaltation and enthusiasm, trying to get up an even greater

speed. When I had passed Strass and was within sight of Unterstrass, the
bicycle chain broke and became hopelessly entangled in the spokes of my
rear wheel. I was catapulted into the ditch. This was the end, without
any doubt. I got up and looked round. No one had observed me. It would
have been too ludicrous to be caught doing this fatal header. I picked the
bicycle up and tried to disentangle the chain from the spokes. Covered
with oil and blood and trembling with disappointment, I looked in what
I took to be was the direction of Salzburg. When all was said and done,
I would have had only another seven or eight miles to cover. Only now
did I realise that I did not know my Auntie Fanny's address. I should
never have found the house with the flower garden. If I had asked, Where
is my Auntie Fanny? or Where does my Auntie Fanny live?—supposing
that I had actually got to Salzburg—there would have been either no
answer at all or else several hundred. I stood there envying the people
passing me in their cars or on their motorbikes and taking no notice
whatever of my distress. At least the back wheel would still turn, and so
it was still possible to push my guardian's bicycle, though admittedly back
to where disaster awaited me and darkness suddenly loomed. In my previous
exuberance I naturally had lost all sense of time, and to make matters
worse a rain storm suddenly came on, making an inferno out of the countryside I had just ridden through in such supreme elation. The rain came
down mercilessly, completely drenching me and turning the road within
seconds into a raging torrent, and as I pushed the bicycle in the downpour
I never stopped crying. Each time the wheel revolved, the buckled spokes
scraped against the frame. It was now completely dark, and I could no
longer see a thing. As always, I thought, I've fallen victim to a temptation
that can only end in utter disaster. It was with the utmost alarm that I
imagined the state my mother must be in, as she went to the police station
at the town hall, furious and at her wit's end, stammering complaints
about her *terrible, dreadful* child. My grandfather, who lived out in the
country on the other side of the town, would know nothing. Once again
I staked everything on him. One thing was clear: there was no question
of my attending school that Monday. I had made off in the most disgraceful
manner, without permission, and what was more I had ruined my guardian's bicycle. What I was now pushing was a useless piece of junk. My
whole body was shaken alternately by the pouring rain and by relentless
fear. In this state I blindly made my way back for several hours. I was
resolved to put everything right; but would that be possible? I had not

changed; my promises were worthless; my good intentions had been just
so many meaningless words. I cursed myself. I wanted to die. But it was
not so simple. I tried to regain some semblance of dignity. I condemned
myself to the supreme penalty. Not to the death penalty—to the supreme
penalty, even though I had no clear idea what that might be. And at once
I became aware of the absurdity of this monstrous game I was playing
with myself. The gravity of my crimes had undoubtedly increased; I felt
this quite clearly. All my previous offences and crimes were nothing compared with this latest one. My truancies, my lies, the traps I set everywhere,
now seemed harmless, as they always did, compared with my latest offence,
my latest crime. I had reached a dangerous stage in my criminal career.
The precious bicycle was ruined, my clothes were dirty and torn; and all
the faith people had placed in me had been destroyed in the most shameful
manner. Suddenly I found the word *remorse* quite misplaced. Pushing my
bicycle through the inferno, I totted up the account from top to bottom,
adding, dividing, subtracting: the sentence that would be meted out to
me was bound to be terrible. My thoughts were persistently dominated
by the word *unforgivable*. What was the good of crying and cursing myself?
I loved my mother, but I was not a good son. Nothing about me was
straightforward, and all the complications I caused her were more than
she could cope with. I was cruel, I was mean, I was sly, and, worst of all,
I was two-faced. Just to think of myself filled me with loathing. If only
I could be at home, I thought, leaning on my mother's shoulder, happy
just to hear her breathing while she read her Tolstoy or another of the
Russian novels she loved! How low I've sunk! It's disgusting! How I have
defiled my very soul! How profoundly I have deceived my mother and my
grandfather! You really are what they call you—*the most dreadful child in
the world!* The world at this moment seemed utterly dark, loathsome and
ugly. If I were at home, I thought, I could go to bed without feeling
ashamed and without a bad conscience. I imagined my mother saying good
night to me and began to cry still more bitterly. Had I still got any shoes
on my feet? It was as though the rain had swilled everything off me,
leaving me with nothing but my misery. But I mustn't give up. I saw a
light, and in the light I slowly perceived the word *inn.* This was my last
hope. My grandfather had always warned me that the world was repulsive,
merciless, and deadly. How right he was! Everything was much worse
than I had thought. I actually wanted to die on the spot. But then I
pushed the bicycle the few yards to the door of the inn, leant it against

the wall, and went in. Inside there was a stage, on which farmers' boys and girls were dancing to the music of a band; the tunes the band played were familiar, but this did not console me. On the contrary, I now felt completely out of it. I was confronted by the whole of human society, and I alone did not belong to it. I was the enemy. I was the criminal. I no longer deserved to be part of it. It was protesting against me. Harmony, fun, security were not for me. The whole world was pointing its finger at me, and that was mortifying. During the dancing no one took any notice of my misery; but then, as the couples left the stage, I was discovered. I was deeply ashamed, but at the same time happy to be spoken to. Where have you come from? Where are you going? Who are your parents? Where are they? Haven't they got a telephone? All right, come and sit down. I sat down. Have something to drink. I had something to drink. Cover yourself up. I covered myself up. I was given a coarse woodman's coat to put round me. The waitress questioned me; I answered her and cried. The child suddenly reverted headlong into childhood. The waitress touched him on the back of his neck. Stroked him. He was saved. But that did not alter the fact that this child was the most dreadful of all children. *You're all I needed!*—that was what my mother was always shouting at me. I can hear it quite clearly even today. A frightful child! My biggest mistake! I cowered in a dark corner of the inn parlour and observed the scene. I was attracted by the naturalness of the people on the stage and in front of it. Here was a world and a society that *showed* itself and behaved quite differently from my own. I did not belong to it, whether I wanted to or not, and my people did not belong to it, whether they wanted to or not. But could it be that some people existed naturally and others artificially? Were these people natural and mine artificial? I was unable to transform this notion into a coherent idea. I loved the sound made by the clarinet, and secretly I listened to nothing else, forming a secret conspiracy with my favourite instrument. I was told that two boys would take me home, but not before midnight. They did as much dancing as they could, and I made friends with them. This friendship began the first moment I noticed them. The waitress kept bringing me things to eat and drink. The people there were all busy with their own affairs, and apart from giving me food they left me alone. I could be happy in these surroundings; I loved inn parlours and their carefree company. But I was not so stupid as to ignore the terrible future in store for me. What awaits me when I leave here will be more horrible than all the horrors I've endured up to now, I thought.

My instinct had never let me down. Even if I was a pathetic bundle of
humanity, still soaked to the skin and cowering in the corner to which I
had been assigned, I still had my little private show, my morality play,
my secret puppet theatre. Not surprisingly, I had fallen asleep by the time
the boys came to get me, rousing me in their rough, uncouth manner.
They picked me up and carried me away from the music and the dancing.
It was an icy-cold, starry night. One of the boys sat me on his bicycle in
front of him, so that I could hold on to the handle-bar, while the other
rode his bicycle with one hand and wheeled mine at the side of it. They
rode at top speed as far as Surberg, where they lived. They did not say a
word; the only sound was their strenuous panting. They set me down in
front of their house. Their mother came out and took me in. She took off
my clothes and hung them up by the stove, which was still hot, then gave
me some milk mixed with honey. She looked after me in a motherly
fashion, but without saying anything; in fact I could tell from her silence
that she strongly disapproved of my conduct. She did not need me to
explain what had happened. There was not much of a mystery to solve.
What will your parents say? she asked. I knew for certain what would
happen to me when I got home. The boys had promised they would take
me back home. When I was dry and no longer shivering with cold, having
got used to the warmth of this unfamiliar but cosy peasant house, I slipped
off the fustian shirt the farmer's wife had put on me and dressed myself
in my own clothes again. The boys picked me up and took me to Traunstein. They dropped me in the Taubenmarkt by the door of our house and
were gone. I did not even have time to thank them. Hardly was I standing
on the ground than they disappeared. I looked up the dark wall of the
house as far as the second floor. Nothing stirred. It was about three o'clock
in the morning. The saddest thing was the sight of my guardian's Steyr-
Waffen bicycle, which the boys had leant against the wall of the house.
Undoubtedly I would have to approach my mother by way of my grandfather, who lived with my grandmother in Ettendorf, in an old farmhouse
only a few hundred yards from a famous place of pilgrimage where every
Easter Monday the villagers stage a cavalcade in honour of St. George,
which is known as St. George's Ride. My mother and I, left to ourselves,
could not have avoided a catastrophe. My grandfather was the authority
to whom everyone deferred, who sorted out every disagreement and whose
word was law. He was the judge, the one who passed sentence. I knew
exactly what it would mean if I rang the bell at home. I was careful not

to ring. I wedged the crippled bicycle between the wall of the house and the wheelbarrow which stood by the door, all the year round, for every conceivable purpose or eventuality, and set off for Ettendorf, which was two or three miles away. I loved the silence and the emptiness of the town. There was already a light at the baker's. I made off out of the Taubenmarkt, down across what were called the Dentist's Steps (where a dentist had plied his trade for as long as anyone could remember), past our grocery store, a tailor's shop, a cobbler's, a funeral director's (every possible trade was represented here), past the gasworks and over the river Traun by way of a wooden bridge, high above which was the railway bridge, to me a miracle of engineering, stretching for some hundred yards across the Traun from east to west. I can still hear my grandfather saying, It's a work of genius, that construction; it's so bold. I recall how, on boring afternoons, I would often place stones on the rails—too small, of course, to impede the gigantic locomotives which my friends from the elementary school and I would have loved to see plunging into the depths. Anarchists of six, seven and eight years old, we did our training on an area of sloping ground by the tracks known as the Wine Slope, spending hours in the hot sun collecting stones and sticks, placing them on the track, and lying in wait. The trains resolutely refused to be derailed and plunge into the depths with all their carriages. They pulverized the stones and sent the sticks flying into the air, while we squatted among the bushes and kept our heads down. We lacked the physical strength to carry out our anarchistic designs, not the mental capacity. Some days we were less radically disposed, and instead of lumps of stone and pieces of wood, we would put small coins on the rails; there was great rejoicing every time they were squashed by an express. One had to place the coins according to a precisely thought-out system in order to get really good results; amateurishly placed coins simply jumped off the rails and were lost in the gravel and undergrowth on the Wine Slope. Very often I imagined the railway bridge collapsing. Even today, in many of my dreams, I have images of the bridge in ruins: the apocalyptic vision of my childhood. I see the first-class carriages hanging by a thread in the swirling river, while corpses and screaming survivors dangle from them in the wind. From my earliest childhood all my dreams have culminated in visions of towns with great gashes running through them, wrecked bridges and trains hanging over chasms. This railway bridge was the mightiest piece of engineering I had seen at the time. If we were to fix just one little packet of dynamite to one of the girders and then detonate it, the whole bridge would inevitably collapse, my grandfather told me. I know now that he was right: one pound of explosives would be enough to demolish the bridge. The idea that a little packet of explosives no bigger than our family Bible would be enough to destroy a bridge well over a hundred yards long fascinated me more than anything else. But it would be necessary, my grandfather said, to detonate it by remote control, in order not to get blown up oneself. Anarchists are the salt of the earth, he often said. This remark fascinated me; it was one of his habitual observations, the full meaning of which—and by this I mean its real significance—I naturally came to understand only gradually. The railway bridge over the Traun, which I contemplated from below as I contemplated my very greatest enormity—an enormity far greater than God, of course, whom I have never been able to make much of at any time in my life—was the biggest thing I knew. And for this very reason I had always speculated on ways of bringing about its collapse. My grandfather had shown me all the possible ways of achieving this. One could destroy anything with explosives if one wanted to. In theory I destroy everything every day, you understand, he said. In theory, he said, it was possible to destroy everything every day, whenever one chose—destroy it, bring it down, wipe it out. This seemed to him the most marvellous idea in the world. I made it my own and have toyed with it all my life. I kill whenever I want, I demolish things whenever I want, I destroy whenever I want. But theory is nothing more than theory, my grandfather would say, lighting his pipe. In the shadow of the railway bridge, on which I used to enjoy igniting my anarchistic ideas, I was on my way to see my grandfather. Grandfathers are our teachers, our real philosophers. They are the people who pull open the curtain that others are always closing. When we are with them, we see things as they really are—not just the auditorium but the stage and all that goes on behind the scenes. For thousands of years grandfathers have taken it upon themselves to create the devil where otherwise there would have been only God. Through them we see the drama in all its fullness, not just a pathetic, bowdlerized fragment, for what it is: pure farce. Grandfathers put their grandchildren's heads where at least there is something interesting to see, even if it is not always easy to understand; and by always insisting on what is essential they save us from the dreary indigence in which, were it not for them, we should undoubtedly soon suffocate. My maternal grandfather saved me from the tedious stench of the tragedy of earth, in which millions upon millions have already suffocated. He pulled me out of the universal bog, fortunately head first, before it was too late, though not without a degree of painful discipline. He drew my attention—before it was too late—to the fact that man is endowed with a head, and he showed me how important this was. He taught me that the ability to walk must be supplemented as soon as possible by the ability to think. So on this night, as always, I went up to Ettendorf to see my grandfather as if I were ascending a holy mountain. Climbing up from the plain, I left behind me everything that was petty and dirty and quite simply nauseating. I left behind me the stench of an airless world dominated by helplessness and depravity. A certain solemnity entered my gait and I breathed a wider air as I walked up the hill to visit my grandfather, the highest authority I recognized. No longer a common criminal, a worthless, vicious character and a shady, corrupt individual, I became a real person whose most notable attribute was a truly sublime pride. Only a highly intelligent person endowed with very special intellectual gifts learns how to ride a bicycle in such a short time and dares to ride to the outskirts of Salzburg. The fact that I failed shortly before reaching my goal does not diminish my achievement. Such were without doubts the thoughts that passed through my mind. Greatness was discernible even in my failure. I prepared myself on my way up the hill; the higher I climbed and the nearer I got to my grandfather, the clearer I became about my achievement. I was not even tired. I was too excited. The only thing that matters is to be active, never inactive. This was a saying of my grandfather's which I constantly bore in mind; even today it determines the way I live. I kept on repeating it to myself as I climbed ever higher. No matter what we do, we must do something, the wise man of the mountain used to say. The active man is the true saint, even if the world brands him as a criminal. In any case the world is corrupt and teeming with horrors of its own. Even a crime, any crime, is preferable to complete inactivity, which is the most detestable thing in the world. And now I had an achievement to report of which I was extraordinarily proud, though I had chosen an extraordinary time to report it. I prepared my story down to the last detail. I was already working on the details when I was a few hundred yards from the house. My grandfather liked people to speak clearly and to the point. He hated all the preliminaries, digressions, and circumlocutions which the rest of the world went in for when it had something to tell. He could not endure the longwindedness of the people around him, who were capable only of amateurish utterance and could count on earning his disapproval whenever they took it upon themselves to say anything to him. I knew he abhorred babble. The semi-educated constantly dish up their stale, unappetizing stodge, he said. He was surrounded only by half-educated people and it sickened him to have to listen to them. To the end of his days he hated their amateurish way of articulating their thoughts. To hear a simple person speak is a benison, he said. He just speaks, he doesn't babble. The more educated people are, the more intolerably they babble. I let myself be guided entirely by these remarks. We can listen to a bricklayer or a woodcutter, but not to an educated person—or a so-called educated person, since there is no such thing as a truly educated person. Unfortunately, the babblers can be heard babbling away incessantly; the others keep quiet because they know perfectly well that there's little to say. I had reached the top of the holy mountain. The morning twilight lent a theatrical effect to my arrival at my grandfather's house. But I dared not go in yet. It was no more than four in the morning. I could not, must not, present myself at once. It would ruin my whole strategy. I did well to consider the matter thoroughly: If I wake my grandparents up, I told myself, I shall be at a disadvantage straight away. Improper behaviour gives offence, and I shall make myself guilty once more. The house, in which my grandparents had lived for several years, belonged to a small farmer who owned six or seven cows and farmed his small plot of land with his wife, who walked with a stoop and was almost totally deaf and dumb. It was almost like heaven to have grandparents who lived on a real farm—mind within matter, as it were. I loved the cow shed and the animals; I loved the farm smells; I loved the farmer and his family. And they loved me. No, it was not just my imagination. They let me watch the cows being milked; they let me feed them and muck them out, and I was allowed to be present when they calved. I was there when the fields were ploughed, the seed sown, and the harvest brought in. In winter I was allowed to sit with the farmer and his wife in their living room. Nowhere was I happier. And here, where I was so happy, my grandfather and grandmother lived too, on the first floor, and that made my happiness complete. From here one had a wide view across to the foothills of the Bavarian Alps, the Hochfelln, the Hochgern, and the Kampenwand. Below, as I knew, lay the Chiemsee. My grandfather used to say that on certain days when there was an east wind one had only to listen properly to hear the bells of Moscow from his balcony. I never heard them, but I was sure there were times when he did. Traunstein lies on a moraine, but Ettendorf is situated much higher. One looked down, so to speak, from the mount of wisdom onto the lowlands of the petty bourgeoisie, over which, as my grandfather never tired of saying, Catholicism waved its brainless sceptre. Everything below Ettendorf was worthy only of contempt. The spirit of the petty bourgeois, the spirit of pettiness in general, of baseness and stupidity. The small shopkeepers, my grandfather would say, huddle like silly sheep round the church and bleat themselves to death, day in, day out. Nothing, he said, was more sickening than a small town, and the type of small town represented by Traunstein was the most sickening of all. One had to go only a few yards into it to be defiled; one had to exchange only a few words with one of its inhabitants and one had to vomit. Either the real country or the big city—that was my grandfather's choice. Unfortunately his son-in-law, my guardian, could find work only in Traunstein, and so, according to my grandfather, we were compelled to exist in this detestable atmosphere. Of course, he himself was in Ettendorf, but if he had to live down there in Traunstein . . . no, he'd rather commit suicide. This was how he talked when we went for walks. Suicide was one of the words that came most naturally to him, one which was familiar to me from my earliest childhood through hearing him use it. I am well versed in the use of the word. There was no conversation he engaged in, no advice he imparted, which did not inevitably lead him to remark that man's most precious possession was his freedom to take leave of the world by suicide, to kill himself when he chose. He himself had speculated on the subject all his life; he had pursued this speculation more passionately than any other, and I took it up myself. At any time, whenever we choose, he said, we can commit suicide—preferably in the most aesthetic way possible. The idea of being able to make oneself scarce, he said, was the only really marvellous idea there was. Your father, he said, when he was well disposed to the person in question (when he was not, he said your guardian), is the breadwinner; you and your mother depend on him—at times we all depend on him. And so we have to accept the fact that he has to be in a dreadful place like Traunstein and earn a living for us. There was no alternative. We are victims of unemployment. This was the only available job for your father [guardian] in the whole of Austria or Germany. How I despise these small-town provincials! How I detest them! But I'm not going to kill myself—not because of these futile people who have a trunk and two legs but no head. He only went down into Traunstein when my mother invited him for a meal. Of all the women I have ever known my mother was the best cook. Home cooking and good plain food are terms which set my teeth on edge, but not where my mother's cooking is concerned. And so two or three times a week he and my grandmother had occasion to go down to Traunstein, which they detested, for a veal cutlet, a roast, or a cottage cheese strudel. The two old people made their way from Ettendorf to Traunstein, heads held high. The farmer and his wife had a grandson of my age who lived in a ground-floor room. His name was Georg, though everyone called him Schorschi, and he went to the elementary school in Surberg, not in Traunstein. He was an additional attraction for me. All this meant that when I was in Traunstein I longed to be in Ettendorf. Schorschi was intelligent; he revered my grandfather and eagerly took in everything he heard him say. And my grandfather loved him. Like me, Schorschi grew up without a father, living solely with his grandparents. It was said that his father saw him now and then, but his mother did not, and I knew nothing about her. The farmer and his wife gave him a peasant upbringing, educating him to absolute frugality, if not deprivation. In addition to attending school, Schorschi had to work hard, but he was a willing worker, and together we brought many a calf into the world. He was stronger than I was, and the image of his grandfather; he had white-blond hair, and, unlike me, he was a genius at sums. He could work out any sum in a matter of seconds. In winter I spent my time almost entirely with him and his grandparents on the ground floor when I was not with mine on the first floor; in fact, when my grandfather was working, he and my grandmother were glad enough to be able to send me downstairs. Schorschi was my friend, my confederate, and my most intimate companion apart from my grandfather. I last saw him a few years ago. By then we were both just forty-five. He had gone mad, and for two years he had not left the house, which he had inherited from his grandparents. He threatened anyone who dared to go up to his quarters on the first floor, where my grandparents had lived. He had let his hair grow for years and was no longer used to talking to anyone. But he was glad to see me and murmured a few words I did not understand. He opened a bottle of Traminer, which we finished off, most of the time in silence. He kept saying that he could see my grandfather quite clearly in front of him, that he still loved and respected him more than anybody else. The simplicity he showed in his degradation put me to shame. I talked about myself, but it meant nothing to him. Everything I said was pointless babble. *You*, I thought, have a clear head, even though physically you're a cripple, while *he* has become a confused, dull-witted wreck which will not be inhabited by a soul for much longer. The soul flickered up fitfully from time to time, in his eyes. It was an eerie scene, but I will not pass over it. The house was full of cobwebs yards long, and the smell of decay hung over every word and every feeling. His father had hanged himself after his electrical business in Munich had gone into liquidation, and that had destroyed the son's life. The grandparents had died, and the house and property had gone to rack and ruin. I could not believe my eyes: surrounding the house formerly so well kept, about a hundred wrecked cars had been dumped and left to their fate. Two men, with beards almost hiding their faces and dressed in overalls stiff with dirt, both pointed to their temples with their index fingers almost simultaneously when I asked after Schorschi. They told me he had not left the first floor for two years. They took him food but were not allowed to go up to his quarters. He still owned the house, although he ought to have been legally incapacitated long ago. They warned me what to expect. But I went in and ventured up to the first floor. The door was opened by a monster, all dirt and hair, but the eyes were still those of beloved Schorschi. At first he did not recognize me and I had to say *Thomas* three times before he understood. This is how a man looks, I thought, when he's completely and utterly given up, but hasn't done away with himself yet. His father did away with himself, but he hasn't, I thought, perhaps precisely because his father did. While speculating in this way I glimpsed through the monstrous figure Schorschi had become, the childhood we had shared. It was still there, alive. . . . So I looked through my friend's bedroom window. He was fast asleep, since he was always overworked and hence overtired, like all farm children. Shall I knock or not? I knocked. Schorschi came to the window and opened it. I can still see the scene clearly. He unlocked the door of the house. I went into his cold room, sat down, and told him my story. It produced the tremendous effect I expected. *Almost as far as Salzburg,* I said. *Not quite, but almost.* I said I had seen the lights of Salzburg but had not known my Auntie Fanny's address. Everything I said evoked admiration, and each new twist in my story increased it. Naturally he had never ridden a Steyr-Waffen bicycle. What a fantastic feeling it was to get it into motion and ride off and away! I enjoyed my own account as if it were being given by a quite different person. It got better as it went on, and I was so inspired by my own excitement at the story I was telling that I added a number of details which were either exaggerations designed to lend it spice, or fresh inventions, not to say lies. Sitting on the stool by the window, opposite Schorschi's bed, I gave him a highly dramatic account which I was convinced was bound to be seen as a very successful work of art, despite the undoubted truth of the facts and events it contained. Where it seemed appropriate I lingered on certain aspects, reinforcing certain points and playing down others, always intent upon building up to the climax of the whole story, never anticipating the crucial points, and never losing sight of myself as the central figure in the drama. I knew what impressed Schorschi and what did not, and it was on this knowledge that I built up my account. Naturally I could not speak too loud, lest I drew the attention of the others in the house to our conversation. It was daylight when I had finished my story. At the end of it I was able, by a few short sentences, to turn my pathetic failure into a triumph. I had succeeded: Schorschi was convinced, that morning, that I was a hero. My grandfather greeted me with a severe expression on his face but at the same time pressed my hand in his as if to say, It's all right. Whatever's happened, it's forgiven. My grandmother served a delicious breakfast. I loved her breakfasts more than anybody else's. They did not ask many questions but were quite simply glad that I was there and that I was well. My grandfather got up and went to work—*to work on his novel.* This I imagined to be something terrible but at the same time quite extraordinary. My grandfather tied his horse-blanket round him with a leather belt and sat down at his desk. My grandmother stood up and shut the padded door. As a child I always had the impression that the two of them were extremely happy. They remained so all their lives. My grandparents were invited to dinner at my mother's that day. This was lucky for me. Holding my grandfather's hand and walking between him and my grandmother, as well protected as I could possibly be, I went down into Traunstein. I was certain of victory. From Ettendorf to Traunstein I walked with my head held high, not hanging it as I had done a few hours earlier when I had walked in the opposite direction. My mother was no match for me. In cases like the present one concerning the Steyr-Waffen bicycle, she used to beat me furiously, usually with the whip she kept on top of the kitchen cupboard. I would cower in the corner of the kitchen or the living room, crying out for help and shielding my head with both hands, aware that I was putting on a superb theatrical performance. She would reach for the whip at the slightest provocation. Since corporal punishment ultimately failed to make any impression on me—a fact which never escaped her— she would try to force me to my knees by saying the most terrible things, and every time she succeeded in wounding me profoundly. She would say such things as *You're all I needed* or *You're the cause of all my unhappiness. Damn you! You've destroyed my whole life. You're to blame for everything. You're the death of me. You're a nothing, I'm ashamed of you! You're as useless as your father. You're worthless. You trouble-maker! You liar!* These are only some of the curses she shouted at me, proving only how helpless she was in dealing with me. She always made me feel that all my life I had stood between her and complete happiness. When she saw me she saw my father, the lover who had deserted her. In me she saw all too plainly the man who had destroyed her. I had the same face, as I know, because I once saw a photograph of my father. The likeness between us was amazing. It was not just that my face was similar to my father's; it was *the same face*. The greatest disappointment of her life, the greatest defeat she ever suffered, was my arrival on the scene. And as long as I was with her, she was confronted with this defeat daily. Naturally I felt her love for me, but at the same time I felt her hatred for my father, which stood in the way of that love. And so this love for me, her illegitimate child, was always suppressed by her hatred of the child's father; it could never develop freely and naturally. In reality my mother did not swear at *me* but at my father, who had deserted her, for whatever reason; when she took the whip to me, she did not beat *me* but the author of her unhappiness. The whip was not just meant for me; every time she used it, it was meant for my father too, who was never talked about by anyone, not even by my grandfather. There was no such person—he did not exist. I very soon stopped asking about my father. My questions immediately made them angry; whatever mood they had been in up to then, my questions about my father cast a blight on it. My father must have been a criminal of quite extraordinary vicious-ness, to judge by everything I heard about him. I loved my mother dearly, and she had at least an equal love for me; but as long as she lived, the development of our mutual love was impeded by the demon I could never see. This invisible man, whose only characteristics seemed to be mendacity and baseness, was a perpetual killjoy. *Long letters, oh yes—but all utterly base. Lots of promises, oh yes—but all lies. Oh yes, your father was a past master at one thing—the art of lying!* That was all my mother told me. Why my grandfather also refused to talk puzzled me, and it still puzzles me. *Brilliant, but rotten to the core!* my mother often said. *In Frankfurt-on-the-Oder he fathered another five children, all of them creatures like you!* And so it went on . . . I had escaped the torture of the whip, at least for the time being.

My grandfather pushed me past my mother, who was furious but said nothing, into what was called the living room, where the meal was waiting. We sat down. My mother was trembling with rage as we ate in silence, but at the same time I could see how desperate she was, and I felt how much I loved her and how much she loved me. At one point she told us she had notified the police. And alerted the whole neighbourhood. In the morning she had discovered what remained of the bicycle against the wall downstairs. A frightful disgrace! And then there was the fact that I had skipped school. I was a failure. If I were to end up as a chief bricklayer, that would be the most anyone could expect of me. She was always threatening me by talking about my becoming a chief bricklayer; it was one of her sharpest weapons, and it always struck home. In fact she's right, I was bound to reflect, for at school I've learnt less than anyone else, and my teachers think I'm quite useless. I was actually incapable of doing the simplest sum; every dictation exercise was a disaster; I was in danger of having to repeat the year. I found little to interest me in what I was taught; it was all infinitely boring—that was the reason for my lack of interest, which was no secret to anybody, least of all my teachers. My grandfather said quite simply that I must pass. How I passed was immaterial. He attached no importance to marks. It was important to move up into the next class, but nothing else mattered. But now I doubted whether I would be able to move up. In the end I was saved by a miracle: all through the year my performance was judged only barely satisfactory or unsatisfactory, but when it came to the end of the year I moved up. This was the mechanism I relied on. My grandfather seemed to have equal faith in it. He did not take at all seriously the debate about my moving up or not, which was thrashed out every time they came for a meal. He maintained that I was of above-average intelligence but that the teachers did not understand this. They were the stupid ones, not I. I was the bright one—they were philistines. Whenever my grandparents came for a meal, my schooling provided a talking-point until my grandfather put an end to the nonsense by observing that I was a genius. On this occasion, because my offence—or, indeed, crime—was of above-average heinousness, they were afraid to bring the matter up: the subject of school was not mentioned. Great care was taken to keep off the main topic of the day. Apart from my mother's remark about informing the police and alerting the whole neighbourhood, I was not mentioned. I cannot remember what they talked about, but at any rate it was not about me. My mother was no good at bringing me up. My grandfather's behaviour on this and other similar occasions was actually fatal—at least if one considers it objectively. My grandfather loved chaos; he was an anarchist, if only in spirit. My mother, on the other hand, spent all her life trying to secure a foothold in the middle-class world, or at least in the world of the lower middle class—an endeavour in which she naturally could not succeed. My grandfather loved anything unusual and extraordinary, anything contradictory or revolutionary. He thrived on contradiction; his whole existence fed on conflict. My mother, in order to be able to assert herself, sought the stability afforded by normality. All her life she longed for a happy, harmonious family. She suffered under the mental and intellectual escapades of her father, which constantly threatened to overwhelm her. She worshipped him all her life, but equally she would have liked to escape from his intellectual influence, which was seen by her as the cause of so much chaos and unfailingly proved destructive. Of course she could not escape. She had to come to terms with this fact, and this resulted in life-long depression. She had long since given up resisting the force of her father's intellect, which everyone around him found exceedingly taxing and a constant challenge. In the person of her much-loved father she revered a despot who, without being aware of it, was out to annihilate her, and in whose proximity it was possible to escape and survive only by subjecting oneself unconditionally to him *because* one loved him. Respect and love, and at the same time the desire to escape, were just not enough for my mother. She longed for normality, although she knew the extent to which it would have diminished our whole way of life; but my grandfather had nothing but scorn and derision and the profoundest contempt for so-called normality, having fled from it at a very early age. It had been utterly out of the question for him to become a master butcher or a wholesale coal merchant; as a teenager he had rejected the notion of slipping into the clothes of the masses, as he put it, and he constantly tried to cultivate the same attitude in me. It is true that a so-called *normal life* would have made many things simpler for my mother. As it was, every day was nothing short of a tightrope act, with the ever-present fear of falling off the rope. We were all continually walking a tightrope and in constant danger of falling off it to our deaths. My guardian, who went to work and earned the money, was a newcomer and, not surprisingly, the least adept on this ever-swaying family tightrope, stretched over an abyss that threatened us with death at any moment and had no safety net to cover it. That was how my grandfather wanted it to be. To this extent we were a circus family of tightrope walkers who never for one moment allowed themselves to get off the rope, and our act became daily more difficult to perform. We were prisoners of the tightrope, exponents of the art of survival; below us lay normality, but we dared not plunge into it, because this, we knew, would have meant certain death. The son-in-law, my guardian, could not go back. His performance earned him only pitying smiles, but he was inevitably stuck on our tightrope, unable to get off. The fascination which my grandfather and his family exercised over my mother's unsuspecting partner was simply too great. There was nothing he could do: he had been taken up onto the tightrope and had to hold his own; he was carried along by the rest, repeatedly saved from falling, and never allowed off. But as long as he lived he never progressed beyond the stage of simply maintaining his foothold; there was no artistry in his performance. Most of the time he dithered over the abyss, and sometimes his cries were to be heard; but the *idiot*—as my grandfather often called him—managed to right himself again and go on with the show. The troupe exploited him for their own purposes. They were adepts at the art of the tightrope and spent all their time admiring themselves; this self-admiration was forced on them in the course of time because they had no spectators, or at least none who kept their eyes on the act. My grandfather came of a family of peasants, small shopkeepers and innkeepers. His father had begun the laborious process of learning to write when he was twenty and had written a letter to his own father from the fortress of Cattaro. He claimed that he had penned it himself, though my grandfather always doubted this. At an early age my grandfather had had serious misgivings about devoting his life to such activities as serving beer, tasting the butter which the farmers brought on their push-carts, and speculating in property year after year, the sole outcome of which was the accumulation of money; and so at the age of about twenty he had renounced his claim to everything that was due to him. His elder sister, Marie, had also seen this brainless routine for what it was and decided it was unworthy of her. As a young woman she had married an artist from Eger, who later became a celebrity in Mexico and is still discussed in the art columns of the big newspapers. She had a daughter by this painter and spent many years in the East, dragging her daughter around with her from pasha to pasha, from sheikh to sheikh, and from bey to bey. Having reached her forties and parted from all her pashas, sheikhs, and beys, and with nothing to show for all her years in the Orient but a quantity of yellowing mementos, she ended up as a mediocre actress at the Court Theatre in Vienna, where she is said to have cut a good figure in farces by Nestroy and even, on one occasion, in Goethe's *Iphigenie*. My great-grandfather built an enormous studio for his son-in-law from Eger against the rock-face of the Marien-klause, near Henndorf, facing on to the Wallersee; this studio is still a sight worth seeing, with its sixty-foot glass windows on which my mother remembered seeing snakes basking. My grandfather's younger sister, Rosina, stayed at home. She was a true, authentic child of the country, so attached to the idyllic rural scene that she was incapable of travelling so much as five miles from Henndorf; in all her life she never once went to Vienna, and probably not to Salzburg either. At the age of three or four, and also when I was older, I used to admire her as the queen of a vast empire devoted to buying and selling. An elder brother of my grandfather, Rudolf, escaped to the forest and became a forester on Uiberacker estates around the Wallersee and the Mondsee. Here, at the age of thirty-two, he committed suicide because he could no longer bear the misery of the world, as he put it in a handwritten note found beside his body, which was found guarded by his dachshund. With the one exception of Rosina, they were all fugitives who had tired of the even tenor of village life. Marie fled to the East, Rudolf direct to heaven, and my grandfather, after a spell in a theological seminary, to Switzerland, where he studied applied science and made common cause with a few like-minded anarchists. It was the time of Lenin and Kropotkin. However, he went to Basel, not Zurich, and grew his hair long. He had frayed trousers, as is shown by photographs taken at the time, and on his nose he wore the notorious pince-nez favoured by the anarchists. But he directed his energy into literature rather than politics. He lived in the house next to the famous Lou Salomé, and he received a monthly supply of butter and sausage from his sister Rosina. His life-long companion, who later became my grandmother, had been forced by her parents into a terrible marriage, which lasted for years, with a Salzburg tailor. She eventually left her husband and two children and went to Basel, where she fell on my grandfather's neck and swore to stay with him forever, no matter where. So it happened that my mother was born in Basel. She was a beautiful child and remained a beauty all her life. I admired my mother and was proud of her. Even as a small child I sensed how helpless she was with me and exploited her helplessness. She had no choice but to take the whip to me. When the blows to my head and other parts proved ineffective, she had recourse to the outbursts I have

already described, the ferocity of which I could not escape. Words were a
hundred times more potent than blows. She chastised me but did not
educate me. She was unable to educate any of her children, either me or
my brother and sister. I was afraid of the whip, but the blows inflicted
by it had no deeper effect. By means of the cruel words she shouted at me
she achieved what she wanted—peace and quiet—but every time they
plunged me into the most terrible pit of suffering, from which I have
never escaped as long as I have lived. *You were all I needed! You are the
death of me!* In my dreams I am still tormented by these words. She was
unaware of the devastating effect they had on me. She needed to release
her tension. Her child was an unendurable monster, a devious child, a
child of the devil. She could never cope with my unhealthy craving for
the sensational. She knew that she had given birth to an extraordinary
child and that his birth would bring terrible consequences. This could
only mean a life of crime. She had enough examples of this in the family.
She was constantly reminded of her own brother, my uncle, who was the
genius of the family and was finally destroyed, according to my grandfather,
because of his infernal *inventiveness.* She pictured me in every possible
reformatory and prison; there was no way of saving me: I was a child who
was doomed to be lost to the powers of evil. She had her own brand of
religion, naturally not entirely Catholic, which would have been impossible
with a father like hers, who had such a low opinion of Catholicism. For
him the Catholic Church was a thoroughly despicable mass movement,
simply an organisation designed to stultify and exploit the peoples of the
world and amass the greatest amount of wealth. As he saw it, the Church
unscrupulously sold a non-existent commodity, the God of goodness, who
was also the God of wickedness. The Church, he believed, exploited the
poorest of the poor in their millions all over the world with the sole aim
of increasing its own wealth, which it invested in enormous industries, as
well as in limitless mountains of money and limitless piles of shares in
almost all the world's banking houses. Anyone who sells non-existent goods
is arraigned and condemned, my grandfather maintained—but not the
Church, which sells God and the Holy Ghost quite openly and with utter
impunity. And the exploiters, my child, the people who pull the strings,
live in princely palaces. The cardinals and archbishops are quite simply
unscrupulous men who take money for nothing. My mother was a believer.
She did not believe in the Church, probably not in God either, whom her
father, throughout his life, repeatedly declared to be dead. But she believed.

She held firm to her belief, even though she felt more and more let down by it, which is what happens to all believers. . . . At the end of the meal, which I can still remember all too clearly, my case did come up for discussion after all. My grandfather launched into a long speech for the defence. School did not matter; therefore it did not matter if I played truant. Schools in general, and elementary schools in particular, were ghastly institutions which destroyed the young before they had begun to develop. Schools actually murdered the children who attended them. And in these German schools stupidity was the rule and brainlessness the guiding spirit. But since there was a legal obligation to send one's children to school, one had to comply with it, even though one knew one was sending them to their ruin. Teachers cause nothing but ruin, my grandfather said. All they teach you is how to become low and base. They are an abomination. Rather than go to school, he said, he preferred his grandson to go to the railway station, buy a platform ticket, and use this platform ticket to travel to Rosenheim or Munich or Freilassing. *That would do him some good,* he said. *School won't. And how base many of the teachers are! Whatever pressure their wives put on them at home they work out on the children at school. I've always loathed teachers. Quite rightly—I've never yet met a teacher who didn't turn out, in a very short time, to be a low and despicable character.* Policemen and teachers spread a foul smell over the surface of the earth. *But we can't abolish them.* Teachers, he said, were all intent upon the corruption and destruction of their pupils' minds. We sent our children to school so that they would become as repulsive as the grown-ups we met every day in the street, the scum of humanity. Admittedly, truancy caused a lot of trouble to those whose duty it was to see that the young were educated. A short note will be enough! he said. A severe sore throat! he exclaimed, whereupon he immediately asked me whether I had seen anybody who might give me away. I shook my head. My mother sat rigidly facing my grandfather and me. My grandfather praised the meal, and my grandmother said it was the best they had had for a long time. Why do the police have to be brought in straight away? my grandfather asked. There was nothing new about these escapades of mine. I had often failed to return home on time, but I had always come back in the end. That's what's so brilliant about him, he said, referring to me. He does things other boys don't do. The bicycle can be repaired—a mere bagatelle. At least he can ride a bicycle now. That was a great advantage, he said. One only had to think of all the things a cyclist could do. You can't ride a bicycle, I can't ride a bicycle, he said to my mother. Nor, he said, could my grandmother. Emil, my guardian, was away, and the bicycle was just rusting away in the hall. Really, it was a brilliant idea of mine to push the bicycle out of the hall and get on it. *And immediately ride off to Salzburg!* he exclaimed. All things considered, it was a quite extraordinary achievement. The only thing you did wrong, he said to me, was to keep quiet about what you were going to do. But he immediately added, Naturally, a plan like that has to remain a secret if it is to succeed. He did not understand how I could be said to have failed. Just think, he said. He gets on a bicycle for the very first time and rides nearly all the way to Salzburg. I personally find that impressive. My mother remained silent: she had no choice. He recounted a number of his own childish escapades. When we make life difficult for our parents, he said, we make something of ourselves. It's the so-called difficult children who make something of themselves. And they are precisely the ones who love their parents most, more than all the others. But parents don't understand this. *You* don't understand it, he said to my mother. Boiled beef was his favourite dish. And the soup which was made from it. I could not understand this, because I hated beef; it made me feel sick. I know now that one gets to like beef only when one is old, not when one is a child. He savoured his food, eating it slowly and turning the whole process into a hedonistic ritual. All these small-town children, what becomes of them? he asked. We come across them in the end as bloated tradesmen who don't know their trade, or as wheeler-dealers with fat bellies who get tanked up every evening. The only poetry these people know is the line their womenfolk embroider on their kitchen towels: *The way to a man's heart is through his stomach.* That's the truth. We should always remember that there's something else in the world apart from the commonplace. But we are surrounded by baseness and cannot avoid being daily suffocated by stupidity. What have I done to be forced to exist in this indescribably filthy hole? And I am one of the lucky ones, he said. Ettendorf isn't Traunstein. When all's said and done, I don't live in a small town; I live in the country. On the other hand, he said, what had he not done to get away from the filth of village life? At the age of seven or eight he had resolved to get out. You had to get out of the filth as soon as possible and not miss the right moment. At first, when his elder brother had gone off into the ghastly forestry business, he had been destined to become a butter wholesaler, a publican and a property-speculator like his father. When they realised that he was not to be relied upon, they sent him off to the theological seminary in Salzburg. *Me a parish priest!* he often exclaimed. At any rate, this was a decisive step towards my escape from the narrow confines into which I'd been born, he said. Coaxing people's wages out of them and getting them drunk in order to augment one's own wealth little by little was not something that attracted him. In Salzburg, he said, he had acquired a taste for *Schopenhauer and Nietzsche. I didn't know such things existed,* he said. My father couldn't even spell, he often said proudly. And I planned novels, enormous novels. No, the child must be inquisitive, and then he will be healthy; one must give his curiosity a free rein. To hobble it all the time is criminal and stupid. The child must follow up his *own* ideas, not those of his educators, who have only worthless ideas. Just think: he travels more than the rest of us—what's more, at no expense, simply on a platform ticket! With this remark, which clearly amused him, he rose from the table. . . . I had always caused difficulties. In 1931, when I was born, it was no accident that my place of birth was Heerlen in the Netherlands, where my mother, on the advice of a friend from Henndorf who was working in Holland, had fled when it became obvious that my appearance on the scene was imminent and that I insisted on being born quickly. It would have been quite impossible for me to be born in a little village like Henndorf: at a time when nobody wanted illegitimate children, it would have led to a scandal and to my mother's being condemned by everyone. My great-aunt Rosina would have thrown her niece Herta, my mother, out of the house, thus blighting the rest of her life with the disgrace of having an illegitimate child and, what is more, the child of a *scoundrel,* as my father was usually called. During her remaining years she would have gone into the village wearing black, and then only to the churchyard and back. My mother must have lived in Henndorf with her aunt Rosina for a time as early as 1930, while her parents were living in the Wernhardtstrasse in Vienna. She loved Henndorf more than any other place in the world and was buried there, by her own wish, in 1950. My father was the son of a local farmer and, as was customary, had learnt a trade, that of carpentry, in addition to the obvious profession of farming. He must have come into close contact—indeed, the closest possible contact—with my mother during this period. About this I have no further knowledge. It is said that they used to meet frequently in a summerhouse in Aunt Rosina's apple orchard. That is really all I know about my pre-history. Now she fled from the scene of her disgrace and went to Holland, where she was put up in Rotterdam by the friend I have already mentioned.

Shortly afterwards she gave birth to a son in a convent in Heerlen which specialized in caring for what were known as fallen girls. When I was born, as I can see from a surviving photograph, I had more hair than I have ever seen on the head of any other new-born baby. I am said to have been a happy child, and my mother, like all mothers, was happy too. Henndorf was spared the scandal, and Aunt Rosina could sleep quietly in her bed. My mother's father, my grandfather, had not the slightest inkling of my existence. For a whole year my mother dared not tell my grandparents in Vienna about my birth. What she was afraid of I do not know. Her father, being a novelist and a philosopher, must not be disturbed in his work; I am convinced that this was the reason why my mother kept me a secret so long. My father never acknowledged me. I could be left only for a short time in the convent near Heerlen. My mother had to come and collect me; she travelled back to Rotterdam carrying me in a small clothes basket borrowed from her friend. As she could not earn a living and be with me at the same time, she had to part with me. The solution was provided by a trawler lying in the harbour of Rotterdam. The trawler-owner's wife fostered a number of children below deck; seven or eight new-born babies hung in hammocks from the wooden ceiling, being lowered from the ceiling on request and shown to their mothers, who appeared once or twice a week. I am told that I cried miserably every time and that while I was on the trawler my face was covered with ugly boils, since there was an incredible stench and impenetrable fumes where the hammocks were hung. But my mother had no choice. She visited me on Sundays, as I know, for throughout the week she worked as a domestic in order to support herself and pay for my accommodation on the ship. The advantage was that in this way she got to know the world, so to speak, and the greatest harbour in Europe was the best place to do this. I do not know much about this period. All the same, I can say that I spent the first year of my life, except for the first few days, entirely on the sea—not *by* the sea but *on* the sea—a fact which constantly gives me cause for reflection and has affected me in every way. All my life it will remain of enormous importance to me. Fundamentally I am a child of the sea: it is only when I am by the water that I can breathe properly, let alone think properly. Naturally no impressions of this period have remained with me; nonetheless I think that my time spent on the sea has affected the whole course of my life. Sometimes, when I breathe in the smell of the sea, I have the feeling that this smell is the earliest thing I can remember. I often reflect, not without pride, that I am a child of the sea, not of the mountains. I do not really feel at home in the mountains; even today I am afraid of being crushed and stifled by them. My ideal landscape is the foreland of the Alps, where I spent most of my childhood, both in Bavaria, near the Chiemsee, and in the region of Salzburg; but that period is extremely remote, extending from the third year of my life to the seventh. Before that, after the first year spent in Holland, I was in Vienna for two years. It was probably when she realised there was no longer any way out that my mother wrote to my grandparents (that is, her parents) from Rotterdam and admitted my existence. She was welcomed in Vienna with open arms. Stowing me once more in the clothes basket, she travelled with me to Vienna; the journey took a whole day and night. From now on I had not only my mother but grandparents too. It was in the Wernhardtstrasse, in the sixteenth district, near the Wilhelminenspital, that I first uttered the word grandfather. I still have a number of pictures from this period. A window looking onto an enormous acacia tree, a steeply sloping street with me on a tricycle riding downhill. Sledging outings with my grandfather under the Ameis-brücke. My grandfather pulling me along past the long iron railings of the Steinhof asylum in a luxurious two-wheeled carriage with a large backrest and armrests and a long wooden handle. There is still a photograph of this in existence. I am supposed, in my second year, to have fallen off my grandmother's Singer sewing machine, on which I had been placed by my uncle. The result was that I spent several days in the Wilhelminenspital with a concussion. I cannot remember this. Only a few isolated images remain with me from this period in Vienna in the care of my grandfather, my grandmother, and my mother, together with my uncle Farald, who brought constant variety into our lives. My grandfather, the writer, spent his time writing; my grandmother worked as a midwife, the profession for which she was trained; my mother earned a living as a domestic and at times as a cook. It was depressing: at the age of seven she had danced in *Snow White* at the court opera and received a medal from the emperor for her performance. At the age of twelve she developed what is called pulmonary apicitis and had to give up the idea of a career as a prima ballerina, for which her father had intended her. He wanted his daughter to make her career in the empire's temple of the muses; she actually had all the qualifications for this, as I know, but she ended up dusting the anterooms and bedrooms of the nouveaux riches in Döbling and working in various kitchens in and around the Währinger Hauptstrasse. Farald was destined to be a philosopher, but he joined the Communist party one night, became a friend and associate of the famous Ernst Fischer, and finally landed himself successively in various prisons in Vienna and the provinces. When I was so small that I had not yet learned to walk, the police were always knocking on the door of our flat in the Wernhardtstrasse to take my uncle away. But he was never at home, since he lived underground, so to speak. His speciality was going out at night, with several comrades selected for the purpose, and putting up large banners across the main streets of the capital, advertising communism as the only future fit for humanity. At this time, when my uncle was about twenty, he made the acquaintance of a hairdresser's assistant by the name of Emil Fabjan, who had just been acquitted of a criminal charge and had a job at a ladies' and gentlemen's hairdresser's near the Maroltingergasse. He made friends with this naïve suburban youth, to whom the world was still complete mystery, and enticed him into joining the party. One day he brought his new comrade with him to the Wernhardtstrasse. My grandfather took a liking to this utterly unspoilt young man, who conceived a great admiration for the writer and marvelled that such people existed. This was how my mother met her future husband, my guardian. It was a time of extreme material hardship, with unemployment at its highest and the suicide rate at its peak. My grandfather is said to have threatened suicide every day and to have kept a loaded revolver under his pillow. It was stupid to give up my inheritance, he said later. A young man goes chasing after some foolish ideal and throws away everything. When, on one occasion, he wrote from Vienna to his sister Rosina to say that he would like to spend a few weeks in her house, which could equally well have been his, to have a break from the frightful conditions in Vienna, she replied by return of post that she had no room available. He often mentioned this disappointment. Farald was not impressed by his father's experience, which was that the idealist who commits himself to a party early in life ultimately finds that he has been cruelly deceived. My grandfather had embraced socialism in his youth and thereby blighted his whole life, and now his son had embraced communism. Every member of the family except the one directly concerned could foresee the consequences. He intensified his alliance with the communists, striking fear and terror into his family. Having drawn Emil Fabjan in too, he also plunged the Fabjans, who lived in the Hasnerstrasse, into a period of terror. To say nothing of the many other families

who were exposed to danger—indeed, mortal danger—by my fanatical
uncle (who along with my grandfather was undoubtedly the brightest of
the family), since everything he did or prompted or staged was illegal.
My uncle's company was always extremely interesting, but it was also
extremely dangerous. His ideal was shattered in the course of time, when
it was far too late and the fragments could no longer be stuck together.
From these years in Vienna, which were such a bitter time for my family,
I have only a few pictures in which I appear well fed and pleased with
things. From a variety of high-chairs, strange period carriages, and sledges,
I can be seen holding sway, always smartly dressed; and on every one of
these pictures (all of them photographs) I appear to have a certain elegance
which even today makes me feel exceedingly proud. This is how the children
of ruling families used to look, I have often thought. So things cannot
have been so bad for me. The landscape around the Wilhelminenberg is
bathed in the mild afternoon sun, and I am the centre of everyone's
attention, demanding total admiration. For my family, who had by then
been living in the Wernhardtstrasse for twenty years, things were probably
at their worst. I have in my possession a number of photographs on which
their suits and dresses hang on them as if they were skeletons. To them
Vienna must have seemed a kind of hell in which everything was at risk
every day. My grandfather wanted to get out of this hell as fast as possible,
even at the cost of going back to the place he had fled from thirty years
earlier. All the same, he had been working during these thirty years, even
though he remained a total failure: true, he had published a novel, though
at his own expense; its title was *Ulla Winblatt,* but this book, he once
told me, had been eaten by a large goat which he and my grandmother
kept at Forstenried near Munich. Being lovers of the romantic, they once
lived there in a forest clearing, which they could not leave for the whole
winter because they were snowed in. The goat was starving even more
than we were, my grandfather said, and it didn't leave one bit of *Ulla
Winblatt* uneaten. He got small jobs as a reader for publishing firms but
immediately gave them up, as he found it distasteful to have to dance
attendance upon some unscrupulous publisher. He was an individualist,
unsuited to living in a community, and therefore unfit for any employment.
Up to the age of fifty-five he earned virtually nothing. He lived off his
wife and daughter, who believed in him unreservedly, and in the end he
lived off his son-in-law as well. My mother married my guardian in 1934
at Seekirchen on the Wallersee, where my family had gone to live at the

beginning of the year under the most bizarre and at the same time most frightful circumstances. My grandfather had finally turned his back on Vienna; subsequently he was surprised that he had had the strength to do so. Their departure from Vienna to the country, to a place only four miles from Henndorf, where they originally came from, must have been fairly sudden, for I recall that we stayed first of all at the railway inn at Seekirchen. We spent several weeks in a guest-room there, with our washing constantly hanging over our heads; and when I said good night (I still folded my hands when I said good night) I could look through a tall window directly onto the lake, which quickly grew dark under the setting sun. We brought nothing with us from Vienna apart from thousands of books, which arrived later—no furniture or other belongings, just two suitcases and our clothes. No doubt the furniture in the Wernhardtstrasse was not worth the cost of transportation. My grandmother loved to tell people that her furniture had never consisted of anything other than cheap sugar chests begged from the grocers' shops near the various apartments she had occupied. The twenty years in Vienna were a terrible experience for my family, because previously, as I know, they had been continually on the move and had changed their address nearly a hundred times. Tiring of this restless life, they had thought to settle in the Wernhardtstrasse in Vienna for good. But now, suddenly, the Wernhardtstrasse too belonged to the past. They were not sorry to leave Vienna, since the hardship there had been too great, and it had become almost impossible to survive from one day to the next. My mother stayed on in Vienna with the husband she had married in Seekirchen. I now saw her only rarely, perhaps two or three times that year. I was looked after entirely by my grandparents. Here, at the railway inn opposite the station, where, beyond the carefully nurtured herb-gardens, there was nothing but bare moorland running down to the lake, began the part of my life of which I have virtually uninterrupted recollections. We had taken just one room on the first floor of the railway inn. My grandmother did the cooking; we probably could not afford to eat downstairs in the inn parlour. My grandfather, whom I loved more than anyone else in the world, suddenly became the city gentleman with the walking stick, who was regarded by everybody with curiosity but also with suspicion—a novelist, a thinker! The contempt he attracted outweighed the admiration. This gentleman could not even afford to take his meals in the parlour. Other people went to work; he went for walks. My grandmother got a job at Hipping Farm, high above Seekirchen, looking after the children and helping with the laundry. She was efficient at everything she put her hand to and soon made friends. She earned enough to keep us. Her skill at sewing, which always earned her universal admiration, could be fully exploited at Hipping Farm. Before long she had become so popular that even the writer, walker, and thinker benefited from it. Suddenly we were respected people in Seekirchen. We moved from the railway inn to the centre of the village, to a dilapidated house which was five hundred years old and only a short walk from the cemetery. We'll stay here, my grandfather said. I was then three. I was convinced that my grandparents and I were quite extraordinary people; every day I got up full of this pretension, in a world whose ghastliness I only dimly sensed, determined to explore it, fathom it, decipher it. I was three and had seen more than other children of my age; I had breathed the air of the North Sea, if not of the Atlantic, for a whole year, as well as the pungent city air of Vienna. Now I was taking deep breaths of the country air around Salzburg, my parents' air. It was here, then, that my father had been born and that my mother had spent her childhood, close to the lake. This lake was to me a completely unsolved mystery and lay at the centre of numerous fairy stories which my grandfather made up specially for me just before bedtime. The world did not consist of walls, as it did in Vienna; it was green in the summer, brown in the autumn, and white in the winter—the seasons were not yet as indeterminate as they are today. From the very beginning my favourite place in Seekirchen was the cemetery, with the pompous tombs and enormous granite gravestones of the well-to-do, the little rusted iron crosses of the poor, and the tiny white wooden crosses on the children's graves. Even at this time the dead were my dearest confidants, whom I could approach freely. For hours I would sit on the curb of some grave and speculate on the nature of being and non-being. Naturally my speculations reached no satisfactory conclusion. The inscriptions on the gravestones inspired tremendous awe in me, especially the word *manufacturer*. What is a manufacturer? I wondered. Or: What is an engineer? I ran home and asked my grandfather about manufacturers and engineers. Then I had an explanation. Every time something seemed obscure and I failed in my own attempt to clarify it, I ran to my grandfather, wherever I happened to be. My grandfather told me I should make a habit of thinking about unsolved questions until the answers came of their own accord; in that way I should benefit more. The questions piled up, and the answers were more and more pieces of the mosaic that made up the great picture of the world. If we were to have all our questions answered for us and finally had all the solutions, we wouldn't have made much progress, my grandfather said. I watched him fondly while he wrote, my grandmother keeping out of his way and quietly calling us to breakfast, dinner, and supper. Being quiet so as not to disturb my grandfather became a regular discipline in the house; while he was alive, quiet was the supreme requirement. Everything had to be spoken quietly; we had to walk quietly and always converse quietly. The head is as fragile as an egg, my grandfather used to say. I saw that this was so and was shaken by the thought. He got up at three in the morning and went for a walk at nine. In the afternoon he worked for two hours between three and five. The walk to the post office was the climax of the day. Would there be a money order for him from Vienna? My mother remitted a large part of the money she earned for my maintenance. Today I know that this is what we lived on in Seekirchen. In addition, my grandmother contributed the proceeds of the sewing and child-minding, etc., that she did at Hipping. I found myself a friend, the only son of a man called Wöhrle, the owner of a cheese dairy and the wealthiest man in the whole area. I had access to a grand house, with marble arcades and large rooms with Persian carpets on the floor. When I had established an eternal bond with my friend, he died, at the age of four, of an inexplicable disease. Now he lay at the spot where only a few days earlier we had played together, in the family tomb, over which a gigantic marble angel spread his wings. I called out his name, but there was no answer. The marble slab lay on top of him and our friendship. For days I went to the cemetery to visit the Wöhrles' tomb, but it was no good: my petitions remained unanswered; I saw that my entreaties were in vain. The flowers had wilted. I knelt there and wept. For the first time in my life I had lost someone. Every second or third house in the village was an inn, but I had not yet been inside one. At dusk they were all packed, and the whole village was full of the music issuing from them. But there was no question of my visiting an inn. I cannot remember ever visiting one with my grandfather. What was denied me during my early time in Seekirchen was to become a regular habit later. As I lay in bed behind the drawn curtains, I used to listen to the sounds coming from the inns. What was it that made all these people so good-humoured that they danced and sang? The moon shone onto my bed, in a big room from whose walls hung shreds of wallpaper with large flower patterns. From my bed I looked directly into the Orient. I slept in a palm garden; I had a mosque by the shore of a blue sea. During the night I could hear the mice under my bed and above it; they came every night, though they had to leave as hungry as they came, because there was nothing for them. I had begun to dream. My dreams centered upon great apartment blocks; these were no doubt images I had brought with me to Seekirchen from Vienna. I was not yet at home here; the Wernhardtstrasse was the scene of my nocturnal imaginings, the Ameisbrücke, the Wilhelminenspital, the Steinhof asylum. But then right in front of the asylum lay the Wallersee; palm trees shot up in the Wernhardtstrasse, finally dwarfing everything else. This at first amused me, but in the end it scared me. I cried out and awoke. A colossal stone had rolled towards my grandfather and crushed him. . . . We did not live in the centre of the village for long. Everything was always described as a provisional arrangement, and this accommodation too was only provisional. One day the three of us—my grandfather, my grandmother, and I—transported our belongings to what was known as the Brewery Hill on an old handcart, which had probably not been acquired solely for this purpose. In front of the old brewery, a derelict building three hundred years old, in whose vaults beer and wine were stored and in which a few desperately poor people (as my grandfather put it) were accommodated at a ludicrously low rent, there stood a small, one-storey wooden house overlooking the village of Seekirchen. It was constructed of railway sleepers and belonged to a farmer who lived near Hipping Farm. It had a curious appearance and sported a large balcony at the front, from which one could look across the village to the lake; on a clear day one could see to the mountains. It was just about the cheapest accommodation in the whole area. We had a splendid view, and under the balcony there was a garden. There were two rooms downstairs and two upstairs, as well as a large flight of steps with a door onto the balcony. I was put between the top of the stairs and the door onto the balcony. From my bed I could see the mountains in the background. Here too the night was dominated by the mice, but by now I was used to them. If I got up in the night, I had to go down the dark staircase, out the front door, and along the wall in all weathers—through the snow in winter—to the privy built onto the house. Through a narrow gap between the boards I could see the gate of the brewery. I was scared when I walked from the front door to the privy and back: my grandfather had told me too many stories about roving gypsies, pedlars, and other criminals who made the area unsafe at night. Getting back into my warm bed was sheer delight. On the ground floor we had a large room which we could all use. Behind it was my grandfather's study, which I was not allowed to enter without express permission. I slept, as I have said, on the first floor at the top of the stairs. Opposite my bed was my grandparents' bedroom; to the right was the entrance to the kitchen, behind which, underneath the roof, was a small cubby-hole which we rather grandly called the dining room and in which, if my memory serves me, there stood a large bucket of dripping; above this hung strings of onions, etc. The produce all came from Hipping Farm, where my grandmother worked. There was no electric light, and so petroleum lamps at first played an important role. Then one day we got electric light; my grandfather must have just had an article accepted for publication, for we also got a Eumig radio, which my grandfather installed in the kitchen on a shelf screwed into the wall, as was then customary. From then on we spent the evenings sitting religiously at the kitchen table, listening in. This radio was to play an important part in our lives a few years later, for it was ultimately responsible for my grandfather's being taken into custody in Traunstein and forced to serve in a Nazi party office set up in a converted monastery. Through my grandmother I was able to visit Hipping Farm. To me this was paradise. The farm had seventy cows together with their young, hordes of pigs, hundreds of hens which fluttered about and clucked away from morning till night, and two or three horses. There was no tractor at that time. In the evening, nearly twenty farm hands ranging from stable lads to scullions and cowgirls, congregated in the workers' quarters, which were larger than our whole house; here, at a centuries-old bench which ran the full length of the room, they washed their faces and the upper parts of their bodies, or just their faces, or just the upper parts of the bodies and their feet, in a row of enamel basins, or combed their brilliantined hair, or just sat and watched. After supper, to which they helped themselves from one large dish, some of them went down into the village, while most went straight to bed, and a few sat at the table and read. There were piles of almanacs and a few novels, with depictions on the covers of knights fighting on horseback or surgeons performing ab-dominal operations. Another pastime was card-playing. About once a week I was allowed to spend the night on the farm, though beforehand I had to carry home the two-litre can of milk that we got from the farm. Usually—at any rate, in autumn—it was quite late when I did this errand, and in any case I had a five-hundred-yard walk, the first half of it down to the stream, then up again on the other side. I used to feel scared. I would set off from the farm at a run and reach the stream as fast as I could in order to be able to get up the slope on the other side, and get home as quickly as possible, taking advantage of the momentum I had built up by straining my lungs. My grandmother would be waiting for the milk and boiled it right away. A particular feat of mine when I was taking the milk home was to swing the can round and round in circles with my right hand, up above my head and down again, without spilling the milk, even though the can had no lid. Once I tried doing it more slowly and was drenched with milk; I had brought on another disaster. Sometimes I spent weeks at Hipping Farm, sleeping next to the stable lads with my new friend, known as Hipping Hansi, the elder of the two owners' two boys. The rooms contained only beds, and on the walls were hooks, from which hung a variety of horse harnesses. The bedcovers were heavy, but we slept on horsehair mattresses and so I know what this is like. At half past four we got up with the stable lads. The cocks were crowing and the horses shaking themselves in their harness. After breakfast in the kitchen, consisting of coffee and a slice of milk-loaf, we went out into the fields. I got to know what farm work was like. Towards midday, I would catch sight of my grandfather in the distance and run across the field to him. In summer he was always dressed in linen clothes and wearing a panama hat. He never walked without a stick. We understood each other. Just a few yards in his company and I was saved. It had been the right thing to leave Vienna. He took a new lease on life. The so-called man of the intellect who had once spent nearly all his time sitting in his study in Wernhardtstrasse, year in, year out, became an indefatigable walker who, unlike any other person I have known, made walking into an art equal to all other arts. I was not always allowed to go for walks with him; most of the time he wanted to be alone and undisturbed, above all when he was in the middle of some substantial project. I mustn't allow myself the least distraction, he would then say. But on those occasions when I was allowed to accompany him, I was the happiest person in the world. I was strictly forbidden to speak, and only rarely did he relax the prohibition—if he had a question, or if I had one. He was my great enlightener, my first and most important one, indeed the only one I have ever had. He would point to animals and plants with his stick and deliver a short lecture on every animal or plant to which his stick drew my attention. It is important to know what one is looking at. Gradually one must learn at least to put a name to everything. One must know where it comes from, what it is. On the other hand, he loathed people who knew, or claimed to know, every-thing. They were the most dangerous people, he said. The important thing was to have an adequate notion of everything. In Vienna his habitual adjectives had been *grey* and *dreadful*. *What dreadful streets, what dreadful people!* And this despite the fact that, like all intellectuals, he was a man of the city—or had become one. At one stage he had had lung trouble, and that may have been what made him decide to leave Vienna for See-kirchen. When he was only twenty-five he had spent a year in Merano with my grandmother on the advice of the doctors. There he had made a complete recovery. This was a miracle, since for months he had been coughing blood and had a large hole in one lung—and I know what that means. It was the discipline that cured me, he used to say. In Merano, in order for them to stay there at all, my grandmother had worked for the family of an English jungle explorer who spent most of the year in Kenya and, according to her, returned to Merano only twice a year, bringing back panther and lion skins. He owned a splendid, castle-like villa in the most beautiful part of Obermais, and it was his wife who persuaded my grandmother to train as a midwife. This stood her in good stead in later life. My grandfather would sit down on a tree-stump and say, Look, there's the church! What would this village be without the church? Or, Look at that bog! What would this wilderness be without that bog? We used to sit for hours, especially on the bank of the Fischach, which flows out of the Wallersee to join the Salzach, and we were completely at one. Always have something great in view: that was his constant exhortation. Fix your eyes on what is highest! Always on what is highest. But what was the highest? When we look around, we find ourselves surrounded only by the ludicrous and the pathetic. We must get away from the ludicrous and the pathetic. Always fix your eyes on what is highest! From then on I always fixed my eyes on what was highest. But I did not know what that was. Did he know? The walks I took with him were entirely taken up with natural history, philosophy, mathematics, and geometry, and the instruc-tion I received made me happy. It was a crying shame, he said, that all the things we knew did not get us any further forward. Life was a tragedy, and the most we could do was to turn it into a comedy. . . . I had a deep friendship with Hipping Hansi. He was my age; my grandfather pro-nounced him highly intelligent and predicted that he would have an intellectual career. He was wrong. Hansi finally had to take over the farm and abandon any intellectual ambitions. When I visit him now, we shake hands and have nothing to say to each other. My memories show, however, that for several years of our lives—and not the least important years; perhaps even the decisive ones—we were all in all to each other, as they say. We were bound together in a conspiracy against our surroundings, which we knew to be beautiful and at the same time evil. We shared the most deadly secrets and made the most outrageous plans. We were constantly in search of the adventures which in our dreams demanded to be realised. We invented a world that had nothing to do with the world around us. We squatted in the hay and told each other about our outward doubts and our inward anxieties. We vied with each other at work, in the fields, the stable, the cow shed, the pigsty and henhouse; and at the age of five we took the milk to the dairy on a one-horse cart. We drove down with the milk and returned with a can of whey. The strict régime imposed by his parents applied to me too. On Hipping Farm order and discipline were paramount; people often treated one another with less consideration than they treated the animals. Hansi's father whipped him at every opportunity with an old leather whip which his own father had used on *him* fifty years earlier. Hansi yelled, and the Hipping people chased me away if he was being punished for a misdemeanour in which I had been a partner. The bounds of toleration at Hipping Farm were soon exceeded. There was nothing to laugh about during working hours, and in the evening most people were too tired to laugh. All the same, it was paradise. And I was conscious of this while I lived there. Under the unrelenting severity of the régime we were, after all, secure; we felt at home. I felt as much at home as I did in our cottage, which was known as Mirtel Cottage, after its owner. It was an enormous empire on which the sun never set. The storms were only brief; the openness with which everything was settled at Hipping Farm was an absolute necessity, and no clouds were allowed to darken the sky. A box on the ears, a touch of the whip, and the matter was settled. The next meal was eaten in an atmosphere of complete normality. On Sundays we had the best curd pancakes I have ever eaten, brought straight onto the table in gigantic frying pans. This was the high point. We went to the early mass dressed in our Sunday best. I used to quake at the comminations that came from the pulpit. I did not understand the spectacle; I was swallowed up every time in the packed congregation, which was forever kneeling down and standing up; I did not know why they did it and did not dare to ask. The incense got up my nose, but it reminded me of death. The words *ashes* and *everlasting life* stuck in my mind. The performance dragged on, and the extras crossed themselves. The main actor, the dean, gave the blessing. Those assisting him bowed every other second, took turns in swinging the thurible, and every now and then struck up some incomprehensible chant. Going to church was my first theatrical experience. I attended my first mass in Seekirchen. Latin! Perhaps that was what my grandfather had meant by the highest? What I enjoyed most was attending what I called black masses—that is, requiem masses, at which black was the predominant colour. Here was the thrill of tragedy, contrasting with the normal Sunday spectacle and its happy ending. I loved the muted voices and the slow pace of the walking, which was suited to tragedy. Funerals began at the house of the deceased; the body lay in state in the hall for three days until it was taken in procession first to the church, then to the cemetery. If a neighbour died, or some well-to-do (or even rich) or influential man, everybody would turn out. They formed a cortège, nearly always a hundred yards long, behind the coffin, which was preceded by the priest and his retinue. The dead, as they lay in state, had distorted faces, very often disfigured by the blood which had oozed out and then dried. It was often useless to bind up the chin; it continued to sag, so that the observer found himself staring into the dark cavity of the deceased's mouth. The dead lay in their Sunday clothes, their hands folded round a rosary. The smell of the dead and of the candles placed on either side of the head was sickly and repellent. Day and night a constant vigil was kept until the funeral. Men and women took turns in telling their beads. One had to reckon on at least three hours before the deceased was in his grave. I was revolted by the punched silver plate on the black coffins, supposedly representing Christ crucified. These funerals made the greatest impression on me. For the first time in my life I saw that people died and were buried and so well covered with earth that they could not possibly infect the living any longer. I still did not believe that I would have to die someday, nor did I believe that my grandfather would die. Everybody dies, but not me, and not my grandfather: of this I was certain. After the funeral the mourners repaired to the inns; the Hipping employees went to the one run by Pommer, who was also a butcher and had his butcher's shop right by the wall of the cemetery, to eat soup and sausages. Two frankfurters in beef noodle soup were the absolute climax of every funeral. The deceased's relatives had their own separate table, where they all sat squeezed together, their clothes smelling of moth-balls. The others sat at other tables, spoon-ing up their soup with gusto, the long white noodles often draping themselves over their black jackets and blouses. These soup-eating sessions at Pommer's, which took place not only after funerals but also after the regular Sunday mass, gave me an incomparable opportunity to study my fellow-countrymen. But I was unquestionably fonder of requiem masses than of normal masses. As many people as possible should die as often as possible: that was what I wanted. I was not yet five when the dean, who was also the headmaster of the elementary school, met me in the street and asked me whether I would like to start school a year early. He had only girls in the class, he said, and he found that boring, but of course I should have to get my grandfather's permission. I at once noticed that the dean regarded my grandfather, whom he had met when they were both out walking, as worthy of the greatest respect; this came out especially in the way he pronounced the word *grandfather*. I'd like to, I told him, but I didn't want to start school without my friend Hipping Hansi. Certainly Hipping Hansi could start school at the same time, I was assured. Hipping Hansi was allowed to do so; neither his parents nor the dean had any objection. My grandfather agreed at once. Mind you, he said, teachers are idiots. I'm warning you against them—don't say I haven't. I was given an old school satchel which was specially dug out of the attic of my grandfather's old home at Henndorf and polished up by my great-aunt Rosina. It was said to have been used by their father. I loved the smell of old leather. The first day at school culminated in the taking of the class photograph, which I still possess. In the middle is the schoolmistress, and underneath are two rows of schoolboys and schoolgirls with typical peasant faces. At the top is the legend *My first day at school*. I am wearing a long, thick jacket buttoned up to the neck and looking more serious and melancholy than the occasion demands. I am sitting in the second row; those in the first all have crossed legs and bare feet. I was probably barefoot too. The children in Seekirchen ran around barefoot from the end of March to the end of October; on Sundays they wore shoes which were so big that they could hardly walk, because they were meant to last for several years; the children had to grow into them. For the beginning of term I got a cape which reached down to my ankles and was made by Janka, the local tailor. I was proud of this cape. Hipping Hansi had no such expensive clothes. When it turned cold, we put on woollen bonnets knitted by our grandmothers and wore stockings made of the same wool. Everything was knitted and tailored for eternity. But I always looked different from the others—more elegant, it seemed to me—and people immediately took notice of me.

During the first few days of school, I recall, we had to do a drawing of a
petroleum lamp; and of all the drawings that were handed in, mine was
the most successful. The teacher stood in front of the blackboard holding
it aloft and said it was the best. I was good at drawing. But I did not
develop this skill, and it became atrophied, like so many others. I was
the teacher's favourite pupil. She spoke to me in a specially kindly tone
of voice, rather more high-pitched than the one she used with the others.
I was extremely fond of my first teacher. Most of the time I sat at my
desk—next to Hipping Hansi, naturally—and gazed admiringly at her.
She wore an English costume and had her hair parted in the middle, which
was then the height of fashion. At the end of my first school year I got a
report containing the words *Works particularly hard;* these were underlined.
I did not know myself how I had managed this. I got nothing but top
marks for the first and last time in my life. In the corner of the schoolroom
stood a gigantic tiled stove heated with logs which the children brought
to school in the morning. Each pupil had one wedged under the flap of
his satchel. The rich children brought big logs, the poor children little
logs. There was nothing laid down about the size. The schoolroom soon
got warm from burning the previous day's logs; the fire was already crack-
ling when lessons began. The stove was then shut, and the warmth lasted
till the following morning. The dean, who was headmaster, needed to
walk only a few yards between the presbytery and the school. The church
too was only a stone's throw away. If the organist was playing the church
organ, it could be heard in the schoolroom. There were four hours of
lessons in the morning and two in the afternoon. The one-hour break at
midday was not long enough for us to get home for dinner and back.
Hipping Hansi and I had dinner at the local hairdresser's, a little damp
one-storey house standing in a garden which was full of dahlias and at its
best in mid-autumn. Day after day the hairdresser's wife cooked for us
alternately noodle soup and gruel. We got a piece of bread as well. My
grandparents paid her for the dinners. For years I went at midday through
the garden gate of Sturmayr the hairdresser to have my dinner. Unfortunately the lessons were not confined to drawing petroleum lamps: we
also had writing and arithmetic. From the beginning I found it all boring.
I probably owed my top marks to the unceasing admiration of my teacher,
not to my ability or my diligence, since I possessed neither. My grandfather
had said that teachers were idiots, miserable wretches and dull-witted
philistines; he had said nothing about the possibility of their being beautiful

like my teacher. If our class had an outing to the lake, it went without saying that I was out in front. If we entered a church, I was the first to go in. In the Corpus Christi procession I was always the one who led the other children and carried the banner with the image of the Virgin Mother on it. In this first year I acquired no new knowledge, but for the first time in my life I had the thrill of being the leading member of a community. It was a tremendous feeling. I revelled in it. I sensed that it was not destined to go on forever. In the second class we had a male teacher, the kind of figure my grandfather had often described to me—lean, despotic, kowtowing to those above him and kicking those below. My run of luck was over. The class was amazed to see how stupid I had become suddenly, almost overnight. I failed in every dictation, every sum, every single exercise. I drew, but I achieved only *a bare pass*. Hipping Hansi's day had come. He had overtaken me. If I got a four, he got a two; if I got a two (which I seldom did) he got a one; and so forth. Now I even regretted starting school early. On the other hand, I reflected, I've got a good start and shall be out of this hell a year earlier. The only subjects that interested me now were drawing and geography. I was enthralled when I read the word London, or Paris or New York, or Bombay or Calcutta. I stayed awake half the night studying Europe, which I had turned to in my atlas, and Asia and America. I walked between the pyramids, strode through Persepolis, and visited the Taj Mahal. I went in and out of skyscrapers and looked down from the top of the Empire State Building at the rest of the world lying at my feet. Basel, my mother's birthplace—what a word! Ilmenau in Thuringia, in Goethe country, where my grandfather had studied applied science! Even today atlases are my favourite reading. Always the same places, always different phantasies. One day I would visit all these places my finger pointed to. *Travelling across the map with one's finger*— for me that was not just a form of words but a rapturous experience. I dreamt about my future journeys, about when and how I should make them. During lessons I spent more time contemplating the chasms between the skyscrapers of Manhattan than the blackboard in front of me, on which the teacher spread out a mathematical wilderness. Suddenly I hated the blackboard and the chalk, which I had previously loved: they brought only misery. My pencils broke because I pressed too hard. I could not write neatly; everything I handed in was illegible. Every few days I lost my sponge and had to spit on the slate and use my elbow to rub off what was written on it; in this way I very soon wore holes in my sleeves. This in

turn annoyed my grandmother, who could not keep up with all the mending, an occupation she normally loved. And so I was soon caught up in a
vicious circle which gradually became a nightmare and caused my throat
to constrict as soon as I woke up in the morning. I slipped back further
and further. Another boy was now the best in the class; another marched
in front; another carried the banner of the Virgin on Corpus Christi Day;
another was publicly praised in front of the blackboard. Now I often had
to line up in front of the teacher's desk to have my hand caned. Most of
the time my hands were swollen. I said nothing at home about my misery.
I hated my new teacher as intensely as I had loved his predecessor. Philistines! My grandfather was right. But what good did that do me? My
second report was marred by several *bare passes*. My grandparents were in
despair. How had I come to get such a report? my grandfather asked.
There was no answer to his question. This can't go on, was his comment
on the whole desperate situation. It did go on, on and on, further and
further downhill. In the third class I came close to having to repeat the
year. But I escaped this disgrace. One day I learned that we were moving,
to Traunstein in Bavaria, a place for which my grandfather could not find
a good word to say, because it was in Germany, and for Germany he had
nothing but condemnation when he was in a bad temper, whether or not
Germany had any relevance to the particular situation. The Germans! he
would exclaim with infinite contempt, though nobody quite knew what
the Germans had to do with whatever happened to have aroused his ire.
The Germans! Scarcely had he uttered this angry exclamation than his
tension relaxed and his demeanour became normal again. His son-in-law
had been unable to find work anywhere but in Bavaria, and Bavaria was
in Germany. The spell in paradise was over. The universal unemployment
in Austria had indirectly driven me out too. A small town in the mountains,
on the Chiemsee! he exclaimed, as if it were a disaster. But we have to
exist! I was to move to Traunstein with my mother and her husband in
advance of my grandparents, who at first did not consider moving at all,
and this made me unhappy. I could not be made to understand that
Seekirchen was at an end. It had been only a temporary stop. To have to
live from now on without my grandfather, under the régime of a stranger
who happened to have married my mother and whom my grandfather
referred to alternately as *your father* and *your guardian,* was quite inconceivable. This was a catastrophe which meant abandoning everything that
had gone to make up my paradise—not only Mirtel Cottage and Hipping

but also Hilda Ritzinger, the crossing-keeper's daughter, who had initiated me into the art of sledging and whose fainting fits I remember as the acme of theatricality. Towards the end of my stay in Seekirchen there were weeks when I spent more time in the crossing-keeper's cottage by the railway line than I did at Hipping. Hilda, like me, was only five years old, and if she wanted a sweetie (as we used to call them) from the kitchen cupboard, she would wait until her mother approached and then fall down in a faint. Her mother would throw herself on the child as she lay on the ground—she was her only child, as may be imagined—and blow air into her mouth to resuscitate her. If I was a witness to such a dramatic event, Hilda would give me a sidelong wink and allow the rescue operation to proceed. She would lie on the ground, pretending to be dead, and come to life only when her mother put a sweetie in her mouth. Her mother would then hug her resuscitated daughter and give her a few more sweeties, and one or two would come my way as well. I recall that I often stayed at Hilda Ritzinger's house, which was some four hundred or five hundred yards from Mirtel Cottage, until after dark. This was not allowed. My grandfather would come to the door of our house and blow a shrill blast on a railwayman's whistle which could be heard down in the valley; this always put an immediate end to my visits. One thing was now clear: my paradise was no longer what it had been. The teacher had managed to turn it into a hell. I had already been too long at Hipping Farm, which in two or three years had changed radically. There was now only one stable lad instead of three, and only two cowgirls instead of five. There were fewer cows and less milk. There was constant talk of war, which failed to break out. The hairdresser's wife died, so there were no more dinners at her house. The old farmer and his wife at Hipping both died and lay in state in the farm annexe within a few weeks of each other. The funeral procession twice made its way down from Hipping to Seekirchen. For some reason the air was no longer as spicy as it had been. My grandfather had become impatient with me. Traunstein—how dreadful! he would exclaim, and retire to his room straight after supper. But there was absolutely no possibility of earning a living here; in Austria we had no chance of survival. All hope was now concentrated not on Traunstein but on a famous author who lived nearby, in my grandparents' home village of Henndorf. I was given to understand that my grandmother had taken a manuscript to the famous man, who was trying to find a publisher for it. We waited. Our walks were no longer relaxing but sheer torture. My grandfather began threatening suicide again. Through the so-called Winter Help scheme we received a few long pea-meal sausages, sugar, and bread. It was depressing to go and collect the bag of provisions at the local administrative offices. I went there with my grandmother. Our only pleasure, if it could be called that, was now the Eumig radio, though it seemed to bring only disturbing news which made my grandfather increasingly gloomy. There was much talk of radical change and of union with Germany, but I had no idea what it was all about. For the first time I heard the words *Hitler* and *National Socialism*. Unfortunately one doesn't stay young, my grandfather said. He was an enthusiastic admirer of Switzerland and had been one for almost thirty years—in fact, ever since he had left that country. *Switzerland is heaven*, he said. *Do we really have to go to Germany? It turns my stomach just to think of it. But then we've no choice.* It was at this time that I saw a real play for the first time in my life, in the assembly room of the Zauner Hotel in Seekirchen. The room was packed, and I was scarcely able to breathe. I stood on a chair against the wall at the back, with Hipping Hansi next to me. On the stage was a completely naked man, tied to the trunk of a tree and being soundly whipped. When the scene was over, everybody clapped and shouted with enthusiasm. I no longer know what kind of play it was. All the same, my first experience of the stage was a shocking one. One day a telegram arrived, informing my grandfather that his novel had been accepted by a publisher in Vienna. The famous man had been as good as his word. The book was published, and my grandfather got a national prize for it. The first and only success had been achieved. My grandfather was fifty-six. The prize-money was sufficient for him to order a winter overcoat from Janka the tailor and get some *tableware fit for human beings,* as he put it. Yes, he said, you shouldn't give in, and you certainly shouldn't give up. My guardian was already in Traunstein, working for Schreiner the hairdresser in the Schaumburgerstrasse. My grandparents were not going to move until my guardian had found them somewhere to live in Traunstein—if possible, my grandfather repeatedly stipulated, *not in Traunstein itself but in the vicinity, out in the country but not too far away.* It was not easy. I was to stay on with my grandparents for a while. I had a period of grace in which to wind up my paradise. I went my various ways, knowing that it was for the very last time. We also visited the so-called literary celebrity in Henndorf. There had been a reconciliation between my grandfather and his sister Rosina, and he was able to set foot inside his family home once more, though not without some misgivings.

He even sat in the guests' garden and counted all the antlers on the wall of the reception room on the ground floor, a room of generous proportions. These were all trophies of his brother, who, as I have mentioned, had committed suicide, on the Zifanken, the highest mountain in the area. What would have become of me, my grandfather said, if I had stayed here and not thrown away my inheritance? Then he immediately added: But what *has* become of me? However you look at it, it's pretty awful. We walked round the house, and my grandfather took me on a tour of all the rooms, from top to bottom, all filled with the most beautiful eighteenth-century furniture. *That's an Empire piece,* he said, examining a chest of drawers—*my mother's chest of drawers,* he said, her favourite one. Or: Napoleon is supposed to have slept in this bed. Then he added: There's hardly a bed Napoleon didn't sleep in! All this could have been mine, but it's absolutely right that I should have nothing, nothing at all, except myself, your grandmother, and you. To think we're going to live in Germany! It was a nightmare. During these months he was often invited by the famous writer, the man who had made possible his first and only success and whose house was frequented almost daily by others no less famous than himself. The famous writer had two daughters with whom I was allowed to play. They were somewhat older than I was and had a log hut in the garden for their own use. The house had once been a mill-house—it was called the *Wiesmühle* or "Meadow Mill"—and had originally belonged to a famous Viennese opera singer who, at the height of his career, had sung the part of Baron Ochs in *Der Rosenkavalier,* only to die shortly afterwards. I was allowed to spend the night in this wooden house with the writer's daughters. The world of these famous people seemed to me quite sensational. As the celebrities arrived, alighted from their cars, and walked up the garden, we children watched in admiration through the upper window of the log hut. Famous actors, writers, sculptors—in fact, artists and intellectuals of all kinds—went in and out of the house. The famous writer was completely different from my grandfather, who, though of course he was also a writer, was not at all famous. Sometimes I was even allowed to sit next to one of these famous people at table. A white-haired gentleman with a blind wife was the focus of the most interesting dinner I ever witnessed as a child. The most celebrated author of his time had no sooner entered the hall than he asked, *Where can one change for dinner?* This impressed me greatly. At table everybody surrounding this enormously famous guest was condemned to silence. All these writers looked quite different from my grandfather, and they were all said to be extremely famous, whereas my grandfather was always said to be completely unknown. My grandfather is completely unknown to this day. First thing in the morning I was allowed to get into what was called my saloon car, the two-wheeled carriage drawn by a long handle, which we had brought from Vienna, and I was pulled to Henndorf by my grandfather or my grandmother, sometimes by both of them, to visit the famous writer and his daughters. Everything a child could dream of awaited me there. The biggest treat of all was a cup of cocoa in the famous writer's kitchen. We made our way as poor people from Seekirchen to Henndorf in the morning, breathed the air of the big wide world, and were back at Seekirchen in the evening. We were poor, but nobody would have known. We all deported ourselves grandly. My grandmother, true to her baptism certificate, looked like a Friulian princess, and my grandfather looked like the thinker he was. They had only a few clothes to their name, but these were of first-class quality. Even if the present made fools of them, there was no mistaking their past. Meanwhile, there had been a fresh disaster. My uncle Farald—as he was called, though his real name was Rudolf—my grandfather's son, had fallen in love with a bricklayer's daughter in Seekirchen and promptly married her. She was a healthy lass, but she came from one of the most disreputable families in the village, a family of inveterate drunkards. Farald, the communist, had become a *free-lance artist* and lived by painting advertising signs for traders, having studied graphic design at an institute in Vienna. He designed colourful labels for processed cheese and painted gigantic index fingers next to shop doorways to draw attention to shopping bargains and special offers, or simply to a toilet located behind the building. He built himself a pile-dwelling in the lake, in the manner of the ancient Germans, and began to work on the various inventions which were to occupy him for the rest of his life. The bricklayer's daughter was the Auntie Fanny whom I set out to visit on my guardian's bicycle without knowing her address, as recounted at the outset of this narrative. She bore him three children, two girls and a boy. The eldest daughter fell to her death one Easter Monday, only two weeks after her marriage, while climbing the Schlenken with her husband. The second daughter also married, but I lost sight of her completely. The son was sent to prison at Garsten for five years at the age of seventeen after he and two like-minded youths had killed a wages clerk from the marble works of Mayr-Melnhof in a wood at Aigen; I believe that when he committed the crime, his mind was totally unbalanced. My grandfather was spared this rapid succession of calamities because they took place after his death and hence do not belong here. I still went for long walks with my grandfather, but we were both completely preoccupied by the thought of leaving Seekirchen and the Wallersee for good. I had arrived at a certain degree of maturity through my close contact with the philosopher and was in fact exceedingly well educated for my age—without, however, falling prey to the fatal fault of megalomania. While my grandfather was acquainting me more and more with all the peculiarities, audacities, and enormities of nature—he had always been my constant teacher—my uncle Farald, down in the village, had completely gone over to the side of the proletariat—*in the vulgarest manner possible,* as my grandfather put it. It made my grandfather very bitter. And it cast a pall over our last weeks and months in Seekirchen. Farald, who had hitherto been a passionate communist, intent on changing the world for the better, who had diced with the political devil day and night in Vienna, now spent most of his time in bed with the bricklayer's daughter, enjoying the peace of the countryside, which was totally unspoilt. My grandfather was assailed by a fit of rage whenever he saw one of my uncle's *paintings* in the village— a large loaf of bread outside a baker's shop, or an elongated lady's shoe outside a shoemaker's. *That's all I needed,* he would say, stabbing the ground with his stick but failing to make it sink in, as he doubtless wished he could on such occasions; then he would stalk off at once. The reputation enjoyed by my grandfather, the thinker—the great man, so to speak— suffered an immediate blow when his son, Farald, turned up at Seekirchen; and by the time the news of his marriage to the bricklayer's daughter came to be known, people no longer greeted him with the same deference as they had done previously, when they knew nothing about his son. Until then they knew only his beautiful Viennese daughter, my mother. At some stage there was a rapprochement between my grandfather's art and that of his son; they were jointly inspired to produce a synthesis of their respective talents in the form of a house sign for Hipping Farm, to which we all owed so much. My grandfather composed some encomiastic verses, and his son inscribed them on parchment paper. They were illuminated by the artist Freumbichler, after which they were framed and soon hung in the main room of the farm. I cannot recall the text, but the gist of it was that Hipping should forever and ever be protected from fire and storm and all other terrible natural forces. The verses still hang in the same place. I now spent a good deal of every day sitting with Hilda Ritzinger outside the crossing-keeper's house, waiting for the Vienna-to-Paris express. On just such a miracle of wheeled technology I was shortly to leave my beloved Seekirchen. I had no idea what Germany was like, and I was not at all impressed by the fact that my guardian had not been able to find work in Austria, but only in Germany—even though I was told it was a mere twenty miles the other side of the border, I did not think about it. After all, the grown-ups must know what to do. The high point of every evening was the Orient Express. The passengers sat by the brightly lit windows, eating their exquisite meals with silver cutlery. For a few seconds I had a glimpse of this world of luxury. Then I began to shiver and ran home. Hipping Hansi was secure, since he had a permanent home on his parents' farm. One day at noon we arrived in Traunstein. My mother had collected me from Mirtel Cottage. Life at my grandparents' was over. From now on I was to live with my mother and my guardian. He had found an apartment for us only a few houses away from his place of work in the Schaumburgerstrasse, on the second floor of number 4, at the corner of the Schaumburgerstrasse and the Taubenmarkt. It was an old house belonging to a rich, elderly widow of long standing by the name of Poschinger, who ran a large funeral business in the ground-floor premises. Over the door of the shop were the words POSCHINGER FUNERAL SERVICES. This was the house in which we were to live from now on. Two chests containing our belongings stood in a big room which from now on we called the living room. My mother and I sat on them and ate a couple of sausages with mustard. It was cold and unfriendly, and the rooms were undecorated. There were only two rooms and a kitchen; the large room, the living room, had two windows looking onto the Schaumburgerstrasse and two looking onto the Taubenmarkt, while the smaller room, the bedroom, had one window looking onto the Schaumburgerstrasse. There was also a cupboard for wood and coal with no window. The water tap was in the passage, at the far end of which, on the Taubenmarkt side, was the toilet. I can't say I was happy. My mother looked desperate. She had brought some furniture from Vienna, which to me seemed comfortable and elegant. Even today it has lost nothing of its comfortableness and elegance. From now on my favourite place to sit was our upholstered chair. I looked out of the windows and saw a completely different world—that of a small town, hitherto unknown to me. I knew the city and I knew the country proper, but I had never before seen a small town. Everything took place according to laws laid down centuries earlier. Everything was regulated by the raising and lowering of the shop blinds and the chiming of the church bells. In the Schaumburgerstrasse the butcher's shop smelt of meat, the baker's of bread; and from Winter the saddler's, which was diagonally opposite, came the smell of hides. We had the apartment decorated, naturally by my uncle Farald, who came over from Seekirchen to Traunstein for the purpose, armed with buckets and brushes. He donned a cap made out of newspaper, such as are worn by house-painters, painted the whole apartment in a few days, cracked a few of his jokes, and disappeared. The apartment smelt of fresh whitewash, and every inch was white. The furniture fitted into the right places more or less automatically. While my uncle was acting the part of decorator, I was reconnoitering the town. What impressed me most was the parish church, which was less than a hundred yards from where we lived. It had enormous vaulting which soared up all round the nave. On the first Sunday I attended mass with my mother, who normally did not go to church at all. It was probably a great feast day, and the nave appeared about to explode under the force of a powerful choir, a full fanfare, and a congregation which was so packed that nobody could possibly have fallen down. At last I thought I understood the meaning of the word gigantic, which my grandfather often used and which had always seemed mysterious. Wherever I went I was recognized as a stranger to the area and from the very start I was nicknamed the Austrian, which was by no means intended as a compliment, since to the Germans Austria meant quite simply nowhere. Hence I came from nowhere. Frau Poschinger had four daughters, three of them living in the house, above us on the third floor or below us on the first. They slept, changed their clothes, and spent Sunday afternoon on the third floor, and they cooked on the first, where they had a little kitchen with a large enamel cooker, and a room next to it where they practised the art of piano-playing. All four sisters played, as was to be expected, and on the wall above the piano hung two large framed photographs of Frau Poschinger and her late husband. It was here that I first heard a piano played, and it was the sound of the piano that emboldened me to knock at the Poschingers' door and to ask to be allowed to witness the music-making with my own eyes and ears. My request was granted. From now on I often sat by the piano and listened to one of the Poschinger daughters playing. Only three of them lived at home; the fourth, I was told, was already a secondary school teacher in Burghausen. She was the pride of the family. Only a few months after we moved into the house, the pride of the family died. A cyst under her arm brought the

secondary teacher's life to an abrupt end. For years afterwards the whole
Poschinger family went around in black, which was not altogether unfitting
in view of the fact that on the ground floor they ran what my grandfather
called a *death shop*. Now only sad pieces were played on the piano, and
these plunged me into the profoundest melancholy. *That's Brahms*, I was
told; *that's Beethoven . . . that's Mozart*. I couldn't tell the difference. I
joined the third class at the elementary school. To reach the school I had
a quarter of an hour's walk through the middle of the town. Diagonally
opposite the school was the prison, which still stands there, a forbidding
building with a ten-foot perimeter wall and heavily barred windows, which
are quite simply square holes. There was consequently something frightening about my daily walk to school. I now had not just one teacher but
several, a different one for each subject. As an Austrian I found it hard to
establish myself. I was the butt of the other children's mockery. I was
punished by the children of the local citizens with their expensive clothes,
who treated me with contempt, though I didn't know why. The teachers
didn't help me; on the contrary, they immediately used me as an occasion
for outbursts of fury. I was more helpless than I had ever been before. I
trembled upon entering the school and cried as I left it. Going to school
was like going to the scaffold, except that my ultimate decapitation was
endlessly postponed. It was a condition of continuous torment. I found
not a single child with whom I could make friends. I tried to ingratiate
myself but was rejected. I was in a terrible state. At home I was incapable
of doing my homework. I was suffering from a kind of paralysis which
even affected my brain. It was no use my mother keeping me in. I sat
there unable to do anything. So I began to lie and tell her I'd finished my
homework. I would flee from the house and walk through the streets and
alleyways, weeping out loud and seeking refuge in the parks and on the
railway embankments. If only I could die! That was my constant thought.
When I remembered Seekirchen I trembled with anguish. When I was
sure nobody could hear me I wept my heart out. I went up to the loft and
looked down at the Taubenmarkt, directly underneath. For the first time
I had the idea of doing away with myself. Repeatedly I stuck my head
through the skylight, but I always drew it in again: I was a coward. I had
no intention of being a lump of flesh lying in the road and disgusting
everybody. I had to go on living, although it seemed impossible. Perhaps
the washing line is my way out, I thought. I worked out a device which
involved attaching the line to a roof-beam and skilfully lowering myself

into the noose. The line broke and I fell down the steps of the loft onto the third floor. Should I jump in front of a car or put my head on the railway track? I had no way out. I played truant from school for the first time, since I suddenly had an overwhelming dread of presenting myself to my teachers without having done my homework. I did not want to go up to the teacher, who would tweak my ears and then, when he got no more fun out of that, give me about ten strokes of the cane on my outstretched hand. I turned back when I reached the gates of the prison, and as I ran away I heard the school bell: lessons had begun. I ran with my schoolbag first down to the Au and then towards the swimming pool. I thought everybody I met must know that I was bunking off school. I drew in my head. I was shivering. I squatted in the grass at the so-called Wochinger-Eck, a popular haunt for walkers, and wept out loud. There was only one thing I wished for in the world: that my grandfather would come to my rescue before it was too late. It seemed like the end. But instead of the end came release. My mother had inspected the farmhouse at Ettendorf and immediately pronounced it ideal for my grandfather. The rent was not high, and the location was superb. It was not far from the town, yet at the same time it was completely rural. It was precisely the kind of country setting that my grandfather thought so important. My mother began to plan how to arrange the accommodation for her parents. That will make a marvellous library, she said. And the southeast room of the house at Ettendorf was in fact turned into a marvellous library only a few weeks after my mother paid the first instalment of the rent and my grandparents moved in. Using his advance royalties, my grandfather employed a joiner to execute the design he himself had made. A truck bringing books and manuscripts arrived in front of the house, and the bookshelves were filled with books. Ever since his earliest youth, since his time in Basel, my grandfather said, he had collected books. They had no money, but they acquired more and more books. Thousands of them. There had been nothing like enough room for them in the study at Mirtel Cottage, so many of them had been stored in the loft. The walls of the study were now covered with books. *I'd no idea I'd accumulated so much intellectual wealth,* he said, *and so much intellectual junk.* Hegel, Kant, and Schopenhauer were to me well-known names, behind which lay enormous mysteries. *And then comes Shakespeare,* my grandfather said. *All of them summits of achievement, unscalable heights.* He sat there smoking his pipe. It had been better after all not to kill myself but to wait for him to come, I told myself. We were opening up a new paradise with Ettendorf at its center, like the one we had had in Seekirchen. Suddenly it didn't matter that it was a Bavarian paradise and not an Austrian one. Memories of Seekirchen, and in my grandfather's case, of Vienna, still dominated our minds. But gradually the transition to the Bavarian idyll was successfully accomplished. It had important points in its favour. It is true it was Catholic—rank Catholic—and Nazi—rank Nazi, but like Seekirchen, it was in the foothills of the Alps and hence suited to my grandfather's purposes: his mind was not oppressed, as he had feared, but liberated, as was later proved. He worked with greater élan than in Seekirchen, and he actually said himself that he had entered a decisive phase in his writing and reached a certain degree of philosophical understanding. I didn't know what that meant. It was always said that he was working on his big novel; and this fact, which was only ever spoken of in a whisper, was underlined by my grandmother, who vouchsafed the further information that it was *going to be over a thousand pages long*. It was completely beyond me how anybody could sit down and write a thousand pages. Even a hundred assembled pages were beyond my comprehension. On the other hand, I can still hear my grandfather saying, *Everything one writes is nonsense.* So how could he think of writing a thousand pages of nonsense? He always had the most incredible ideas, but he always felt that these ideas were the cause of his failure. We all fail, he said time and again. That is the thought that most occupies my mind too. Naturally, I had no idea what failure was, what it meant, what it could mean, though I myself was already going through a process of failure, non-stop failure; at school I failed at everything with incredible consistency. My efforts were of no avail; my repeated fresh starts and attempts to improve never got beyond the first stage. My teachers had no patience and pushed me deeper into the morass when they should have been pulling me out of it. They kicked me wherever they could. They too took a liking to my nickname "the Austrian"; they used it to torment me, persecuting me day and night, so that I no longer had any respite whatever. I added wrongly, divided wrongly, and soon could not tell top from bottom. My handwriting was so bad that whenever my work was handed in, it was held up as a glaring example of thoughtlessness and negligence. Hardly a day passed when I did not have to go to the front of the class for a few strokes of the cane. I knew what they were for, but I did not know how I came to deserve them. I was soon put down among the so-called dunces, the gang of hopeless blockheads, who believed that I was one of them. There was no

way for me to escape. The so-called clever pupils shunned me. I soon saw
that I belonged neither to the one group nor to the other, that I did not
fit into any group. In addition to this, I did not have respected parents;
I was, so to speak, the offspring of a poor, fly-by-night family. We did
not have a house, only lodgings, and that said everything. To live in
lodgings and not to have your own house was a death warrant in Traunstein
right from the beginning. We had three children from the orphanage in
our class, and they were the ones I felt closest to. They were brought to
school every morning, holding hands, by one of the nuns from the orphanage, which was in the road leading to the Au, and they wore coarse
grey coats and trousers similar to those worn by prisoners. They always
had close-cropped hair and were basically ignored by their classmates; they
made a nuisance of themselves, but nobody got into a fight with them.
During breaks the rich children ate enormous apples and thickly buttered
slices of bread, while I and my fellow-sufferers from the orphanage had to
make do with a piece of dry bread. We were four silent conspirators. I
was a consistent failure, and I gradually stopped making any effort. Even
my grandfather knew of no way out. Being with him was my compensation.
As soon as I could, I would run across the Taubenmarkt, down the Schnitz-
elbaum Steps to the gasworks and past the gasworks to Ettendorf. That
took a quarter of an hour. Panting for breath, I would fall into my grandfather's arms. While Schorschi still had to work—he went to school in
Surberg, the community to which Ettendorf belonged—I was allowed to
accompany my grandfather on his so-called evening constitutional. My
mother had never attended any school, public or private, since she had
been destined to become a prima ballerina and had had only one teacher
in her childhood, my grandfather, who taught her at home. Why did I
have to go to school? Only because the law had changed! I did not understand this. I did not understand the world; I understood nothing,
nothing made sense any longer. I heard what my grandfather said, but it
did not help me in dealing with my teachers. I was not as stupid as the
others, but I was unfit for school. My lack of interest in what I was taught
at school caused me to fall further and further down in the class. Although
my grandfather was now present and Ettendorf had become the holy mountain, my daily place of pilgrimage, I was still squirming wretchedly in
the nets of the school, in the fangs of the teachers. Soon I shall suffocate,
I thought. I turned back again outside the school gate, having been struck
once more by the idea of buying myself a platform ticket. I used to get

one from the machine for ten pfennigs, walk through the barrier, and board a train, any train. My first journey took me to Waging. The train passed directly below my grandparents' house at Ettendorf; I cried as we passed it. The engine gave off steam as if in some supreme effort. The route lay through woods, ravines, marshes, and meadows. I pictured my place in the classroom: it was empty. After travelling in a large curve, the train passed along an avenue of poplars and pulled into Waging. It'll be the third lesson by now, I thought. The teacher, furious at my absence, grew into a monster. Waging was a quiet and totally unpretentious place, popular because of its lake, which was shallow and hence always quite warm. But dreary. The lake was surrounded by reeds, and when one went into the water one found oneself wading in a kind of brown soup. But I was impressed by the fact that this place, which only made me feel sadder than I was already, had its own railway, with not only third-class but second-class carriages too. In some way, I told myself, the place must have an importance which was not immediately apparent. On my return journey I employed the same method as on the outward trip: I got myself a platform ticket from the machine and was able to go through the barrier with no trouble. I knew that the conductor remained sitting on the platform of the last coach and did not check the passengers. Had he come down the train, I would have hidden in the toilet; but he did not come. At about the time when school ended, I turned up at home. My mother knew nothing about my excursion. I threw my schoolbag on the kitchen bench and sat down to my dinner. I put on an act, but I did not play it well enough, and my mother at once became suspicious. Finally I confessed my enormity. Before my mother could reach for the whip, which had already found its place on the kitchen cupboard, I jumped up and crouched in the corner by the door. She whipped me so long that one of the Poschinger sisters came rushing upstairs to find out the reason for my pitiful cries. It was Elli, the eldest. My mother had stopped hitting me, but the whip was still shaking in her hand. Elli Poschinger asked what I'd done this time. I really was a dreadful child, a trouble-maker, as she put it. Elli Poschinger, who had set herself up, so to speak, as my mother's assistant, used the word *trouble-maker* several times. This word cut me to the quick. From this moment, when she first uttered the word *trouble-maker,* I was afraid of Elli Poschinger. She was a huge, strong woman, but thoroughly good-natured, though I was not to know this. She was the first of the Poschinger girls to marry, but she lost her husband in the war, only a few weeks later. As chance would have it, he was last seen alive by my guardian, of all people, who, like him, was serving in the Montenegrin karst. My guardian would often go and sit with Elli Poschinger when she felt the need to give vent to her grief. He would talk about her husband and say, *He was looking out of a hole in the rock*—whereupon Elli Poschinger invariably burst into tears. I was the most talented child but at the same time the least able where school was concerned. My talents were not, as one might have thought, conducive to my school progress but were in the highest degree detrimental to it. Fundamentally I was more advanced than the others, and the knowledge I had brought with me from Seekirchen was far more extensive than what my classmates had to learn. My misfortune was that I was unable to rid myself of my positively unhealthy aversion to school, which my grandfather had inculcated into me; all my ideas about school were coloured by my grandfather's maxim about school being geared to produce stupidity and philistinism, and this determined my entire attitude. My mother talked to the teachers, and they predicted nothing but disaster for me. My mother blamed everything on our move. My grandfather defended me and not the school. Every day I descended into hell, whence I returned to the purgatory of the Schaumburgerstrasse and then, in the afternoon, to the holy mountain of my grandfather. Every morning I took my school things with me and ran down the holy mountain straight into hell. There the devils tormented me ever more outrageously. At this time Austria suddenly became part of Germany, and the word Austria was no longer allowed to be uttered. People here had long ago given up the traditional greeting *Grüssgott* in favour of *Heil Hitler,* and in Traunstein on Sundays one no longer saw the hordes of the faithful at prayer but the hordes of brown-shirts screaming their heads off. There had been none of these in Austria. At a rally held in Traunstein in 1939, tens of thousands of brown-shirts paraded in the town square with hundreds of flags belonging to different Nazi groups. They sang The Horst Wessel Song and *Es zittern die morschen Knochen*. The climax of the ceremony—to which I had gone first thing in the morning, prompted by my thirst for sensation and my anxiety not to miss anything—was to be a speech by Giesler, the Gauleiter of Munich. I can still see Giesler climbing onto the platform and beginning to rant. I did not understand a word, as the loudspeakers which were placed all round the square to transmit Giesler's speech produced only a tremendous croaking noise. Suddenly Gauleiter Giesler collapsed and disappeared behind the speaker's desk like an ochre-

coloured doll. Immediately the word went round the crowd that he had
had a heart attack. The tens of thousands marched off, and peace reigned
once more in the town square. That evening on the radio we heard the
official confirmation of Gauleiter Giesler's death. At this rally I was not
yet a member of the Nazi Young People's organisation, a junior branch
of the Hitler Youth. Shortly afterwards I was. Without having been asked,
I was one day made to parade in the yard of the senior school, which stands
next to the prison, together with a number of other children of my age,
in front of a junior group leader. The Young People wore black corduroy
trousers and brown shirts; round the collar they wore a black neckerchief
which had to be pulled through a plaited leather ring on the chest. They
also wore white knee-length socks. Thinking that corduroy was quite
simply corduroy, my grandmother had a pair of trousers made for me by
the firm of Teufel in the town square, the leading outfitters, who had a
resident tailor; but she had them made of brown corduroy, since she
preferred brown to black. When I turned up on parade, the only new
member of the Young People wearing brown corduroy trousers instead of
the black worn by all the others, the junior group leader boxed my ears
and chased me from the yard with the order to appear next time in the
regulation black corduroy trousers. A black pair was now made for me in
great haste. The Young People's organisation was more dreadful than
school. I was soon fed up with constantly singing the same brainless songs
and marching down the same streets yelling my head off. I hated the so-
called pre-military training; I was not suited to playing at war. My family
implored me to endure these Young People's torture sessions, though
without telling me why I should; and to please them I did so. I was used
to being independent and spending the greater part of my time alone; I
hated the herd and loathed the masses—hundreds and thousands of voices
bellowing from one great communal mouth. The only thing about the
Young People that impressed me was the absolutely rainproof brown hood
they wore. I was not in the least troubled by the fact that brown was the
party colour. My grandfather found the Young People's organisation appalling, *but you must go to it—that's my dearest wish,* he said, *even if it costs
you the greatest effort of will.* I was soon sick of the whole thing. My one
chance lay in my skill at running. I always came first, whether it was in
the fifty metres, the hundred metres, or the five hundred metres. I found
that in these competitions, held twice a year, I was unreservedly admired.
I was placed on a pedestal and honoured, while the leader fixed a victor's

pin to my chest. I went home wearing it proudly. This saved me from
being ostracized. I won several victor's pins. On one occasion I won the
swimming championship and got a pin for that too. But having pins stuck
to my chest did not in the least diminish my loathing for the Young
People's organisation and its tyranny. Suddenly, as the boy wonder at
running, I was able to allow myself more liberties than the others, and I
exploited this to the full. Formerly I had run fast only because I was scared,
scared to death. The torment was lessened by winning my first pin. But
I found the whole thing utterly dreary. Of politics I still understood
nothing; everything to do with the Young People went against the grain.
My miraculous running achievements were appreciated only within the
organisation, where they brought me great advantages, but no notice was
taken of them at school. There my situation remained as intolerable as
ever. I was clumsy at giving the Hitler salute and was boxed round the
ears. I dozed off during the German lesson and was given ten of the best
with the cane. I was punished by being made to cover dozens of pages
with the line *I must pay attention*. My tormentors were enormously inventive.
But these were not just my teachers: my classmates tormented me too.
Perhaps I'm too stuck up, I thought. Or the direct opposite? Try as I
might, there was no solution. The educational horizon darkened. At this
time we were visited about twice a month in the Schaumburgerstrasse by
a lady called Dr. Popp, who had been married to a local doctor and lived
near the hospital; she used to bring us second-hand underclothes, socks,
and other articles in a large leather bag, together with what was known
as a health cake. She wore a tight costume, and her straight hair was
gathered up in a large bun at the back of her head. She had a first-floor
office in the Marienstrasse, where she sat behind a desk and looked me up
and down when I went there to collect a charity parcel, for we were
registered as a poor family in Traunstein and supported by the welfare
services. I was scared of this woman and at first incapable of saying a word
when confronted by her. I found it profoundly distasteful to have to say
thank you after the parcel was handed to me. I trembled with rage when
I had to go to see Dr. Popp, and I trembled even more at the humiliation
of having to accept charity at her hands. The underclothes filled me with
horror, and the health cake stuck in my gullet. My mother had nothing
against Dr. Popp. You must be nice to the lady, she said. My grandfather,
sitting in aloof eminence on the holy mountain, did not trouble himself
about such trivial matters, but I was in danger of being suffocated by

them. They came so thick and fast that I could no longer breathe. But Dr. Popp scared me more than anything else; I suspected that something was afoot, though I could not make out just what it was. I was not mistaken. One day Dr. Popp appeared at the Taubenmarkt entrance to our flat in the Schaumburgerstrasse and told my mother she was going to send me away for a rest—*to a home in the middle of the woods. The boy needs a change of air.* To my dismay my mother was thrilled by Dr. Popp's news. She expressed her thanks in advance and took hold of Dr. Popp's hands, while this lady directed her merciless and penetrating gaze at me. As soon as she had gone I wanted to shout out *No!* but I did not have the strength. My mother probably immediately found it a relief to learn that I was going to be out of the way for a while. She herself no longer had the strength to deal with me. I could no longer be controlled. There were daily rows, which sometimes culminated in a kitchen window being broken by the cups and pans my mother threw at it when she realised that the whip was no longer effective. I could see her desperation myself, and I cannot blame her. For a long time she had been unable to control me. She was completely exhausted by the child she could no longer tame. Only the prospect of not having me around her for a while made her feel liberated, though not happy. This fact depressed me; I could not understand how my mother, as it seemed to me, could want her own child to go to the devil. My dismay was even greater when my grandfather raised no objection to this holiday *in the middle of the woods.* He had seen Dr. Popp only briefly and found her appalling, but he assured me, *this woman only wants what is best for you.* Now I was completely deserted. Again I was plunged into the deepest gloom and thought of suicide. What prevented me from throwing myself out of the loft window or hanging myself or poisoning myself with my mother's sleeping powders was my reluctance to cause my grandfather the anguish of knowing that he had lost his grandson through his own negligence. It was only my love for my grandfather that stopped me from committing suicide as a child. But for this it would have been easy. All in all, the world was for years an intolerable burden which constantly threatened to crush me. But at the last moment I always recoiled from killing myself and accepted my fate. The time of my departure drew near; my underclothes were washed, my clothes cleaned, and my shoes taken to the cobbler for mending. I was to go to Saalfelden, a place in the mountains near Salzburg, not far away. On the evening before I left, Dr. Popp appeared with a large papier-mâché sign with a string attached, which I was to wear round my neck so that it would be clearly visible on my chest. On it were written my name and destination. It's only a two-hour journey, through delightful scenery, my grandfather said. You'll enjoy it, you'll see. What actually happened was quite different. The train did not go in the Salzburg direction, to Saalfelden, but in the Munich direction, to Saalfeld in Thuringia. My family had not read the sign carefully enough. It was dark when I left. I had been deceived. Traunstein disappeared, and the train sped through the marshes and swamps beside the Chiemsee in a westerly direction. Never before had I ridden in such a splendid train; the seats were upholstered, and we picked up speed from second to second almost noiselessly. At first I was able to control my feelings, but then I was overcome by tears at the shock of finding that I was on the way to Saalfeld, not Saalfelden. I can still hear them telling me that Uncle Farald would be coming to see me in two weeks' time. Everything had been a mistake—perhaps even a cruel trap. About Thuringia I knew nothing except that it lay in the north. I was plunged into the utmost misery. If my family knew I was going to Saalfeld and not Saalfelden, they had tricked me; if they did not know, then they were guilty of unpardonable carelessness. I was suddenly prepared to believe anything of them. I cursed them and would have dearly loved to die there and then. I cried my eyes out as we sped away from my home in the ever darkening night, a home which I now saw in its true and terrible colours. Even my grandfather was included in my suspicions and the curses to which they gave rise. The compartment I was sitting in, like several others in the red diesel train, was filled with fellow sufferers, though they did not share my despair but seemed enthusiastic about the adventure that had just begun. For most of them it was their very first train journey, whereas I had years of train travel behind me; dozens of times I had got on a train and steamed off, with or without a platform ticket. I had always succeeded in evading discovery, and in this way I had got to know all the lines leading away from Traunstein; even the one to Munich was familiar to me. My family could not plead the slightest extenuating circumstance; consciously or unconsciously they had behaved reprehensibly towards me. I was profoundly shocked by their negligence in confusing Saalfelden with Saalfeld, since it meant sending their supposedly much-loved son and grandson on a journey to an uncertain destination, without making sure what that destination really was. The nurse who was in charge of our group put her head into our compartment and counted us. Then she noticed that I was crying. *Boys don't cry,* she

said. Nobody else was crying, she said; all the others were starting the
journey happy and cheerful—a happy journey, she said—and I was the
only one who wasn't. That was the first reproach. Then she saw that,
unlike the others, I had no food to eat on the journey. *Oh, you poor boy!*
she exclaimed, *what parents you must have, letting you go on a long journey
with nothing to eat! What parents!* she repeated. That cut me to the quick.
I was incapable of telling her that my family thought I was going only to
Saalfelden, in the mountains near Salzburg, not to Saalfeld in Thuringia.
I was suddenly a poor boy, and a collection was made for me. In the end
I had more apples and sandwiches than all the others. All the children
were from the southeastern part of Upper Bavaria; they were real working-
class children with pale faces and broad accents. They were poorly and
tastelessly dressed. No sooner was the train in motion than they began to
eat. *Poor boy!* the nurse said to me and held my hands for a while. Suddenly
I was calm, having ceased to cry, though not because I felt secure in her
hands but because I was appalled and disgusted. I began to eat like all
the others. We were told we should be breaking our journey in Munich;
we were to be put up for the night in private houses, after which we would
continue our journey next morning from Munich to Saalfeld via Bamberg
and Lichtenfels. In the end my curiosity overcame my despair and I looked
eagerly out of the window. In Munich, as I could see from my seat by the
window, the night sky was transected by innumerable searchlights intended
for aerial defence. I had never seen a sight like it. Everybody crowded to
the window to observe all the rays probing the night sky. Up to now no
bombs had fallen on Munich. The sight of these columns of light was my
first experience of war. I had not been particularly affected by the fact that
my guardian had been called up a long time before, in the first place for
service in Poland; but the spectacle of the searchlights was something
tremendous. In Munich five of us were billeted in one flat, where an old
woman was waiting to give us supper. After we had had our supper, we
went to bed behind a glass door covered by beautiful old tapestries with
Oriental patterns. As may be imagined, it was a sleepless night. That was
a blessing, since for the first time in ages, being unable or unwilling to
sleep, I did not wet the bed. For I had been a bed-wetter for some time;
in addition to being a trouble-maker I had in due course become a bed-
wetter. There was not a single night at home when I did not wake up—
deeply distressed, as may be imagined—on a wet sheet. There are reasons
for bed-wetting, but at that time I had no idea what they were. As soon

as I woke up I would be utterly miserable, trembling with fear. Hardly had I got up, trying to cover up my disgrace with the blanket, than my mother would furiously whip off the blanket and throw the sheet over my face. It went on for months, in fact for years. I had a new name, the most mortifying of all: the bed-wetter! When I came home from school and was half-way up the Schaumburgerstrasse, I could see my sheet, with its large yellow stain, hanging out of the window. My mother hung my wet sheets out of the window, one day on the side looking onto the Schaumburger-strasse, next day on the side overlooking the Taubenmarkt, *to deter other children, and show them all what you are!* she said. I could do nothing to counter this humiliation. My bed-wetting gradually became worse. When I woke up, it was always too late. I recall that for years I not only wet the bed but constantly wet my trousers during the day. In winter, not daring to go home because of my disgrace, I would walk round the town for hours, freezing and shivering, hoping that my underclothes would dry in due course; but this was a vain hope. The insides of my thighs were constantly chapped and inflamed with urine. Every step I took was torture. Accidents happened constantly—in church, at skiing, everywhere and all the time. When I went to confession, to which I was sent by my mother, it would happen while I was on my knees reciting my sins. When I left the confessional, I saw the puddle on the floor and felt ashamed. And it happened before I entered the school gate if I had to speak to one of my so-called betters. And always at night. I can still hear my mother saying to Dr. Popp, *He's a bed-wetter, I'm at my wits' end.* I think it was this revelation which led to my being sent off to Saalfeld. Everybody in the Taubenmarkt and the Schaumburgerstrasse knew I was a bed-wetter, for every day my mother would hoist the flag which proclaimed my disgrace. I would come home from school hanging my head, and there it was, fluttering in the breeze, telling all and sundry what I was. And so I was ashamed in front of all and sundry; it may not have been true that everybody knew I wet the bed, but I believed it was. And naturally accidents happened during lessons at school too, if they had not already happened outside the gate. During this night in Munich, for the first time for ages, I did not wet the bed. The sheet remained dry. But for ages to come, that was the last and only occasion. Today I know that what seemed to me, during these years of bed-wetting, to be something completely unnatural and alarmingly abnormal was in fact a perfectly natural outcome of my cir-cumstances. When my mother admitted to Dr. Westermayer, our family

doctor, that she was entirely at her wits' end about my bed-wetting, he
only shrugged his shoulders. When I was ill, this fat Dr. Westermayer
would bend over me, without removing his glowing cigar from his mouth,
and listen to my breathing, with his great sweaty head resting on my
chest. Doctors have no idea what to do; they only note what is wrong.
On one occasion I was lucky enough to be woken by my urge to pass water
before it happened. I got out of bed and managed to reach the closet just
in time, but in the morning it turned out that I had confused the door
of the wash-cupboard with that of the closet, since both were alike. I was
doubly horrified, and my punishment was dreadful. The night in Munich
was filled with all the desperate thoughts one can imagine a child having.
Early in the morning the five of us, all with our cardboard signs round
our necks, crowded into one compartment of an express bound for Berlin.
The line from Munich to Bamberg, Lichtenfels, and beyond was not yet
electrified, and the train was hauled by one of the giant Borsig engines.
For most of the journey the landscape was hidden by a cloud of stinking
black smoke. Whenever the train stopped, our heads were at the windows.
We already knew one another's names, where we all came from, what our
parents were, and what our families did. Why are you called Bernhard if
your father is called Fabjan? I was asked, not for the first time. I had
already had to endure it thousands of times before. I explained that my
father was not really my father, but my guardian, and that I had not been
adopted. Had I been adopted, I would be called Fabjan and not Bernhard.
My real father was still alive, but I knew nothing of his whereabouts or
indeed anything about him. I had never seen him. My companions could
make nothing of what I told them about myself, but it was more extraordinary than what they had to tell. I had a grandfather, I said, who was a
writer and whom I loved more than anybody else. They had no idea what
a writer was. Their grandfathers were tilers and bricklayers. I explained
to them that a writer spent his time writing, writing manuscripts. But
"manuscript" was another word they had never heard. There was no point
in going on. In Saalfeld we formed a fairly large group on the station
platform; there were possibly about fifty or more of us, lined up in threes
behind the nurse. I had a feeling that she paid more attention to me than
she did to the others. I thought: She knows who and what I am, a shocking
character, a bed-wetter and trouble-maker and more besides. I did not
dare to look her straight in the eye. Did my family know I was now in
Saalfeld and not Saalfelden? As I now know, they only learned this a week

after my departure, from a picture postcard of Saalfeld which I sent the very next day after my arrival to set their minds at rest, as we were all instructed to do by the nurse. They were greatly alarmed. They had made a mistake which I shall not forget as long as I live. The children's holiday home lay in the middle of the forest—Dr. Popp had told the truth—in a large clearing. Part of it was a half-timbered building with a number of gables and turrets; perhaps it had once been a hunting lodge. But though it was called a children's holiday home, it was actually nothing of the sort but—as I now know, having been back there forty years later—*a home for maladjusted children.* It seemed as though I had come to an idyllic spot. There were a lot of small rooms with bunk beds. I was given a top bunk. The day began with the raising of the swastika flag, which flew in the courtyard until dark. We had to parade round the flagstaff, raise our hands in the Hitler salute, and shout "Heil Hitler" when the flag had been hoisted. At nightfall the flag was lowered again, and again we had to parade in the same way; when the flag had been lowered, we again had to raise our hands and give the Hitler salute. Once it had been raised, we had to form threes and march off. We had to sing the songs we were taught in the first few days. I can no longer remember what the songs were, though the one we sang most often centred upon the word *Steigerwald.* The countryside was beautiful but not exciting. The food was good. We had two "instructors" who took charge of us from the very beginning, after we had been handed over by the nurses. The proceedings began with a talk about punctuality, cleanliness, and obedience—about exactly how to raise our hands when giving the Hitler salute, and so forth. It was my misfortune to be revealed as a bed-wetter on the very first night. The method of treatment used on me in Saalfeld was to display my sheet with the large yellow stain in the breakfast-room and announce that it was mine. But this was not the only way in which the bed-wetter was punished: he did not get any of the so-called "sweet soup" like the others—he got no breakfast at all. This "sweet soup" was a mixture of milk, flour, and cocoa served in soup plates, and I adored it. The more often I was denied it— and that was almost every day—the more I longed for it. I suffered this deprivation throughout my stay at Saalfeld because I could not be cured of my bed-wetting. I was given medicines, but they did no good. It was depressing to see my sheet stretched out in the breakfast-room every morning and to sit there without any breakfast. I was a disgrace, and the friends I made in the first few days were my friends no longer. I was eyed with

suspicion and a certain amount of malicious glee. Nobody wanted to sit
next to a bed-wetter; nobody wanted to have anything to do with a bed-
wetter; and, naturally, nobody wanted to sleep in the same room as a bed-
wetter. I was suddenly more isolated than ever before. Every two weeks
we were allowed to write home, but we had to send cheerful news. It is
no longer possible today to imagine how profoundly desperate I was. On
an empty stomach I shouted "Heil Hitler" as the flag was lowered and
took part in the marching, singing the song about the Steigerwald. I had
entered a new hell. But I had one companion in my suffering. His name
was Quehenberger, a name I shall not forget as long as I live. This was a
boy suffering from rickets, with deformed hands and legs. He was as thin
as a rake. He was the most pitiful figure imaginable, and it was pathetic
to see him shouting "Heil Hitler" and marching through the Thuringian
Forest. Every night he had a far worse accident than I did: he was doubly
incontinent. I can remember exactly how dreadful it was: in the washroom
downstairs, where the cellars were, Quehenberger had his soiled sheet
wrapped round his head, while I had a white powder applied to my chapped
thighs round the testicles. I had found a friend, someone who was much
more of a victim than I was. Naturally, the instructors and nurses often
spoke words of encouragement to us, but most of the time they could not
control themselves and treated us badly. German boys don't cry! And in
the Thuringian Forest I did hardly anything but cry. Where Quehenberger
and I were concerned, the skill of the instructors and the nurses failed.
Instead of improving, our condition became worse. I longed to be back
in Traunstein, and above all in Ettendorf with my grandfather; but months
passed before the torture was over. Any mention of Thuringia, especially
of the Thuringian Forest, is still capable of striking terror into me. Three
years ago I revisited this scene of my deepest despair on my way to Weimar
and Leipzig. I had not expected to find it again, but it actually existed,
completely unchanged. The children who were now accommodated in the
half-timbered building, just as we had been, had left their shoes, which
were wet from marching, on the wooden fence by the entrance. The only
difference is that the building no longer stands in a clearing, since the
wood all around it has been cleared, so that it is now surrounded by fields.
As I drove there in my car, having enquired about the location of the
holiday home in Saalfeld (which was quite different from the way I remembered it), I was stopped a few times by the so-called People's Police.
In Saalfeld I learned that it was not a holiday home but *a home for maladjusted*

children. I was allowed to pass. I had an Austrian number plate, which seemed to them suspicious. But I was there forty years ago, I told the man whom I approached in the town square of Saalfeld. He simply shook his head, turned away, and walked off. I looked at the children's shoes and boots placed on the fence, and at once an instructor appeared. The washroom is down there, I said, and the instructor confirmed it. Up there are the bedrooms. Through there is the breakfast room. Nothing had changed. On the flagpost hung the flag of the German Democratic Republic. The instructor was a young man and had been talking to me for only a few minutes when he was summoned by a whistle from an obviously senior colleague who was looking out of an upstairs window. It was time for me to leave. I continued my journey to Weimar and Leipzig. I ought not to have visited this scene of terror, I thought at the time. Today I think differently. It is a good thing I did. Times and methods do not change. This was yet another proof. The days spent in the home were all alike. In the mornings we marched up and down in all directions. In the afternoons there were lessons on all the elementary school subjects. Here too I suffered from the same paralysis as before. A few cards arrived from my mother and my grandfather. I cried over these cards to such an extent that the writing became illegible. I had them under my pillow when I went to sleep. Before going to sleep I had only two wishes: to be allowed to have sweet soup for breakfast and to be back with my grandfather soon. A few weeks before I left the home the nurses rehearsed a Christmas play with us. I was given the part of an angel, a very minor part, since I was not trusted to do anything properly. I had only two or three sentences to say, but all the same I did have a scene to myself. All my life I had had the greatest difficulty in learning things by heart; I could not remember even the shortest text. Even today I cannot imagine how actors manage to learn a long text, sometimes running to a hundred pages. It will always remain a mystery to me. At all events I had the greatest difficulty in learning and memorizing two sentences in the course of two or three weeks. Then came the dress rehearsal at which everything went well. But when the performance came and it was time for me to make my entrance, the nurse who had dreamt up the play unexpectedly prodded me in the back and propelled me into the hall. I managed to stay on my feet, but I could not utter a word. In my bewilderment I stretched out my arms (which were meant to be wings) as I had been instructed, but the words would not come. Then the authoress grabbed hold of the pink underslip belonging to her, which she had put on me to serve as the angel's costume, and dragged me off the stage. I ended up on a bench in the corridor. The play continued. Everything went well; only the angel was a failure. He sat outside in the corridor and wept while inside the hall the curtain fell and the applause rang out. The one thing that stands out in my memory as my greatest experience in the Thuringian Forest is a visit to a grotto near Rudolstadt. We were taken up in an elevator into the interior of a gigantic crystal mountain. Never in my whole life had I seen colours of more exquisite beauty. This was the fairy-tale world I had always longed to see. Every now and then we would come across large crystals lying on the ground all over the area. I took some samples back home with me. Another thing I enjoyed was the local chocolate: in Saalfeld there was the famous Mauxion chocolate factory, and all over the town there were automatic machines which delivered a bar of this incomparable delicacy for ten pfennigs. All our pocket money ended up in these machines. Even today I can see myself as clearly as if it were yesterday—not over forty years ago—marching through the Thuringian Forest and singing as I marched. We cleaned our shoes in the courtyard with a cream called *Schmollpasta,* which was brought along by some boys who joined us from Vienna. When I got home I had a baby brother. We all loved him. Two years later a sister arrived, and we all loved her too. The theatre of war had now spread to Russia, and my guardian was fighting somewhere between Kiev and Moscow. My uncle Farald wrote to us from Mosjøen and Narvik, where he was said to be serving with the mountain infantry. He was the joker of his outfit: in large community halls near the North Cape whole companies are supposed to have fallen about at his jokes. He got onto the staff of General Dietl. There was no trace left of the erstwhile communist. He sent us reindeer skins from Trondheim and elk antlers from Murmansk. We got a large number of photographs showing him dressed up as a Lapp. When he or my guardian was on leave, I walked proudly beside him down the Schaumburgerstrasse. Both wore decorations on their uniforms. The men of military age were serving in all theatres of war, in the north, south, east, and west, and there was daily mourning for the many who had fallen. The parish church bell was tolled both for those who died in civilian dress at home and for those who fell for the fatherland in what was called a foreign field. Pfenninger the sexton, who lived opposite the church in a little house which belonged to it, suffered from arthritis and had completely deformed fingers, and so one day he asked me to toll the bell for him. I had to throw the whole weight of my body onto the rope in order to get the bell to ring. I was given five pfennigs for every time I tolled it. Old Pfenninger's arthritis became more and more severe, and my trade increasingly flourished as scores of Traunstein's citizens fell in enemy territory. The war also brought a tremendous increase in general mortality. I not only had to toll the bell; I also had to hang out wood-framed blackboards for notices on the two main doors of the church—on these the names and ages of the deceased and the fallen were entered in chalk, which old Pfenninger could use only with great effort. I loved the Pfenningers' house. Not only did I get my earnings there; I was also given something good to eat, since old Frau Pfenninger was a superb cook. Even as a child I was fairly keen on money, and I was always running to old Pfenninger to ask whether anybody else had died. From my point of view there could not be enough deaths. When the blackboards were full up, there was a pleasant jingle of coins in my pockets. I had no scruples whatever. In the *Münchner Neueste Nachrichten*, the newspaper taken by the Poschinger family, there were whole pages devoted to the names of those killed on active service or in the bombing. It was the period of the so-called *terror attacks*. When the air-raid warning sounded, we could think of nothing better to do than shelter in the hall, where we remained until the all-clear. We squatted in front of the door leading directly from the hall to the death shop. I created an imaginary world of horror for myself from the dozens of long shrouds which hung from the shelves, some of them made of cheap crepe paper, others from artificial silk. Black veils, black jackets, and black skirts swung eerily in the draught which blew through the cracks in the side of the house facing the Schaumburgerstrasse. The Poschingers were doing more business than at any other time in their lives. But they did not benefit from the money they made, since money would no longer buy anything. For the first time in his life my grandfather earned some money: two books were printed (in Holland, not in Germany, it was said mysteriously), but he was unable to buy anything with the money, which he solemnly invested in the local savings bank. One day he got wind of a bargain. He read in the Traunstein paper that there was an easel for sale near Ruhpolding. *Painting,* he said, *that would suit you. An artistic activity!* He underlined the advertisement several times in red. We took the train to Ruhpolding and asked the way to the house where the easel awaited us. An ancient monstrosity, partly rotten, stood in a hallway that was almost totally dark. It was a great disappointment. We bought the easel, which we were told was once used by the famous painter Leibl, and it was transported, under the most difficult circumstances, to Traunstein. My grandfather paid for it in cash. On the way home, somewhere near Siegsdorf, my grandfather said, *Perhaps painting's the thing for you. You're extremely talented at drawing. You must do something artistic.* The easel was duly delivered a few days later and unloaded in the Schaumburgerstrasse. It had completely fallen apart. Shortly afterwards we burnt it in our living room stove. There was no more talk of painting. I wrote poems. They were about war and its heroes. I had an inkling that they were bad, and so I gave up. Suddenly, because there was so much talk of heroism, I tried to make myself into a hero. The best prospect for this was afforded by the Young People's organisation. I improved my performance in the various racing disciplines. Possibly my athletic fame had spread to the school after all, for people there began to take notice of it as a consequence of my wearing my victor's pins quite openly, even in class. I had won more pins than any of the others. Although I did not yet suspect it, I already *was* the school hero. I did not pay any more attention, I was no better than before; but the marks I got told of my progress at school. *Toughness* was the decisive word used at the time, and I took advantage of it. Suddenly the boy whom all had shunned was sought out by everyone. At this period, although it did not strike me at first, I gave up wetting the bed. I was the hero now, no longer the bedwetter. On one occasion I gave a tremendously exciting display of my heroism in front of hundreds of schoolchildren on the cinder track in the Au. I had run the hundred metres in record time and went on immediately to win the five hundred metres. I had won two victor's pins. The crowd went wild. I was a gladiator. The homage of the crowd made me feel good, and I ingeniously spun it out. But when I tried to do another small lap that same day, after everybody had left the sports field, I slipped and fell full-length on the cinder track, gashing my chin, forehead and both knees. I limped home from the Au by way of the steps by the cinema and through various side streets and back yards. Nobody was at home but Elli Poschinger. I must have been a pathetic sight. Elli Poschinger put me right in no time. She placed me on the cold kitchen range and began very dexterously, as I still recall precisely, to cut away loose fragments of flesh from my knees with a pair of large tailor's scissors. When she had treated the gaping wounds with spirit she said, *So, that's done!* She wrapped seemingly endless bandages round my knees, and after bathing the wounds on my chin and forehead she stuck plasters on them. Next day the victors were to be honoured. At the ceremony that morning I did full justice to the hero I now was. I lived up to the heroic image perfectly. My heroism was clearly to be seen in the form of two extravagantly large bandages. I wore them with pride, despite the extreme pain I was in, though of this I gave not the least hint. The only mementos I have today of this moment of glory are two large scars on my knees. Elli Poschinger made me immortal, at least for as long as I live. When I was eleven, Inge Winter, the youngest daughter of Winter the saddler, taught me the facts of life, or at any rate tried to, on the balcony overlooking her father's yard. I now had a second girl-friend, a successor to Hilda Ritzinger, who had meanwhile been forgotten and whose doings no longer interested me. I went down to the river Traun with Inge, did gymnastics with her on the struts of the railway bridge, and went running with her past the tennis courts to Bad Empfing, which was only a short walk from the cemetery in the wood. There I was again and again amazed by the grandiose tomb of the Poschingers. Maria, the latest of them to die (the one who had been a secondary school teacher in Burghausen), was pictured on a large photograph which leant against the granite. When one called into the tomb, a terrible echo came out. I often visited the mortuary chapel with my grandmother. The road led past the cemetery, which was rapidly increasing in size, to Wang. In Wang, on my early bicycle rides, I had got to know a farmer's wife from whom, all through the war, I was able to obtain a whole jug of milk as well as butter and dripping. I used to take her our unused tobacco coupons. I loved the old woman, who had every imaginable kind of flower in her little back garden. The whole house smelt of strange herbs, and on all the window-sills and cupboards there were large jars full of medicinal juices, jams, and honey. The Steyr-Waffen bicycle now had its time of glory. I was constantly painting it with silver paint and riding it all over the countryside around Traunstein, as far as Trostberg in one direction and Teisendorf in the other. I always wore a rucksack. When I had collected enough food—and I was nearly always successful—I was naturally welcomed with open arms on my return. Inge Winter not only introduced me to sex, a subject which was never mentioned at home, at least not in my presence; she also had entrée, as the daughter of a respected Traunstein citizen, to all the so-called better-class houses in the town. She took me with her wherever she went, and I soon got to know all these houses from the inside as well as from the outside. In summer I used to pick strawberries with her in an orchard the Winters owned near the barracks; we picked enormous basketsful, and I used to eat my fill. Her sister Barbara, the second eldest of the Winter children, was attending the secondary school and was said to be the cleverest of the family. One day Barbara attended mass at the parish church and went mad at the climax of the service. She went into the pulpit and proclaimed *a great joy*. She was taken to a clinic and from there to a lunatic asylum, after which she disappeared. The cleverest people are constantly in danger of going mad, my grandfather said. Unable to do anything with the money he had by now received from various publishers, he arranged for me to have violin lessons. I went to a violinist whose wife was Spanish; she looked just as I imagined a Spaniard should look—black-haired, and with a sophisticated curl in the middle of her forehead. It was said that she had been a concert-singer. I did not want to play the violin—I hated the instrument; but my grandfather saw me as a virtuoso violinist. He told me about Niccolò Paganini and extolled the great virtuosos. A whole world is opening up before you, he said. Just think, you may play in the world's most famous concert halls—in Vienna, Paris, Madrid, and—who knows?—one day even in New York. I loved hearing others play the violin, but I hated my own playing, and so it remained. On one occasion, not long before Christmas, it was snowing hard, and being in high spirits, I was jumping about for some reason in the town square. I was carrying the envelope which contained the monthly fee for my violin lessons and inadvertently threw the five-mark piece into a pile of snow. All my efforts to find it were in vain. In March, when the snow had gone, I found it again. There it was suddenly, gleaming. *I* had found it; nobody else had. I don't know whose idea it was, but one day I started delivering bread for Hilger, the baker opposite our apartment. I started work at half past five in the morning. At Hilger's bakery a large white linen bag was loaded onto my back; it was stuffed with dozens of little linen bags full of rolls and salt sticks ordered by the customers. These I hung on various door-handles throughout the town before going to school. In this way I earned my pocket money and was allowed to take home with me six items of my choice. And so we got half our breakfast for nothing. Once a week I had to push a two-wheeled cart loaded with large loaves up to the theological college on the hill overlooking Haslach; this was almost beyond my physical powers, but these were always exceeded by my ambition. Of course, the return journey downhill with the empty cart was always a joy. I can picture my mother and me in summer, pushing a small handcart through the town. I felt this to be a tremendous disgrace. We were on our way to the surrounding woods to collect the bark left behind by the woodcutters; we used the bark as fuel in winter. The loft was half-full of bark, which dried there very quickly. Usually I went alone. I loaded the handcart with as much bark as possible, and it was hard work pulling it. Coming downhill from the barracks, I rode on it, controlling the steering handle with my legs, until I reached the town. But we were not the only people who collected bark in this way. Many people found it necessary. It was nothing out of the ordinary. Unlike Inge Winter and the other middle-class children, I was given no money to spend at the annual fair in the Au; I had to earn it myself. I got myself employed by the hour on the roundabout; along with other children I went round in a circle, like the donkey at the well, hundreds, perhaps thousands of times to keep the roundabout moving, with nothing to look at but the turf which was trampled by my own feet and those of my toiling companions. With my earnings I tried my skill in the shooting gallery. I was afraid of the roundabout. The only time I rode on it I at once began to feel sick and had to vomit in midair. I marvelled at it from below. I marvelled at the hundreds of glass and china vases one could shoot, the jumping jacks, and the top hats. Once I was employed for days at a stall selling rubber shoe-soles. As payment I was given a dozen soles, a centimetre thick, to take home. Long after the war was over we were still wearing these rubber soles, nailed onto our wooden shoes, for the age of leather soles was long since past. We had a visit from the Busch Circus in the Au, and I decided I wanted to be an animal tamer; but having seen the enormous open mouths of the lions, I changed my mind. There was an air-raid warning almost every night, and later we had them in the daytime too. The flights of bombers, often well over a hundred of them, grouped above our heads and turned towards Munich to drop their deadly loads there. All the interesting things were now taking place in the air, in all weathers. We saw and heard them and were scared. One glorious day around noon, when my grandmother was sitting at the sewing machine in our apartment in the Schaumburgerstrasse, the roar of a bomber formation made us look out of the window. The American planes, in formations of six, gleamed in the sky on their rigid course towards Munich. Suddenly, from a still greater height, a German plane, a Messerschmidt 109, appeared and in no time shot down one of the silver giants. My grandmother and I saw the bomber drop out of formation and finally, with tremendous force, break into three parts which landed at widely separated spots. At the same time there were several white points indicating the members of the crew who had bailed out by parachute. It was a spectacle of unrelieved tragedy. Our stark noonday picture showed several parachutes which failed to open: we could see the black dots falling to earth faster than the parts of the plane. Other parachutes opened but caught fire for some reason and burnt out in no time, falling to earth with the crew-members attached to them. All this had no effect whatever on the bomber formation as a whole. It flew on to Munich. The town was too far away for us to hear the detonation. My grandmother, sensing excitement, got hold of me and ran with me to catch the next train to Waging, where she suspected the parts of the destroyed plane would have landed. She was right. At Otting, a place of pilgrimage situated on a hill, one stop before Waging, the remains were still smoking. One of the bomber's two enormous wings, about a hundred feet long, had fallen directly onto a pigsty, setting it on fire and killing about a hundred pigs. There was an unimaginable stench in the air when we at last arrived, out of breath, at the top of the hill. It was winter, and the air was icy. We had had to trudge through deep snow from the station up to the village. The inhabitants of Otting stood looking at the wreckage and finding fresh fragments of it. Great holes were to be seen in the snow, where the bodies of the Canadians (as they turned out to be) lay shattered after falling from the sky. I was horrified. Everywhere the snow was spattered with blood. There's an arm! I said, and on the arm was a watch. I no longer enjoyed the sight of war. What had been merely a sensation I now saw from a different angle. I wanted to see nothing more of war, which had now shown its horrible face to us, having until now been known only from a distance. We went back to Traunstein. I sought comfort from my grandfather. He had nothing to say. In the evening he and my grandmother sat in a corner of the room listening to a Swiss radio station. At the end of February and the beginning of March Schorschi and I spent our afternoons dragging the dead deer and their young out of their last retreats. We dug ditches and buried the frozen carcasses in them. I spent whatever time I could in Ettendorf. When my great-aunt Rosina died, my grandfather, her brother, went to Henndorf to attend the funeral. He had kept away from his birthplace in recent years. After the so-called funeral feast, which the mourners ate in the large assembly room of the family hotel, Rosina's younger sister, the much-travelled artist's widow, is said to have launched into a speech in which she repeatedly referred to herself as a *German woman. She referred to herself nonstop as a German woman, inspired by her new ideal, National Socialism. That was too much for me in the end, so I jumped up and said, Do you know what you are? You're not a German woman, you're a German sow!* They never saw each other again. They broke with each other over National Socialism. Marie was later paralysed by a stroke and finally went mad. When I visited her in the Weitloffgasse in Vienna just before her death, she was sitting in a chair specially made for her by a carpenter from Währing, burbling about her dear brother who had died a long time ago. After returning from the funeral of his sister Rosina (whose whole estate passed on her death to her daughter-in-law Justine), my grandfather was so disgusted—not just by what things had come to in his home village—that he exclaimed, The whole place stinks! Under most of the names on the gravestones in the cemetery they had engraved the words *party member.* After the war these dreadful words were removed. Again it was a notice in the *Traunsteiner Zeitung* that brought about a change in my existence: a commercial college in Passau advertised itself in the newspaper as an excellent institution. *That's just the thing for you,* my grandfather said. He bought two first-class tickets and we went to Passau. Instead of sitting in first class, we had to stand for about four hours till beyond Wels—and in a packed corridor. The journey in the military furlough train—there were hardly any others—was torture. When the train drew into Passau, we looked out of the window, and all we could see were grey walls and coal merchants' signs. My grandfather had booked a room for several nights in the famous *Passauer Wolf* hotel. But as we emerged from the station, he was so disgusted by what he had by then seen of Passau that he said, *No, this is no town for you. Passau's definitely not for you.* Next day we visited the commercial college, and I did the necessary entrance test—just because we happened to be there, for no other reason. I was now thirteen. Two months after our visit to Passau, long after we had forgotten all about it, we were reminded of this nightmarish journey by a letter from the college, which informed my grandfather that his grandson had passed the entrance test *with distinction.* My grandfather put his hand to his head and said, What a good thing it's not Passau! What a good thing I've decided to send you to Salzburg!

AN INDICATION OF THE CAUSE

Two thousand people every year attempt to put an end to their lives in the province of Salzburg. A tenth of these suicide attempts are successful. This means that in Austria, which together with Hungary and Sweden has the highest suicide rate in the world, Salzburg holds the national record.

SALZBURGER NACHRICHTEN, 6 May 1975

2

GRÜNKRANZ

WITH ITS POPULATION made up of two categories of people, those who do business and those upon whom they prey, the city has only a painful life to offer the young person who goes there to learn and to study; for sooner or later anyone who lives there, whatever his constitution, becomes disturbed and is eventually deranged and destroyed by the city, often in the most deadly and insidious manner. The extreme weather conditions have an unfailingly irritating, enervating, and sickening effect on the inhabitants, an effect which is compounded by the devastating influence of the Salzburg architecture. Consciously or unconsciously, these unfortunate inhabitants are all victims of the climate prevailing in the Alpine foothills, *to which they are relentlessly exposed, and which causes actual mental and physical damage, constantly undermining their constitution* and engendering a breed of irritating, enervating, and sickening human beings, given to insolence and insult and endowed with every kind of baseness and viciousness. The climate and the architecture conspire to produce a race of citizens who pursue their petty preoccupations, their stupidities and idiocies, their unscrupulous deals and melancholy obsessions within the cold damp walls of the city, and to provide an inexhaustible source of income for medical practitioners and funeral directors of every possible and impossible variety. Thirty years ago, when I myself went to Salzburg to learn and to study, I was prepared to love the city, but experience taught me to hate it. The adolescent boy, who had been condemned to spend his formative years in the city, against his will but by the choice of those responsible for his education, had been mentally and sentimentally predisposed in its favour, only to find himself a prisoner: on the one hand, a prisoner in the endless show trial staged to vindicate its world-wide fame—itself nothing more than a squalid device for making money and yet more money out of the exploitation of beauty—and on the other, a prisoner of the poverty and helplessness which afflicted his childhood and youth and became for him an impregnable fortress of anxiety and terror. Of Salzburg and the existence it afforded him at the time, he has—to put it neither too crudely nor too lightly—nothing but dismal memories, memories of experiences which darkened his youthful development and cast a fatal blight over his whole subsequent existence. In the face of lies, slander, and hypocrisy, he has to tell himself as he writes down this account, intended as an indication of what he experienced, that this city has shaped his whole nature, determined his whole way of thinking, and always exercised a malign and injurious influence on his mind and temperament, above all in those two decades of despair in which he was drilled and hectored into maturity, being constantly punished, directly or indirectly, for crimes and offences of which he was not guilty—decades in which any sensitivity or sensibility he possessed was ruthlessly trodden under foot and not the least effort was made to foster his creative ability. This period of study was without doubt the most terrible time of his life, during which he paid a high price, probably the highest possible price, for the continuance of his existence; and it is with this period and the feelings he had at this period that the present account is concerned. The city has never deserved or requited the love and affection he was prepared to bring to it, as a predisposition inherited from his elders; it has constantly and consistently rejected and repulsed him right up to the present day, striking him when he was defenceless and incapable of striking back. It is a city that has always dealt cruelly with anyone creative, hounding him, persecuting him, and ultimately destroying him; and had I myself not been able to turn my back on it at the crucial moment, when, despite the most extreme nervous tension and mental derangement, my life could still be saved, I should have gone the way of so many creative spirits who have lived in the city—of many to whom I was once intimately attached—and suddenly done away with myself, as so many have done in Salzburg, or else I should have perished slowly and wretchedly within its walls, gradually suffocating, like so many others, in its stifling and inhuman atmosphere. True, I have often had reason to love and appreciate this uniquely beautiful city, the city of my ancestors, famed for its architecture, one of the wonders of art, and for its setting, one of the wonders of nature; but no sooner have my love and appreciation been aroused than they have been stifled by the brainlessness of the inhabitants, who mindlessly reproduce their kind year in, year out, as well as by their vicious laws and the even more vicious manner in which they interpret these laws. My own unaided resources were no match for the petty bourgeois logic which prevails in this city as in no other. Everything here is opposed to whatever is creative; and it remains true, no matter how vehemently the contrary is asserted, that this city is built on hypocrisy and that its greatest passion is hatred of the intellect and the spirit: wherever imagination is so much as glimpsed, it is rooted out. Salzburg is a deceitful façade, a monument to the world's mendacity, behind which creativity and the creative artist are doomed to atrophy, disintegration, and death. This city of my fathers is in reality a terminal disease which its inhabitants acquire through heredity or contagion. If they fail to leave at the right moment, they sooner or later either commit suicide, directly or indirectly, or perish slowly and wretchedly on this lethal soil with its archiepiscopal architecture and its mindless blend of National Socialism and Catholicism. Anyone who is familiar with the city knows it to be a cemetery of fantasy and desire, beautiful on the surface but horrifying underneath. Whoever goes there to learn and to study, trying to find his way around and expecting to meet with some kind of justice, soon discovers that this city, renowned the world over for beauty and edification, as well as for the celebration of what is known as Great Art at its annual festival, is in truth nothing but a chill museum of death, open to every kind of disease and depravity, in which he finds himself ruthlessly confronted by every conceivable and inconceivable obstacle designed to sap his energies and to impair and inhibit his intellectual talents. What was at first a place of natural beauty and matchless architecture soon becomes a vile and impenetrable jungle of human viciousness, and when he goes through the streets they are no longer filled with music but with the moral filth of those who people them. Suddenly finding himself cheated of all he hoped for, he reacts in accordance with his age, not just with disenchantment but with horror; and for all this, even for shattering his whole life, the city can produce its deadly arguments. The thirteen-year-old boy (and here I am describing how I *felt* at the time and the way I *think* now, having endured the full severity of such an experience) suddenly finds himself in a filthy dormitory stinking of old damp walls, old grubby bedclothes, and young unwashed bodies at the boarding house in the Schrannengasse. He shares this dormitory with thirty-four other boys of the same age. For weeks he cannot sleep, because he cannot understand why he is suddenly forced to occupy this filthy, stinking dormitory, since nobody has explained to him that it is necessary for his education, and he can only feel betrayed. During his sleepless nights he is able to observe the neglected state of the dormitories in educational establishments, of the establishments themselves, and of the children housed in them——children from rural communities like himself, shunted off by their parents to be disciplined by the state. Yet unlike himself, as it seems to him during these nights of enforced observation, these children have no difficulty in turning their exhaustion into sleep, while he, in a state of far greater *exhaustion,* in fact in a state of permanent *distress,* is unable to catch a moment's sleep. The nights are interminable periods of anxiety and despair, during which everything he sees and hears, everything he becomes aware of in his state of constant alarm, provides fuel for fresh despair. To the new boy the boarding house seems like a prison, ingeniously designed to afflict him and his whole existence and built solely for the *infamous purpose of oppressing his spirit*. In this prison everyone and everything is controlled by Grünkranz, the warden, and his assistants (the equivalent of prison warders). Absolute obedience and subordination are required of the pupils, the subordination of the weak to the strong—to Grünkranz and his assistants—and no answering back is tolerated. Being imprisoned in the boarding house means enduring increasingly severe punishment, which in the end produces utter hopelessness. The new boy cannot conceive how those who loved him, as he always believed they did, could have thrown him into this state-run prison in full knowledge of what they were doing. It is in the very nature of things that the main thought which occupies his mind during the first few days is *the thought of suicide*. Simply to snuff out his life and his existence, to escape from the necessity of living and existing, to put an end to his misery and helplessness by jumping out of a window or hanging himself—perhaps, in the shoe closet on the ground floor—seems the only reasonable course; but he does not take it. Whenever he is in the shoe closet practising the fiddle (Grünkranz having allocated the closet to him for this purpose) his thoughts turn to suicide. The closet offers him ample opportunities to hang himself, and there is no difficulty about getting hold of a rope. As early as the second day he tries to hang himself with his braces, only to abandon the attempt and carry on practising the violin instead. From now on, entering the shoe closet means entering upon the idea of suicide. The closet is filled with rows of sweaty shoes belonging to the boys, ranged along rotten wooden shelves. Just below the ceiling there is a hole which lets in only the foul air from the kitchen. In the shoe closet he is all alone—alone with his thoughts of suicide, which come to him as soon as he starts practising. It is without doubt the most dreadful room in the building, but it affords him a refuge, an opportunity to be alone with himself under the pretext of practising the violin. And he practises so loudly on his violin that he fears the shoe closet may explode at any moment. Playing the violin comes easily to him. He plays with the utmost virtuosity, if not with the utmost precision, and as he plays he is totally absorbed in the idea of suicide. Even before entering the boarding house he had been trained in thoughts of suicide, for throughout his childhood spent with his grandfather he had been taught to speculate on the subject. Although he was aware that he would never achieve much on the violin, the daily routine of playing the instrument and the daily study of Ševčik's exercises furnished him with a welcome excuse for being alone in the shoe closet, which no one else was allowed to enter while he was practising: on the door hung a notice in Frau Grünkranz's hand, with the words NO ENTRY—MUSIC PRACTICE. Every day he longed for a respite from the exhaustion brought on by the educational torture of the boarding house, for the chance to withdraw to the dreadful shoe closet in order to play his fiddle and pursue his thoughts of suicide. He had an idiosyncratic style of playing which fostered such thoughts, and the music he produced on his fiddle was of the most virtuoso kind, though it bore no relation to what was prescribed by Ševčik, or for that matter to the exercises set by Steiner, his violin teacher. It was in fact a device for escaping every day after dinner from the company of the other boys and from the whole routine of the boarding house. It was purely and simply a means of being alone. It had nothing to do with the real study of the violin, which he had been obliged to take up but detested because he had no wish to learn. This hour of violin practice in the shoe closet, which was almost completely dark and pervaded by the smell of leather and sweat from the rows of shoes reaching from floor to ceiling, was *his only possible escape*. As soon as he entered the shoe closet he began to meditate upon suicide; and the more he concentrated on his playing, the more intensely was he obsessed with suicide. He actually made many suicide attempts in the shoe closet, but they were never carried *too far*. He experimented with his braces and with pieces of rope; but these experiments, like the hundreds of others he made with the numerous hooks on the wall of the closet, were always broken off at the crucial moment and followed by deliberate concentration on his playing. He would quite consciously break off his thoughts of suicide and concentrate on the increasingly fascinating possibilities of the fiddle, which in time became less a musical instrument than an instrument for switching on and switching off his suicidal meditations and suicidal inclinations. According to Steiner his playing was, on the one hand, highly musical, and on the other—again according to Steiner—totally undisciplined when it came to observing the rules. Its only purpose, especially in the shoe closet, was to facilitate his suicidal speculations; that was all. He was plainly incapable of following Steiner's instructions and making progress on the violin, in the actual study of the violin. His speculations on suicide, which preoccupied him almost continuously both in the boarding house and outside it and from which he could not escape at this time and in this city, no matter how hard he tried and no matter what his momentary state of mind, were linked more with his violin and his playing of the violin than with anything else. They were set in motion *by the very thought of playing the violin,* and they intensified when he took the instrument out of its case and began to play it. This was a mechanism to which he was eventually obliged to surrender himself of and which did not stop until the violin was finally destroyed. Later on, when he thought of the shoe closet, he often wondered whether it would not have been better, supposing he had had the courage, to end his existence there and then, to wipe out his whole future, no matter what it held in store for him, by committing suicide, than to prolong an existence which in any case was of dubious value. And now I know what the future held in store. But he was always too weak to make such a decision. Many boys actually did commit suicide at the boarding house in the Schrannengasse, though, curiously enough, none of them did so in the shoe closet, which would have been the ideal place: they all threw themselves out of windows in the dormitory or the lavatories or hanged themselves from the showers in the washroom. They were able to summon up the necessary courage, but *he never had the strength, the decisiveness, or firmness of character required for suicide.* During the short time he spent there during the Nazi period—between his arrival in autumn 1943 and his departure in autumn 1944—four pupils at the boarding house actually killed themselves by jumping out of windows or hanging themselves (how many others must have done so before and since!), and many others living in the city, having set off for school, were driven by unendurable despair to deviate from their usual route and throw themselves down from one of the hills, usually the Mönchsberg, onto *the asphalt of the Müllner Hauptstrasse—the suicide street,* as I used to call it. I often saw shattered bodies lying in this street, the bodies of schoolchildren and others, though mainly schoolchildren, lumps of flesh wrapped in bright-coloured clothes appropriate to the time of year. Today, thirty years later, I read reports at regular intervals (though more frequently in spring and autumn) about schoolchildren and others who have committed suicide. Every year there are dozens of such reports, though the real number of suicides runs into hundreds, as I have reason to know. It is probably true that in boarding establishments, especially those with exceedingly sadistic régimes and exceedingly bad climatic conditions, like the one in the Schrannengasse, the subject which preoccupies the minds of the pupils is suicide—in other words, a completely unscientific subject, not one of the mass of subjects on the syllabus but one with which they are all intensely concerned. Of course the truth is that suicide and the idea of suicide are pre-eminently scientific subjects, though this is a fact which our hypocritical society cannot comprehend. Living with one's fellow pupils has always meant living with the idea of suicide: the idea of suicide comes first, the subjects on the syllabus second. I was by no means the only pupil who was obliged to spend the greater part of his time contemplating suicide. This was forced on me on the one hand by the brutality, ruthlessness, and utter viciousness that surrounded me, on the other by the extreme sensibility and vulnerability that is inherent in all young people. The time of one's life spent in learning and study is above all a time for thinking about suicide—whoever denies this has forgotten everything. The times I walked through the city thinking only of suicide, of blotting out my existence, wondering where and how I should do it, whether alone or in compact with others! There must have been hundreds of times. But these thoughts and speculations, prompted by everything I experienced in the city, led me back time and again to the prison of the boarding house. Every boy privately harboured the thought of suicide; it was the only thought that was both enduring and potent. Some were *immediately destroyed* by it, others *merely broken,* broken for the rest of their lives. The idea of suicide and the phenomenon of suicide were continually debated, but always *in silence.* And again and again we had a real suicide in our midst. I will not mention their names, most of which I have forgotten anyway; but I saw all of them hanging or lying shattered on the ground, the ultimate proof of the terrible suffering they had endured. I know of a number of burials at the Communal Cemetery and Maxglan Cemetery where boys of thirteen, fourteen, fifteen, or sixteen, having been done to death by society, were unceremoniously *dumped in the ground, not properly buried,* for in this strictly Catholic city suicides were naturally not given a proper burial but simply dumped in a hole and covered with earth in utterly depressing circumstances, which shed a most revealing light on humanity. These two cemeteries are full of evidence to prove my recollections correct. I am thankful to say that these recollections are in no way distorted, but here I must confine myself to giving simply an indication of what I remember. Grünkranz, wearing his officer's boots, would stand in silence at the dumping site together with the dead boy's relatives, dressed in pompous black and with expressions of shame and horror on their faces. Also present were the dead boy's classmates, the only ones present who knew the truth in all its horror. I can see them all watching the proceedings at these makeshift burials, and I can hear the words used by the bereaved relatives, those supposedly responsible for the suicide's education, as they tried to dissociate themselves from him as the wooden coffin was lowered into the ground. No priest would have anything to do with the funeral of a suicide in a city like Salzburg, which was not only completely possessed by a mindless Catholicism and completely dominated by the Church, but also, at that time, in thrall to Nazism. Early spring, which makes its entrance in fever and decay, always claimed its victims, more numerous here than anywhere else in the world, and so did late autumn. Those most liable to suicide have always been the young: young people who have been cast off by parents and guardians and sent away to learn and to study, but who spend their time brooding upon self-extinction and self-annihilation—young people for whom everything is still true and real and who come to grief because the truth and the reality are too terrible to bear. Any one of us could have commited suicide. In some cases we could see clear signs of what was coming; in others we could not, though we were rarely deceived. When one of our number suddenly became too weak to bear the terrible burden of the world within him and the world without, being no longer capable of keeping these two oppressive forces in equilibrium—when suddenly, from a certain moment on, everything about him and within him pointed to suicide, his resolve becoming apparent and soon alarmingly obvious in his whole demeanour—in such circumstances we were always prepared for the terrible but quite logical outcome, the suicide of one of our fellow pupils and fellow sufferers, and we were never taken by surprise. The warden and his assistants, on the other hand, never once became aware of this *preparatory phase of suicide*, even though the external symptoms had been developing over a considerable period and were plain for all to see; and so naturally the suicide of one of their charges was always a blow to them—or so they pretended. The warden always reacted as though he were horrified, yet at the same time as though he had somehow been impudently deceived by the hapless victim. He always reacted without any compassion to the suicide of one of his charges, in a manner which we all found disgusting. With the cold egoism of the true Nazi he would blame the dead boy as if he had been guilty of some offence, though of course he was always guiltless, for no guilt attaches to a suicide; all the guilt lies

with the world around him, in this case the Catholic-Nazi world in which
he had lived, which had crushed him and finally driven him to take his
own life, no matter what the immediate cause may have been, or the
hundreds and thousands of causes. Anything at any time might have been
a motive for suicide in an institution officially called a *National Socialist
Home for Boys*, especially one like the boarding house in the Schrannengasse,
where any sensitive boy might be tempted or seduced into suicide and *a
large percentage was bound to succumb*. The facts are always frightening, and
in all of us fear of the facts is constantly at work, constantly being fuelled;
but this morbid fear must not lead us to conceal the facts and so to falsify
the whole of human history—which is of course part of natural history—
and pass it on in falsified form just because it is customary to do so, when
we know that all history is falsified and always transmitted in falsified
form. Up to now he had always believed what people told him, but it
soon became clear to him that he had been sent to the boarding house for
his own destruction and annihilation, not for the careful nurturing of his
faculties of thought, perception, and feeling, as he had been repeatedly
assured by his family, and this despite the fact that they were quite aware
that this was the most shameful, treacherous, and criminal of all the lies
employed by those responsible for a child's education. In particular he
could not understand his grandfather, upon whom this responsibility de-
volved, his guardian having been called up into the army, the so-called
German defence forces, with which he served throughout the war in Yugoslavia. I now know that my grandfather had no choice but to send me
to the boarding house in the Schrannengasse and to the Andräschule, the
city's main school, in preparation for the grammar school, unless he wanted
me to have no secondary education at all and hence no subsequent university
education. While the city fell short of glorifying every aspect of Nazi
totalitarianism, it always gave it considerable support, and even without
Nazi totalitarianism the city's all-pervasive influence was in any case bound
to have a demoralizing, destructive, and deadening effect on anyone young
and helpless. It was pointless to think of escaping when the only escape
was suicide, and it was for this reason that many young people, having
been hectored and bullied by Nazi totalitarianism and having seen their
whole existence shattered, chose to throw it away by jumping out of a
window or off one of the cliffs of the Mönchsberg—thus making *short work
of it* in the truest and most basic sense of the phrase—rather than let
themselves be ground down gradually by the education system prevailing

throughout the land, a system dedicated to a pedagogical plan which was based on sado-fascism and conformed to the rules governing the art of human education and human annihilation in the Greater Germany of the time. For even if a boy was allowed to leave the boarding house and so escape—and I am speaking here as one who did—the sentence he had already served in this kind of educational prison ensured that he would be destroyed for the rest of his life, for the rest of his questionable existence, and that, whoever he was and whatever he became, he would never get over the indignity he had suffered but would remain without hope, a *hopelessly lost soul,* even if he were to go on living for many years, no matter where, no matter as what. As a schoolboy I was haunted chiefly by two fears. One was the fear of everything and everybody at the boarding house, but especially of Grünkranz, who, with low military cunning, was always appearing from nowhere to hand out punishments. He was a model officer, of both the army and the SA, whom I hardly ever saw in civilian clothes but nearly always in his captain's uniform or his SA uniform, an archetypal Nazi who also conducted a male-voice choir in Salzburg and who was probably incapable, as I now realize, of coping with his sexual tensions and perverted sadistic urges. My other fear was fear of the war, with which we had long been familiarized by reports in the newspapers or from relatives on leave from the forces, such as my guardian, stationed in the Balkans, or my uncle, serving in Norway. The latter I always remember as a brilliant communist and inventor—he remained an inventor throughout his life— who always put extraordinary and dangerous thoughts into my head and confronted me with incredible and dangerous ideas, a truly creative spirit, though a flawed and unstable personality. We had been aware of the war as a *nightmare* at second hand which was being played out a long way away, engulfing the whole of Europe and devouring many human lives; but now it was suddenly brought home to us by the almost daily air-raid warnings. Caught up as I was *in and between* these two fears, this period at the boarding house inevitably became a time of mortal danger for me. What I studied in class was forced into the background, on the one hand by my fear of the National Socialist Grünkranz, on the other by my fear of war, in the shape of hundreds and thousands of droning, menacing aircraft which daily darkened the cloudless sky; for the greater part of our time was no longer spent working at our lessons in the Andräschule or the study rooms, but in the air-raid shelters, which we had seen being driven, over a period of months, into the two hills of the city by forced labour from abroad, mainly

Russian, French, Polish, and Czech prisoners working under inhuman conditions. These shelters were enormous tunnels, hundreds of yards long, into which the populace streamed every day, at first hesitantly and out of curiosity but later, after the first air-raids on Salzburg, in their thousands out of fear and terror. In these dark caverns we witnessed the most terrible scenes, very often scenes of death, for the air supply was inadequate, and I often found myself sharing these dark, wet tunnels first with dozens and then gradually with hundreds of men, women, and children who had fainted. I can still see the thousands of people who had taken refuge in them anxiously standing, squatting, or lying there, pressed close together. The shelters underneath the hills afforded protection from the bombs, but many people died there of suffocation or fright, and I saw many of the victims being dragged out dead. Sometimes a whole succession of people fainted immediately after entering the shelter in the Glockengasse, the one we ourselves always used. All the pupils from the boarding house were marched there by boys who had been detailed to lead us—older boys from our school—together with hundreds and thousands of children from other schools. We were marched to the shelter along the Wolf Dietrich-Strasse, past the Hexenturm and along the Linzergasse and the Glockengasse. When people fainted in the shelter, they had to be dragged out immediately if their lives were to be saved. Several large buses containing stretchers and blankets were permanently parked by the entrances to the shelters. Those who had fainted were taken to the buses, but there was usually not enough room for all of them, and those who could not be accommodated in the buses were laid on the ground in the open air in front of the entrances, while those in the buses were driven through the city to the Neutor. Here the buses were parked, their occupants still inside, until the all-clear was sounded, by which time some of those inside were already dead. I myself fainted in the Glockengasse shelter on two occasions and was dragged into one of these buses and driven to the Neutor, but on each occasion I quickly recovered in the fresh air and was able to observe what went on at the Neutor—how helpless women and children gradually regained consciousness or quite simply failed to do so. It was never possible to ascertain whether those who did not recover had died of suffocation or of fear. These people who died of suffocation or fear were the first victims of the air attacks—or terror attacks, as they were called—even before a single bomb had fallen on Salzburg. By the time this happened, in mid-October 1944, at noon on a completely clear autumn day, a large number of people had

already died in this way. They were the first victims of the air-raids, later
to be joined by the many hundreds or thousands killed by the bombs. We
schoolboys were afraid of an *actual* bombing raid on our city, which had
been entirely spared until that day in October, yet at the same time we
secretly longed for the *actual experience* of an air attack. We had not yet
experienced such a terrible event, though we knew that hundreds of other
towns in Germany and Austria had been bombed, many of them having
been completely destroyed and obliterated. For the facts had not been
concealed from us—indeed they had been forced upon our attention daily
in all their terrible authenticity by countless personal accounts and newspaper reports—and the truth is that in our adolescent curiosity we wanted
our city to be bombed too. Then it happened—I think it was the sev-
enteenth of October. That day, as on hundreds of previous occasions, we
had gone straight to the shelter in the Glockengasse by way of the Wolf
Dietrich-Strasse, without entering or leaving the school. We had witnessed
the by now familiar but still horrifying proceedings in the shelter with all
the eagerness for sensation that is typical of the young: we had seen the
fear of those standing, sitting, or lying there, mostly children, teenagers,
women, and old men—all of them more or less bewildered, in spite of
the fact that their lives had for so long been completely dominated by the
terrible events of the war—suspiciously eying one another all the time in
their universal helplessness, in that permanent state of watchfulness induced
by the war, as if this were the only thing that kept them alive, apathetically
watching everything with eyes dimmed by fear and hunger, the grown-
ups accepting largely with indifference everything that happened, helpless
to influence it. Like us, they had long since become accustomed to seeing
people die in the shelter; they had long since come to accept the shelter,
with all its horror and darkness, as their daily place of resort and come to
terms with the continual humiliation and indignity to which they were
subjected. That day, at a time when normally the all-clear would already
have sounded, we suddenly heard a rumbling and felt an extraordinary
shaking of the earth. This was followed by complete silence throughout
the shelter. People looked at each other, saying nothing; but from the way
they kept silent it was possible to gather that what they had been fearing
for months had now happened—and in fact, after the tremor and the
quarter of an hour's silence that followed it, word quickly spread that
bombs had fallen on the city. After the all-clear, people pushed their way
out of the shelter more urgently than usual, anxious to see for themselves

what had happened. When we got into the open, however, nothing had changed, and we concluded that the talk of the town's being bombed had been just another rumour. We at once doubted the truth of what we had heard and once more persuaded ourselves that this city, described as one of the most beautiful in the world, would never be bombed—a conviction which many people in the town actually held. There was a clear greyish-blue sky, and I could neither see nor hear any evidence of an air attack. Suddenly it was reported after all that the old city—that is, the part of the city lying on the opposite bank of the Salzach—had been destroyed. *Everything* had been destroyed, it was said, and so we set off down the Linzergasse at a run. We could now hear all kinds of sirens and alarm bells from ambulances and fire engines; and after running across the Bergstrasse behind the Gablerbräu and into the Makartplatz, we saw the first signs of destruction. The streets were strewn with broken glass and rubble, and the air carried the distinctive smell of total war. A direct hit had turned the so-called Mozart House into a smoking pile of rubble, and the surrounding buildings, as we saw at once, were badly damaged. Terrible though the sight was, nobody stopped. We all ran on, expecting to find scenes of far greater destruction in the old city, where we suspected that most of the damage had taken place and from which there emanated all kinds of noises and unfamiliar smells indicating a greater degree of devastation. Until we had crossed the Staatsbrücke I had been unable to see any change in the familiar sights, but in the Old Market, as I could already see from some distance away, Slama's, the well-known and highly reputed gentlemen's outfitters, had been severely damaged. (This was the shop where my grandfather used to buy his clothes whenever he had the money and the opportunity.) All the windows, including the display windows, were smashed, and the clothes in the window display, which had still been highly desirable despite their inferior wartime quality, were all in shreds. To my amazement none of the people I saw in the Old Market took any notice of Slama's; they went on running in the direction of the Residenzplatz. I was with a number of other boys from the boarding house, and as soon as we turned the corner by Slama's, I knew what it was that had made people rush on without stopping: the cathedral had been hit by a so-called aerial mine, and the dome had crashed into the nave. We had reached the Residenzplatz at just the right moment: an enormous cloud of dust hung over the ruined cathedral, and where the dome had been there was a great gaping hole the size of the dome itself. From the corner by Slama's we had a direct view of the great paintings which had adorned the walls of the dome and were now for the most part savagely destroyed, what remained of them standing out against the clear blue sky in the light of the afternoon sun. It was as though this gigantic building, which dominated the lower part of the city, had had its back ripped open and were bleeding from a terrible wound. The whole square below the cathedral was strewn with fragments of masonry, and the people who had come running like us from all quarters gazed in amazement at this unparalleled and unquestionably fascinating picture, which to me seemed monstrously *beautiful* and not in the least frightening. Suddenly *confronted* with the absolute savagery of war, yet at the same time *fascinated* by the monstrous sight before my eyes, I stood for several minutes silently contemplating the scene of destruction presented by the square with its brutally mutilated cathedral—a scene created only a short while before, which had still not quite come to rest and was so overwhelming that I was unable to take it in. Then we followed the others into the Kaigasse, which had been almost entirely destroyed by the bombing. For a long time we stood rooted to the ground in front of the huge piles of smoking rubble, under which many people were said to be buried, probably dead. We looked at the piles of rubble and the people desperately searching for survivors. What I was witnessing was the utter helplessness of those who are suddenly pitched into war, people who are utterly defenceless and humiliated, and who are suddenly made aware of their helplessness and futility. Gradually more and more rescue teams arrived, and, suddenly remembering the rules of the boarding house, we decided to turn back. Even so, we made our way not back to the Schrannengasse but to the Gstättengasse, where the damage was reported to be just as great as in the Kaigasse. In the Gstättengasse, to the left of the Mönchsberg elevator, stood an ancient house which at that time belonged to relatives of mine—a master tailor who lived in it with his family and who employed twenty-two sewing machines and their operators in his business. I could see that almost all the buildings apart from theirs had been totally destroyed. They had undoubtedly been at home at the time of the air-raid, but I soon ascertained that they were still alive. On the way to the Gstättengasse I stepped on something soft lying on the pavement in front of the Bürgerspital Church. At first sight I took it to be a doll's hand, and so did my companions, but in fact it was the severed hand of a child. It was the sight of this child's hand that quite suddenly transformed this first attack on the city by American bombers from the *sensation* it had been up to then—a sensation which produced a state of feverish excitement in the boy I was at the time—into an *atrocity*, an enormity. We were all alarmed (there were several of us) by what we had found outside the Bürgerspital Church, and so we ran back across the Staatsbrücke, though against our better judgment we did not return to the boarding house but ran to the station and turned into the Fanny-von-Lehnert-Strasse. Here the Co-operative Building had been bombed and many of the employees killed. When we saw the rows of bodies covered by sheets, their bare feet visible on the dusty grass behind the iron railings of the so-called Co-op, and when for the first time we saw the trucks arriving in the Fanny-von-Lehnert-Strasse with enormous consignments of coffins, the sensation suddenly lost all its fascination, forever. To this day I cannot forget the sight of those bodies covered with sheets, lying on the grass in front of the Co-op; and whenever I am anywhere near the station I can see these bodies and hear the desperate voices of the relatives; and the smell of burnt flesh, both animal and human, still attaches to the terrible picture I recall of the Fanny-von-Lehnert-Strasse. My experience of what happened in the Fanny-von-Lehnert-Strasse decisively affected my whole life. The street still has the same name, and the Co-operative Building has been rebuilt on the same site; but today, if I question people who live or work there, none of them knows anything about what I saw in the Fanny-von-Lehnert-Strasse at that time. Time makes its witnesses forget. People then lived in a perpetual state of fear. American planes were almost continually overhead, and everyone in the city was accustomed to going to the air-raid shelters. Many no longer troubled to undress at night, so that in the event of an alert they would be able to pack a bag or a suitcase with all the essentials and go to the shelters. However, many people in the city thought it sufficient to go down into their cellars, believing themselves safe there; but if bombs fell on the houses, the cellars were turned into graves. There were soon more air-raid warnings during the daytime than during the night, because by now the Americans had un-impeded freedom of the air, which appeared to have been completely abandoned by the Germans. Swarms of bombers now flew over the city in broad daylight, heading for targets in Germany, and towards the end of 1944 the drone and roar of enemy bombers was *only rarely heard at night*. But we still had air-raid warnings at night. We would jump out of our beds, put on our clothes, and make our way to the shelters through completely blacked-out streets. We would arrive at the shelters to find them filled with people from the city, for many went there in the evening, even before there had been a warning, taking all their belongings with them, since they preferred to spend the whole night in the shelters rather than wait for the warning and be woken up and driven through the streets to the shelters by the howling of the sirens. Because of the many deaths in Salzburg resulting from the first raid, people now streamed in thousands to the shelters, those black holes in the cliffs, glistening with moisture, which were in fact a danger to life because they gave rise to a great many deadly diseases. Many lost their lives *through visiting these unhealthy, disease-ridden shelters.* I remember being wakened one night by the howl of the sirens. Without thinking, I ran past the other boys into the toilet, then back into the dormitory, where I lay down again and immediately fell asleep, only to be wakened shortly afterwards by a blow on the head. Grünkranz had hit me on the head with his flashlight. I jumped up and stood in front of him, trembling all over. Then, by the light of Grünkranz's flashlight, I saw that all the beds in the dormitory were empty. Only then did I remember that there had been an air-raid warning and that everybody had gone to the shelter. Instead of getting dressed like the others I had gone to the toilet, and then, forgetting the air-raid warning, had groped my way back to my bed through the silent dormitory in complete darkness, imagining that everyone was asleep. I had got into bed and immediately fallen asleep, all by myself in the enormous dormitory, while the others had been in the shelter for ages. Grünkranz, in his capacity as air-raid warden, had discovered me on his rounds and simply roused me with a blow from his flashlight. He boxed my ears and ordered me to get dressed, saying that he would think up a punishment for my offence (probably going without breakfast for two days) before ordering me down into the air-raid shelter in the cellar. There was nobody there but his wife, a person I trusted. Frau Grünkranz was sitting in a corner of the cellar, and she let me sit down next to her. She was a motherly woman, and she protected me whenever she could. I told her what had happened, how I had got up like all the others but, instead of getting dressed and going with them to the shelter, had gone to the toilet and then, having returned to the dormitory, forgotten about the air-raid warning and gone back to bed. This, I said, had made her husband angry. I did not tell her that the warden had hit me on the head with his flashlight to wake me up, only that I had been told I should be punished. No bombs fell that night. The repeated air-raid warnings played havoc with the rules of the boarding house. Whatever activity we were engaged in was immediately dropped when the alarm was sounded, and everybody made for the shelter. Even while the sirens were still wailing, streams of people were making their way to the shelters, where there were always dreadful scenes of violence at the entrances. People forced their way in with all their inborn brutality, which they no longer troubled to restrain, and forced their way out with equal brutality, so that the weak were often quite simply trampled underfoot. Most people by now had their accustomed places in the shelters, having formed themselves into groups, and the same people were always to be seen together, hundreds of groups squatting for hours on the stone floor. Sometimes, when the air supply gave out and they fainted one after the other, people would start to scream, and then it would become quiet again—so quiet that one imagined that the thousands of people in the shelters must have died. Those who fainted were laid out on long wooden tables placed there for the purpose before being dragged out of the shelters. I can still recall large numbers of naked female bodies lying on these tables, with ambulance women and ambulance men massaging them to keep them alive. Sometimes we too were called upon to massage them under the direction of the ambulance personnel. The pale host of the starving and dying became more and more ghostly with every day and every night that passed. Squatting in the darkness of the shelters, in an atmosphere of hopelessness and fear, they talked of nothing but death. The terrible events of the war, which they had either experienced themselves or heard of from others, and the thousands of deaths reported from all quarters, from the whole of Germany and Europe, were the constant topics of intense discussion. In the prevailing darkness of the shelters they spoke uninhibitedly about the collapse of Germany and about the present situation, which was by rapid degrees developing into the greatest catastrophe the world had known, and they stopped talking only when they were totally exhausted. Very often they were all overcome by a terrible exhaustion, and most of them would lie asleep in long rows against the walls, heaps of humanity under a layer of clothes, often completely indifferent to their fellow men and women, who could be heard and seen dying in their midst. We schoolboys spent the greater part of our time in the shelters. There was soon no question of studying, let alone learning anything, though frantic efforts were made to maintain the routine of the boarding house. Although, for instance, we often did not return from the shelters until five o'clock in the morning, we still had to get up at six in order to wash and be in the study-room

on the dot of half past. In our state of utter exhaustion, however, there
was no question of using the study-room for study, and by breakfast we
often had to set off again for the shelters. In this way we often missed
going to school or attending lessons for days on end. When I think back,
I can see myself doing little else at this time but going along the Wolf
Dietrich-Strasse to the shelters and back from the shelters along the Wolf
Dietrich-Strasse to the boarding house, always in a large group. And the
meals, which daily got worse and took place at increasingly irregular times,
were simply intervals of waiting before the next visit to the shelters. There
were hardly any lessons at the Andräschule by now, because the school
was closed as soon as the so-called *preliminary alert* was given, the pupils
being told to leave the school and go to the shelters; and there was a
preliminary alert every day at about nine o'clock, so that the eight o'clock
lesson consisted solely of waiting for the preliminary alert to be given at
nine. None of the teachers embarked upon any real teaching: everybody
simply waited for the preliminary warning and the exodus to the shelters.
We no longer unpacked our schoolbags but simply kept them ready to
hand on our desks, while the masters killed the time between eight and
nine by commenting on newspaper reports or talking about who had died,
or else by describing how many famous German cities had been destroyed.
As far as I was concerned, however, I always managed not to miss my
English lessons and my violin lessons, since the time between two and
four was usually free of air-raid warnings. Steiner, my violin teacher,
continued to teach me on the third floor of his house as if nothing had
happened, whereas my English teacher, a lady from Hanover, now gave
me lessons in the dark ground-floor room of a public house in the Linzergasse. Then one day, probably after the second air-raid on the city, the
public house where I had gone for my lessons was nothing but a pile of
rubble. I had no idea that it had been destroyed and had gone there as
usual for my coaching. Suddenly I found myself standing before a pile of
rubble and was told by somebody whom I did not know, but who obviously
knew me, that all the inhabitants of the house, including my English
teacher, were buried under the rubble. As I stood there listening to what
the stranger was saying, I thought about my English teacher from Hanover,
who was now dead. Having been totally bombed out in Hanover (this was
the term used to describe a person who had lost everything in an air-raid
or so-called terror attack), she had fled to Salzburg to escape the bombing,
only to lose not just all her possessions—once more—but her life too. A

cinema now stands on the site of the public house where I used to have lessons with the lady from Hanover; and whenever I speak to people about what happened, nobody knows what I am talking about. In fact everybody seems to have lost all recollection of the many houses that were destroyed and the many people who were killed, or else they no longer want to know when someone tries to remind them. When I visit the city today, I always ask people what they recall of that terrible period, but they react by shaking their heads. To me these shocking experiences are as vivid now as if they had happened only yesterday. Whenever I visit the city, I suddenly remember sounds and smells which they, it seems, have blotted out of their memories. When I speak to people who are old inhabitants of the city who must have been through what I went through, I meet only with extreme annoyance, ignorance, and forgetfulness. It is like being confronted with a concerted determination not to know, and I find this offensive— offensive to the spirit. As I stood in front of the ruins of the public house— or rather the pile of rubble where it had once been—my English teacher from Hanover suddenly no more than a memory, I did not even cry, though I felt like crying. Then all at once I realised that I was holding an envelope containing the money my grandfather owed her for her efforts at teaching me English. I wondered whether it might not be better to tell them at home that I had given the money to my English teacher, the lady from Hanover, *before her terrible death*. I do not know what I did, and therefore cannot say, but I probably did tell them that I had paid the lady for my lessons before she died. So suddenly I had no more English lessons, only violin lessons. During these I would follow the instructions of Steiner, who was a strict and nervous man, and attend to his orders; but all the time my thoughts were on anything but the lessons, and consequently I made no progress. I spent my whole time gazing down at the St. Sebastian Cemetery, at the fine, domed mausoleum of Archbishop Wolf Dietrich, and at the graves, monuments, and tombs, some of which with time had begun to gape and sent out a strange chill which made me shudder. I looked down at the arcades inscribed with the names of Salzburg citizens, some of whom were related to my family. I always loved visiting cemeteries. It was a taste I had acquired from my maternal grandmother, who had a passion for visiting cemeteries but above all for visiting mortuary chapels, where the dead lay in state. When I was a small child, she had often taken me to visit cemeteries and view the dead, no matter who they were—not necessarily relatives but simply dead people lying in state. They always fascinated her, and she tried to pass on this *passionate fascination* to me, but I was always scared when she lifted me up to look at the dead. I can still see her taking me into the mortuary chapels and lifting me up to see the dead lying in state, holding me up as long as she could and saying: You see! You see! You see! until I began to cry, then putting me down again and gazing for a long time at the dead before we left. Several times a week my grandmother would take me to the cemeteries and mortuary chapels. She visited the cemeteries regularly, first to see the graves of her relatives, and then for a long time to view all the other graves and tombs. There was probably not one that escaped her notice. She knew everything about them—what they looked like and what condition they were in— and she was conversant with all the names on them and thus had an inexhaustible topic of conversation for any company. I probably owe my own fascination for cemeteries to my grandmother, who trained me more thoroughly in visiting cemeteries, inspecting graves, and observing the dead lying in state than in anything else. She had what she called her favourite cemeteries, and she continually went back to those which marked various stages in her life—in Merano and Munich, in Basel, in Ilmenau in Thuringia, in Speyer and Vienna, as well as in Salzburg, where her favourite was not St. Peter's, which has often been called the most beautiful in the world, but the Communal Cemetery, where most of my relatives and dead companions are buried. But to me the St. Sebastian Cemetery has always been the eeriest and hence the most fascinating. I have often spent hours there all alone, meditating longingly on death. During my violin lessons I would look down at the St. Sebastian Cemetery and think to myself, If only Steiner would leave me in peace—if only I could be down there by myself, walking from grave to grave as my grandmother taught me to do, thinking about the dead and about death, observing the world of nature on the graves and in between them, a nature isolated from the world outside yet still proclaiming the seasons and their changes! The cemetery was left open, the former owners of the burial plots being no longer concerned about their property. I would often sit down on a fallen gravestone to calm myself after escaping from the boarding house. During my lessons, which were both practical and theoretical, Steiner taught me first on a three-quarter fiddle, then on a full-sized one. He would play me each individual passage from Ševčik, on which he based his instruction, and I then had to play it back to him. Always Ševčik. But then we gradually progressed to classical sonatas and other pieces. He was nearly always angry over my lack of concentration, over the resistance I put up, my perverse reluctance to *learn* how to play, and he would punish me by rapping my fingers with his bow at predetermined but unpredictable moments, the intervals between the raps being dictated by his own temperament, which with time had come to be entirely dominated by rhythm. Although I had the greatest desire to play the fiddle, the greatest desire to make music, I detested any form of theory and systematic learning, which meant constantly attending to the rules and so making headway in the study of the violin. I felt that my playing was of the most virtuoso kind, yet I could not play anything properly from music. This never failed to incense Steiner, and I was constantly amazed that he went on with my lessons instead of suddenly discontinuing them and sending me home in ignominy and disgrace, fiddle and all. To a layman's ears the music I produced must have seemed utterly weird, but to mine it seemed highly accomplished and exciting, though it was entirely my own invention and bore no relation to the mathematics of musical structure, being a product of what Steiner repeatedly called my *highly musical ear,* itself a function of my *highly musical sensitivity* (as Steiner used to tell my grandfather when he took me to my lessons), a function of my *highly musical talent.* But the music I played was intended only for my own satisfaction, being fundamentally amateurish and conceived as an accompaniment to my melancholy broodings, and naturally this blocked any progress I might have made in the study of the violin, which ought to have been pursued properly. In short, despite my virtuosity I was never able to play from music, and this was bound, in time, not only to annoy Steiner but to make him permanently angry with me. My musical talent was undoubtedly of a high order, but so too was my lack of discipline, what Steiner called my lack of concentration. My lessons with Steiner served only to underline the increasing futility of his efforts. My violin lessons and my English lessons had given me a quite legitimate pretext for getting away from the boarding house at regular intervals, but quite apart from this consideration, the alternation between these two very different disciplines afforded a welcome contrast. Not only did they compensate me in some measure for the stringency and indignity I had to endure in the Schrannengasse; they also provided me with a contrast between the lady in the Linzergasse who taught me English, who always put me at my ease and took the greatest pains to teach me, and who was in any case a kindly person of whom I grew increasingly fond, and Steiner in the Wolf Dietrich-Strasse, who only tormented and depressed me; be-

tween English twice a week and the violin twice a week. Losing both the
lady from Hanover and my English lessons threw me completely off balance,
for the violin lessons in the Wolf Dietrich-Strasse alone, without the
English lessons in the Linzergasse, afforded no contrast, nor did they
compensate me for the boarding house and all it meant to me, which I
have already indicated; by themselves they only reinforced what I already
had to endure at the boarding house. It was undoubtedly my grandfather's
wish to make an artist of me; the fact that I was *artistic* misled him into
setting himself the aim of turning me into an *artist*. Loving his grandson
as he did—and having that love fully reciprocated as long as he lived—
he tried every means he knew to turn me into an artist, to convert an
artistic person into an artist, into a musician or a painter—for later, after
I had left the boarding house, he sent me to a painter to learn painting.
During my childhood and youth he would talk to me over and over again
about the greatest artists—about Mozart and Rembrandt, Beethoven and
Leonardo, Bruckner and Delacroix—constantly telling me about the great
men he admired, constantly drawing my attention, even when I was a
child, to everything that was *great,* constantly pointing out greatness and
trying to explain to me what it was. But with every violin lesson it became
increasingly obvious that it was futile to teach me the art of playing the
violin. I wanted to make progress for his sake, since I loved him. I wanted
to achieve something in the art of the violin, but it was not enough for
me merely to want to please my grandfather, merely to want to fulfill his
ambitions for me by becoming an *artist* on the violin. Every lesson was a
miserable failure, and Steiner invariably reacted to my failure by calling
it *criminal:* it was the greatest crime, he said repeatedly, for a person *with
such a highly musical temperament* to refuse to concentrate: *lack of concentration
was criminal.* It was clear to both of us (and it struck me as appalling) that
the fees my grandfather paid for my violin lessons were just money down
the drain; but Steiner said he liked my grandfather too much to tell him
to his face that he should give up all hope of my ever becoming proficient
on the violin. Moreover, he probably thought that, after all, at this time
of chaos, with the end of the war in sight, nothing mattered in the slightest,
including the whole question of me and my lessons. I was depressed, but
I still often made my way past the Hexenturm and into the Wolf-Dietrich-
Strasse and back—and in any event the violin was the *precious instrument
of my melancholy,* giving me access to the shoe closet, as I have already
indicated, and to everything associated with it. Although I had a great

number of relatives in the city, whom I had gone to visit as a child (chiefly with my grandmother) and who lived in many of the old houses on both banks of the Salzach—I may say that I was, and still am, related to hundreds of Salzburg citizens—I never had the slightest desire to visit them. I felt instinctively that it would be pointless. What would I have gained by complaining about my misery to these relatives, who, *as I can now see and no longer simply feel instinctively,* as I did then, were completely shut up in their stolid everyday preoccupations? I would have met with sheer incomprehension, just as I would today if I were to visit them. The boy who had once done the rounds of these relatives (some of them very wealthy) on all kinds of family occasions, holding his grandmother's hand, had probably seen through them all immediately and reacted correctly: he never visited them again. True, they led quite profitable and prosperous lives behind their walls in all these old streets, but he did not visit them. He had found them repellent from the start, and over the decades they have remained repellent. Interested only in their possessions, concerned with their reputations, and absorbed in their brainless Catholicism or National Socialism, they would not have had anything to say to the boy from the boarding house, let alone have helped him had he asked them for help. On the contrary, had he gone to see them, even in a state of extreme despair, he would only have been rebuffed and utterly crushed by them. The inhabitants of the city are totally cold; meanness is their daily bread and squalid calculation their characteristic trait. It was clear to him that he would have encountered only complete incomprehension from such people, and so he never went to visit them. And so it was that with more relatives in the city than anyone else at the boarding house—most of the boys having no relatives at all in Salzburg—I was the most isolated of them all. Not once, not even in my greatest affliction, did I set foot in the house of a single one of my relatives. I often passed their houses, but I never went in. There were countless reasons for visiting them, but in the end there was one overriding reason for not doing so: I simply could not permit myself to have any dealings with these people, who in the past had shown so little understanding and so much inhumanity and been deadened and drained of all warmth by the cold, deadly atmosphere of the city. My grandfather had been grossly deceived and disappointed by his relatives in Salzburg. They had cheated him in every way and caused him the profoundest unhappiness when he had thought to turn to them for help. When he got into difficulties as a student and could see no way out of them, and later when he fell on bad times abroad and came back home a complete wreck, forced to return to his own country and his own home town— moreover, in the most dreadful and pitiful circumstances—he had hoped for help from these people; but all he got, from his own relatives and from the inhabitants of Salzburg in general, was calumny and contempt. The story of his death reached its climax in circumstances which were both sad and ludicrous but in any case typical of the city and of those who inhabit it and conduct its affairs. For ten days my grandfather lay in state at the cemetery in Maxglan, but was refused burial by the parish priest on the grounds that he had not been married in church. His widow and son (my grandmother and uncle) went to all possible lengths to arrange a burial in the Maxglan cemetery, where he was officially entitled to be buried and where he had wished to be buried, but permission was refused. No other cemetery was prepared to bury him except the Communal Cemetery, which he had disliked intensely. None of the Catholic cemeteries in the city would accept him; my grandmother and uncle went to all of them to seek per- mission for my grandfather to be buried, but none would accept him because he had not been married in church. And this was 1949! Finally my uncle, his son, went to see the archbishop and told him that as he did not know what to do with my grandfather's body—which was now in an advanced state of decomposition after being refused burial by all the Catholic ceme- teries in the city—he was going to place it in front of the door of the archbishop's palace. Only then did the archbishop give permission for my grandfather to be buried at Maxglan. The funeral was probably one of the saddest the city has seen and took place under the most embarrassing circumstances imaginable. I did not attend it because at the time I was in hospital with a serious lung disease. Today my grandfather's grave is what is known as an honoured grave. The city has always rejected those spirits it could not understand and has never taken them back under any circumstances, as I know from experience. I found the city increasingly intolerable as a result of hundreds of sad, squalid, appalling, and mortifying experiences, and essentially it has remained intolerable to this day. To pretend otherwise would be untrue, hypocritical, and dishonest, and it is imperative that I should set down this record now and not later—I must set it down now, while I am still capable of fully recreating my experience as a child and an adolescent in Salzburg, of recreating it with all the factualness and scrupulous regard for truth which are necessary if I am to give a true indication of what it was like to be a schoolboy there. I have to seize this moment when it is still possible for me to say what has to be said, to indicate what has to be indicated, and so vindicate, if only partially, the truth as it was then, the true facts and the true reality. For all too soon the time may come when everything that was unpleasant will be unwarrantably mitigated and appear in a pleasanter light; and whatever Salzburg was to me as a schoolboy, it was never a pleasant or tolerable place, and I should not wish to spare it now by falsifying the true picture. All I ever had from the city was torment: as a child and an adolescent I was never allowed any pleasure, happiness, or security. The city was never what it is claimed to be by those who are commercially motivated or quite simply irresponsible—a place where a young person is secure and bound to find happiness. I can count on my fingers the pleasant and happy moments I had there, and they were dearly bought. The reason why I rate this period even today as the darkest and altogether the most agonizing I have known is not that it coincided with the war—with all the devastation that war brought to the surface of the earth and those living on it, with the wartime mentality dedicated to the violation of man and nature, and with the descent of darkness over Germany and the whole of Europe. Nor does the reason lie in my fatal hypersensitivity to natural conditions, which was intensified during those dark days and left me wholly at the mercy of all natural conditions. The reason lay—and lies—in the deadly spirit of the city, a spirit which is deadly not only to me, and in the lethal soil on which it is built. It is the very beauty of the city and its landscape, a beauty of which everyone speaks—continually, thoughtlessly, and in quite impermissible terms—that constitutes *the deadly element in this lethal soil.* Those who are linked to this city and its landscape by their birth or by some other circumstance for which they are not responsible and so find themselves bound to it by the force of nature are constantly crushed by this world-famous beauty. Such world-famous beauty is a deadly force when combined with such an inhuman climate. And it is here that I am at home, here on this lethal soil from which I sprang. In this city and its surroundings I am more at home than others; and whenever I walk through the city today, imagining that it has nothing to do with me because I wish to have nothing to do with it, the fact remains that everything about me, everything within me, *derives from this city.* I am bound to it by a terrible, indissoluble bond. My whole being has its origin in this city and this landscape. Do what I will, think what I will, I become more and more conscious of this fact, and one day this consciousness will grow so intense that it will destroy me. Everything within me is at the mercy of this city of my origin. Things which I now find endurable and can easily ignore were unendurable and could not possibly be ignored in my school-days: I am speaking of the state of utter inadequacy and helplessness which afflicted me *as a boy* and afflicts everybody at this vulnerable age. To put it quite simply: during that time my spirit was almost broken; and nobody, *not one single person, perceived this darkening of my spirit, this virtual destruction of my spirit*. No one saw that I was suffering from *a disease, a mortal disease,* and nothing was done to alleviate it. The young person I was then became increasingly unhappy through being at the mercy of everything and every-body at the school and the boarding house, but especially of Grünkranz and his assistants. This unhappiness was compounded by the wartime conditions and the hostility he felt towards his family as a consequence of these conditions, as well as by the fact that there was nowhere in the city where he could find the least protection. Soon his only remaining hope was that the boarding house would be closed down—a possibility which was spoken of after the second raid but did not become reality until well after the fourth or fifth. After the third raid my grandmother came and took me home to the country. This raid, the heaviest of all, was witnessed by my grandparents from the safety of their house at Ettendorf near Traun-stein, twenty-three miles away, where they learned of the devastation it had caused. This was the raid which completely destroyed the ancient *Schranne,* a medieval market-hall with a great vaulted roof which stood right opposite the boarding house. At the moment when it was destroyed I was not in one of the shelters but for some reason in the cellar of the boarding house with Grünkranz and his wife. None of the other pupils was there. It seemed nothing short of a *miracle* that we got out of the cellar and back to ground level after this raid, for many people in the surrounding buildings were killed. After the raid there was utter havoc throughout the city. The dust of destruction was still in the air when I discovered that my locker in the first-floor corridor had been destroyed and that my violin, which I kept in the locker, had had its neck broken off. I remember being delighted, despite the horror of the air-raid, at the destruction of my violin, for this could only mean the end of my career on the instrument, which I loved but at the same time detested. For a long time there was no possibility of obtaining another, and I have never played the violin again from that day to this. The period between the first and third raids was undoubtedly the *most calamitous* time for me. We were still roused from our sleep by Grünkranz flinging open the door of the dormitory and ordering us out of our beds, and even today I still sometimes have visions of this Nazi creature, always standing in the doorway in his highly polished jackboots, pressing with all his might against the door-frame and screaming *Good morning!* into the dormitory. I can still see the boys rushing past him as he stands there half-blocking the doorway. I can still see them rushing into the washroom and up to the washbasin like animals, each in his own way, the most brutal always beating the others to it. There was not enough room for them all at the washbasin, which was seven or eight yards long and not unlike a manger, and so the stronger boys always got in first, the weaker ones last. The strong always pushed the weak out of the way, thus making sure of their places at the long washbasin and under the showers. They could spend as long as they liked washing themselves and cleaning their teeth, whereas the weaker boys usually did not manage to wash or clean their teeth properly, since only a quarter of an hour was allowed for ablutions. I was not one of the strong and so was always at a disadvantage. We still had to assemble in the day-room to hear the news, standing there listening to dispatches from the various theatres of war. On Sundays we still had to don our Hitler Youth uniforms and sing Hitler Youth songs. We were still subjected to all Grünkranz's relentless severity and insolence and became more and more afraid of the man, though he had now begun to be afraid himself, as we could tell from his behaviour, the look on his face, and his whole manner, because his National Socialist dreams and designs were not working out and would probably very soon be destroyed, as he was no doubt constantly aware. Fearing that all his hopes were at an end, he once more summoned up all the brutality and viciousness he could command and vented them on us. We still went to the Andräschule for lessons, though no longer regularly and for no more than a few hours every week. In fact there no longer were any lessons: we simply sat around in the classroom in a state of fright, waiting for the preliminary air-raid warning and what then ensued: the rush from the classroom, the procedure of forming up in the corridors and the schoolyard, filing off, and running along the Wolf Dietrich-Strasse into the Glockengasse and then into the shelters. We were still confronted with the plight of those who sought refuge there but often found only sudden death. We were still confronted with screaming children, hysterical women, and old people crying quietly to themselves. I still had my violin lessons, and so I was still subjected to Steiner's tyranny and withering comments, still obliged to make my depressing journeys along the Wolf Dietrich-Strasse to and from his house. I still had to read textbooks I had no wish to read, to write things in my exercise books I had no wish to write, and to assimilate knowledge which I found repugnant. We were still roused from our beds at night, though often not by the air-raid warning but by the first flights of bombers, and we were often surprised in broad daylight to see bomber formations in the sky before the air-raid warning had joined in the drone of their engines—a fact which indicated the complete chaos that had overtaken the system of news transmission. The newspapers were full of horrific war pictures. So-called total war was getting closer and closer and had now made itself felt even in Salzburg, so putting an end, once and for all, to the notion that the city would not be bombed. And the news of fathers and uncles serving at the front was not good. At this time many boys in the boarding house lost fathers and uncles, and reports of men killed in action came thick and fast. It was a long time since I had had news of my guardian, who was serving in Yugoslavia, or of my uncle, who had been in the army in Norway throughout the war. The post no longer functioned properly, and the news it brought was always bad and sometimes alarming—in many cases the death of a close relative. Yet behind the walls of many houses in the city we still heard Nazi songs being sung, and we still sang them ourselves in the day-room, conducted by Grünkranz, the old choir-director, his long arms bent inwards at the elbow and moving jerkily in time with the rhythm. Every two months I went to spend the weekend with my grandparents, and while I was there I learned what was really happening during these final stages of the war. My grandfather, I recall, used to sit with the curtains drawn, listening to the news bulletins broadcast by foreign stations, especially Swiss stations. I often sat with him, observing the effect the news had on him as he listened intently, though I understood none of it myself. Listening to foreign stations was forbidden, and the fact that my grandparents did so was no secret to their neighbours. My grandfather was reported to the authorities and taken into custody in a former monastery not far from his home and now used as a camp by the SS. I still had to appear in the study-room a quarter of an hour after getting up in order to prepare for lessons at the Andräschule, though none of us knew *what* to prepare, since there no longer were any lessons, properly speaking. I was still becoming more and more scared of Grünkranz, who would call out my name and box my ears for no reason at all whenever he encountered me—he would suddenly appear from nowhere, call out my name, and box my ears, as though my sudden appearance, wherever it happened to be, were an obvious reason for boxing my ears. Not a week went by when I did not have my ears boxed several times, but mostly it happened when I arrived late in the study-room in the morning because I had been repeatedly pushed out of the way in the dormitory and the washroom, then again in the dormitory and in the corridors, by the brutality of the stronger boys. And what happened to me happened to others among the weaker pupils, those who could not defend themselve and were daily victimized by the strong, or by those just slightly stronger than themselves. The weak—or weaker—pupils, whose weakness nearly always resulted in unpunctuality, were fair game for Grünkranz and always had their ears boxed. He used and abused this weak—or simply weakened—*human material* (this was the Nazi phrase he employed) to satisfy his sick sadistic needs. The city was still teeming with refugees. Every day saw the arrival of hundreds, if not thousands, of new refugees. The fronts were closing in, and more and more military personnel joined the civilian population. A state of extreme tension existed among the inhabitants, and even we could see that the situation was explosive. Everything pointed to the fact that the war was lost. My grandfather had said this for ages, but of course there was no such talk at the boarding house. On the contrary, Grünkranz contrived to radiate a mood of triumph, though by now he was desperate and nobody believed him, not even at the boarding house. I always felt sorry for his wife, for she had probably always had to suffer under this man. By now he had become a totally malign character, and his wife had to suffer more than anyone else from his malignity. As I recall, the former Staatsbrücke had long since been destroyed and was now replaced by a wooden emergency bridge. This was the largest construction site in the city, and I can still see the Russian prisoners of war, who were employed as forced labour, hanging on to the piers of the bridge, dressed in dirty grey quilted clothing, compelled by ruthless mining engineers and site foremen to go on working even though they were starving. Many of these Russians are said to have fallen into the Salzach from sheer exhaustion and to have been washed downriver. The city suddenly presented a sorry appearance, having become just another German town exposed to attack from the air. It rapidly lost its looks and became progressively uglier during the course of a few weeks and months in the autumn of 1944. Few windows were left undamaged, and whole rows of houses had no windows at all, just cardboard or plywood shutterings, and all the shop displays had been removed. By now everything was *makeshift*. Yet as a consequence of the ugliness and ruin which had rapidly overtaken the city, disfigured as it now was by the air-raids and the resulting destruction and reduced to utter chaos by the thousands of invading refugees, it suddenly acquired something of a human face, so that I was now able, as at no time before or since, to feel a real and intense affection for it. Now, in the hour of its greatest distress, the city had suddenly become what it had never been before, a real living entity. However great its despair, it was suddenly alive. The dead museum of beauty, which is what this deceitful city had always been up to this moment of its greatest despair, was suddenly imbued with genuine humanity. In this hour of extreme desperation and hopelessness its stony stolidity suddenly became endurable and I found myself able to love it. At this time the citizens lived simply for the next distribution of rations, intent only upon surviving and not caring how. Their pretensions were gone. They had been utterly deserted, and this was clear for all to see. Everybody realised that the war would be over in a very short time, yet even now few were prepared to admit it. At this time I was confronted by the sight of hundreds of men who had been wounded in the war, soldiers mutilated in battle; I became aware of the utter stupidity and obscenity of war and of the wretched plight of its victims. Yet amid all the chaos that reigned in the city I still had my violin lessons, and on Thursday evenings we still had to go to the sportsground wearing our uniforms, to be hectored by Grünkranz on the grass or the cinder track. Only one thing about me impressed him, though naturally not for long. When it came to the annual athletic competitions I was unbeatable in the fifty metres, hundred metres, five hundred metres, and thousand metres. Twice I mounted the platform specially set up on the Gnigl sportsground for the ceremony of decorating the victors of the games, to receive pins for the events I had won—which meant all the running events. But to Grünkranz my prowess at running was a thorn in the flesh. My victories were due quite simply to my long legs and to the boundless fear of losing which filled me while I was running. I never enjoyed any sporting activity—indeed I always hated sport and still do. All ages, and in particular all governments, have always attached the greatest importance to sport. And for good reason, for sport diverts, dupes, and dulls the masses. Dictatorships in particular know perfectly well why they unfailingly promote sport. As my grandfather used to say, whoever promotes sport has the support of the masses, and whoever promotes culture has the masses against him. Hence all governments are in favour of sport and opposed to culture. The Nazi dictatorship, like any other, became powerful through mass sport and almost succeeded in ruling the world. All states in all ages have used sport as a means of manipulating the masses. There is no state, however small and insignificant, that will not sacrifice *everything* for the sake of sport. Yet how grotesque it was that as we made our way to the Gnigl sportsground to compete for our athletic awards we passed hundreds of severely wounded war victims, many of them almost totally crippled, who were being reloaded at the railway station like tiresome, badly packaged goods! Our whole treatment of human beings is grotesque, and nothing is more grotesque than war and all its concomitant circumstances. Even in Salzburg there was an enormous notice over the concourse of the railway station stating that WHEELS MUST TURN FOR VICTORY. One day it fell apart and simply collapsed on the heads of the hundreds of dead underneath. The third air-raid was the most terrible of all. I can no longer remember why I was not in the shelter but in the cellar in the Schrannengasse. Perhaps I had been in the shoe closet when the warning was sounded, practising the violin and pursuing my fantasies and dreams and thoughts of suicide. There were in fact many occasions when I did not hear the sirens because I was playing the fiddle in the shoe closet, absorbed in my fantasies and dreams and thoughts of suicide. No sound could penetrate into the shoe closet—it was as though it was hermetically sealed in order to promote my fantasies and dreams and thoughts of suicide. Suddenly I found myself in the cellar with Grünkranz and his wife, who had probably rushed down there at top speed, just as I had. This time I escaped being punished by Grünkranz for my slackness and lack of discipline. The violent explosions caused by bombs and aerial mines landing right next to the boarding house hurled us against the walls. Grünkranz was probably too frightened himself to give much thought to punishing me; but while I was pressed to the wall in the protective arms of Frau Grünkranz, scared to death and just hoping to survive, I was still waiting for Grünkranz to remember that I was to be punished for not hearing the warning or for ignoring it and not going to the shelter. The punishment, moreover, was bound to be severe and exemplary. However, Grünkranz never did punish me for infringing the air-raid regulations. When we emerged from the cellar and reached ground-level we could at first see nothing, being unable to open our eyes for all the dust and sulphurous fumes. When we were finally able to open them we were horrified by what we saw: the *Schranne* had split into four large sections, so that the great building, which had been about a hundred or a hundred and twenty yards in length, looked like a slaughtered beast, the vaulting having split or caved in to form a huge open belly. The Andräkirche gradually became visible behind it as the dust first rose, then sank back and finally settled. The church was completely mutilated, but that was no cause for regret, since it had always been an eyesore, and at the time everyone agreed that it was a pity the Andräkirche had not been destroyed completely. But it had not, and after the war it was rebuilt—one of the biggest mistakes that could have been made. On the other hand the *Schranne*, that huge medieval monster of a building, was damaged beyond repair. It was said that at the *Schrannenwirt*, an inn just three houses away from the boarding house, about a hundred customers had gone up onto the roof because it was such a fine, clear day and because they were curious to see the spectacle—which was always fascinating—of the bomber formations glinting and glistening high up in the sky. All these sightseers were killed; their bodies were never recovered but, like many hundreds of others, simply pushed down into the rubble, which was then levelled off. A private house now stands on the spot, and when I ask people what happened there, nobody knows. The damage to our own building, the boarding house, was fairly serious, but not sufficient to warrant its closure. We all set about clearing away the dust and the fragments of masonry hurled through the windows from the *Schranne*, and in a short time all the rooms were once more accessible and inhabitable. Several lockers, mine included, were badly damaged. My violin was destroyed, and my few items of clothing were largely in shreds. The air-raid had caused a great deal of damage throughout the city and cost many hundreds of lives, though I was too taken up with what I had lost to appreciate the extent of the damage. Only two or at the most three hours after the raid, my grandmother suddenly turned up. We packed those of my belongings which could still be used; after that we left and were very soon back at my grandparents' house in Ettendorf. The trains were still running, and so I gave up being a boarder. For weeks, in fact for months—until shortly before the end of the year—I travelled from Traunstein to Salzburg by train. I remember all these journeys in minute detail. Usually they did not take me right to school, for no sooner had I arrived at the station in Salzburg (which had by now been completely gutted by bombs) than I was confronted with the fact that there had been an air-raid warning long before, and so I would make my way straight to the shelter. Whether or not the time I spent in the shelter coincided with an air-raid, it was always so long that there was no point in going to school afterwards. And so, after leaving the shelter, I would simply make a tour of the city, where every day I came upon fresh scenes of devastation. It was not long before the whole city, including the old quarter, was full of such scenes. It seemed that more houses and public buildings had been destroyed or seriously damaged than had survived intact. For hours I would wander backwards and forwards with my schoolbag, utterly fascinated by the experience of total war, which had suddenly overtaken the city. I would sit somewhere on a pile of rubble or a protruding wall from which I had a good view of the devastation and of the human beings who could no longer cope with it; sitting there I was able to contemplate the spectacle of human despair, indignity, and annihilation. It was at this time, as I observed the most appalling misery which existed in the city—about which nobody now knows anything or wants to know anything—that I learned through direct experience how terrible life and existence are in general and how little value they have in wartime: precisely no value at all. This knowledge and experience were to remain with me throughout my life. The whole enormity of war, the crime of all crimes, was borne in upon me. For months I travelled to school by train, though I hardly ever got as far as the school. I would arrive at the railway station, by now little more than a shell, in which hundreds, if not thousands, of people had been killed. Entering it on foot immediately after an air attack, I saw many dead bodies. I travelled on the same train as another boy from my school, who came from Frei-lassing, and together we would make our way between huge bomb craters. We became experts at spotting dead bodies. The station was one enormous bombed site, and we often stood around there, nobody paying any attention to us, and watched the railwaymen as they searched and dug for bodies and deposited what they found on the few remaining pieces of level ground. On one occasion I saw whole rows of bodies laid out side by side where the station toilets now stand. By now the city had become grey and ghostly, and it seemed as though the only goods transported through the streets were consignments of coffins. These were carried in trucks and in cars fuelled by wood gas with boilers welded into their backs. In the final weeks before the schools were closed I only rarely travelled all the way to Salzburg by train. The train usually stopped before Freilassing, the pas-sengers jumping out and taking cover in the woods on both sides of the track. The train would be attacked by British twin-engined fighter-

bombers, and I can still hear the rattle of the cannon-fire as clearly as I
did then. Branches of trees flew through the air, while among those in
hiding in the woods there prevailed a silence and fear to which they had
long since grown accustomed. Squatting on the damp ground and keeping
my head down, though keenly on the look-out for enemy planes, I ate the
apple and the black bread which my grandmother or my mother had packed
in my schoolbag. When the planes had gone, everyone ran back and got
into the train, which now resumed its journey for a distance, though not
as far as Salzburg, since the tracks had long since been ripped up. Often
the train could not proceed at all because the engine had been set on fire
and the driver killed by the British gunners. As a rule, however, it was
not the trains bound for Salzburg that were attacked but those bound for
Munich. I preferred to travel home on the so-called furlough trains while
they were still running. These were expresses which had white boards on
the carriages marked by a diagonal blue line. Strictly speaking, it was
forbidden for civilians to use them, but it had long been a habit among
schoolchildren. The trains were so crowded that one could get on and off
only by climbing through the windows. I usually rode from Salzburg to
Traunstein on the connecting platform between the coaches, squeezed
between soldiers and refugees, and it required the greatest effort to board
the train at Salzburg and to alight at Traunstein. These trains were attacked
from the air almost every other day. The British in their Lightnings would
open fire on the engine, kill the driver, and fly off. The engines would
burn out, and bodies of the drivers would be taken to the nearest crossing-
keeper's house and left there. I saw many of them through the basement
windows of crossing-keepers' houses—with bullet wounds in their skulls
or their heads completely shattered. I can see them still—the dark blue
railwayman's uniform and the shattered railwayman's head behind the
basement window. Contact with death had become an everyday experience.
In late autumn the schools were closed. So too, I heard, was the boarding
house, and my train journeys to Salzburg, which always terminated before
Freilassing, came to an end. I lived alternately with my mother in Traunstein and with my grandparents in Ettendorf, which was not far away.
But I was not long without employment. After only a few days I started
work with Schlecht and Weininger, a gardening firm in Traunstein. I took
to the job immediately and kept it until spring—until April 18, to be
precise. During this time I came to know and love gardening in all its
possible and impossible forms. Then, on April 18, thousands of bombs

fell on the little town of Traunstein, and in the space of a few minutes the area round the station was completely destroyed. The plot which Schlecht and Meininger occupied behind the station was now a mass of huge bomb craters, and the building where the firm had its offices was so badly damaged that it could no longer be used. Hundreds of bodies were laid out in the station road and then carried in makeshift soft-wood coffins to the cemetery in the woods, where they were buried in a mass grave, since most could not be identified. This little town on the Traun had suffered one of the most horrific and senseless bombing attacks, just a few days before the end of the war. I went back once more from Traunstein to Salzburg, probably to collect a few clothes I had forgotten. I can see myself walking with my grandmother through the devastated city, which was now populated only by deranged and starving people, going with her to knock on the doors of relatives, and going in to see them if they were still alive. The boarding house was locked, a third of the building having been destroyed since I had last seen it. Half of the dormitory where I had known the most terrible conditions and had my most terrible dreams had been demolished by a bomb and hurled into the yard. I have not been able to discover what became of Grünkranz and his wife, nor have I ever heard anything more about any of my fellow pupils.

UNCLE FRANZ

We are brought forth, but we are not brought up. Having brought us forth, our procreators proceed to treat us with all the mindless ineptitude it requires to destroy the new human being they have made. During the first three years of his life they contrive to ruin whatever potential he was born with, not knowing the least thing about him—except perhaps that he was produced unthinkingly and irresponsibly—and not realizing that in producing him they were committing the greatest possible crime. Having brought us into the world in sheer *base ignorance*, our procreators—that is, our parents—are at a loss to know how to deal with us once we are there. All their attempts at dealing with us end in failure, and they soon give up, though never soon enough—never before they have succeeded in destroying us. For the first three years of our lives are the decisive years, and of these three years our parents and procreators do not know anything, do not wish to know anything, cannot know anything, because for centuries everything has been done to foster this atrocious ignorance. In these three years we are destroyed and annihilated by it for the term of our natural lives, and the truth is that we only ever have dealings with others who were destroyed and annihilated in their earliest years by base, ignorant, and unenlightened parents. The new human being is whelped like an animal, and his mother ensures his undoing by continuing to treat him like an animal. All our dealings are with animals whelped by their mothers, not with human beings, animals which were destroyed and annihilated as human beings in the earliest months and years of their lives by the brute ignorance of their mothers. Yet no blame attaches to the mothers, since they were never enlightened. Society has no interest in enlightenment, no intention of enlightening its members. Every government in every country and every state has an interest in keeping society unenlightened, for if society were once enlightened it would very soon destroy them. Society has remained unenlightened for centuries and will remain so for centuries to come, because to enlighten it would be to destroy it. And so we always find ourselves dealing with unenlightened procreators of unenlightened children who in their turn will become unenlightened adults, condemned to live out their lives in utter ignorance. Whatever methods are employed in educating the new human beings born into the world, their education is bound to lead to their ruin, since it is inevitably in the hands of utterly base, ignorant, and irresponsible educators—who are educators *in name only* and cannot be anything more. This all takes place in the very first days, weeks, months, and years of the child's life, for what he receives and perceives in this early period determines what he will be and what he will remain throughout his life, and, as we know, not a single life is lived which has not already been disturbed and destroyed, no existence is led which has not already been destroyed and annihilated. There are no true parents, only criminals whose crime consists in bringing new human beings into the world and then abusing them in the most brainless and mindless fashion. And they are supported in their criminal behaviour by all the world's governments. For no government has any use for someone who is *enlightened and thus actually in tune with the times*, because he would naturally be opposed to its purposes. It is thus inevitable that untold millions of weak-minded people will continue to produce untold millions of weak-minded offspring, probably for decades and possibly for centuries. The new human being, in the first three years of his life, is made by his procreators or those acting on their behalf into what he will be and cannot help being throughout his life—an unhappy person, a totally unhappy human being. And this holds true whether or not he acknowledges his unhappiness, whether or not he has the strength to acknowledge it and draw the necessary consequences, whether or not he gives the matter a moment's thought, for, as we know, most of these unhappy people never do give a moment's thought to their condition throughout their whole life or their whole existence. From the moment of his birth the new-born child is at the mercy of these witless and unenlightened procreators or parents, who turn him into a witless and unenlightened person in their own image. During the hundreds and thousands of years that human society has existed, this outrageous and unbelievable process has become an unvarying custom, and society, having grown accustomed to it, has no intention of abandoning it. On the contrary, it has become more and more engrained, and never more so than in our own age, for at no time in the past have the millions and billions of human beings who make up the world's population been produced more casually and thoughtlessly, more shamelessly and irresponsibly, than in our own day, and this despite the fact that society has long been aware that unless this process, which is a scandal of world-wide dimensions, is brought to a halt, it will mean the end of human society. But the enlightened spirits fail to transmit their enlightenment, and it is beyond all doubt that human society is bent upon self-destruction. My parents behaved no differently from the rest but mindlessly conformed with the rest of humanity throughout the world, producing a human being and then applying themselves, from the moment of his procreation, to turning him into a half-wit and destroying his humanity. Everything in this human being, as in any other, was destroyed and annihilated in the first three years—buried and covered up with rubble so brutally that it took him thirty years to clear away the rubble under which he was buried and become once more the human being he had undoubtedly been in the first moment of his life, the human being whom these parents proceeded to bury under the mental and emotional detritus of centuries. Even at the risk of being thought mad, we must not be afraid to say that our parents, like theirs before them, were guilty of the crime of procreation, which means the crime of creating unhappiness, of conspiring with others to increase the unhappiness of an increasingly unhappy world. Man is made and brought forth by a purely animal process and continues to be treated as an animal—whether he is loved, pampered, or tormented—by his utterly mindless and unenlightened parents or by those acting on their behalf, in pursuance of their own selfish ends. Lacking any real love, any capacity or willingness to bring him up properly, they feed him and treat him like an animal until gradually his principal *emotional* and nervous faculties are crushed and destroyed. It is at this point that one of the greatest agents of destruction, the Church (or religion generally), sets about destroying his *soul*, while the schools, acting on the authority and under the orders of the governments of all states throughout the world, apply themselves to murdering his *mind*. I was now at the Johanneum, this being the new name for the old building which had once been a National Socialist establishment but was now a strictly Catholic one and had once more been rendered inhabitable while I had been living with my grandparents. During the few months since the end of the war the former *National Socialist Home for Boys* had been transformed into the *strictly Catholic Johanneum*, and I was one of the few inmates who had previously been a boarder at the National Socialist Home for Boys. I now attended the grammar school, not the main school, or Andräschule, as I had done previously. Grünkranz had disappeared, having probably been imprisoned because of his National Socialist past—at all events, I never saw him again—and in his place a Catholic priest, who was always called simply *Uncle Franz*, had been set in authority over us as the new warden. Another priest, about forty years old, acted as Uncle Franz's assistant and was known as the prefect. He spoke a very clipped German and was the Catholic heir to the mantle of the National Socialist Grünkranz. He was just as much feared and hated as Grünkranz had been, and probably a similar character, and we all found him repellent. Only minimal repairs had been carried out on the building. The half-destroyed dormitory had been restored, the roof repaired, and the window-panes replaced. The front of the building had been given a new coat of paint, and when one looked out of the window one no longer saw the old *Schranne* but a pile of rubble which had subsided under numerous rain storms, and beyond it the ruined Andräkirche. Nothing had been done to this church, because the city had been unable to decide whether to rebuild it as it had been before, to rebuild it in a modified form, or to demolish it. The last course would have been the best. Inside the boarding house I could find no striking changes, but the so-called day-room, where we had formerly been instructed in National Socialism, had been turned into a chapel. In the place which had been occupied by the speaker's desk, at which Grünkranz had stood before the end of the war and held forth to us about the Greater Germany, there now stood an altar; where Hitler's portrait had once hung on the wall, there was now a large cross, and in place of the piano at which Grünkranz had accompanied our singing of National Socialist songs like *Die Fahne hoch* or *Es zittern die morschen Knochen*, there now stood a harmonium. The room had not even been repainted—obviously there was not enough money available—and where the cross now hung there was a conspicuous white patch on the grey surface of the wall where for years Hitler's portrait had been. We no longer sang *Die Fahne hoch* and *Es zittern die morschen Knochen*, and we no longer stood to attention to hear special announcements on the radio. Instead we sang *Meerstern, ich grüsse dich* or *Grosser Gott, wir loben dich* to an accompaniment on the harmonium. Nor did we any longer tumble out of our beds at six o'clock and rush first to the washroom, then to the study-room, to hear the early morning news from the Führer's headquarters. We now rushed into the chapel to receive holy communion. The pupils actually went to communion every day—in other words, more than three hundred times a year, which was probably enough to last each of us a lifetime. The outward signs of National Socialism had in fact been entirely obliterated in Salzburg, as though this terrible period had never been. Catholicism now emerged again after being suppressed, and the Americans were in control of everything. There was far more hardship now than there had been before. People had nothing to eat and only the shabbiest and most basic clothing. During the day they worked at removing the huge mountains of rubble, and in the evening they streamed into the churches. The colour of the ruling party was once more Catholic black, as it had been before the war, no longer Nazi brown. Everywhere there was scaffolding, and on it were people trying to erect walls, but it was a long, laborious, heart-breaking process. Scaffolding went up in the cathedral too, and work soon began on restoring the dome. The hospitals were filled to overflowing, no longer with crippled soldiers and air-raid victims but with thousands of others who were half-starving or dying of hunger and despair. For years the city was pervaded by the smell of decomposition, since it proved simplest to leave the dead undisturbed, buried under the restored buildings. Only after an interval of months was it possible to appreciate the full extent of the destruction the city had suffered. Suddenly its inhabitants were seized by a deep dismay, for the damage seemed beyond repair. For years the city remained nothing but a pile of rubble emitting the sickly stench of decomposition, yet all the church towers remained standing, as if in mockery. It was as though the citizens used these church towers to pull themselves slowly back onto their feet. There was still nothing but toil and hopelessness, for whatever hope there had been at the end of the war was gradually eroded by numerous setbacks and increasing starvation. Crime rose to unprecedented levels; in the immediate post-war period there was far greater fear abroad than ever before, since hunger might drive anyone to kill. People were murdered for a piece of bread or because they still owned a rucksack. All who could looked to their own safety, and most people managed to do this by forgoing almost everything. Even in this city one saw hardly anything but ruins, and people scurrying about in the ruins looking for whatever they could find. It was only hunger that brought people out into the streets—whole hordes of them appearing in the streets on mornings when a fresh supply of rations was announced. The city was infested by rats. The sexual excesses of the occupying troops spread *fear and terror* among the inhabitants. Most of them were still living off what they had looted in the final days of the war, but their spirits were kept up by an enormous barter-trade in food and clothes. A friend of my mother's from Leipzig was employed in the food distribution centre at Traunstein, and through her I was able to arrange for a truckload of potatoes to be brought across the border to Salzburg. Thanks to this consignment of potatoes, amounting to several thousand kilos, the Johanneum was able to keep itself above water for some time. Everybody in Salzburg was half-starved and reduced to begging from the Americans for the luxury of having enough to eat. In the fresh hopelessness which suddenly set in after the so-called liberation and the brief period of relief which followed the end of the Nazi reign of terror, the city seemed for years to be entirely run down and weary of life. It was as though the citizens had surrendered not only the city but themselves, and few could summon up the courage or the strength to combat the universal despair. They were simply overwhelmed by the indignity to which they were subjected and the almost total annihilation resulting from it. But this can be no more than an indication. This time I had voluntarily crossed the border into Austria, which was once more a free country, and returned to the boarding house on my own initiative. The border between Germany and Austria had been restored and remained closed for months after the war—in fact it was still *hermetically* sealed two years after the war had ended. I had been living in Traunstein, where my guardian had found work in 1938 and where first my mother and then my grandparents had subsequently settled, since at that time he was the only member of the family who earned any money. My boarding fees were paid by my uncle, who lived in Salzburg and who, as I have already indicated, was a brilliant communist and life-long inventor. It was natural for me, in the late summer of 1945, to try to take up where I had left off in the autumn of 1944, and there was no difficulty about my being accepted by the *grammar school*. I had spent the intervening period mainly with my grandparents at Ettendorf, which is a place of pilgrimage in the woods near Traunstein. At first I had worked as a gardener for the firm of Schlecht and Weininger, until the terrible air-raid on Traunstein which took place, as I have already indicated, on April 18. I was thus in Traunstein when the war ended. I remember how Marshal Kesselring, having fled from the Americans and been trapped by them in Traunstein, barricaded himself in the town hall under the protection of the last of his SS troops, and how the Americans delivered an ultimatum to the mayor of Traunstein demanding the surrender of the town, which would otherwise be destroyed. I remember how a single American soldier, with a pistol in each hand and two others in his enormous trouser pockets, walked into the town from the west, quite alone and quite unmolested. When nothing happened to him, the rest of the American troops entered the town, which was now full of white flags—freshly washed bedsheets and bedcovers hoisted on broomsticks. The town was completely quiet, Kesselring and the SS having withdrawn into the surrounding hills. But I am not concerned here with this period. Perhaps I should mention the drawing lessons which my grandfather arranged for me with an old man who lived in the poor-house at Traunstein and wore an enormous stiff paper collar. For my drawing lessons this man used to take me up into the hills which rose behind the poor-house in the direction of Sparz. He would sit with me there under the trees, looking down at the town and making drawings of it, sometimes taking in every possible detail but very often just the silhouette. I have the pleasantest memories of these drawing lessons. They were, like my violin lessons and my later clarinet lessons, simply desperate attempts by my grandfather to make sure that my artistic talent did not become atrophied and that no aspect of it was left *untried*. I learnt French from a young Frenchman who had been stranded in Traunstein, and another taught me English. Now, after the most eventful year of my life (of which this is not the place to speak), I had crossed the border once more and returned to the *foreign country which was my home*. I was back at the boarding house, which was no longer a National Socialist institution but a Catholic one. At first the only difference I could see was the replacement of Hitler's portrait by the cross of Christ

and of Grünkranz by Uncle Franz. The day began at six o'clock and ended
at nine. Being now a year older, I no longer slept in the largest dormitory
with its thirty-five beds but in the second largest, which had fourteen or
fifteen. Many details of the life we led still reminded me of the National
Socialist era, which I had always loathed, on the basis both of my own
perceptions and of opinions expressed by my grandfather, who had nothing
but contempt and condemnation for National Socialism. However, the
speed with which the boarding house and its institutions had been restored
made me overlook these remaining traces of what I felt to be a wholly evil
period. Yet what struck me most was the quiet that reigned here now,
by contrast with the final months of the war. The night was once more a
time for sleeping, no longer a time for fear. But in my dreams, for years
to come, I was still startled out of my sleep by the sound of the air-raid
sirens, of the women and children screaming in the shelters, of the aircraft
droning and roaring overhead, and of the huge explosions and detonations
that rocked the whole earth. I still have these dreams today. Uncle Franz
was a good-natured person and utterly convinced of the Catholicism he
felt called upon to inculcate into us all the time, but his benevolence
barricaded itself behind the malevolence of the prefect. This man, whom
Uncle Franz had no doubt appointed, had a hatred of humanity which he
vented on us and which manifested itself in his facial expression, like the
perpetual menace of divine punishment. I can still see him today, his arms
crossed behind his back, walking backwards and forwards between the
desks, on the look-out for some slackening of concentration in one of the
pupils. Once he had discovered a real slackening of concentration in a
pupil, or simply a bit of slackness (and he seldom failed to discover some
such slackening or some such slackness), he would punch the unsuspecting
offender on the back of the head. I was no longer afraid of a man like the
prefect, who was in no way inferior to Grünkranz when it came to systematic sadism. Suddenly I was less afraid than the other boys—probably
because my fear had for years been schooled to respect the intense relationship between power and impotence and had entered into everything I
was capable of feeling and thinking. At the Johanneum, therefore, I was
less afraid of the methods now used by the prefect, which were essentially
no different from those of Grünkranz, than I had been when they were
used by Grünkranz himself; but the new boys were filled with *the greatest
fear*. I had come to terms with this sadistic ritual of punishment, and while
it was painful when I was on the receiving end, it no longer had the same

destructive and annihilating effect, because I had been destroyed and annihilated already. I was able to observe an almost total identity between the punitive measures employed in the boarding house under the former National Socialist régime and those in use under the present Catholic régime. Here, in the Catholic boarding house, we had another Grünkranz under a different name, no longer wearing military or SA boots but black clerical bootees, no longer dressed in a grey or brown uniform jacket but in a black one, no longer sporting gleaming shoulder straps but a paper collar. Grünkranz had played the same role in the Nazi period the prefect now played, and the pastoral care which had formerly been the province of Frau Grünkranz had passed to Uncle Franz. For the truth of the matter was that although this *good-natured* priest with his pink peasant's face was the warden, he had contrived to transfer all the real power to the prefect, as we all realized at once and were never allowed to forget. Thus from the very beginning it appeared to me that although Uncle Franz was always described as *a very kind man*, he was actually an unreliable character, if not—behind his show of good nature—a disgusting individual. All day long the name Uncle Franz could be heard shouted, spoken, or whispered all over the building, thus deceiving people, especially visitors, into thinking that the boarding house was enveloped in a cosy Catholic charm, which was, in fact, non-existent. However, Uncle Franz's insecurity often worked to my advantage—and to the advantage of others—in that at times he really was what everyone knew him to be: a man who *could not say no*. All the same, he and the prefect made a good team, and between them they conducted their Catholic reign of terror in the Schrannengasse as efficiently as Grünkranz had conducted his National Socialist one. At this point I must repeat that I am recording, or simply sketching or indicating, how *I felt* then, not how I *think* now, for what I felt then is different from what I think now, and the difficulty is to record and to indicate my former feelings and my present thoughts in such a way that they correspond to the facts of my youth, to my experience as a schoolboy, even if they cannot always do full justice to them. At any rate I intend to try. In the prefect I always saw the spirit of Grünkranz, entirely undiminished. Grünkranz himself had vanished from the post-war scene—for all I know he was probably in prison—but to me he was always present in the person of the prefect. Even in his physical bearing the prefect resembled Grünkranz. Nearly everything about the man (and probably within him too) was similar. It would probably be true to say that, *like Grünkranz*, he was a thoroughly unhappy man, and for this reason alone it was an act of criminal irresponsibility to give him full control of an institution like the one in the Schrannengasse. For he did in fact control it, he was *the real warden*, whereas Uncle Franz, who was the warden on paper, had no say at all. It was of course irresponsible, not to say despicable, for dear old Uncle Franz to place the pupils at the mercy of such a frustrated character, for he knew perfectly well how the prefect operated. However, Uncle Franz was such a weak and defective character that he needed some sort of machine for breaking the spirits of others and destroying their characters if he was to survive at the boarding house, and so from his point of view he had chosen the right man. Fundamentally there was no difference whatever between the National Socialist system and the Catholic system there. Everything simply had a different veneer and a different name, but in the end the effect was the same. After our morning ablutions, which were just as perfunctory as in the Nazi period, we now made our daily pilgrimage to the *chapel* to hear mass and receive holy communion, just as we had previously gone to the day-room to hear the news and receive instructions from Grünkranz. We now sang hymns where we had previously sung Nazi songs; and the course of our day, Catholic fashion, followed the same essentially inhuman pattern of routine punishment as it had under the Nazi régime. Whereas then we had stood to attention at the refectory tables waiting for Grünkranz to say Heil Hitler, after which we were allowed to sit down and start our meal, we now stood to attention waiting for Uncle Franz to say grace, after which we were allowed to sit down and start eating. Most of the boys had been given a Catholic upbringing by their parents, just as their predecessors had been given a National Socialist one. I had been given neither, for my grandparents, with whom I grew up, had never caught either of these malignant diseases. Having had it constantly drummed into me by my grandfather that I must not let myself be impressed by either variety of idiocy, the Catholic or the Nazi, I was never in the slightest danger of succumbing to such weakness of mind or character, though this was exceedingly difficult in an ambience like that of Salzburg, which had been completely permeated and poisoned by both, and more especially in one like that of the boarding house in the Schrannengasse. Swallowing and gulping down the body of Christ every day— in other words, about three hundred times a year—was essentially no different from rendering daily homage to Adolf Hitler. While the two figures are totally different, I had the impression that at any rate the ceremonial was the same in intent and effect. And I was soon confirmed in my suspicion that our relations with Jesus Christ were in reality no different from those we had had with Adolf Hitler six months or a year earlier. When we consider the songs and choruses that are sung to the honour and glory of any so-called extraordinary personality, no matter whom—songs and choruses like those we used to sing at the boarding house during the Nazi period and later—we are bound to admit that, with slight differences in the wording, the texts are always the same and are always sung to the same music. All in all these songs and choruses are simply an expression of stupidity, baseness, and lack of character on the part of those who sing them. The voice one hears in these songs and choruses is the voice of inanity—universal, world-wide inanity. All the educational crimes perpetrated against the young in educational establishments the world over are perpetrated in the name of some extraordinary personality, whether his name is Hitler or Jesus or whatever. Such capital crimes against the young are committed in the name of some character who is celebrated in song, and there will always be extraordinary personalities of one kind or another who are celebrated in song, and such capital crimes will go on being committed against the young in the cause of education, which by its very nature cannot be anything other than a capital crime, whatever its particular effects may be. Thus both at the boarding house and in the city—which has been appositely dubbed the *German Rome*—we were daily subjected to educational ruin and educational death, first in the name of Adolf Hitler, then after the war in the name of Jesus Christ; and National Socialism had the same devastating effect on all these young people as Catholicism had later. A young person is bound to be lonely if he grows up in this city and this landscape, in this solidly Catholic-National Socialist atmosphere; but having been born into this atmosphere, he cannot escape, whether or not he acknowledges the fact, whether or not he even knows it. Wherever we look, we see only Catholicism or National Socialism, and almost everywhere in the city these combine to produce conditions which are calculated to disturb, derange, and destroy the minds and the lives of those who live in it. Even at the risk of once more making oneself look ridiculous in the eyes of all these blinkered inhabitants, even at the risk of making oneself impossible in the truest sense of the word, it must be said that this is a city which has been ruthlessly ground down by Catholicism in the course of many centuries and brutally violated by National Socialism in the course of a few years, and that it never fails of its effect. A young person born and brought up here almost invariably grows up to be either a Catholic or a National Socialist, and so when we have dealings with people in the city, we only ever find ourselves dealing with either hundred-percent Catholics or hundred-percent National Socialists, the minority who are neither being ludicrously small. All the year round, therefore, the spirit of this city is in reality a Catholic-Nazi *denial of the spirit*; all else is a lie. In summer, under the name of the Salzburg Festival, it makes a hypocritical pretension to universality, when so-called universal art is pressed into service to disguise this perverted denial of the spirit; and indeed everything that goes on here in summer is merely deceit and hypocrisy set to music and performed for all it is worth by various combinations of instruments. So-called Great Art is exploited every summer by the city and its inhabitants simply for squalid commercial gain. The festival is mounted to conceal the real squalor for a few months. But this too I can only indicate, for this is neither the time nor the place for a full analysis of the city then and now. Whoever undertakes such an analysis will need the ability to think clearly—heaven help him! Thus many centuries and a few years have combined to invest this city with a character which is not just intolerable but has to be described as sick and perverted, a character in which there is no room for any constituent other than Catholicism and National Socialism. This character was manifested daily in all its frightening authenticity in the life of the boarding house where we grew up and were in the end crushed between Catholicism and National Socialism, between Hitler and Jesus Christ, who were simply a couple of interchangeable transfer pictures for the stultification of the masses. It is therefore of paramount importance to be on one's guard and avoid being bluffed, for in this city the confidence trick has been developed into a fine art, and every year thousands and tens of thousands, if not hundreds of thousands, are duped by it. The widespread belief in the innocuousness of the petty bourgeois is in reality a gross misconception to which one all too easily falls prey and which can often lead to universal disaster, as we have reason to know. The people of Salzburg have learnt nothing from experience: National Socialism could easily supersede Catholicism overnight. All the pre-conditions are there. In fact the balance between the two is so precarious that it might at any moment tip in favour of National Socialism. Yet although this idea is constantly in the air, anyone who expresses it is declared to be a fool, just as he is if he expresses any other dangerous ideas that are in the air, and just as anyone is who expresses what he thinks and feels. What I give here are simply indications of thoughts and feelings which cause me constant unease (to put it no more strongly than that) and never give me a moment's rest. The grammar school had always been strictly Catholic; even though it became a *state* grammar school again when it was re-opened in 1945, having been closed in 1938. But then the Austrian state has always called itself a *Catholic state*, and we were taught, as I recall, almost exclusively by Catholic masters, the one exception being the mathematics master. In schools like this, more Catholicism is taught than anything else, since every subject is taught as a Catholic subject, just as in the Nazi period every subject was taught as a National Socialist subject, as though the only worthwhile knowledge were National Socialist or Catholic. After being subjected in the main school to the Nazi lie about history, the prevailing one at the time, I was now subjected to the Catholic lie. However, my grandfather had sharpened my perception, and so I escaped being infected, difficult though it was not to be infected and to become a Catholic after the war, having been a Nazi before it ended. Both National Socialism and Catholicism are infectious diseases, diseases of the mind, but I succumbed to neither, since my grandfather had taken care to *immunize* me against them. Nonetheless I suffered under them, though not *from* them, as only a child of my age could suffer. To this day the thoroughly Catholic Uncle Franz and the thoroughly National Socialist Grünkranz have remained for me the perfect examples of these two human types, and as long as I live they will typify the two universal attitudes of mind which have given the world more cause for suffering than for rejoicing. Uncle Franz was the very quintessence of Catholicism, just as Grünkranz had been of National Socialism; in every Catholic I see Uncle Franz, and in every National Socialist I see Grünkranz. And in many of the citizens of Salzburg I see the prefect, who for me was a Catholic *and* a National Socialist rolled into one, representing a type and a mentality more common in Salzburg than any other and still predominant there today. Even those who call themselves socialists—which is a concept quite *incompatible* with the Alpine terrain, especially in the Salzburg region—display a mixture of National Socialist and Catholic traits. This human amalgam can be recognized any day by any visitor to the city. The grammar school, unlike the main school during the war, was a highly efficient teaching machine, entirely untouched by extraneous influences, a good specimen for studying the spiritual entrails of the civic body of Salzburg: what revealed itself upon inspection here as in other grammar schools, especially to the pupil, the victim of the system, was the spirit of bygone centuries. This building with its long corridors and whitewashed arches, which had been the old university and was more like a monastery than a school, inspired awe and reverence in me when I first entered it—that is to say, when I first moved up from the main school, the Andräschule, to this superior secondary school and was suddenly admitted to the higher orders which had always been associated with this *venerable house.* It was borne in upon me that now, as I entered the school and climbed the marble staircase every day, I too, like the building, belonged to a higher plane of existence. And indeed what young person would not, upon entering this building from the surrounding streets, or, like me, from the woods and the countryside, have felt a certain pride as he took his first official steps in this austere pile, which (so one is constantly told) has always supplied the nation's élite? But awe and reverence, which in any case restrict the mind, soon vanished in the first few weeks of term, and what had seemed to me before entering the school (and what had seemed to my grandfather, who had wanted me to enter it) to be a great step forward, turned out to be a great disappointment. The methods employed in this institution, which so self-consciously called itself a grammar school—and even more self-consciously a state grammar school, which is what it still calls itself—were in all essentials the same as those used in the main school, the Andräschule, which it affected to despise; and after systematically observing what went on at the grammar school I very soon conceived a strong aversion to everything about it. The masters were simply the servants of a corrupt and essentially philistine society, which meant that they were just as corrupt and philistine themselves, and their pupils were expected to grow up to be corrupt and philistine in their turn. The teaching I received took me further and further away from any natural mental development. I found myself gripped in the intolerable vice of an educational machine which purveyed history as a dead subject while pretending that it was vitally important, and I noted in myself a resumption of the destructive process which had been broken off when I stopped attending the main school. Once more I was facing disaster, and having recognized the grammar school for what it was—quite simply a machine for the mutilation of my mind—it was not long before everything within me revolted against it. Moreover, I developed a marked distaste for the teaching staff, who were depressingly narrow-minded and without exception products of the stale learning that had been passed down for centuries, as well as for all my fellow pupils, who exploited their lower- or upper-middle-class status as a weapon against everything and with whom I was never able to establish any real contact. Repelled by their bourgeois attitudes, I soon withdrew into myself, while they, conversely, were repelled by my undoubtedly unhealthy dislike of them (and their bourgeois attitudes), and soon excluded me from their company. The result was that I was once more thrown upon my own resources and forced permanently onto the defensive, and this permanent *defensiveness* in its turn bred in me constant fear and anxiety. This does not mean, however, that I was unable to help myself. On the contrary, I gained increasing strength from being constantly put under pressure, not only by the masters but by the other boys, whose background, as I have indicated, was quite different from mine. Having to fend for myself against all and sundry meant that in due course I no longer allowed myself to be attacked and browbeaten but simply let things ride, aware by now that I should not be at the grammar school forever. I soon lost interest in everything that was taught there, and this loss of interest was reflected in my first term's marks. I soon came to regard attendance at the grammar school as a vexatious imposition which I could not yet escape and hence had to endure for a time. My only real interest was in *geography, a completely useless subject*, drawing, and music, together with history, a subject that has always fascinated me. No other subject aroused the slightest interest in me, and I soon came to regard school—though at that time only instinctively—as what I now know it to be: an institution for the destruction of the mind. However, if I was to achieve anything out of the ordinary—which I naturally wanted to do—I had to complete my grammar school education. This had been continually impressed upon me, and so, despite my total lack of interest and the utter revulsion I felt for the grammar school and all its works, I tried to master its requirements. This, however, proved increasingly hopeless, though I was careful to conceal the fact from my grandfather, who had stressed the need for me to complete my grammar school education if I did not want to be trampled upon by society—and I was fully aware of what that meant. He knew nothing of my almost complete inadequacy at school, of which I never breathed a word on my fortnightly visits to Traunstein or Ettendorf. Once every two weeks I left the boarding house at about three o'clock in the morning, through a window in the corridor which was left open for me, and went home. This meant walking about eight miles to the frontier, which I crossed in the early morning light at a point near the Wartberg

inn, halfway between Salzburg and Grossgmain—where I was always afraid
of being spotted by the frontier officials. Every two weeks I made my way
through the cold, dark, and seemingly dead city, branching off at Vieh-
hausen, crossing the border by way of the moor beyond Wartberg and
making for Marzoll. From there I walked to Piding, a little Bavarian
village, where, in possession of both an Austrian and a German identity
card, I boarded a train and travelled first to Freilassing and then to Traunstein. These journeys across the border were necessary because I had no
one in Salzburg to do my washing and no one I could talk to. They were
necessary also because any young person, if possible, goes as often as he
can to see the one person he knows and loves best—in my case, my
grandfather. My mother also lived in Traunstein with my half-brother
and half-sister, the children of my guardian, her husband, who was now
back from Yugoslavia after serving there *in the war.* I often went on weekends to see my uncle in Salzburg too (he was the life-long communist
and inventor of saucepans that did not boil over, water-driven motors, and
such like), but usually I spent weekends with my grandparents and my
mother in Traunstein and Ettendorf. Once over the border, I got out
my German identity card; after crossing in the other direction I got out
my Austrian identity card. In this way I had official authorization to reside
in both countries at a time when all so-called cross-border traffic was strictly
prohibited, and probably only a boy of my age could have crossed the
border so often—and nearly always unmolested—in one direction on Saturday morning and in the other on Sunday evening. At this time the
boarding house accommodated not only boys who attended the grammar
school but others who did not, including a number of young craftsmen.
One day I got to know a young man there who later turned up as a customs
official. I had already crossed the border dozens of times near Wartberg,
where there was no border post, but from now on this young customs
official took me across the border at Siezenheim, where he was stationed,
under the very eyes of his Austrian and Bavarian colleagues. This is how
he did it. On Friday evening I would walk to Siezenheim and spend the
night there in a little house on the edge of the woods; this house belonged
to a carpenter called Allberger, who had served in Norway with my uncle
during the war—*on General Dietl's staff,* it was always said. There I was
given some warm milk and put to bed. The carpenter's mother would
wake me at about four o'clock in the morning, and I would get up, have
breakfast, and then walk alone through the woods to the border hut, where

I would knock on the window. The young customs official would then come out wearing a large cape, and as had been arranged previously, I would immediately climb onto his back and he would carry me, under the cover of his cape, over the narrow border bridge to the German bank of the river Saalach. Here I would get down off his back and quickly run off through the woods to Ainring, where there was a railway station. From there I would travel to Freilassing and then on to Traunstein. On Sunday evening the whole procedure was repeated in reverse, the time of my arrival in the woods near Ainring being prearranged with the greatest precision. It always worked. Since my grandparents lived in the country, they had no need of bread coupons, and so I always brought some for the customs official in return for his help. On several occasions, however, I was caught, and on one I was locked up and actually taken in the dark like a criminal— I was then fourteen or fifteen, I can't remember exactly how old—to the customs house at Marzoll, and from there to the one at Wals. I was made to walk in front of a border guard who carried a gun with the safety-catch off. My protestation that I was simply a schoolboy from Salzburg and had lost my way was of no avail. And on one occasion my guardian was arrested at Traunstein by the Americans; for days he did not know why. The reason was that I always carried a rucksack full of letters from Austria to Germany, most of them containing packets of saccharin, which was obtainable in Austria but not in Germany. There was at that time no postal service between the two countries in either direction. The recipients had to send their replies to our address in Traunstein, my guardian's address, so that they could be delivered by me in Austria. My guardian spent two weeks in the Traunstein jail because of this postal service of mine, and he probably never forgave me for getting him into trouble: after all, I was the one who started the service and the only one responsible for it. I ran it for almost two years. These journeys across the border were the scariest experiences of my life. Once I took my half-brother with me from Traunstein and across the border at Marzoll without telling my mother or my grandparents. He was seven at the time. Why I should have taken it into my head to do such a thing I cannot imagine. It certainly caused great alarm to my family. Naturally I did not fully appreciate the consequences of what I was doing. However, I had no difficulty crossing the border with my little brother, whom I deposited with my horrified uncle in Salzburg—after all, what would I have done with him at the boarding house? I probably took him back across the border *illegally* on the following Saturday when I returned to Traunstein, where no doubt the direst consequences awaited me. It was an utterly weird period in which people were *not responsible* for their actions and constantly did the most *outrageous* and *unbelievable* things. Montaigne writes that it is a miserable thing to be in a place where everything you see occupies and concerns you. Elsewhere he writes: Yet my mind was ceaselessly moved and formed true and open judgments concerning the objects around me, which it would digest without any help or communication. And amongst other things I verily believe it would have proved altogether incapable and unfit to yield unto force or stoop into violence. And again he writes: I greedily long to make myself known, and I care not at what rate, provided it be truly. And again: There is no description so hard, nor so profitable, as is the description of a man's own life; yet must a man handsomely trim up, yea and dispose and range himself to appear in public. Now I continually trick up myself; for I incessantly describe myself. I do not write my own acts, but myself and my essence. And again: Many a matter which propriety and reason would forbid me to disclose I have made known for the instruction of others. And again: For my part I am resolved to dare to say all that I dare to do; even thoughts that are not to be published displease me. And again: If I desire to know myself it is to know myself as I really am; I take stock of myself. These and other sentences I often heard quoted to me by my grandfather the writer, though without understanding them, when I was out walking with him. He loved Montaigne, and it is a love I share. I spent more time with my grandfather than with my mother, with whom my relations were always difficult, ultimately because she found my very existence incomprehensible and was never able to come to terms with it. My father, a farmer's son who worked as a carpenter, had deserted her and shown no further concern for either her or me. Towards the end of the war he was killed or murdered at Frankfurt-on-the-Oder in circumstances which I have never been able to discover to this day. I learned this from his father, my paternal grandfather, whom I saw only once in my life— unlike my father, whom I *never saw even once*. My mother died in October 1950 as a result of the war, a victim of her family, by whom she was worn down and in the end virtually killed. I always found it extremely difficult to live with my mother, *whose nature I am to this day quite unable to describe*. I cannot even give an indication of her character, and even today I find it impossible *to comprehend even approximately* the eventful life she led, which came to an end when she was only forty-six. I cannot do justice to this remarkable woman, who devoted herself to the children she had by my guardian. (He was never my stepfather because he never officially adopted me and so he remained simply my guardian.) As a result of these family circumstances I spent more time with my grandparents than with my mother, for it was with them that I found all the love, affection, and understanding I could find nowhere else, and so I grew up entirely under the undemonstrative care of my grandfather. My pleasantest memories are of going for walks with him. We used to walk for hours in the country, and I would listen to his observations, by means of which he gradually taught me the art of observation. I was attentive to everything he pointed out to me—indeed, I may justifiably regard the time spent with my grandfather as the only useful education I had, for it had a decisive effect on my whole life. It was he and no other who taught me about life, who acquainted me with life by first acquainting me with nature. Everything I know I owe to this man, who decisively influenced my whole life and my whole existence and who himself was taught by Montaigne, just as I in turn was taught by *him*. My grandfather was quite familiar with the conditions and circumstances prevailing in Salzburg, for his parents had sent him there to study. He had attended the theological seminary in the Priesterhausgasse, where he was made to suffer the same conditions as I was to suffer fifty years later at the boarding house in the Schrannengasse. He had broken loose and gone to Basel to lead the dangerous life of an anarchist like Kropotkin, which was outrageous conduct at the time, just before the turn of the century. He spent two decades as an anarchist together with his wife, my grandmother, always sought by the police and often arrested and imprisoned. In the middle of this period, in 1904, my mother was born in Basel. Some time later my uncle was born in Munich, where the young couple had moved meanwhile, probably in flight from the police. This son, my uncle, was a revolutionary all his life. As a communist in Vienna at the age of sixteen, he spent most of his time either in prison or on the run, and throughout his life he remained true to his communist ideals. All through his life he was obsessed with communism, which can never become a reality but must always remain a fantasy in extraordinary minds like my uncle's—a fantasy, moreover, which is bound to bring them lifelong unhappiness. My uncle in fact came to grief in the most tragic and terrible circumstances. But this, like everything I record here, can only be indicated. Probably it was my grandfather's experience of studying in Salzburg which made him so determined to send me there to study.

However, he could not have foreseen that his grandson too was doomed to failure there. He could not have understood this in advance—or perhaps he did understand it but could not fully grasp it—and when it happened, it probably seemed to him like a dreadful re-enactment of his own failure. His object was without doubt to secure for his grandson what he himself had never had: a *proper education* in Salzburg, which was his home town and mine. It pained him when I was forced to disappoint him. Yet was I not bound to fail after the education he had given me throughout my childhood and early adolescence? But my grandfather was still quite un-aware of the reality, which was not yet accomplished but already predict-able: that I should not attend the grammar school for long, because I was not only not making progress but falling behind, and because I was grad-ually losing any desire to learn anything. There came a point when I detested the school and everything connected with it; I was educationally *lost.* Yet for many months—for one and a half years, in fact—I forced myself to accept this intolerable situation and went on attending school despite my absolute conviction that I had no chance of making progress and despite the constant humiliation and depression I had to endure. Every day I walked through the vegetable market and entered the building, which had by now become unendurable in every detail. It was like entering hell every day. And I had a second hell—in the boarding house in the Schrannengasse. I was thus commuting between one hell and another; all I felt was despair, though I did not give the slightest hint of this to anybody. My grandmother was the daughter of a prosperous Salzburg family and had relatives all over the city, who owned fine old houses—and still do. She often encouraged me to visit these relatives, who were my relatives too, but I never acted on this suggestion. I had too great a distrust of all these business people with whom I could claim relationship to go through their heavy iron doors and expose myself to their endless destructive curiosity and suspicion. My grandmother herself had told me time and again about the dreadful childhood and youth she had spent in this awful city among all these relatives, who were as cold as the city itself. She had had anything but a happy childhood and was married off at seventeen by her parents, a prosperous business couple, to a wealthy Salz-burg master tailor of forty. It was natural for her to break loose suddenly at the age of twenty-one and join my grandfather in Basel, leaving her three children behind in order to escape from an unloved and exceedingly brutal husband and a marriage which was no more than a business arrangement. She had met my grandfather when he was at the seminary in the Priesterhausgasse, which she could see from her apartment; and having followed this extraordinary man to Basel, she remained his companion for life. My grandmother was a brave woman, and she was the only one of us who retained anything like a real enjoyment of life, which remained undiminished until the end of her life. However, her life ended quite miserably in an enormous ward in the Salzburg Nerve Clinic, crammed with thirty or more half-rusted iron beds. I saw her a few days before she died, surrounded by helpless geriatric patients who were demented and dying. She could still hear what I said to her but could no longer understand me. She did nothing but weep all the time. This visit to my grandmother is probably my most painful memory. But she had led an unbelievably rich life. She had travelled all over Europe, both with and without my grandfather. She knew almost every town in Germany, Switzerland, and France, and I never knew anyone else who could tell such fascinating stories. She lived to be eighty-nine, but even at that age there was still much she could have told me. She had experienced more than any of us, and her memory remained clear almost to the end. At the end her home town showed itself in its very worst light: she was stuck in a hospital and finally in the madhouse by incompetent doctors and let down by everybody— literally everybody, including her relatives, to end her life in an enormous hospital ward unfit for human beings and filled only with the dying. This is how all my closest relatives finally returned to the earth of this city and the surrounding country from which they sprang. But it is pointless to visit the graves of my mother, my grandparents, and my uncle; it simply calls up unbearable memories and brings on debilitating depression. This public declaration, however, binds me to keep myself within my course, as Montaigne says. I am greedy of making myself known, he says, and I care not to how many, provided it be truly; or, to say better, I hunger for nothing; but I am mortally afraid of being mistaken by those who come to learn my name. All my previous conditioning disqualified me for the grammar school *even before* I entered it. I should never have gone there, but it was my grandfather's wish, and I wanted to fulfill it. Indeed, I at first summoned up all my strength in order to fulfill it for his sake, not for mine. I would rather have slaved away in one of the numerous businesses owned by my relatives than attend the grammar school, but of course I complied with my grandfather's wish. I did not feel that I would gain any incidental advantage by attending the grammar school as my grandfather suddenly felt—which was contrary to his normal way of thinking, though this is how people have always thought for as long as there have been grammar schools. The truth is that I entered the grammar school absolutely sure of being a failure. The grammar school machine was bound to have a destructive effect on me and my whole personality, but for my grandfather it had to be the grammar school and nothing else: he himself had attended a *technical school*, not a *grammar* school, and so his grandson had to attend a grammar school since he, for whatever reasons, had not been allowed to. The fact that I had been accepted as a regular pupil at the grammar school was of the greatest importance to him: *through me* he had now achieved what he had not been able to achieve himself, and through him, so to speak, I had entered upon the first and all-important stage of an educated life, and that meant a better life. Yet as soon as I entered the school, everything inside me told me I was bound to be a failure, because I did not belong here, being disqualified by my previous upbringing. Those who did belong in the grammar school—in other words, more or less all the pupils—felt at once that it was their natural home, whereas for me it was just an institution, a building, never a home. To me it stood for everything that was contrary to my own nature. My grandparents and my mother were proud of the fact that I was at the grammar school, that I had been accepted by an institution where, according to the general belief, they take a nobody and turn him, in the course of eight years, into an educated person, a better class of person, a distinguished and extraordinary person, or at any rate an unusual person. They did not conceal their pride, whereas I was already convinced that it was quite wrong for me to go to the grammar school in the first place, since my whole make-up was wrong—I was just not grammar school material. My grandfather of all people ought to have known that he himself had disqualified me for this kind of school as a preparation for life by the training he had given me. How could I have suddenly fitted in at a school like this when in fact I had been carefully and painstakingly educated by him all my life to reject all *conventional* education. He was *the only teacher I acknowledged*, and in many respects this is still so. Hence the very fact that my grandfather had sent me to a so-called secondary school and exposed me to the rigours of life in Salzburg was bound to seem like a betrayal. But I had always carried out his requirements, I had always obeyed his orders; there has never been another person whose wishes I have always complied with and whose orders I have always unconditionally obeyed. In sending me to Salzburg and placing me at the mercy of the boarding house, in sending me first to the main school and then to the grammar school, he was acting out of character. It was the only time he ever acted inconsistently towards me, and of all the inconsistencies he could have been guilty of, this was the only one which could have had such a shattering effect on his grandson. Indeed, it had a devastating effect because it ran counter not only to his way of thinking but to my way of feeling. For him it was quite simply a surrender to a life-long dream, but he lived to see that it had been an error and to rue it bitterly. The primary schools I had attended, at Seekirchen on the Wallersee and at Traunstein, had posed no threat to me, for as long as I was near my grandfather and constantly within reach of his enlightening influence, I was never at the mercy of these primary or elementary schools. I could attend them with a fair degree of casualness, and they never did me any harm; but this sudden switch in my grandfather's attitude, his deciding that it was necessary for me to attend a so-called "higher" school, caused me intense mental anguish. It was so unlike him. The masters struck me as poor, pathetic individuals. How could they ever have had anything to say to me? They were the very personification of insecurity, inconsistency, and spiritual indigence. How could anything they had to say have been of the slightest use to me? For more than a decade my grandfather had trained me in physiognomy, and now I had an opportunity to make use of my training. The results were dismal in the extreme. The masters were afraid on the one hand of the headmaster, a man by the name of Schnitzer, and on the other of their family circumstances, to which they were condemned for life. They had nothing to say to me, and the relations between us in fact amounted to little more than mutual contempt and the one-sided infliction of continual punishment. I soon became accustomed to being punished all the time—whether I had deserved it or not—and was quickly reduced to a perpetual state of humiliation and degradation. I despised these masters and in time came to hate them, for all they ever did, as far as I could see, was to unload their revolting historical slops over my head every day (though they regarded these slops as some kind of higher knowledge) as if from some enormous, inexhaustible bucket. This was the activity they engaged in every day, without giving a moment's thought to the consequences. With the well-known schoolmasterly demeanour and the well-known schoolmasterly mindlessness they quite mechanically *destroyed* the pupils committed to their charge by their teaching, which was simply a state-ordained means for demoralizing and destroying

the minds of the young and, with hideous inevitability, eventually annihilating them completely. These masters were simply sick men, whose
sickness reached explosion point in lessons. To be a grammar school master
one has to be mindless or sick, or rather mindless *and* sick, for what they
teach day after day, what they constantly unload over their victims' heads
is nothing but mindlessness and sickness—knowledge that has been passed
down and become putrid over the centuries and now amounts to a mental
disease which is transmitted to the pupils and must inevitably stifle all
thought in every one of them. The activity which goes on in schools, and
especially in secondary schools, consists of constantly cramming the pupil
full of putrid, useless knowledge and so turning his whole nature into *the
antithesis of all that is natural*. The result is that whenever we have dealings
with the products of such schools, we find ourselves dealing with unnatural
people, whose real nature the schools have managed to destroy. Secondary
schools, and, above all, grammar schools, serve only to putrefy human
nature, and it is time we considered abolishing these centres of putrefaction,
as in fact they should be, because it has long been obvious that they are
nothing but centres for the putrefaction of human nature. They deserve
to be abolished. The world would be better off if all these so-called middle
schools, grammar schools, secondary schools, and so on were abolished
and we were to confine education to elementary schools and universities.
For elementary schools are not destructive—they do not destroy anything
in a young person's *nature*; and universities are there for those who are
suited to the pursuit of learning and would be equipped for a higher
education even without having attended a secondary school. Secondary
schools, on the other hand, should be abolished because they bring inevitable ruin upon a large proportion of the young. Our educational system
has become sick over the centuries, and the young who are forced into it
are infected and become sick in their millions, with no prospect of a cure.
If society wishes to change, it must change its educational system, because
if it does not change, if it does not impose some restriction on itself and
acquiesce to a large extent in its own abolition, it will assuredly be at an
end. As for the educational system, it must be changed *fundamentally*.
Changing a bit here and a bit there is not enough. *Everything* should be
changed—unless we want to see the earth populated *solely by unnatural
people who have been destroyed through the wilful flouting of nature*. And the first
institutions to be abolished should be the secondary schools, in which
millions of young people are placed every year to face sickness and anni-

hilation. If the world is to be *renewed*, the new world will be one in which there is only *elementary education for the masses* and *higher education for the few*. This new world will have liberated itself from the convulsions of centuries by abolishing secondary education and so getting rid of grammar schools. Whenever I arrive in the city today, I at once find myself in a mental or emotional state—or, rather, a mental *and* emotional state— which gives rise to instant depression or at least to instant irritation. Even twenty years later I sense a drop in the barometric pressure and begin *to wonder what is the cause* of this mental or emotional state, this mental *and* emotional state. I am not forced into it any longer, but again and again I am engulfed by it, either in reality or in imagination, often without knowing why—expecting something while at the same time knowing that there is nothing to expect here. This state of mind is quite devastating, and over and over again I tell myself that it is due to my experiences. I won't get into this state again; I won't go back to the city, either in reality or in imagination. It is not enough to have a clear head and to be able to think straight about this architecture and landscape, which are irrevocably bound to me as I am to them, no doubt for the rest of my life, by my origins, my childhood, and my youth. No amount of clear thinking can cope with the mental debility which unfailingly afflicts me, contrary to all reason, for longer or shorter spells whenever I enter this city, by whatever means and from whatever direction. As soon as I arrive here, a mental and temperamental *change* comes over me and I relapse into this mental and temperamental *state* which has always been destructive and may well prove fatal. Much that seems light and perspicuous and, at my present age, altogether tolerable is suddenly no longer light but oppressive, no longer perspicuous but obscure, and made altogether intolerable by the whole burden of a heredity which even today arouses nothing but fear in my mind. My childhood and youth were difficult in every way, leading to depression and derangement, a period of development which, as indicated in these pages, had overwhelming consequences and left me with a confused sense of having been reprimanded for reasons which remain obscure to this day, but in a manner which has left a lasting mark. I am not finished with this city of my childhood and youth. Whenever I visit it I am still de- fenceless, incapable of the slightest resistance, entirely at its mercy. I spent twenty years away from the city, in every possible place and every possible landscape; and during these twenty years I experienced and studied many things—*because of the city, always trying to counteract its influence*, as I know—

only to discard them again after strenuous study. But none of this is of
any avail against this state of mind which comes upon me whenever I
return. Whenever I arrive in the city, I find myself in the same state,
always feeling the same hostility, enmity, helplessness, and wretchedness;
the walls have not changed, the people have not changed, and the atmosphere is the same atmosphere which crushed and stifled everything
within me when I was a helpless child. I hear the same voices and the
same noises; I smell the same smells and see the same colours. Everything
combines to ensure the immediate resumption of *this progressive sickness
which absence only seemed to have halted* but which in fact continues unabated,
proof against any remedy. It is really *a process of dying, which resumes as soon
as I return, as soon as I take my first steps and think my first thoughts.* Once more
I breathe the deadly air peculiar to this city and hear the deadly voices.
Once more I go where I no longer ought to go, revisiting my childhood
and youth. Once more, against my better judgment, I hear the base opinions
of base people and find myself, against my better judgment, speaking when
I ought *not* to speak and keeping silent when I ought *not* to keep silent.
The beauty for which my home town is famous—like the beauty of any
town—is merely the means by which its baseness, irresponsibility, narrowmindedness, and megalomania make themselves felt with such extreme and
pitiless intensity. As Montaigne says, I study myself more than anything
else. That is my metaphysics and my physics. I am myself the king of the
matter I treat, and I am accountable to no one. There were two people at
the grammar school whom I recall more clearly than any others. One was
a fellow pupil crippled by infantile paralysis, the son of an architect with
an office in one of the old houses on the left bank of the Salzach, blackened
by damp up to the third or fourth floor, with tall arches and walls a yard
thick. I often visited the house myself for remedial exercises in mathematics, which I found I could do better in collaboration with the crippled
boy than I could by myself. He used to help me with my geometrical
diagrams too, and I would often visit his house at least once a week. The
other was the geography master, a small, bald, and utterly insignificant
man called Pittioni, who was the laughing stock of the whole school. Even
the other masters, his colleagues, made fun of Pittioni, who was ugly and
was made to suffer for his ugliness like no other man I have known. During
my time at the school he was the butt of everyone's mockery and scorn,
an inexhaustible source of malicious jokes; and he gradually became for
me the central figure of the school; and from whatever point of view I

consider it today, he remains the central figure, a frightening example of readiness for sacrifice—on the part of the individual and on the part of a whole brutal society which thoughtlessly and unscrupulously abuses him. Pittioni illustrated the individual's capacity for pain and suffering on the one hand and the vileness and viciousness of the society around him on the other. The crippled schoolboy and Pittioni were for me the most important figures at the school; it was they who brought out, in the most depressing manner, all that was worst in a ruthless society, in this case a school community. Observing them, I was able to study the community's inventiveness in devising fresh cruelties with which to torment its victims. I was also able to study the helplessness of the victims in the face of each new affliction, the increasing harm they suffered, their systematic destruction and annihilation, which became more terrible with every day that passed. Every school, being a community, has its victims, and during my time at the grammar school the victims were the geography master and the architect's crippled son. All the baseness of society, all its natural cruelty and viciousness—all its sickness, in fact—were daily vented on these two; it was they who brought it all to explosion point. Afflicted as they were by ugliness or deformity—two afflictions which no society or community can tolerate—they were made to look ridiculous every day, and this continuous ridicule turned them into objects of contempt, sources of endless amusement for masters and pupils alike. Whenever people are thrown together—but especially when they are thrown together in tremendous numbers, as they are in a school—the suffering of one or more individuals like the architect's crippled son or the geography master becomes a focus of vicious entertainment of a quite disgusting and perverted kind. So it was at the grammar school. There was nobody who did not participate in the entertainment, for the supposedly healthy members of any society enjoy such entertainment—whether secretly or not, whether openly or behind a mask of hypocrisy—at the expense of the suffering, the crippled, and the sick. In such a community, such an institution, a victim is always sought and always found, and if he is not a victim already, from the start, he will *in any case be made into one*. In establishments like the grammar school or the boarding house the community always sees to that. It is not difficult to spot a so-called mental or physical disability in a person and to make him, because of this so-called mental or physical disability, the focus of everybody's amusement. Wherever human beings are thrown together, one of them at once becomes a laughing stock, a source of malicious mirth, whether the mirth is uproarious or restrained, surreptitious, soundless. Society never rests content until one of the many— or of the few—has been selected as its victim and has become the target of every pointing finger. The community always seeks out its weakest member and exposes him to its pitiless laughter, to repeated and ever more exquisite torture by ridicule and mockery; and it always shows itself supremely inventive in constantly devising fresh refinements. We need only look at what goes on in families: there is always one member of a family who is mocked and ridiculed. Wherever *three* are gathered together, there is always *one* in the midst who is mocked and ridiculed. Society cannot exist without one or more such victims. It always derives its amusement from one individual or a small number of individuals in its midst. We see this happening all our lives. And the victims go on being exploited until they are destroyed. In the cases of the crippled schoolboy and Pittioni I was able to observe *the degree of viciousness which society or the community can reach in the process of mocking, destroying, and annihilating its victims. It always reaches the very highest degree and then often goes one better, casually killing the victim in the process.* Any sympathy felt for the victim is sympathy only in name; it is really no more than bad conscience on the part of the individual at the cruel behaviour indulged in by others, behaviour in which he is in fact just as keenly involved by *behaving cruelly* himself. No extenuation can be pleaded. Examples of cruelty, viciousness, and ruthlessness practised by the community against its victims to provide itself with entertainment run into hundreds and thousands, as we know, and the victims are invariably driven to the extremity of despair. Society tries out every variety of cruelty and viciousness on its victims and goes on experimenting until it has killed them. As invariably happens in nature, the weakened elements in the organism, the weakened substances, are the first to be attacked, exploited, killed off, and eliminated. And of all the organisms there are human society is the basest, being the most cunning. And the passing of centuries has brought not the slightest change: on the contrary, methods have become more refined and hence more appalling and more infamous. Morality is a lie. Inwardly the so-called healthy person gloats over the sick or the crippled. Pittioni's arrival at school every morning at once set in motion a torture mechanism designed specially for him, in which he was made to suffer all morning and half the afternoon; and when he left school to go back his home in the Müllner Hauptstrasse, he simply escaped from one torture mechanism at school to another at home, for Pittioni's home life, as I know, was hell. He was a married man with three or four children, and I often have visions of him walking in front of his wife, pushing a pram with his smallest or youngest child in it, walking desperately through the city on a Saturday or Sunday afternoon. Punished by ugliness all his life for nothing he had ever done, spawned by his parents and exposed to the pitiless gaze of society as an object of scorn and contempt, Pittioni was simply a victim of the society to which he belonged. It was plain to see that he had long ago come to terms with the role he was called upon to perform in it: to entertain it by his ugliness and inadequacy. He was quite simply one of society's victims, just as many others are society's victims, though we are not prepared to admit that this is so, and hypocritically pretend that in fact things are quite different. And he was a superb geography teacher, probably the best the school has ever had, if not altogether the most remarkable teacher it has ever had; for all the other masters, *with their boundless health*, were no more than average and in no way his equal. I often think and dream about the tormented Pittioni. It is true that everything about the man was ridiculous in the extreme, but this very ridiculousness amounted to a species of greatness which dwarfed all the others at the school. After lessons, when everyone had left and the school was empty, the architect's crippled son would still be waiting at his desk, which he shared with me. Condemned to almost total immobility, he had to wait for his mother or sister to come and lift him out of his seat and put him in his wheelchair. He had long been accustomed to this procedure. Very often—and not just because I sat next to him—I would while away the time with him. As we waited we would spend the time telling each other about the lives we led. I would tell him whatever seemed worth recounting about the boarding house and he would tell me about his life at home. Sometimes his mother was delayed, and his elder sister too sometimes arrived as much as an hour late. These periods of waiting naturally tended to drag, and very often I felt like getting up and going back to the boarding house, through the vegetable market and over the bridge; but the obvious friendship my classmate showed me in everything he said and did always stopped me leaving. When his mother or sister came up to the classroom to collect him, she always brought with her a load of fruit or vegetables she had just bought in the vegetable market next to the school. She hung her purchases on the wheelchair, lifted the crippled boy into it, and, with my help, carried him, wheelchair, fruit, vegetables, and all out of the classroom and down the wide marble stairs.

By the time she had reached the first floor her load had become too heavy, and she would put it down in front of the war memorial for a rest. At this point I usually took my leave and ran off. In this way I often arrived late at the boarding house, where I found only a cold meal waiting for me and a severe reprimand from the prefect. The other boys were sons of prosperous shopkeepers (the father of one owned Denkstein's, the shoe shop) or of doctors and bank officials. Very often today I find myself standing in front of a shop with a familiar name on the door, and then I recall that I went to school with the owner. Or I read in the newspaper about judges who attended the grammar school with me, or about lawyers or mill-owners who were in my class. There are several doctors among my former classmates. Most of these classmates went to the grammar school in order to follow in their fathers' footsteps and have since taken over their fathers' businesses and offices. But there is not another whom I recall as clearly as the architect's crippled son, whom I will refrain from naming. When I think of the grammar school, it is this crippled boy and the ridiculous and incredibly ugly geography master who spring immediately to mind. This establishment, which is set in the middle of the town and therefore surrounded by some of the finest architecture ever created, became gradually more and more oppressive, until suddenly I could endure it no longer. But before I finally left the grammar school—and the boarding house in the Schrannengasse—of my own volition, I still had much misery and unhappiness to endure. At the time I saw myself as being in league with the two people I have described—the crippled boy and Pittioni. But I was different from them: their unhappiness was plain for all to see, while mine was hidden deep inside me. Being by nature introverted, I had the advantage of being able to conceal my unhappiness and go largely un-molested. Whereas the architect's son and the geography master never went unmolested throughout their lives, I could always hide my unhap-piness under the surface and make it invisible; and the unhappier I was, the less it showed in my behaviour and demeanour. My nature has not altered: I can nearly always manage to conceal my true inward condition by presenting a front which betrays no hint of my real feelings. This ability brings great relief. Though I still walked to the grammar school every morning from the boarding house in the Schrannengasse, I knew that I should not be doing so much longer; but of this thought, which occupied my mind to the point of obsession, I did not speak a word to anyone. On the contrary, since I knew that I was going to leave the grammar school, and hence the boarding house and secondary education altogether, I took care to give the impression that everything was in order. The consequences of this decision became more and more a matter of indifference to me. I can't even spare my grandfather this blow, I thought. I knew that I was going to leave of my own free will, even though I did not know exactly how or in what circumstances. All I knew was that I was going to put an end to this whole situation which had caused me so many years of humiliation and torment. It must have struck people that I had suddenly learnt discipline and now only rarely drew attention to myself; for some time the prefect and his superior, Uncle Franz, had had no trouble from me. I had suddenly taken to subordinating myself completely and was even making progress at school, though this was only because I knew for certain that this time of suffering would soon be at an end. I now often went up alone onto the two hills in the city, thinking of little else but putting an end to my days at the grammar school. Lying under a tree or sitting on a rock, I would give myself up to observing the city, which suddenly seemed beautiful even to me. It was now just a matter of time, perhaps a very short time, before my suffering in secondary education would be over; inwardly I had already escaped from this period of suffering. At the end of 1946 my grandparents, my mother, my guardian, and the children suddenly returned to Salzburg overnight because they wanted to be Austrians and not Germans. The German authorities had issued an ultimatum that they must either accept German citizenship overnight or return overnight to Austria, and they had responded to it by returning to Austria and so to Salzburg. Within three days I had found them an apartment in the Mülln district; and, having barricaded myself in the apartment for fear of being ejected by others in search of lodgings, I was able to wait there and receive them. Profiting from the chaotic conditions into which we were plunged by our decision to remain Austrians and not become Germans, I left the boarding house, though I continued for some time yet to attend the grammar school. Inwardly, however, I had long since freed myself from it; and one day as I was walking to school—a walk which took me along the Reichenhaller Strasse—I decided not to go to the grammar school but to go to the labour exchange instead. The labour exchange sent me that very morning to Podlaha's grocery store on the Scherzhauserfeld Project, where I began a three-year apprenticeship without saying a word about it to my family. I was now fifteen years old.

THE CELLAR

An Escape

*It is an irregular
uncertain motion,
perpetual, patternless
and without aim.*

MONTAIGNE

3

I FOUND *the other people* by going *in the opposite direction*, no longer to the odious grammar school but to the apprenticeship which was the saving of me; by flouting the dictates of reason and no longer walking to the centre of the city with the civil servant's son but along the Rudolf-Biebl-Strasse to its outskirts with the journeyman locksmith from next door; by taking not the route through the wild gardens and past the ornate villas to the academy of the middle class and the lower middle class but the one which led past the institutes for the blind and the deaf and dumb, across the railway tracks and through the allotments, past the wooden paling of the sportsground by Lehen Asylum, to the academy of the poor and the outsiders, the academy of the mad and allegedly mad, on the Scherzhauserfeld Project—the roughest and most dangerous district of the city of Salzburg and the source of most of its criminal cases—to the grocery store owned by Karl Podlaha, a sensitive Viennese character whose life had been destroyed, who had wanted to be a musician but remained a small shopkeeper for the rest of his days. The procedure of being taken on as his apprentice was over in no time. Herr Podlaha came into the side office where I was waiting for him, took one look at me, and said I could start work straight away if I wanted. He opened the door of the cupboard and took out one of his shopcoats, saying it might fit me. I slipped it on. It did not fit, but it would do for me to wear provisionally. Podlaha repeated the word provisionally several times, then thought for a moment and took me out through the shop, which was crowded with customers, into the street and to the house next door, where the storeroom was. My new master took down a broom from the storeroom door and handed it to me, telling me to spend the time until twelve o'clock sweeping up. At twelve, he said, he would talk to me about the rest of the work. Left alone in the dark storeroom, with its strange mixture of smells and the damp that is a feature of storerooms in general, I had time to think back over everything that had happened. I had given the woman official at the labour exchange a hard time, but the result was that within an hour I had got what I wanted: an apprenticeship on the Scherzhauserfeld Project, where I could be *usefully* employed, working for human beings among human beings. I felt I had escaped from one of the greatest idiocies invented by man, the grammar school. Suddenly I felt that my existence was *a useful existence* again. I had escaped from a nightmare. Already I pictured myself packing flour, dripping, sugar, potatoes, semolina, and bread into people's shopping bags, and I was happy. I had executed an about-turn halfway along

the Reichenhaller Strasse and gone to the labour exchange, where I had
given the woman official a hard time. She had offered me any number of
addresses, but at first none *in the opposite direction*. I wanted to go *in the
opposite direction*. I swept up in the storeroom; then at twelve o'clock, as I
had been told to do, I locked up and went round to the shop. Herr Podlaha
introduced me to Herbert, the assistant, and Karl, the apprentice. He said
he did not want to know anything about me; all I had to do was complete
the formalities and, for the rest, make myself *useful*. He suddenly came
out with the word *useful*, though without giving it any special emphasis,
as though it were a favourite word of his. As for me, it was my motto. I
felt I had just come to the end of a period of uselessness, a period of
misery, a dreadful phase in my life. Two possibilities had been open to
me, as I can still see clearly today: one was to kill myself—and I was not
brave enough for that; the other was to quit the grammar school without
further ado. I did not kill myself but got myself an apprenticeship. Life
went on. The reaction I met with at home was partly apathy—from my
mother and my guardian—and partly extreme understanding and sympathy—from my grandfather. They at once accepted the changed situation,
without a moment's discussion. For a long time I had been left to my own
devices. Just *how* alone I had been I realized only at this moment. The
effect would have been the same whether, having taken hold of my own
existence, I had thrown it out of the window or thrown it at my family's
feet. I put my schoolbag in the corner, just as it was, and did not touch
it again. My grandfather managed to hide his disappointment. He now
dreamt of my becoming a high-powered businessman—a capacity, he said,
which might give my genius greater scope than any other intellectual
capacity. He blamed my failure on the circumstances of the times, on the
fact that I had been born into the unhappiest period possible, the lowest
point in human history, from which, as far as one could judge, there was
no longer any escape. Suddenly, after having had a lifelong contempt for
businessmen, a contempt based on intimate personal experience, he now
saw them as an honourable class, membership of which was not incompatible with greatness. I myself had no ideas about my future. I did not
know what I wanted to be. I did not want to be anything—I had quite
simply made myself useful. Quite suddenly and unexpectedly this thought
afforded me a refuge. For years I had gone to the learning factory and sat
at the learning machine, only to have my ears deafened and my mind
deranged. Now, suddenly, I was among human beings again, people who

knew nothing of the learning factory and had not been corrupted by the learning machine because they had never come into contact with it. What I was seeing now I immediately loved and was able to take seriously. There were days when hundreds of people came to the shop, when the cellar was stormed at eight in the morning, like a veritable food-fortress, by the hungry and the half-starved. These alternated with other days which belonged to the old, the lonely, and the female drunks. Whatever the day, Karl Podlaha's grocery store was the central point of the project; there was nowhere else for people to congregate, no bar, no coffee-house, only buildings which were constructed in such a way as to destroy the lives of their occupants, so dreary and repulsive that any personality was bound to disintegrate and atrophy within them. The women called at the cellar shop even when they had no purchases to make, for no practical reason at all. All of them were liable to turn up at any time of the day for want of anything better to do, just to exchange a few words with another person. It was clear as soon as they appeared at the top of the concrete steps—and it became abundantly clear when they came down into the shop—that they had simply fled from their dreadful homes to find respite, a chance to live. For many of those living in the project the cellar proved again and again to be their last and only refuge. Many of them were in the habit of calling in every day, sometimes several times a day, to make some small purchase—two ounces of butter, for instance—not because they were short of money but because these frequent visits to the cellar were a vital necessity to them, affording them the opportunity to escape from surroundings which were in some cases quite deadly. That they had no ulterior motive was proved by their embarrassment when they came down the steps. It was only now, in the first few days spent in my new surroundings, that I again had direct and immediate access to human company. Such direct and immediate access had been denied me for years. First my mind and then my spirit had been all but stifled by the deadly pressure of school and enforced learning, and for years I had had only an indistinct perception, through the fog created by this forced learning, of whatever lay outside the school and its constraints. Now I was seeing human beings again and had direct contact with them. For years I had existed among books and set texts and among people who had nothing in their heads but books and set texts. I had been surrounded by the stale smell of mouldering, desiccated history, all the time feeling as though I had become part of history myself. Now I was living in the present, with all its smells and stringencies. I had made my decision, and this is what I had discovered. I was alive again, after being dead for years. Most of my real qualities, the positive features of my character, came to the surface again within my first few days in the cellar, after being buried and stifled for years by the odious educational methods to which I had been subjected. They developed spontaneously in the new environment, the quality of which was determined on the one hand by my colleagues in the shop, on the other by the customers as human beings, the human beings who were our customers; but what brought out the best in me was above all the tremendous *usefulness*, which I at once appreciated, of the intense relationship between these two sets of human beings. This was the setting in which I did my work, and from the very first moment my work gave me pleasure. I began my apprenticeship just as a new series of ration coupons was called up, and it was only a few hours before my duties ceased to be confined to sweeping the floor and keeping the shop tidy: toward evening, when my colleagues began to show signs of fatigue, I was put to the test and took a hand in serving the customers. I passed the test. *Right from the start I did not just wish to be useful—I really* was *useful, and my usefulness was noted,* just as previously, up to the time of my starting work in the cellar, my uselessness had been noted. By deciding on an apprenticeship, I reflected, I've succeeded in putting an end to my uselessness, which has been going on for as long as I've been alive. And today I know that my years spent in the cellar were the most useful years of my life. I now know also that those which preceded them were not wholly useless, though at the time, having just been taken on as a member of Podlaha's team in the cellar, I was one hundred percent convinced of the uselessness of all that had gone before. Right from the beginning my time in the cellar was a precious time, not one which dragged on endlessly and pointlessly, tormenting my mind and deadening my nerves and affording no hope. I was suddenly leading an *intense, natural, and useful* existence. The difficulties that presented themselves were overcome at once; in fact there were basically no difficulties, because whatever I was faced with was of my own choosing. Everything served to distance me from the life I had led up to now, since it was the exact opposite in nearly every way. In my very first days in the cellar the life I had led previously was ruthlessly unmasked and revealed for what it was and what I had for years felt it to be—a terrible time, a time of terror. Everything was revealed as a deception, an error, and that was what I wanted. Having previously believed I had no future of any kind, I now knew I had one, and suddenly every moment brought fascination, a feeling that had been deadened long ago. I no longer had to try and persuade myself that I had a future, as so often in the past, I had one. I had got my life back again. And all at once I had it entirely within my grasp. All I had had to do, I reflected, was an about-turn in the Reichenhaller Strasse; I had simply had to get myself apprenticed instead of going on to the grammar school, to go to the cellar instead of the palace of learning. In the Scherzhauserfeld Project I saw the kind of people I had always heard about but never seen. I knew from what my grandfather had told me that such unfortunate people existed, people who were victims of poverty and despair, but I had never seen them at close quarters. The civic authorities did everything possible to suppress any knowledge of the conditions in the Scherzhauserfeld Project, but reports were carried by the newspapers, and later, as legal correspondent for the *Demokratisches Volksblatt*, I myself had to write reports every week about people from the Scherzhauserfeld Project who appeared before the courts. Most of them were known to me from the time of my apprenticeship in the cellar, and even then it could have been foreseen that they would one day end up in court. The reason why they are now in court, I would reflect during the proceedings, is bound up with all the things I know only too well from my time in the cellar. The judges did not know what I knew, and they did not trouble to enquire closely into the life of the accused: they treated all cases alike, confining themselves to the documents of each case and to the so-called incontrovertible facts, passing sentence without any knowledge of the person they were sentencing, of his background and history, or of the society which had made him a criminal and led to his being branded as one in court. The judges confined themselves almost exclusively to the documents in the case, thus destroying the human being who had been brought before them by applying their brutal, unthinking, and unfeeling laws, laws which were indeed inimical to any thought or feeling. At least once a day the whole life and existence of some human being arraigned before the court would be destroyed by some judge's ill temper. This was—and is—a terrible observation to make. But this is not the proper time for a sketch of the judiciary. All I wish to say is that years after my apprenticeship in the cellar had come to an end, I still came across many of my former customers in the dock; and whenever I open a newspaper I am confronted by names I know from the cellar, by the fates of individuals I once knew there—people from the Scherzhauserfeld Project who used to get themselves into the court reports—and still do, thirty years after I served my apprenticeship. I knew why I had made the woman at the labour exchange take out dozens of cards from her card-index: it was because I wanted to go *in the opposite direction*. This was the phrase I had repeated to myself over and over again on my way to the labour exchange. Again and again I had used the phrase *in the opposite direction*. The woman did not understand what I meant, for I actually told her that I wanted to go *in the opposite direction*. She probably thought I was out of my mind, for I used the phrase to her several times. How can she possibly understand me, I thought, when she knows nothing about me, not the slightest thing? Driven to desperation by me and her card-index, she offered me a number of apprenticeships, but none of them was *in the opposite direction* and I had to turn them down. I did not just want to go in a *different* direction—it had to be the *opposite* direction, a compromise being no longer possible. So the woman had to go on taking cards out of her card-index and I had to go on rejecting the addresses on the cards, because I refused to compromise: I wanted to go *in the opposite direction*, not just a different one. The woman was as kind as she could possibly be, and she probably started off by producing her best addresses. She regarded an address in the city centre—for instance, that of one of the largest and most highly esteemed clothing stores—as the best address of all, and she quite simply could not understand why I was not interested in it. All she wanted to do was to fix me up with a good position, but I did not want to be fixed up with a good position. I wanted to go *in the opposite direction*. I kept on telling her this, but she was not to be put off and went on taking what she regarded as good addresses out of her card-index. I can still hear her reading out the best-known and most celebrated addresses in the city, addresses which are known to everybody, but they did not interest me. As soon as I entered her office I had told her that it must be a shop frequented by *a lot of people*, but I was unable to explain to her what I meant by *the opposite direction*. I told her that for many years I had gone into the city along the Reichenhaller Strasse on my way to the grammar school but that now I wanted to go *in the opposite direction*. The two of us—she with her good nature and I with my singlemindedness—went on playing this card-index game for over half an hour: she would take out a card and read off the address, which I would then turn down. I turned down every address because none of those she took out of her card-index was the one I was looking for. *Not one* of the many addresses I rejected (and at that time, unlike today, there were hundreds of vacancies for apprentices in Salzburg) was *in the opposite direction*, which was what I wanted. They were the best addresses imaginable, but there was none *in the opposite direction* until Karl Podlaha's shop on the Scherzhauserfeld Project came up. This was an address which, unlike the others, the woman hesitated to produce from her card-index. From her point of view, as I saw at once, it was one that simply could not be considered. It was only with distaste that she could bring herself to read out Podlaha's address and utter Podlaha's name, only with distaste that she gave me the precise address and pronounced the words *Scherzhauserfeld Project*. She found these words utterly repugnant and had to force herself to utter them. But this, she said, was an address I should probably not consider for a moment. She did not actually say *This is an address you can't possibly consider*, but her whole manner told me unmistakably that this is what she meant. Yet I did consider Podlaha's address, for it was the one address which lay precisely *in the opposite direction*. As far as I could judge, the woman did not believe me when I told her this *was* the right address for me, the one I had been looking for. The very words *Scherzhauserfeld Project*, which had made her naturally recoil in horror, had a powerful fascination for me, and I kept repeating them, just to gauge her reaction, which was one of extreme pain. She repeatedly looked me in the face and simultaneously heard me say the words *Scherzhauserfeld Project*, and she was horrified that I should be making a mental note of precisely this address. She wanted to take out more cards from her card-index, but I told her I was satisfied with the address she had given me; it was the right one, I said, and if I was not taken on at this address I would come back and ask her for another like it, another *in the opposite direction*, like Podlaha's on the *Scherzhauserfeld Project*. The woman was on the one hand glad to have satisfied me but on the other hand horrified at the workings of my mind, of which I had allowed her a glimpse. She had sought out he very best addresses from her card-index, thus providing me with opportunities for getting on in the world, and I had plumped for what she considered the very worst address. Not that she warned me against going to the Scherzhauserfeld Project, but I sensed that she detested the very name of it, and that the name Podlaha was profoundly repugnant to her. Moreover, she had the utmost contempt for what I myself had called *the opposite direction*, and as soon as I made to go in this direction, disregarding all her well-meaning advice (and she must have seen how serious I was about Podlaha's address on the Scherzhauserfeld Project), she had nothing but contempt left for me. It was quite incomprehensible to her that an obviously intelligent young person who had until two or three hours ago been a grammar school boy could reject what to her were the best possible positions on offer, quite fantastic positions in her eyes, and settle for the very worst, one that was quite dreadful and horrifying and beneath contempt, unless of course I was suffering (as she may have thought) from some dreadful, momentary fever of the brain—and probably her only recourse was to refuse to take me seriously any longer. Merely a passing phase, she probably thought to herself as I left her office, the sort of thing that happens to schoolboys during puberty. However, I never went back, and that must have made her think again. A confused schoolboy suffering from a fever of the brain, she probably thought—nothing uncommon; he probably got over it long ago. But in all probability she immediately forgot all about me. The mechanism of school had never meant anything to me, nor had the people connected with it, whereas I immediately found myself intensely attracted by everything connected with the cellar. Everything in the cellar and everything connected with the cellar aroused fascination in me; yet it was more than just fascination—it was a sense of belonging, of fervent commitment. I felt that I belonged to the cellar and all of its people, whereas I had never felt that I belonged to the world of the school. The Reichenhaller Strasse, as I now saw, had never been *my* street, the one that led in *my* direction. My street was the Rudolf-Biebl-Strasse. *It* led in my direction: when I walked along *it*, past the Lehen post office, past the Bulgarians' vegetable gardens, past the paling of the sportsground and through the Project, I was going *my* way, to *my* people, whereas nothing that lay in the other direction was ever mine. I may go so far as to say that the route which took me along the Reichenhaller Strasse was the route which always took me, with the greatest ruthlessness imaginable, away from myself, into daily horrors which might suddenly have led to fatal consequences. The Rudolf-Biebl-Strasse was the street that led me *to myself*. Walking along it every day to the Scherzhauserfeld Project and the cellar, I would think: Now I'm going to myself, and every day I get closer and closer to myself, whereas if I happened to be walking along the Reichenhaller Strasse, I could not help thinking that I was going away from myself, out of myself, to a place where I did not want to be. This was the route that had been forced upon me by those who brought me up, those who directed my steps and were entrusted with the management of my fortune, my *mental* and *physical* fortune, and never did anything but mismanage it. They had chosen this route for me and ordained that I should follow it—and they brooked no contradiction. Then all of a sudden I had done an about-turn and gone along the Gaswerkgasse, past the Fischer von Erlach Hospital, to the labour exchange. And as soon as I was set on this route, having executed my about-turn, I was struck by the thought that I was *now on the right route*. Every morning for years I had woken up thinking that I must break away from the route onto which I had been forced by those who brought me up and managed my affairs, but I had always lacked the strength to do anything. For so many years I had been forced to take this route against my will, all the time enduring extreme mental and nervous tension, until quite suddenly I found the strength to break away from it and do a complete about-turn, something of which I was the last to believe myself capable. But to do such an about-turn one has to have arrived at the point where one's mental and emotional energy has reached an absolute peak and where no other option is open but to do an about-turn or to kill oneself, when one's resistance to everything one has to endure—to everything that has to be endured by a person such as I was at this time—is at its most intense and its most deadly. Such a moment is crucial for our survival; we simply have to pit ourselves against everything or quite simply cease to exist. I had the strength to pit myself against everything, and when I made my way to the labour exchange in the Gaswerkgasse I was pitting myself *against everything*. While the learning machine in the city was once more claiming its senseless victims, I had escaped from it by doing my about-turn in the Reichenhaller Strasse. In a split second I had decided that I no longer wanted to be one of its thousands and hundreds of thousands and millions of victims. I had turned in my tracks, leaving the civil servant's son to walk to school by himself. That morning I had been far too conscious of what my own feebleness had cost me to be able to give in yet again; I did not want to throw myself off the Mönchsberg—I wanted to live. And so that morning I did an about-turn and ran for dear life in the direction of Mülln and Lehen. I ran faster and faster, leaving the whole deadly routine of recent years behind me, leaving absolutely everything behind me, once and for all. When I fled into the labour exchange I was in fact in a state of mortal fear. I did not walk into the building as most people do—I *fled* into it in mortal fear. In the course of just a few minutes I had stood *everything within me* on its head and pitted it *against everything else*. In this state of mind I ran through the streets of Mülln and Lehen and arrived at the labour exchange in a

state of mortal fear. *It's now or never*, I told myself. It was clear to me that
it had to be done that moment. I had suffered too many injuries to allow
myself to hesitate any longer. As I climbed the stairs I thought to myself:
I still have to get through this labour exchange, this revolting building
that fills me with fright and stinks of every kind of poverty, this abominable
building where the stench of dying existences is stronger than in any
other—when I've done that I shall be saved. I won't leave this horrible
building, I told myself, until I've been sent for an apprenticeship, a position
that will make it possible for me to survive. With this thought in my
mind I entered the office of the woman official who dealt with apprenticeship applications. I had no idea what kind of apprenticeship I wanted,
but the longer I stood there facing the woman official, the clearer it became
to me that only one kind of apprenticeship would do: one that would bring
me into contact with as many people as possible, and as *usefully* as possible.
As she searched around in her card-index I became certain of one thing: I
wanted a job in a grocery store. Jobs which involved being thrown upon
one's own company most of the time, as one is in all manual trades, would
not do for me, because I wanted to be among human beings, as many
human beings as possible, under the most stimulating conditions, and I
wanted to be as useful as possible. It is a curious feature of human beings
in general that they find it difficult to make themselves understood, and
the consequence is often a total lack of understanding. The woman did
not understand me, but by the time I had made a complete nuisance of
myself she had cottoned on to what I was after. It was only then, when
she had decided that I was quite insufferable, that she produced the card
with Herr Podlaha's address on it. She had thought all along that I was
out of my mind and not taken me seriously. But now she had had enough
and wanted rid of me, so to put an end to our tête-à-tête, as it were, she
took Podlaha's address out of the card-index. Maybe she reckoned that I
was acting under the influence of some fever on the brain and that my
problems would sort themselves out in a few hours. Whatever she may
have thought, I was determined to get an address from her which was
promising enough for me to be able to take my leave of her. She doubted
the seriousness of my intentions and probably had doubts about my sanity
too. Puberty produces strange aberrations, and one of these might well
lead a young grammar school boy to run to the labour exchange and demand
the address of a grocer, believing that such an address would make him
happy or at least tide him over the next few hours or help him to live

through a day that had become unbearable. As far as I was concerned, however, my intention was unalterable. It may be that I suddenly let myself drop from the high wire I had been walking at school, with all its appalling pressures, down into the real world represented by an apprenticeship in a grocery store. I still did not know who or what lay behind Podlaha's address in the Scherzhauserfeld Project, so I took my leave of the woman in the office and left the labour exchange. I ran out into the Gaswerkgasse and across to the Scherzhauserfeld Project, which until then I had known only by repute as *the* rough area of Salzburg; but it was precisely this rough area that held such an irresistible attraction for me, so I ran as fast as I could and in no time I had found the shop. I went straight down into the cellar and introduced myself. Suddenly I found myself sitting at Podlaha's desk in the narrow side office next to the shop. To think that the boys at the grammar school are now merely schoolboys, I reflected, warming to the impressions which Karl Podlaha's cellar-shop made on me. Perhaps my future lies in this cellar, I thought; and the more I was taken up with the idea of staying in the cellar, the clearer it became to me that my decision had been the right one. In next to no time I had escaped from the society I had belonged to up to that point and had entered Herr Podlaha's cellar. Now I was sitting there waiting for him to say the decisive word. He was a man of medium height, somewhat plump, and neither particularly friendly nor particularly unfriendly, and this was the man from whom I was demanding nothing less than that he should rescue my existence. What kind of impression had I made on this man, who was addressed simply as Boss, as I could hear through the slightly open door to the shop, and whose voice was soft and yet at the same time reassuring? The quarter of an hour I spent sitting alone increasingly reinforced my desire to be apprenticed to Herr Podlaha, who struck me as an intelligent man and far from vulgar. At school I had always found it exceedingly hard, and in most cases impossible, to make contact with either the masters or the other boys. A tension had always existed between myself and others, leading not just to a degree of aloofness but to almost constant enmity and hostility. In the course of time I had drifted into a state of quite hopeless isolation; and even at home, though I found it just possible to make contact with the other members of my family, I could only ever do so with the greatest difficulty. In the cellar, by contrast, I had no such difficulty. Indeed, I was amazed to find that I had no difficulties at all either with my colleagues or with the customers from the project, with whom I was on the best of terms and had a perfect mutual understanding right from the start. I did not have the slightest problem in making conversation and getting along with the inhabitants of the Scherzhauserfeld Project. I soon became familiar with the scene of my daily existence and activity. I gradually got to know almost all the inhabitants, starting of course with the wives of the factory workers, miners, tramway employees, and railwaymen, and also their children. I visited their homes, at first through helping them carry their shopping home when it was too heavy for them. I got to know the Scherzhauserfeld Project from the inside by carrying shopping bags filled with purchases or humping hundred-pound sacks of potatoes to the various housing blocks; and during the many conversations I had with them I was able to observe the way these people lived. Talking to the women and children who called in at the cellar, I got to know about the menfolk who were waiting for them at home, the babies and old people who were waiting for them at home; and it was not long before I knew every block, not just from the outside but from the inside too. And I got to know the language that was used in the project, a quite different language from the one I was accustomed to hearing at home and in the city, and quite different also from the one that was spoken in the rest of Lehen. In the Scherzhauserfeld Project people spoke a clearer and more robust language than they did in Lehen, and I was soon able to talk to the inhabitants in *their* language, because I was able to think *their* thoughts. Everyone here was on standby, and the way people thought in the Scherzhauserfeld Project was the way people think when they are on standby. The Scherzhauserfeld Project was a perpetual blot on the city's landscape, and the city fathers were fully aware of this blot. The Scherzhauserfeld Project, this blot on the face of Salzburg, was constantly cropping up in the columns of the daily newspapers in the form of reports about criminal proceedings or about palliative measures taken by the provincial government. And those who inhabited this blot on the Salzburg landscape were aware that they all constituted a blot on the landscape. They became progressively more of a blot. Here one could find all the things that the city tried to hush up and suppress, all the things that the normal person flees from if he is in a position to flee. This was Salzburg's black spot, and to this day the Scherzhauserfeld Project is Salzburg's black spot, of which the city is ashamed whenever it is reminded of it, a single black spot made up of poverty and consequently of hunger, crime, and dirt. But these people had long since come to terms with this black spot

of theirs. Though they were on standby, they were not really standing by
for anything any longer. They had been abandoned and forgotten—repeatedly appeased and then once more forgotten. The Scherzhauserfeld
Project, the black spot of Salzburg, only ever became an issue when political
elections were due, but as soon as the elections were over the black spot
was forgotten again, with the same regularity as the elections themselves.
Yet through decades of shared misery, and under the deadly pressure of
the contempt in which they were held by the rest of the city's inhabitants—
in whom the very mention of the Scherzhauserfeld Project brought a sickening pain to the pit of the stomach—they had developed their own brand
of pride. They were proud of their fate and their origins, and when it came
right down to it they were proud of their black spot, which one local
newspaper, the *Salzburger Volksblatt*, also called *the biggest stain on the face
of the city*. To live in the Scherzhauserfeld Project was to live in the middle
of a black spot and a stain. The view of the city generally was that this
was where the lepers lived, and to speak of the Scherzhauserfeld Project
was equivalent to speaking of criminals or, to be more precise, of jailbirds
and drunks, or even of drunken jailbirds. The whole city gave the Scherzhauserfeld Project a wide berth. To come from there and actually want
something meant a sentence of death. Branded as a criminal ghetto, the
Scherzhauserfeld Project was the only district which brought the rest of
the city nothing but crime; and if someone left the project, it could mean
only one thing—that a criminal was on the loose in the city. People did
not mince their words when expressing such views, and hence the people
from the Scherzhauserfeld Project had always been chary of showing their
faces. After decades of vilification and contempt they had inevitably come
to believe that they really were what everyone called them, *criminal scum*;
and it is not surprising that from some point in the distant past, some
four or five decades ago, the Scherzhauserfeld Project had been the regular
supplier of fodder for the Salzburg law courts, an inexhaustible source of
raw material for Austria's prisons and penitentiaries. The police and the
courts had been kept busy by the Scherzhauserfeld Project for decades, but
not the city council; and to the so-called social services the Scherzhauserfeld
Project simply served as an alibi to cover up its boundless incompetence.
Even today, well over thirty years since I worked there, I have only to
open a Salzburg newspaper to read about the link that still exists between
the Scherzhauserfeld Project and practically all the city's criminal trials—
trials for manslaughter and murder. When I think back more than thirty

years, it occurs to me that conditions can only have become worse. Where thirty years ago there were fields, there are now apartment blocks and tower blocks, excrescences of our mindless and unimaginative age, an age that is inimical to the mind and the imagination. When I went to work there, I used to walk across fields, past the institute for the blind and the institute for the deaf and dumb, past the Lehen post office, along ordinary gravel paths and through countless natural smells that have vanished—the smell of grass and earth and pools—where now there is only the stultifying stench of exhaust fumes. Between the city and the Scherzhauserfeld Project—as if the city were anxious to keep its distance—there lay a belt of fields and meadows, with here and there a few crudely constructed pigsties, here and there a larger or smaller refugee camp, odd dwellings occupied by eccentric dog-owners of both sexes, and shacks housing prostitutes and drunks whom the city had disgorged at some time. In the middle of these fields, at what it judged a sufficient distance from itself, the city had built a low-cost, soul-destroying housing project to house its social rejects, its poorest, most neglected, and most down-and-out citizens, who were naturally at the same time the sickest and most desperate—its human waste, in other words. It sited the project just far enough away to avoid being confronted by it, so that anyone who wished could go through life without knowing about this project, which was reminiscent of the penal settlements in Siberia—and not just because of the way the blocks were numbered. In the middle of each of the single-storey blocks a flight of several steps led up into a narrow entrance hall giving access on both sides to the individual dwellings, which no one today could call apartments. Each of these consisted of one or two rooms, those with two rooms being occupied by the largest families. The water tap was in the hall, and there was a single, shared lavatory. The walls of these blocks were made of sheets of asbestos held together with cheap mortar. Only the three-storey blocks were built of brick, and these were occupied by what might be called the privileged members of the proletariat. Our grocery store was in the cellar of one of these three-storey buildings. Every day brought a scene of family violence, and at least once a day the police van came round the corner. The ambulance would arrive to rescue someone who had been half-killed or stabbed, and the hearse would come to collect someone who had died wretchedly in his bed or someone who had been murdered. The children spent most of their time on the streets—the only streets in Salzburg that had no names—screaming and shouting because in the streets they had room to scream and shout, and with their screaming and shouting they drowned the awful silence that reigned in the Scherzhauserfeld Project, a silence that would have been deadly had they not screamed and shouted. At home I tried to give some indication of what I saw; but, as always happens when one tells people about something shocking and appalling, something inhuman and utterly horrifying, they did not believe me. They did not want to hear about it, and, as always, they called the terrible truth a lie. But one must not stop telling people the truth; and the shocking and appalling things one observes must under no circumstances be suppressed or even doctored. My task can be no more than to pass on my observations, whatever effect they produce, always to report whatever observations seem to me worth passing on, whatever I see around me or can still see with the eye of memory when I look back, as I am doing now, to thirty years ago. Many things are no longer clear, while others are all *too* clear, as though they took place only yesterday. The people one speaks to try to protect themselves by refusing to believe, and they often refuse to believe the most obvious facts. People refuse to be troubled by the trouble-maker. All my life I have been a trouble-maker, and I shall go on being the trouble-maker my relatives always said I was. As far back as I can remember, my mother used to call me a trouble-maker, and so did my guardian and my brother and sister. I still am a trouble-maker, with every breath I draw and in every line I write. Throughout my life my very existence has always made trouble. I have always troubled and irritated people. Everything I write, everything I do, is a source of trouble and irritation. My whole life, my whole existence, has consisted of troubling and irritating others, by drawing attention to facts that trouble and irritate them. Some people leave others in peace, while others—of whom I am one—cause them trouble and irritation. I am not the sort of person who leaves others in peace, and I have no wish to be. Writing about the Scherzhauserfeld Project today is a way of making trouble for the civic authorities of Salzburg: recalling the Scherzhauserfeld Project causes irritation. I can remember my time as an apprentice; I regard it as the most important period of my life, and it is natural that I should remember this human limbo, which was my private name for the Scherzhauserfeld Project. Whenever I went there I did not say, I'm going to the Scherzhauserfeld Project, I said, I'm going into limbo. Every day I went into the limbo which the city authorities had built for their rejects. I told myself at the time that if there was such a place as limbo, it would probably look like the Scherzhauserfeld Project. Those were the days when I still believed in hell. Since I no longer do, the proper name for the Scherzhauserfeld Project must have been hell, since nothing could have been worse for those who lived there. For all those human beings there was no salvation, and every day I saw them perish, young and old alike. They had diseases I had never heard of, all of them deadly, and they committed the most terrible crimes. Most of them were born to rags and died in rags. All their lives they dressed in overalls. They procreated children in a state of delirium, then killed them in an advanced state of imbecility which resulted from their latent despair. There were days when the air I breathed was heavy with the smell of all those inhabitants of the Scherzhauserfeld Project who were rotting away alive. Chance, I reflected, has led me into limbo (or hell). No one who is unfamiliar with this limbo (or hell) has any idea what it was like and hence is not qualified to speak. Truth, it seems to me, is known only to the person who is affected by it; and if he chooses to communicate it to others, he automatically becomes a liar. Whatever is communicated can only be falsehood and falsification; hence it is only falsehoods and falsifications that are communicated. The aspiration for truth, like every other aspiration, is the quickest way to arrive at falsehoods and falsifications with regard to any state of affairs. And to write about a period of one's life, no matter how remote or how recent, no matter how long or how short, means accumulating hundreds and thousands and millions of falsehoods and falsifications, all of which are familiar to the writer describing the period as truths and nothing but truths. His memory adheres precisely to the events and their precise chronology, but what emerges is something quite different from what things were really like. The description makes something clear which accords with the describer's *aspiration* for truth but not with the truth itself, for truth is quite impossible to communicate. We describe an object and believe that we have described it *truthfully* and *faithfully*, only to discover that it is not the truth. We make a state of affairs clear, yet it is never the state of affairs we wished to make clear but always a different one. We are bound to say that we have never communicated anything that was the truth, yet throughout our lives we have never stopped trying to communicate the truth. We wish to tell the truth but fail to do so. We describe something truthfully, but our description is something other than the truth. We ought to be able to see existence as the state of affairs we wish to describe, but however hard we try we can never see this state of affairs through our description.

Knowing this to be so, we ought to have given up wishing to write the truth long ago and so given up writing altogether. Since it is not possible to communicate and hence to demonstrate the truth, we have contented ourselves with wishing to write and describe the truth, as well as to tell the truth, even though we know that the truth can never be told. The truth which we know is, from the point of view of logic, a lie, and this lie, since we cannot circumvent it, is the truth. What is described here is the truth, and yet at the same time it is not the truth, because it cannot be. In all the years we have spent reading, we have never encountered a single truth, even if again and again what we have read has been factual. Again and again it was lies in the form of truth and truth in the form of lies, etc. What matters is *whether we want to lie or to tell and write the truth*, even though it never can be the truth and never is the truth. Throughout my life I have always wanted to tell the truth, even though I now know that it was all a lie. In the end all that matters is the truth-content of the lie. For a long time reason has forbidden me to tell and write the truth, because that only means telling and writing a lie; but writing is a vital necessity for me, and this is the reason why I write, even if everything I write is bound to be nothing but lies which are conveyed through me as truth. Of course we may demand truth, but if we are honest with ourselves we know that there is no such thing as truth. What is described here is the truth, and at the same time it is not, for the simple reason that truth is only a pious wish on our part. If I am asked why I have chosen to write about my time as an apprentice now and not later, when I might be able to give a freer and more dispassionate account of it, I can easily answer the question: I have learnt from the newspapers that the city is proposing to tear down the Scherzhauserfeld Project, to dismantle the fifty-year-old testimony of the bricks and asbestos, to raze this limbo—or hell, if you prefer—to the ground, and to demolish the walls in which for decades so much useless misery has been endured. A brief notice in the press has once more set in motion a mechanism in my head which came to a halt a long time ago, the mechanism of memory by which I recall the Scherzhauserfeld Project, that appalling human settlement which was the stepchild of the city and perpetually shunned by each and every citizen. To say one came *from* or lived *in* the Scherzhauserfeld Project or worked on the Scherzhau-serfeld Project or had anything whatever to do with the Scherzhauserfeld Project was enough to excite alarm and revulsion all round. It was a stigma to come from there or to have anything to do with a place that nobody could possibly come from or have anything at all to do with, and all the inhabitants of the Scherzhauserfeld Project bore this stigma throughout their lives. They bore it until they were dead—dead because they ended up in the madhouse or in prison or in the cemetery. Even the children were born into this state of mind, feeling that it was somehow impermissible to come from the Scherzhauserfeld Project. And they suffered from this stigma all their lives, and those who have not yet been ruined by it will be caught up by it sooner or later, even though they may deny it. The Scherzhauserfeld Project was on the one hand a ghetto of despair, on the other a ghetto of shame. One could tell that people came from the Scherzhauserfeld Project simply by looking at them, just as in all towns— and especially in big cities—the trained observer can tell what district a person comes from, and the trained observer knows as soon as he meets somebody whether he comes from the local purgatory, the local limbo, or the local hell. In the city of Salzburg, which has never admitted to having a limbo in its midst, let alone a hell, one could recognize the denizens of limbo or hell from a distance—lost, confused creatures who scurried along furtively, each one of them manifestly unhappy both outwardly and inwardly. They were the real outsiders in the most elementary sense of the term, branded unmistakably as inhabitants of the Scherzhauserfeld Project. The state, the city, and the Church had long since failed in their obligations to these people and given up. The inhabitants of the Scherzhauserfeld Project had been given up and abandoned—and not just by the world around them, the perverse, deceitful, and fastidious society of the city, but by themselves: the inhabitants of the Scherzhauserfeld had given themselves up long ago. All who met them treated them as though they had the plague. The moment they entered one of the shops in the city they were put down; the moment they set foot inside an office they were humiliated and put down; the moment they appeared in court they were summarily sentenced and that was the end of them. Salzburg society as a whole regarded the Scherzhauserfeld Project as a leper colony, and so did its inhabitants; as a penal colony, and so did its inhabitants; as a death sentence, and so did its inhabitants. Life became atrophied here and amounted in reality merely to a creeping death, yet a few hundred yards away affluence and pleasure were rolling off the assembly lines in a perverse city which gave itself the air of being the sole ruler of the world. All these people in the Scherzhauserfeld Project were fully aware that it was pointless to want to break out and seek a better life elsewhere, and the instances of those who had tried to break out and seek a better life demonstrate that such attempts could only lead to still deeper despair and still greater isolation. Those who did go away either perished in the world outside—because wherever they went and whatever they did they never ceased to belong to the Scherzhauserfeld Project—or else they returned to the Project, to end their lives in even greater wretchedness than those who had stayed at home. One of them tried his luck as an actor in every possible town in Austria and Germany, only to come back several years later *as a complete wreck* (these were his mother's words), utterly emaciated and scarcely a human being any longer, let alone the good-looking man he had certainly been (at least according to his mother), and die in convulsions on his mother's rotting sofa. One became a professional dancing host; one went to America and another to Australia, just like hundreds of others over the years—but they came back to the Scherzhauserfeld Project, where they finally went to pieces and died. Their mothers and fathers just waited for it to happen. They all followed a circuitous route, which very often took them to foreign countries, but led only to disintegration and death; and meanwhile their parents, their brothers and sisters and other relatives, drank themselves to death at home. The children were born into families who drank themselves into a mindless stupor and spent whole days in a delirium of despair, so that from the very beginning of their lives they were bound to be demoralized and destroyed. In the course of their appalling lives the girls hardly ever achieved anything better than a job as a charwoman, while the boys seldom became anything more exalted than a workman's mate or a coalminer, and they were always changing their jobs and taking refuge in sickness and crime. Their appalling lives amounted simply to a perpetual alternation between sickness and crime right up to the day they died. They lived out their existence in a constant welter of accusations: in order to gain some sort of relief, in order to be able to breathe, they blamed everyone and everything—God, the world, one another. They all existed in a ceaseless *delirium of accusation and blame which amounted to a deadly disease*. Basically all they had was demoralization and destruction; this was all they existed on, and all their time was spent in demoralizing and destroying one another. Their existence was fraught with all the deadly intensity of despair, and both men and women sought refuge alternately in hospitals, asylums, and prisons. At first I could not understand the offensiveness of certain customers—which did not make them any worse or any better than the others; I just could not make it out. I missed the point of their double-edged,

triple-edged, or multi-edged remarks and turns of phrase, but it took me
only a few days to realize what they were talking about and why. They
spoke about things that were naturally not mentioned openly by people
in the city, and it soon became clear to me why this open way of talking
seemed sensible and more appealing than the silent hypocrisy of others.
In no time at all I naturally became familiar with the so-called indecent
remarks and turns of phrase that were current in the Scherzhauserfeld
Project in hundreds and thousands of variations. These people never minced
their words. I very soon got used to this *openness*, and after a few weeks
and months I was often able to outdo them all in inventiveness on this
score and did not hold back. In the Scherzhauserfeld Project I could give
my fertile imagination free rein as I was never allowed to do at home, and
not surprisingly it went down well. Once I had familiarized myself with
the regular conversational techniques and the commonest topics discussed
in the cellar, I never looked back. I exploited the full range of my mental
virtuosity and was able to put even the most hardened practitioner in the
shade. Thanks to my youthfulness and the boyish charm I had at the time,
as well as my ready command of a rich and varied vocabulary embracing
all shades and nuances of meaning, I was made. There were five main
topics of conversation in the cellar—food, sex, the war, the Americans,
and—in a quite separate compartment from these—the atomic bomb, the
effect of which on the Japanese city of Hiroshima still obsessed everyone.
The question of food and how to come by it preoccupied them all day and
night, and naturally there were hundreds of routes and channels for obtaining it. The official channel was by way of ration coupons, which became
valid at intervals depending on the supply and availability of certain food-
stuffs, their validity being announced in the press and over the radio. There
were also, however, unofficial channels, underground routes leading to the
Americans, for example, and to subterfuge and theft. The whole nation
had in fact turned criminal, in the strict sense of the word, in order to
survive. In the cellar too not everything was strictly legitimate. Some
people obtained more than they were strictly entitled to, and even the boss
was caught out, despite his faith in the efficacy of hushing everything up.
A gold wrist-watch might be traded for two pound-packets of butter. The
employees of the wholesalers often succumbed to attempts at bribery made
by small shopkeepers, among whom our boss was by no means the least
skilful. And who in fact did behave with complete probity in those days?
Criminal tendencies where food was concerned were the most conspicuous

natural characteristic of everybody. The crime of obtaining food to which one was not entitled was one that everybody committed. They were scared of the atomic bomb, and of the Americans they spoke on the one hand with impotent disdain and on the other with obsequiousness. Their favourite topic was the war. The women talked about their husbands, and the husbands about the theatres of war where they had served. The women were at their most communicative when telling about their husbands' wounds, and the men always steered the conversation round to Smolensk, Stalingrad, Calais, El Alamein, and Narvik. And in spite of having heard it all hundreds of times before, we still had to return to these theatres of war every day—and as for their wounds, we knew all about them, down to the smallest and most insignificant details. One woman, for instance, related again and again in great detail how her husband's bladder no longer functioned properly because his testicles had been grazed by shrapnel at Sevastopol. The women talked about their husbands' time in captivity and gave us, as it were, second-hand accounts of the conditions in the Russian, American, and British camps. In the minds of ordinary men theatres of war represent high points in their lives, no matter whether they are associated with victory or defeat. Anyone who had a father and an uncle was constantly being told of nothing but their deeds of valour. Even their defeats became deeds of valour, and all the dirty and disreputable things they had done in the war became, when it was over, so many decorations to be pinned unashamedly to the horizon of their memories. The women displayed the most passionate involvement as they told us in the cellar about their husbands' deeds of valour and the atrocities committed by the enemy. The repatriated prisoners of war spoke grandiloquently of heroism. Only those who were actually crippled for life remained silent and could scarcely be induced to say a word. We children soon knew all there was to know about the pioneers and the mountain infantry, and after a certain time we were always hearing the same stories about Narvik and Trondheim, about Calais and Jajce and Oppeln and Königsberg. The men brought their empty rum bottles to the cellar, and while they were having them filled they would lean against the counter and discourse on the history of the war. Their theatre had been the roar of gunfire and the sight of corpses, the multi-rocket-launcher and the Leopard tank, General Dietl and Field Marshal Paulus. They blamed the débâcle alternately on Hitler and Churchill, though Churchill came in for more of the blame than Hitler. And they talked almost non-stop about how they had got back home after the war and how remarkable it was that they had got back at all—and they probably dreamt about it all when they had no one to tell. The war was only superficially over: in everyone's mind it was still raging. Everyone knew how defeat could have been avoided, yet on the other hand they had all foreseen it. Whenever somebody leant against the counter and related his war experiences as though they were the quintessence of all that was important and significant in human affairs, we had a member of the general staff at the counter. The exceptions were the silent figures with only one arm or with no legs or with metal plates in their heads. They could not be drawn on the subject of the war, and most of them left the cellar the moment the talk turned to the war. The war was always topic number one among the men. War is the poetry of men, by which they seek to gain attention and relief throughout their lives. They all took refuge, each in his own way, in viciousness and depravity and regenerated themselves in a state of complete and pitiful apathy. From an early age they had learned to hate, and in the Scherzhauserfeld Project hatred was developed to a fine art as a means to be used against everything. Hatred breeds hatred, and they hated one another and the rest of the world unremittingly to the point of exhaustion. And their states of exhaustion served only as means to an end, the end being self-destruction; in these states of exhaustion they devised new miseries for themselves, new sicknesses and new crimes. They fled from one misery to another, one misfortune to another, each one deeper and more inescapable than the last, and they always made sure of taking someone else with them. They fled into the world outside, but the world outside dealt only deadly blows, and they were soon beaten back. They fled into fantasies which eventually turned out to be nightmares; into debts, which were the quickest way to prison; into febrile imaginings from which they emerged utterly drained of energy. They fled into dreams and fancies which left them perilously debilitated. These denizens of limbo, which was in all truth nothing short of hell, were cheated at every turn of any chances they had. It was in the nature of things that they had no chances at all, except the chance of ruin. There were only two ways to put an end to this existence: either they could kill themselves at a given moment or they could take to their beds and die at a given moment. The will to live or exist was paraded here and there in grotesque guise, even in the Scherzhauserfeld Project, and only made the conditions in limbo (which in reality was hell) even more appalling. At regular intervals, especially on weekends, music could be heard coming from a few of the windows—

the sound of an accordion, a zither, a trumpet, and now and then there was singing—but all this gaiety was of a macabre kind. The singer who had sung his folksong so beautifully one evening was carried out of the house in a coffin the very next day just as I was shutting up the shop; the woman who had placed the zither hanged herself not long afterwards; and the trumpet-player ended up in the tuberculosis clinic at Grafenhof in the Pongau. The climax of the year was carnival: on Shrove Tuesday, having bought themselves every possible kind of mask and made themselves comic or scary costumes, they would rush excitedly to and fro in the project as though they had taken leave of their senses for the day, believing that no one could recognize them, though in fact each of them could readily be recognized. You know that drunken voice, I would think to myself; you know that limp. But woe betide anyone who told them he had recognized them. They would come into the shop in their fancy dress with their familiar rum bottles and get a litre for nothing. Since they brought so many children into the world—more than were born in any other district of the city—they qualified for the highest burial record too. They made regular excursions into the Big Wide World to attend funerals at the Communal Cemetery or Liefering Cemetery when one of their number had died. With a few exceptions they ended their earthly courses in a shared grave or a mass grave. After the interment they treated themselves to a funeral feast consisting of all kinds of food and delicacies bought on credit at our shop. Very few of our customers paid cash: they all had a so-called credit slate, and many delayed payment for months, until Herr Podlaha ran out of patience. Then they either paid up or took their business to the other grocer in the Scherzhauserfeld Project, until they were no longer welcome there either, after which they would come back and pay up. The other grocer did not keep a slate and never took the risk of giving his customers any credit; the price he paid was to have a much more modest turnover. In fact he could hardly exist on his turnover. Podlaha's generosity—or rather his commercial cunning—stood him in good stead: nearly everybody in the Project bought his goods, and the reason why they bought so many of them was that they were so desperate: all these denizens of the Scherzhauserfeld limbo or hell believed that by constantly buying and consuming food and delicacies they could make their despair more endurable, and it is a well-known fact that the poorest and most unfortunate people buy most and eat most and in doing so buy and eat their way into ever deadlier despair. They unloaded nearly all the money they had in our shop. On pay days the shop was almost denuded of goods and the storeroom half depleted. They all had large numbers of children and hence many ration coupons; and whatever was not on ration, and therefore was freely available, they bought sight unseen in large quantities—above all, things they did not need, and our boss showed great inventiveness in the way he stocked up with such useless goods: whenever they were available on the cheap, he brought in hundreds of objects such as cast-iron candlesticks or wine-dispensers, all of which were purchased by his customers, though they had no use for either, since they did not burn candles and drank their wine straight from the bottle, without recourse to glasses. No matter how dreadful or useless the objects were, they were bought up in no time. From a business point of view this was an ideal time for a man like Podlaha: everyone in the Scherzhauserfeld Project was seized by an obsessive craze for buying. Podlaha was the cleverest person I have ever known when it came to disposing of goods; he could have sold anything on the most favourable terms and had nothing left on his hands. But he was not just a good commercial calculator; he was also good-natured. He was not just out to do business, and it was not just for commercial reasons that he had opened his shop in the Scherzhauserfeld Project; he could have opened one anywhere he chose. Absurd though it may seem, he had been attracted by the Scherzhauserfeld Project as a refuge, possibly for reasons similar to mine. The Scherzhauserfeld Project was a refuge for him after his failure in Vienna, as it was for me. After taking a commercial course he had wanted to study music at the Academy and make it his principal career, but the war had forced him to give up his studies and say good-bye to the Academy and all the hopes connected with it. He had not come to Salzburg simply to do business: he was an intelligent man and far too sensitive for that. His reversion to the career for which he was originally trained was simply a way out of his personal plight. He was qualified by his training to run a grocery store, and it was probably instinct which led him to open one not just *in* Salzburg, but *on the outskirts, in the Scherzhauserfeld Project*, which must have had an attraction for him too, as it was bound to have for anyone repelled by the so-called normal world, and Podlaha had been repelled by it just as I had. In cases like ours the next step is quite naturally the one that leads into limbo or hell. He probably felt, as I did, that he was one of the beneficiaries of limbo or hell. Podlaha too was an outsider— just how much of an outsider I did not learn until much later. He knew the right way to deal with the customers, especially the women, who valued the conversations they had with him, and I learned a great deal from him about how to get on with people. Here in the project he was able to maintain his independence, which was just as important to him as mine was to me, by opening a business in the cellar, which he was able to furnish and equip to his liking; in this way he could live his own life as an outsider, isolated from the normal world. He did not live in the project but with an uncle in another part of the city. It was this uncle, I suspect, who had made it possible for him to move from Vienna to Salzburg and had used the influence he had in Salzburg to remove some of the obstacles which even then faced a Viennese who wanted to open a business in Salzburg. Podlaha always dreamt about music—he probably dreamt about it incessantly—but he led the life of a small grocer. He may have felt himself to be a musician, which he undoubtedly was, though he was no longer a practising musician and no longer played an instrument. All day long he dreamt of being a musician, but he never became anything but a grocer. By nature he and I had much in common; how much we had in common I realize only now, but this is not the time to speak of it. Chance—if there is such a thing—had brought together two people, Podlaha and myself, who resembled each other even in the smallest details of character. There was a close affinity between us, and our two existences ran parallel in a number of important respects. Whenever he found his life as a grocer irksome or indeed unbearable, as he often did, he would say that he had really wanted to be a musician, always using the same words and adopting the same accusatory tone. He had taken a commercial course to please his parents, but he had wanted a musical career, the height of his ambition having been to play in the Vienna Philharmonic. His plans had been frustrated by the war, and instead of playing the tuba or the trumpet in the Vienna Philharmonic he had been thankful to find refuge in the Scherzhauserfeld Project, in the same cellar where I myself found refuge a few years later. Podlaha lacked the stolidity of other members of his trade, who are constantly impelled by financial greed; I even had the impression that money was of no great importance to this man, who loved going for walks—or at least not of prime importance. When I had been working in the cellar for only a few hours, he drew my attention to certain people with whom I was to *go easy*, one of them being a woman of about sixty or sixty-five called Frau Laukesch or Lukesch, who had been coming to the cellar for years with her rum bottle and whose son had tried to make a career for himself as a popular actor in a converted beer cellar in Schallmoos, though he had naturally ended up simply as a drunk. Podlaha enjoyed business, just as I always did, and in fact I know that I should have become a competent and by no means unsuccessful businessman had I wished. However, he did not exploit the situation of the denizens of limbo or hell. He could have exploited them right, left, and centre, as they say, but instead he behaved honestly. He dealt with his customers firmly but always correctly, and he showed special consideration to the older women and the children. Where necessary, he took on the role of psychological counsellor, dispensing advice and medicaments, and there were many occasions when he was able to avert some personal or family tragedy. He taught me more than anyone else about the art of human relations, and I am convinced that I owe to Podlaha, and my observation of his daily dealings with the people who came to the cellar, my ability to get on easily with the so-called common people. He was a good teacher, not only in commercial matters but in matters concerning people. Whereas others find everything connected with human relations difficult, I have never experienced any such difficulty since my apprenticeship with Podlaha. I was of course extremely receptive. My whole term as an apprentice in the cellar was a period of observation, and it was from my grandfather that I had learned the art of observing everything intensely. After the individual tutoring I had had from my grandfather I do not think I could have had a better second teacher than Podlaha. My grandfather had taught me how to be alone and self-sufficient; Podlaha taught me how to mix with people, with a large number and variety of people. My grandfather had given me an ideal introduction to the school of philosophy—ideal because it came so early—while Podlaha, in the Scherzhauserfeld Project, introduced me to the greatest of all schools: the school of absolute reality. These two schools which I attended early in my life had a decisive effect on its subsequent course, each complementing the other and providing me to this day with a basis for my further development. The cellar-shop catered to the necessities of life and was itself *a vital necessity for my life*. I immediately realized this, and everything had to be subordinated to this realization. At home they noticed the change that had come over me ever since I had started my apprenticeship. I told them simply that I would not be going to school any longer but to a grocery store. When I told them it was in the Scherzhauserfeld Project they did not believe me, but they had to come to terms with the fact. I actually *did* go to the Scherzhauserfeld Project when I set off from home at half past seven in the morning with the

journeyman locksmith from next door (who, incidentally, was later to
become an extraordinarily gifted actor and has since appeared in almost
every theatre in Germany). I had made my decision independently, entirely
on my own, having been left alone for years by those responsible for
bringing me up. They had been at a loss to know what to do with me
and had written me off. They had no ideas about my future. Sensing that
they themselves had no future, how were they to envisage mine? All they
had was their misery and the effects of the post-war calamity which had
engulfed them and with which they were unable to cope. All they could
do was stare at it. They spent all their time staring at their own calamity,
which they called the post-war calamity, and did nothing about it. They
were already half-demented through staring at this calamity of theirs, their
post-war calamity. The family was never a real family because all its
members, as long as they lived, were totally hostile to the concept of
family. It was a collection of relatives living in a single set of rooms which
they still had at their disposal, nine people who could not stand the sight
of one another any longer and who expected to be kept alive solely by my
mother and her husband, my guardian. They expected my guardian to
earn the money to keep all nine and my mother to cook for all nine every
day. They loathed the conditions they lived in but did nothing to change
them. Everyone in time got on everyone else's nerves, and it was not long
before the hopelessness of their situation had drained them of all their
mental and emotional energy. The one thing that pleased them was that
one of their number had made himself independent. They were not interested in where he had come by this independence—they did not care.
I suddenly realized that I could have done whatever I liked so long as I
supported myself and made no further demands on them. But, after all,
I was only sixteen when I decided to swap the grammar school for Herr
Podlaha's cellar. From the age of sixteen and for the rest of my life I earned
my own living. From that moment on I did not cost them another penny.
From the age of sixteen I had no more cause for gratitude. And for this I
am thankful. I preferred to go into limbo—or hell—rather than to stay
on at the grammar school and have to rely on my family. However, they
too benefited from my new area of activity. I was able to come to their
rescue by providing them with food, not always on a strictly legitimate
basis. Coming to their rescue often amounted to nothing more than bringing home a white loaf or a desiccated sausage or a can of jam. My grandfather, on whom I had pinned *all* my hopes, had himself come to the end

of the road and could no longer point me the way ahead. What I had learnt from him was suddenly of use only as far as my imagination was concerned and had no bearing upon my practical life. And so all at once I felt myself deserted by the one person I had trusted one hundred percent. He had tried to compel me to do something I was quite unwilling to do. Basically, something had happened which was bound to happen: the grammar school, where I was concerned, had ended in a *reductio ad absurdum*, and the educational disaster I had suffered was the fault of my grandfather, who had carried his instruction in how to be alone to quite preposterous lengths. Nobody can live in solitude and isolation, which inevitably lead to ruin, a fact which we see confirmed by the deadly society we live in. Unless I wanted to be ruined I had to break with the one person who meant everything to me, and this meant breaking with everything. I made the break quite abruptly, not knowing what the consequences would be but knowing it had to be made. Perhaps I could have stayed on at the grammar school for years, daily renewing my alliance with the same madness and absurdity, prolonging for years the deadly revulsion I felt for everything; but in the end I should have had to make the break—by which time it would probably have been not just a break with the school and everything connected with that miserable institution (which amounted to almost everything in my life except the resolve I had made) but with life itself. It would have meant finally ruling off an existence that was almost lost anyway. For ages my life had been intolerable, but *the time had not been ripe for making the break.* I had not been able to foresee when the time would be ripe, and when at last it was, I was so much taken by surprise that I did not know what had come over me when I did my about-turn in the Reichenhaller Strasse. I had just bought myself new schoolbooks and exercise books, and my grandfather was once more trying to find someone to coach me in mathematics. I thought I was going to have to put up interminably with my guardian's curses, with being cursed every day by those who provided for me, with being intimidated and reduced to abjection by their curses. Then suddenly I made the break. My attention was fixed on the civil servant's house, where the civil servant's son was waiting for me. In a moment I'll ring the bell, I thought, and my fellow pupil will come to the door and join me. This boy had only one arm, his left arm having been ripped off by a bazooka abandoned by the Germans somewhere in a forest in Upper Austria. We'll walk the rest of the way along the Reichenhaller Strasse, I thought, as far as the Neutor, then we'll go through the Neutor and past the Sacellum to the grammar school. At this moment I turned in my tracks and ran *in the opposite direction*, across the Aiglhof meadows, through Mülln and into the Gaswerkgasse. And from that day to this I have neither seen nor heard anything more of the civil servant's son, and for years I never set foot again in the Reichenhaller Strasse. For years I avoided going through the Neutor, and even today I would find it impossible to enter the grammar school. The fact that from one moment to the next I had turned myself from a pupil at the grammar school into an apprentice in a grocery store must have caused the profoundest dismay to my grandfather, and probably to my mother as well. As for the others, they were probably indifferent to the problem. To my guardian it was a cause of unalloyed relief; according to him, he would not have minded whatever I had done—even if I had become an apprentice bricklayer he would not have objected. His reaction was understandable: he was weighed down by the chaos existing among all the people he had to support single-handed. He could afford to be indifferent—he was not being cynical. As for my uncle, my grandfather's son, my decision to leave school and the fact that I had taken a commercial apprenticeship confirmed him in his suspicion that *I had run away from the grammar school because I was no good.* He was jealous of me because my grandfather loved me but had always had misgivings about *him*, his own son, and this was probably why he felt his suspicions confirmed. Be that as it may, I did not quit the grammar school because I was no good but because I loathed it. However, there was no way of making him understand this. My grandfather alone understood my reasons and had some idea of what was going on inside me. He saw my switch from the grammar school to an apprenticeship as a transitional move, and very soon after my revelation he was fully convinced of the usefulness of a commercial apprenticeship, even though he was unable or unwilling to tell me why. I had his blessing for my work in the cellar and for the new life I had begun in surroundings which were not entirely without danger to myself. I was assured of his love and affection and needed nothing more. Once again I had my grandfather by my side to protect me. It was probably because of him and the sense I had of his authority that I had been able to make my bold decision, which everyone else regarded as a mistake. He had had great plans for me and had spoken of them repeatedly, to me and to others, and now I had ended up as an apprentice in a grocery store in a cellar in the Scherzhauserfeld Project. The moment Herr Podlaha took me on I was free. I *was* free and I *felt* free. I did everything and went on doing everything of my own *free* will. Previously I had done everything against my will, but now I did everything freely and without reluctance, enjoying whatever I did. Not that I believed I had found the meaning of life, or even a particular meaning that made sense to me; yet I knew my decision had been the right one. Today I am bound to say that the one moment which was decisive for my later life was the one when I did my about-turn in the Reichenhaller Strasse. Without it I should probably have had no later life. The circumstances which finally crushed and killed my grandfather and my mother would have crushed and killed me too. As a pupil at the grammar school I should have been crushed and killed: as an apprentice in the cellar in the Scherzhauserfeld Project, under the régime and supervision of Karl Podlaha, I survived. The cellar was my one refuge, limbo (or hell) my one salvation. One day a week (I can no longer remember which) I had to attend the technical college, at the so-called Neues Borromäum in Parsch. The teachers there were quite different from those at the grammar school. They were local businessmen who were employed as teachers for obvious reasons relating to their merit and reputation and whose appointment at the technical college assured them of a pension for life. Because of their total concern with the present and their familiarity with what went on around them in the real world, they won my confidence. The subject-matter of the instruction engaged my interest, being entirely new to me, and to my surprise I found that I was receptive to the commercial variety of mathematics. Mathematics had never interested me at the grammar school but only bored and depressed me, yet at the technical college I suddenly and unexpectedly found it fascinating. Quite by chance I recently came across one of my exercise books from this period, and I find that its contents make sense, even though they are now very remote and I am no longer conversant with such formulations as "The supplier receives a certificate of change of title" or "We sell goods forward" or "We pay a bill on maturity." I did not greatly enjoy attending college, even though I paid only short visits to the Neues Borromäum, and these were often interrupted for fairly long periods—when I had no time to attend because there was a sudden flood of customers due to a new call-up of ration coupons or because my time was fully occupied with clearing up the storeroom. There were no schoolboys at the college, only apprentices who did not wish to be schoolboys. And the teachers were basically not teachers but businessmen or so-called *economic experts*; they were to a large extent just as vain and stolid as the masters at the grammar school, but less insufferable. After the educational trauma I had suffered (unlike the other apprentices, who had not known the hell of grammar school but had only attended the main school, in some cases only the elementary school) I was not enthusiastic about these days I spent under instruction. Here too a mood of narrowmindedness, pettiness, vanity, and mendacity prevailed, but it was all less shattering, less tense and unnatural, than the excesses of the classical grammar school. Above all, the tone, if rough, was straightforward—the tone used by people engaged in trade, those who fight on the economic front. The mendacity one met with here was less extreme than at the grammar school, and what was taught here was of immediate utility, unlike what one learned at the grammar school, which was never going to be of any conceivable use. At the technical college I had no difficulties with my fellow students and soon made friends. What surprised me most was to find myself suddenly belonging to the commercial class. This was borne in upon me above all at the college. It was an undeniable fact. And I did not wish to deny it. I remember the commercial mathematics teacher, a man called Wilhelm who walked with a limp, and Rihs the engineer, who owned a paint shop—two completely different but complementary characters who set the tone of the college while I was a student there. Their influence was useful to me, and whatever liking I was forced to deny the one, because he was a wholly unlikeable person, I was able to give the other. Here too, as is always the case with human relations, I found myself able to exist within the dangerous borderland between sympathy and antipathy and to profit from the experience. The work of a commercial apprentice is not confined to keeping the shop and the storeroom clean and tidy, nor to the habit he acquires of breathing in flour dust every day, an occupational hazard which arises from constantly carrying and emptying bags of flour and semolina and can often lead to lung disease, thus bringing many an apprenticeship to an abrupt end. It does not consist solely of the orderly routine of a grocery store like the cellar-shop in the Scherzhauserfeld Project: first of all unlocking and pushing back the concertina grille, then unlocking the shop door and letting the boss, the employees, and the customers into the shop, in which everything had been made spotless and all the containers topped up the previous evening, often by dint of hours of work put in after closing time—all of it involving the meticulous performance of numerous small tasks requiring conscientious devotion and a methodical, mathematically inclined memory. These jobs and hundreds

of others equally important have to be carried out daily. In my day there
was in addition the enormous task of dealing with the ration coupons,
which required great precision and attention to detail; these had to be cut
out whenever a purchase was made and stuck onto a sheet of wrapping
paper every evening after the shop closed. Quite apart from continually
lugging bags around and filling bottles and grading potatoes and sorting
fruit and vegetables and making up bags of coffee and tea and slicing
butter and cheese; quite apart from the feats of skill required to pour
vinegar and oil and every other possible liquid such as rum and wine and
fruit juice into every possible kind of bottle, all with impossibly narrow
necks; quite apart from having to be constantly on the look-out for mould
and decay, for vermin, for excessive cold and excessive warmth; quite apart
from perpetually unloading all kinds of deliveries, sometimes making
hundreds of journeys a day from the shop to the storeroom and back,
cutting bread and making breadcrumbs, keeping the ham fresh and the
eggs cool; quite apart from dusting the shelves daily and rushing to and
fro between the refrigerator and the counter, between the potato boxes and
the counter and between each of the shelves and the counter; apart from
continually washing and drying one's hands and using knives that have to
be sharpened every day and forks and spoons that have to be cleaned every
day and jars that have to be washed out every day; and apart from cleaning
the windows and mopping the floor and waging a continual war against
flies and gnats and horseflies and wasps and cobwebs on the walls—quite
apart from all this, the most vital requirement was never to slacken in
one's attentiveness to the customers, always to be polite and friendly and
obliging and to engage them in conversation, constantly keeping oneself
in practice, in a word to satisfy them all the time and never, not even for
a moment, to let up in one's eagerness to help: on the one hand to meet
the wishes of the customers and at the same time never for a moment to
neglect the interests of the business. Tidiness and cleanliness were imperative. The customers and the boss had to be kept happy all the time, and
at the end of the day the takings had to be correct. To my own surprise,
to the surprise of my colleagues and to the amazement of the boss himself,
I very quickly mastered the job and had no difficulty in doing whatever
was right and expected of me. Moreover, I got on well with everyone, and
the cheerfulness I brought to the cellar proved infectious. I do not know
where I got this sudden capacity to be cheerful and to infect others with
my cheerfulness. I had always had it in me, and now it was no longer

stifled but had free rein again. Many people came into the cellar to have a laugh with me. I had a friendly manner and a quick wit which was never lost on the customers. Whenever the boss went to get supplies from the wholesalers, he could confidently leave me alone in the cellar for whole days if Karl the apprentice was sick and Herbert the assistant out of the shop for some other reason. I was soon able to cope with the customers single-handed and was quite unperturbed if there were dozens of them crowded in front of the counter. I dealt with each in turn, calmly and with one hundred percent efficiency, totally absorbed in my work and at the same time in love with it. The boss knew he could rely on me. There were days when a new call-up of ration coupons brought a massive onslaught of customers and I kept it under control without difficulty all by myself. The simple fact was that I enjoyed my work: I had wanted to be useful, and I had got my wish. And the satisfaction I got from my job was plain to everyone I had dealings with in the cellar. I had had no idea that life could be so happy on days when I had so much to do that nobody was prepared to believe I could cope with it all alone. The shop counter in the cellar was like the captain's bridge, from which I commanded everything perfectly when I was left in sole charge as a result of one of Karl's ailments or one of Herbert's love affairs, which more and more frequently led him to miss work. Herr Podlaha valued my self-sufficiency; intelligence and practical skills seldom go together as well as they did in me. In addition I had a naturally open manner and the ability to be happy and cheerful whenever necessary; I did not have to hide my feelings; on the contrary I showed them quite openly. For years I had been unaware of all these abilities and positive qualities, which suddenly surfaced again in the cellar in the Scherzhauserfeld Project in the most refreshingly extrovert fashion. At such times, when I was in sole charge of the shop, I was completely happy. There I was, at the centre of things, not only selling our groceries and other wares but also giving everyone who came into the shop, as an additional free gift, so to speak, a share in my rediscovered *joie de vivre*. On Saturdays, after the weekly clean-up in the shop, I arrived home pretty well exhausted, bringing with me white loaves, potatoes, sugar, and flour or whatever I had been asked to get. I would walk home through the streets of the project, which at that hour were always filled with the same smells of cooking (especially the smell of soup), past the sportsground with its almost completely rotten paling as far as the Lehen post office, through the dirty puddles and the rank unmown grass in front of the post office and past the makeshift fences of the Bulgarian gardeners, whom I often watched through the fence as they worked, reminding me of the gardening job I had had for a year at Traunstein. I used to think as I watched them that gardening would also have been a suitable occupation for me. Had the bomb-craters not put an end, in 1945, to the gardening firm of Schlecht and Weininger, where I learned so much, perhaps—who knows?—I should now be a gardener. Gardening is one of the best occupations for both mind and body, affording the best escape from melancholy and discontent, melancholy and discontent being the most conspicuous characteristics of human nature. The Bulgarians were able to make very little land yield large quantities of fruit and vegetables, and their produce was always of the highest quality, because they actually used their heads as well as their hands when they worked, and because they were not afraid of any amount of work, their whole lives being concentrated solely on the land they tilled. Often on my way home from the Scherzhauserfeld Project I would go into the gardens (where today there are apartment blocks) and talk to the Bulgarians, and every time I did so the observations I made proved useful. My route then took me across to the institute for the deaf and dumb with its tall trees and tastefully disposed glasshouses, in which the inmates spent the whole day working under the care of white-wimpled nuns, and then across the railway line. I had the choice of either crossing the tracks or going through the underpass, but if I had time I chose the prohibited route across the tracks. Saturdays took me away from the shop, away from the Scherzhauserfeld Project, and back into a state of melancholy. Even before I had left the project silence had fallen on it, broken only by the rattle of crockery and cutlery to be heard through the windows, a silence that meant one thing: it is Saturday, nobody is at work, people are lying around in their apartments on their sofas or their beds, not knowing what to do with their free time. The afternoon silence lasted until three, when they began to quarrel, and then some of them would rush out of the houses into the open air, very often swearing and screaming, desperation written all over their faces. I always felt that Saturday afternoon was a dangerous time for everyone. This mood of desperation, to which most of the inhabitants fell victim to the most alarming extent, resulted from dissatisfaction with themselves and with everything and everybody, as well as from the sudden awareness that they were being exploited and that their lives were entirely pointless. Most people are used to their work, to some kind of regular occupation; and when work stops they momentarily lose their sense of purpose and succumb to a state of morbid despair. This is as true of the individual as it is of the mass. They imagine they are recouping their spent energy, but in reality they find themselves in a vacuum, and this drives them half-demented. The result is that on Saturday afternoons they get the maddest ideas and everything they attempt turns out unsatisfactorily. They start moving furniture around—wardrobes and chests of drawers, tables and armchairs, even their beds. They take their clothes onto their balconies to brush them, and they clean their shoes as if they had suddenly gone mad. The women get up on the window-sills and the men go down to the cellar and stir up the dust with their brooms. Whole families take it into their heads that they must tidy up their living quarters, and so they fall upon the contents of their apartments and try to make order; but they succeed only in creating disorder in their minds. Or else they take to their beds and nurse their ailments, taking refuge in their diseases, permanent diseases which they become aware of again on Saturday afternoon when work is over. The doctors know all about this and are more in demand on Saturday afternoons than at any other time. When work stops, the diseases start; there are sudden pains, the well-known Saturday headache, the Saturday afternoon palpitations, fainting fits, outbreaks of fury. The diseases are suppressed and assuaged during the week by working or by being occupied in some way. On Saturday afternoon they make themselves felt again, and the sufferer is at once thrown off balance. And if he has stopped work at midday and becomes aware soon afterwards of his true situation, which is in every case a hopeless situation, no matter who he is, what he is, or where he is, he has to admit to himself that he is unhappy, even if to others he pretends the opposite. The fact that there are a few happy people who are not thrown off balance by Saturday only proves the rule. Fundamentally Saturday is a day people fear even more than Sunday, for on Saturday they know that Sunday is still to come, and Sunday is the most terrible day of all; but Sunday is followed by Monday, a working day, and this makes it endurable. Saturday is frightful, Sunday is terrible, and Monday brings release. To pretend that this is not so is malevolent and stupid. On Saturday the storm gathers, on Sunday it breaks, and on Monday the calm returns. Human beings do not like freedom—to say otherwise is to lie. They do not know what to do with their freedom. No sooner are they free than they occupy themselves with opening chests of drawers full of clothes and underclothes, sorting out old papers and looking for photographs, documents, and letters, or else they start digging their gardens, or set off quite pointlessly and aimlessly in some direction or other, whatever the weather, and call it going for a walk. And wherever there are children around, they are brought into the well-known activity known as killing time, to be provoked, beaten, and boxed round the ears in order to restore the chaos that brings release. On the other hand, what can be more dreadful than the Saturday afternoon walk to visit friends and relatives, an occasion which satisfies curiosity but destroys good relations? And if people read, all they are really doing is tormenting themselves with a self-imposed punishment; and nothing is more ridiculous than sport, the most popular alibi so far devised to account for the utter futility of the individual. The weekend is murder for everyone and death for every family. On Saturday, when work is over, the individual—hence everybody—suddenly finds himself entirely alone, for the truth of the matter is that the only company people have throughout their lives is their work—they have their occupation and nothing else. No human being can be a substitute for another's work. No one goes to pieces when he loses another human being, not even if he loses the person who matters most, the most important person in his life, the one he loves most; but if he is deprived of his work or occupation it is not long before he lies down and dies. Diseases arise when people are not fully occupied, when they have too little to do. People should complain not of having too much to do but of having too little. When work is reduced, diseases increase; unhappiness takes hold of everyone when work is reduced. To this extent work, though in itself pointless, nevertheless has a point, an essential purpose. What one observed first of all on Saturday afternoons was the characteristic silence, the calm before the storm. Then suddenly people would rush into the street, having remembered their friends, or the existence of nature, or the fact that there was a cinema show or a circus. Or else they would flee to their gardens and start turning the soil. But whatever they did, they invariably did it because they were disappointed. Quite clearly, anyone who did not take refuge in some activity but believed that he could bridge the gap in his normal activity by merely pursuing his reflections, using meditation as a means to fend off the danger that this posed to his state of mind—a state of mind which might easily put his life at risk—soon put himself wholly at the mercy of his personal unhappiness. Saturday was always the day for suicides, and anyone who has attended the courts for any length of time knows that eighty percent of murder victims meet their deaths on Saturdays. All through the week everything that is calculated to make a person discontented and unhappy, because his mind is concentrated to such an extent on his discontent and unhappiness, remains suppressed; but on Saturday, when work is over, this discontent and unhappiness return—with a vengeance. And on Saturday everyone tries to unload his discontent and unhappiness onto someone else. When work is over, he takes his discontent and unhappiness home, where nothing but discontent and unhappiness await him, and unloads them there. The consequence of this is that Saturday has a devastating effect on every human being. Where a number of human beings live together, as in families, they find life unendurable and there is bound to be an explosion; and the situation of the person who is completely alone and hence lonely and isolated, is no less appalling. Saturday is the real killer, a fact which is made unbearably clear on Sundays; then Monday comes and all the discontent and unhappiness is put off until the following Saturday, until the next deterioration in everybody's mental state. I myself hated Saturday and Sunday; I dreaded them because these were the days when I was quite ruthlessly confronted with the misery of my family, nine people in three rooms, getting on one another's nerves from morning till night, dependent on my guardian's meagre earnings and my mother's cooking, constantly hungry and with nothing to wear. As I recall, they were so short of clothes that they used to swap shoes and coats and trousers so that each in turn could go out into the street looking decent. My grandfather had the smallest room to himself, but it was so small that he could scarcely turn around in it. There he spent his time among his books, with all his ideas that had come to nothing, disgusted by the world around him. Most of the time he sat at his desk, wrapped in the old grey horse-blanket to save firewood (which was almost non-existent), without really being able to work. For days on end he would lock himself in his room, as I know, while his wife, my grandmother, waited to hear the shot from the pistol he kept on his desk—on his desk during the day and under his pillow at night. She was afraid of hearing the shot. We had all heard him threaten suicide again and again. He had no money and not the least strength left, and like the rest of us he was starving. It was the bitterest time we ever knew, two years after the end of the war; and he had absolutely nothing left but hopelessness. My guardian worked at his job for a pittance. At this time I had my bed in the entrance hall right next to the door, because there was simply nowhere else to put me. In such circumstances there was no question of my being able to sleep undisturbed, and so on most mornings I went to work completely unrested. And when my uncle and his wife moved out and there were seven of us left, my mother took in a Tyrolean violinist who practised non-stop, in order to have a source of income with which to provide for all the mouths she had to feed. There was nothing for me to laugh about at home. Our existence could not have been more difficult, and there was just no way out. The end of the war had brought us all together in this apartment to show us how dreadful life was. However, this is not the place to describe in detail the horrors of our domestic life. In fact I must refrain from dwelling on it; I must resist the temptation to write down my recollections of something that was simply indescribable. By comparison I found everything else a joke. Perhaps the reason for my invariable good humour in the cellar was my knowledge of what I had escaped from every morning. *Home for me was hell*, from which I was saved every day by my journey to the Scherzhauserfeld Project, which I will now go back to calling *limbo*. My home was at least as appalling as all the so-called homes in the Scherzhauserfeld Project. Just as I escaped from home every day by walking to work along the Rudolf-Biebl-Strasse *to* the Scherzhauserfeld Project, those who lived there escaped, if they had the strength and the opportunity to do so, by walking to some job *outside* the Scherzhauserfeld Project. Most, however, no longer had the strength, just as none of my family, with the exception of my guardian, any longer had the strength. Most of the people in the Scherzhauserfeld Project had no strength left. They went mad or they died, or else they went mad *and* died, as my relatives did. But that is another story. The one thing that saved me on Saturdays and Sundays was walking for hours with my grandfather, going up onto the Mönchsberg with him if he felt strong enough—and he seldom did, since he was by now a very sick man. How perverse it had been, on top of all these appalling conditions at home, to send me to the grammar school! Even now as I looked back, it all seemed like a senseless nightmare. In reality the conditions in my own home were more dreadful and appalling than any in the Scherzhauserfeld Project. The denizens of limbo thought they were in hell, but they were not—*I* was in hell. But I told them nothing about this: it would have ruined the position of trust I enjoyed after I had been in the cellar only a short while. I said nothing about the utterly chaotic conditions at home; on the contrary, I painted a reassuring picture of my family and my home for my colleagues in the cellar and especially for Herr Podlaha. In order to protect myself I falsified the picture and never gave the slightest hint of what my home was really like—pathetic and hopeless. To keep quiet about something is not to lie, and I kept quiet about nearly everything. When I left home, where I was always depressed, I took a deep breath and quickened my pace, running as if for dear life along the Rudolf-Biebl-Strasse and down to the Scherzhauserfeld Project. Having left home sad and disconsolate, I arrived at the Scherzhauserfeld Project in a cheerful mood. The distance I had to walk was just enough to turn my dejected mood into one of cheerfulness. It was a pleasant downhill walk, and the air was fresh and spicy. Now and then I would walk up onto the Mönchsberg by myself and lie down in the grass under a tree to write poems or to go through the lessons I had to learn for college, learning about the hundreds of kinds of coffee and tea that grew in all parts of the world or doing either simple or unusually difficult calculations involving interest rates, wholesale margins, bills of exchange, and the latest credit conditions. And on the last pages of my exercise books I drew the doorways and interiors of shops I imagined myself owning one day. I had become involved with rice and semolina, with Russian tea and Brazilian coffee, without putting up any resistance—or at least with far less repugnance than I had felt for Alexander, Caesar, Virgil, and the like. On weekends I became conscious of the tremendous tension that existed between the two worlds I inhabited, my home and the cellar, and of what it meant to endure this tension. Every morning at three o'clock my grandfather made a fresh start on *The Valley of the Seven Courts*, which he planned as a book of five hundred manuscript pages. For years now the need to press on with this task had got him up at three o'clock to resume the struggle with death. Debilitated all his life by a serious lung condition, he had made it his custom to start the day at three in the morning by addressing himself to the terrible task that faces the fanatical writer and philosopher, wrapping himself in his horse-blanket and fastening it round his body with an old leather belt. At three o'clock I would hear him in his room as he resumed his fight against the impossible, against the utter hopelessness of the writer's task. Of course at that time I knew nothing of the cruel futility and hopelessness of such an undertaking; but I was a sensitive boy, and I loved my grandfather more than any person in the world, and as I lay in bed in the hall by the door I would listen attentively to the sounds that came from his room, signalling as they did a fresh triumph over the fear of death and a fresh resumption of the desperate struggle to complete what he referred to as his principal work. I was not yet familiar with the pointlessness and futility of principal works; but at sixteen or seventeen I had some inkling, through being constantly close to my grandfather, of the monstrous effort involved in literary endeavour and indeed in all artistic, intellectual, and philosophical endeavour. I admired my grandfather's toughness, tenacity, and tireless energy as he wrestled with all the thoughts he had written down and those he had not, because I admired everything about him; yet at the same time I was aware of the truly terrifying madness in which a man like my grandfather must have landed himself, and of the furious speed at which he was inevitably driving his life into a human and philosophical cul-de-sac. He was to have become a priest and a bishop, and he himself had wanted to be a politician, either a socialist, or a communist; but like all who try their hand at writing, he became disappointed with all these impossible categories and became a writer, philosophizing about all these categories and idiocies and philosophies and inevitably ending up as a lone eccentric absorbed in his writing. At three o'clock in the morning I could hear him begin the day's proceedings behind the padded door of his room. His situation was utterly hopeless, but he went on fighting, even after forty years of total failure which would have made anyone else give up long before. He had not given up. The more obvious and unbearable his failure became, the more obsessed he became with the subject that had become his life's work. He was an uncommunicative person and he hated society. He had incarcerated himself with his writing, with his literary task, yet he allowed himself the freedom of being alone and subordinating everything else to his life's work. All his life he made those around him suffer, above all his wife, my grandmother, but also my mother; it was their tireless devotion that made it possible for him to live in this state of total creative isolation. What they gave him they paid for from their own lives, and they could not have paid a higher price. At three o'clock he rose with the bakers and the railwaymen and sat down at his desk. I would listen and, hearing him moving, turn onto my side again. The knowledge that my grandfather was already up and working, with only the padded door between him and me—that he was close to me and *still alive*—made me happy every morning. My uncle emerged at about five o'clock from the room he shared with my grandmother, my mother, and my brother and sister, separated from them by a large cardboard screen, and woke me up. Life went on like this for years. He would go down into the cellar, where he carried out his experiments, and get on with his inventions. He always intended to apply for patents for them, and indeed he did apply for patents; they were supposed to bring him wealth and security, which was of course a pipe-dream, if not true madness. I got up at about six, got myself ready, and had breakfast in the kitchen with my mother and my guardian. Sometimes breakfast was rudely interrupted by an explosion in the cellar when one of my uncle's experiments went wrong and shook the kitchen floor. Normally, however, we all kept as quiet as possible so as not to disturb my grandfather, who had already been working for hours. We would never have dared to speak too loudly or even make the slightest sound that might have caused irritation. We all went on tiptoe in order not to hold up the work in progress on *The Valley of the Seven Courts*. My grandfather's good nature had its limits; where his work was concerned he was unforgiving, and we often found him to be an absolute tyrant. He was capable at times of a positively devastating hardness and asperity, especially towards the women—his wife and daughter. But everyone respected him more than anyone else and made it possible for him to do as he pleased, and everyone loved him. They believed in him and guarded his privacy. He came from the country and had a positively suicidal distrust of anything to do with town life. He had a hatred of civilisation which coloured all his thoughts and feelings as well as everything he wrote. He had been brought up in the country, and it had been a big step when he left it for the wider world; but finding the world an uncomfortable and repellent place, he had soon turned his back on it and retreated into the fastness of his own obstinacy. He could not believe that nothing ever changed. My guardian left the house at about seven. He was just over thirty and supported us all. To me at the age of sixteen or seventeen he naturally seemed very grown up, almost an old man. That was his misfortune. The fact that at the time he was expected to meet the most monstrous demands, working to support the whole family and its numerous hangers-on, was something I did not understand. At about half past seven I myself left to go to the Scherzhauserfeld Project, to the cellar-shop. All in all, the circumstances at home were unbearable because there was no prospect of their improving. We were imprisoned in misery and want, and hence I considered myself extremely lucky to be able to escape every day across the fields and meadows to the Scherzhauserfeld Project. In Podlaha I quite suddenly and unexpectedly had a teacher again, one whom I could accept. I knew little about his background except that he came from Vienna, that he had wanted to be a musician and had become a small shopkeeper, which I know he remained. He taught me all the things I

could not learn from my grandfather, about the real world of the present.
By observing him attentively, more attentively than he realized, I learned
how to cope with everyday life and how to assert myself, something I had
never learnt even from my grandfather. I learned that unremitting self-
discipline was the pre-condition for getting on in everyday life: getting
everything straight not only in one's own mind but in all the most trifling
matters of day-to-day existence. In him I had a teacher who did not have
to force his knowledge and his personality onto me and from whom I was
eager to learn, without being browbeaten or made to feel ashamed. He
was unaware of his role as my teacher in those areas which were most
important to me and unconnected with my commercial apprenticeship.
Whatever had to be learnt in that area I soon mastered, for I had a real
commercial instinct which always stood me in good stead in the shop.
The important thing Podlaha taught me was that one should seek the
greatest involvement in one's dealings with other people yet at the same
time keep one's distance. He was an expert in the matter of human relations,
and that was something I could never have learnt from my grandfather,
who had isolated himself and gradually all those around him—his wife,
my mother and her husband, their children, and consequently me too.
My grandfather was quite incapable of making contact with people, whatever their origin, background, or nature, whereas Podlaha could make
contact with anybody. I owe it to him that I have never since had difficulties
in making contacts, and that is a great advantage, a vital advantage. My
grandfather taught me to observe people from a distance: Podlaha brought
me face to face with them. I was now able to do both. Podlaha, however,
unlike my grandfather, never lost his self-confidence. Podlaha was not a
lone eccentric: he was always surrounded by people. My grandfather, on
the other hand, was a complete loner, even though he had a family, whereas
Podlaha had none. Unlike my grandfather, Podlaha had not let himself
be destroyed by those who had destroyed his hopes. But I do not want to
compare my grandfather with Podlaha—that would be absurd. They had
nothing to do with each other and never saw each other, nor did they ever
show any interest in meeting each other. As a teacher Podlaha filled in
the gaps left by my grandfather. I was his apprentice, but the really
important things I learned from him, the real benefit I derived from the
time I spent with him, extended far beyond this. During this time he
gave me an insight into human possibilities I had never dreamt of, *the
alternative human possibilities*. Somebody tells me now that the Scherzhau-

serfeld Project is going to be demolished, quietly and without publicity. When I heard this I thought for a moment of going back to see it once more, something I had intended to do for years—setting out from the Gaswerkgasse and revisiting the cellar-shop. On one occasion five or six years ago I went and looked into the cellar through the concertina grille, which is still there, and the tall windows. The shop had been closed for a long time, apparently because it had ceased to be profitable. The grille was rusty and the doors were locked, but inside nothing had changed except that, by contrast with the time when I worked there, everything was unimaginably dirty. So Podlaha decided to give it up one day, I thought as I stood there wondering whether or not I was being observed—probably because he no longer saw any point in staying on. A number of large stores have opened in the neighbourhood; so-called supermarkets have sprung up out of the ground in Lehen, and what were once fields are now a built-up area. Where I once walked to work every day there are now grey, impersonal concrete blocks housing tens of thousands of people. It was a quarter of a century since I had last visited the Scherzhauserfeld Project, but the smells and the noises had not changed. As I stood there looking into the shop, I wondered how I had done it—how I had carried sacks weighing nearly two hundred pounds out of the storeroom, up the storeroom steps, then round the corner and down the steps into the shop. I had carried hundreds, in fact thousands, of sacks of flour, semolina, sugar, and potatoes up and down these steps. It had not been easy, but I had done it. I had opened the grille and let the crowd of customers into the shop. I had served all these hundreds and thousands of customers who probably still lived in the project, though now they would all be twenty-five years older. I used to open the door to them, wrap up their bread, slice their sausage, and put their packets of butter in their shopping bags. How often I had made mistakes in calculating what they owed, especially when there was a new call-up of ration coupons, sometimes to the boss's advantage, sometimes to theirs! On such occasions I had had to put up with any number of complaints. I had given many of them more than their coupons entitled them to because I was sorry for them. I had not always been strictly honest. I stood there wondering what had become of this or that child. I could still visualize some of the old faces, even the most inconspicuous details. I could hear all the voices, see the hands counting the money and the legs of the customers passing the window of the side office. I remembered myself surreptitiously stuffing a sausage sandwich or a few apples into some woman's shopping bag. Who cared now? I remembered how clever I had been at pouring raspberry juice into their bottles, and the accident I had once had with a sack of corn cobs weighing a hundred and fifty pounds when I caught it against the corner of the block and the contents spilled down the steps in the rain. I remembered how Karl the apprentice had been repeatedly caught stealing by the boss and his assistant, how he had disappeared overnight, and how his mother had come to the shop in despair to plead for him. But Karl never turned up again. He joined the Foreign Legion. The boss never engaged another apprentice; I was the last. Herbert opened his own coffee-roasting establishment in the city. Half my time as an apprentice had been spent alone with the boss. That had been a success: we had worked well together. We got on well with each other; we respected each other. I was in the shop and did all the work, and when there was a call-up of ration coupons I easily controlled the hundreds of customers by my cheerful self-confidence while the boss fetched the goods to the counter. I had even been able to deal with the difficult customers—with Frau Laukesch or Lukesch, for instance, whose son had got stuck in a hopeless career as a popular actor in the beer-cellar, as I have mentioned already, and committed suicide one day. Shortly afterwards Frau Laukesch or Lukesch killed herself too. And the woman who had lived alone directly over the shop—I have forgotten her name—was strangled, as I read in a newspaper twenty years after I ended my apprenticeship. I looked up at the windows. Perhaps her children lived there now. I can see her now, I thought. She used to wear a rust-coloured blouse and was never seen without a hat. The woman next door I had once seen later as a shy cloakroom attendant at the Festival Concert Hall. I looked into the shop and could see myself standing behind the counter. I could hear my loud laughter and the others bursting into still louder laughter. The crunch of the tires behind me—that was the boss's car drawing up outside the cellar. I used to run out of the shop and up the steps to help him unload the goods and carry them down into the cellar. He would tell me he had bought too many onions, too many tomatoes, too many apples—they would all go rotten. He would have to leave again as flour was selling at a good price. Where he went to buy this flour I do not know. He would sit in the shop, sweeping and mopping the floor and sorting through the crates of potatoes and tomatoes. I would take the rotten fruit and vegetables up the steps and round the corner and tip it all into the dustbin. Is the storeroom locked? I would check the padlock and take the empty buckets back to the shop. The boss would be in the side office cashing up. Sometimes we spent half the night in the office, sticking the ration coupons onto sheets of packing paper, as we were required to do. As I looked into the shop, which was now unbelievably dusty and dirty, all the indications were that nobody had been inside it for years. I remembered the women staggering down the steps with their rum bottles, almost falling over as they came into the shop, and planting their bottles on the counter. With great skill I would fill them, even though I had instructions not to let this or that woman have any more rum, either because she had run up too many debts or because she had made too much of a racket in the project after finishing off the contents of her last bottle. Podlaha did not want trouble; he did not want bad publicity for his shop. If they were not given any drink, they used to threaten to kill him. He would throw them out, and they would crawl up the steps on all fours, cursing all the time, and return the next day. If someone died—and there was a death in the project nearly every week— the boss would attend the funeral, not in a black suit but wearing a black tie. The black tie hung in the cupboard in the side office where the shopcoats were kept. He only needed to put it on and go. Everyone who died had been a customer of his. The shop was the local meeting place. In the mornings there would be five, six, or even seven prams standing behind the rails at the top of the steps while the mothers chatted in the shop. I made them sandwiches of rolls and slices of sausage and gradually got them to buy every possible kind of sweet. First one, then another, would remember something she had to buy. In the winter they were all attracted to our two electric space heaters. Most of them had no heating at home. I stood there by the door looking into the shop and only now became aware that I was standing in a huge pile of rotting leaves. For years the leaves had been blown down here from the trees in the project, and nobody cared. Clearly nobody was interested in the shop any longer. It was no longer a viable proposition. Podlaha had given it up many years ago. He had not even taken the space heaters, or the shelves, or the counter of which he was so proud and which he had designed himself, as he had the shelves, which were so practical. In the shop were posters advertising goods that have not been available for twenty years. Podlaha had connections with the Americans, though what these connections were I do not know. Sometimes a black man would turn up at the shop, disappear into the side office, and leave after fifteen or thirty minutes. Podlaha still had a mother

in Vienna at the time. She was perhaps sixty—no age at all, though to
me it seemed ancient—and he always spent Christmas Eve with her in
Vienna; in summer she came to stay with him in Salzburg for a few days
or a few weeks. She was a smart woman. Podlaha used to like me, I
reflected, and I liked him. He had a lot of trouble with the older apprentice,
Karl. Karl spent four or five years in the Foreign Legion, then one day he
suddenly turned up again in Salzburg, and I ran into him in the middle
of the city. He recognized me at once. Since then I have heard nothing
of him. Herbert, the assistant, was always kind to me. He never needled
me. No one in the cellar behaved sadistically. In summer it was cold and
in winter pleasantly warm, thanks to the space heaters. Naturally I had
to do the roughest and, so to speak, the lowliest jobs; but I had a strong
constitution, and I had no difficulty heaving one-hundred-and-fifty-pound
sacks onto my back—sacks of maize, for instance—and carrying them. I
never felt it degrading to perform any of the hundreds and thousands of
tasks required of me. When I had finished cleaning the windows and made
them all sparkle, a car would always drive through the puddle above the
shop door and undo all my work. Undoubtedly there were still many
people in the Scherzhauserfeld Project whom I would have known, and
many of them would have known me. All I had to do was to enter one of
the blocks, but I did not do so. Several times it seemed to me that this
or that voice behind me was familiar. What a life they lead here! I thought.
Apart from the dirt there's nothing in the cellar. Even the rats and mice
that came into the cellar when I worked there have gone away. There's
nothing left for them either. What do the old people do now that there's
no grocery store in the cellar and it's too far for them to go to the super-
market? The children who used to play ball over there, I thought, will
have grown up long ago. I wonder what has become of them. How many
of the older people are still alive? I knew all the many cracks in the walls,
but now they were bigger. I heard the same names being called out, but
they belonged to different children. Perhaps a few of them have made a
success of their lives? They have not got rid of the stigma of belonging to
the Scherzhauserfeld Project, of being the *dregs of humanity*, as I have heard
them called time and again. No restaurant in the city would have employed
a girl from the Scherzhauserfeld Project as a waitress. No shop in the city
would have trained a man from the Scherzhauserfeld Project as a salesman.
A few of the men worked on the railway—that was the very best the
Scherzhauserfeld Project could rise to in my time. If there was any support

for a political party, it was the Communist party. But in this city the communists have never been more than a ludicrously small minority, a little club that is treated with derision. Almost certainly there was nobody from the Scherzhauserfeld Project even in the fire brigade. I can remember one man who was a conductor on a petrol bus and another on a trolley bus. On the way home from work (insofar as they had any work) in the evening the men would come into the cellar to buy beer and radishes. They came in their overalls, and until well into autumn they went barefoot or else they wore wooden clogs and no socks. They were usually already drunk and asked after their wives. The teenage girls kept company with the Americans day and night. The Americans gave their girl-friends from the project loads of chocolate and nylon stockings and nylon blouses and all the rest of the luxury junk that suddenly flooded into Europe with their arrival. The girls all painted their faces like Chinese dolls, and their high-heeled shoes gave them an impudent and at the same time comic gait. They came down into our shop with an air of arrogance, since they were the lucky ones who no longer had to rely on it, having *got off* with an American. Families with daughters pushed them, if they needed any push-ing, into the arms of the Americans—there was the so-called Rainbow Division, as I recall, which was stationed in Salzburg—after which they had no more worries, for a time at least, and incurred the hostility of others who were less fortunate. Even in the Scherzhauserfeld Project the Americans were a disaster. The little girls were transformed overnight into little Americans. Some girls from the project were killed by Americans. There were several sensational trials by court martial at the Lehen barracks. The uniformed murderers were found guilty and vanished from the scene, back to America. Significantly, there had been no Nazis in the Scherz-hauserfeld Project, but naturally even the fact that they had been opposed to the Nazis did its inhabitants no good when the war was over: their conditions remained wretched and to most observers disgusting. Individual communists and what the National Socialists called *antisocial elements* had been rooted out, even in the Scherzhauserfeld Project. The Nazis had sorted out from the *Scherzhauserfeld scum* what they believed to be *the worst elements*, as they felt free to call them (and feel free to call them once more) and sent them off to be gassed or otherwise disposed of. The minority is once more afraid. But anyone who says such a thing is sure to be immediately accused of lying. In the Scherzhauserfeld Project there were no National Socialists—or were there? The social outcasts are also political outcasts.

To a few dozen families in the Scherzhauserfeld Project the Americans brought an immense improvement in their standard of living—at the price of the pretty girls, or of some who were less pretty, but sad. In the Scherzhauserfeld Project, that limbo or hell, I never heard it said that anybody had *had a lucky escape* under Hitler, but in the rest of the city I have heard it said over and over again. And I hear it being said again today. In the Scherzhauserfeld Project no one has lucky escapes. They are constantly vulnerable, and no one protects them. They are left to themselves, and they know it. It is not a question of whether the people in the Scherzhauserfeld Project were less happy than those in the city, because this is an unanswerable question. The question of happiness is always unanswerable: we can make comparisons and we can speculate, but we must not be tempted to answer it. Everyone is happy and no one is happy, just as everyone is unhappy and no one is unhappy. What do we learn from what we see? We often ask about happiness, because it is the one question that occupies us incessantly all our lives. But if we are wise we refrain from answering it, unless we want to get even more of our own dirt on ourselves than we have already. What I was seeking was something different, something I had not known before, something that might be stimulating and exciting, and I found it in the Scherzhauserfeld Project. I did not go there out of any feeling of pity: I have always detested pity, and especially self-pity. I did not permit myself to feel pity; my only motive was the will to survive. Having come so close to putting an end to my life, *for every possible reason*, I had the idea of breaking away from the path I had taken for many years because I was too stupid and too unimaginative to choose another, and because I had been set upon this path by those who brought me up to fulfill the dreary ambitions they entertained on my behalf. I did an about-turn and ran back along the Reichenhaller Strasse. At first I simply ran back, without knowing where I was heading. From this moment on it's got to be something different, I thought—in my excitement this was the only thought in my head— something that is the very opposite of what I have done up to now. And the labour exchange in the Gaswerkgasse was exactly in the opposite direction. Under no circumstances would I have turned again and gone in any other direction. The farthest point in the opposite direction was the Scherzhauserfeld Project, and it was on this farthest point that I set my sights. The Scherzhauserfeld Project was the farthest point in every respect, not just geographically. There was nothing there to remind me even remotely of the city and of everything in the city that had tormented me for years and driven me to despair, to thinking of scarcely anything but suicide. Here there was no mathematics master, no Latin master, no Greek master, and no despotic headmaster to make me catch my breath whenever he appeared. Here there was *no deadly institution*. Here one did not continually have to keep oneself under control, keep one's head down, dissimulate and lie in order to survive. Here I was not constantly exposed to the disapproving looks I had found so deadly. Here no outrageous and inhuman demands were made on me. Here I was not turned into a learning and thinking machine. Here I could be myself. And all the others could be themselves. Here people were not constantly being pressed into an artificial mould as they were in the city, in a manner that daily grew more sophisticated. They were left in peace, and from the very first moment I set foot on the Scherzhauserfeld Project I too was left in peace. One could not only think one's own thoughts: and one could express them, when and how one liked and as loudly as one liked. One was not in constant danger of being attacked for being headstrong. One's personality was suddenly no longer suppressed and crushed by the rules of the bourgeois social apparatus, an apparatus designed to destroy human beings. In towns where stupidity reaches such alarming proportions as it does in Salzburg, human beings are constantly tweaked and shaken, constantly hammered and filed into shape, and they go on being hammered and filed into shape until there is nothing left of the original human being but a revolting, tasteless artifact. In towns of medium size (I will say nothing of small towns, where everything is grotesque) every effort is directed toward turning human beings into artifacts. Everything in these towns is opposed to human nature; even the young are nothing more than artifacts from A to Z. The human species today can preserve itself only in the unadulterated country or in the unadulterated big city—only in the unadulterated country, which still exists, or in the unadulterated big city, which also exists. In such conditions one still finds natural human beings—beyond the Hausruck or in London, for instance, and as far as Europe is concerned one probably finds them nowhere else. For in Europe today London is the only genuine big city; admittedly it is not on the continent, but it is in Europe all the same; and beyond the Hausruck I can still find the unadulterated country. Everywhere else in Europe one finds only artificial human beings, people whom the schools have turned into artifacts. Whoever we meet in the rest of Europe turns out to be an artificial human being, a tasteless replica of the real thing. The number of such products runs into millions and—who knows?—will perhaps shortly run into billions; and all their movements are controlled by various educational systems, which are in reality pitiless, insatiable, man-eating monsters. All the time our ears are assailed, if we are still capable of using them, by the sickening din of mass-produced marionettes with not a single natural human being among them. It is possible that in the Scherzhauserfeld Project I experienced the Hausruck or London effect, but I was not conscious of this at the time. I had obeyed my instinct and gone in the opposite direction. At the height of my despair and revulsion I had instinctively gone in the right direction and, as I have said, started running. I had finally abandoned the wrong direction and started running at full speed in the right one. I was running away from everything I had previously been connected with—from my school and my teachers, from the city of my school and my teachers, from the loved and unloved relatives who had brought me up and managed my life, from all the people who had irritated me and made my life a misery, from the whole chaos of my own past. I ran away from it all at top speed. Anyone who has done an about-turn runs away at top speed and goes on running, not knowing where he is running to if he is running in the opposite direction. I ran to the Scherzhauserfeld Project, but I did not know what it was like; I could do no more than guess what it was like until I saw that it was just as I had imagined it. My running away might have resulted in complete self-destruction and self-annihilation, but I was in luck. I had arrived among the right people at the right moment. I had staked all on one card, as I was to do again and again, and I struck lucky—because I was not prepared to give in for one moment, because I did not allow myself to weaken. What would have happened, I wonder, if I had listened to the woman at the labour exchange, who, after only a few minutes, had called my application crazy and told me to go home? What would have happened if I had done as she told me, without resisting? I'll stay in her office, I told myself, until she's given me the right address. She had not understood me, but I knew she would give me the right address before I left the office. I would not leave her office until she had. I was determined to make her give me *the right address in the opposite direction*. I would have forced her to. She was probably used to having desperate schoolboys coming to her, wanting to change their poisoned lives or their terrible existences and then weakening as soon as they were in her presence. All the people we know whose lives have been destroyed have weakened and given in at the crucial moment, but we must not give in at the crucial moment. So all at once she picked the right address out of her card-index, and for me this was the big draw. Karl Podlaha, Scherzhauserfeld Project, block B. Clutching my big draw, I ran off and could not fail to strike lucky. At first it was hard in the cellar, I have to admit. Shall I be able, I wondered, to meet the demands that will suddenly be made of a young and highly sensitive person in a shop like this? Shall I be able to do it right? Was I not quite unused to physical work? Had it not always been an effort to carry my schoolbag along the Reichenhaller Strasse and through the Neutor to the grammar school? Should I be able to cope with all these people I did not know, whose ways were entirely unfamiliar to me? And did I not know that arithmetic was not my strong point? To say nothing of *mental* arithmetic. What madness! Unloading truckloads of potatoes in the pouring rain all by myself, using only a heavy iron shovel? Moving them to the storeroom? And moving crates of dripping and crates of artificial honey and bags of sugar up the storeroom steps and down into the cellar? Was I the kind of boy who could place himself unconditionally at the mercy of a completely unknown employer, an employer who had been unable to conceal the harder features in his face? Shall I be able to hold my own against the coarseness of the assistant and the hostility of Karl the apprentice, which I thought I detected the moment I arrived? Against all these people whose behaviour struck me as so mean and inconsiderate when they came into the shop? I was able to perform all the tasks I was set, and in no time all the difficulties proved easy to overcome. I had drawn a winner. Knowing this, and surprised by the physical and mental abilities I possessed, I threw myself into my apprenticeship with gusto. It paid off. The milieu of the small shopkeeper was not new to me: Rosina, my grandfather's younger sister, had run a general store in her parents' house at Henndorf, and one of the high points of my childhood had been helping in my great-aunt's general store when she was serving. There were still sugar loaves wrapped in blue paper; it was the period of rowing vests and petroleum lamps, the period before 1938. At the age of three, four, and five I was crazy about sweets, like all children; and also like all children, I was equipped with the most sophisticated powers of observation—and so my favourite place in Henndorf was always my great-aunt's general store, in addition to which she ran a sizeable restaurant and a small farm. My grandfather had declined to take over this property, which should have come to him after the suicide of his elder brother, who had been a forester.

Wishing to spend his life in the big cities of Germany and unwilling to be lumbered with property, he had let it go to his sister Rosina. My grandfather told me that his brother the forester, of whom I have a number of photographs, shot himself at the highest point on the Zifanken, leaving a suicide note at the spot where he killed himself in which he gave an explanation of sorts for taking his own life: he was going to shoot himself, he wrote, because he could *no longer endure human misery*. My great-aunt Rosina knew how to keep me fully occupied: she would let me do whatever I wanted in her shop—open and close the drawers, carry bottles to and fro between the shop and the storeroom—and as a special treat she would let me sell small items to the customers. My passion for commerce dated from this period. But Karl Podlaha's cellar had nothing else in common with my great-aunt's general store. The smells were different: there was not the typical smell of general store; there were no longer any sugar loaves or petroleum lamps; and rowing vests had long since gone out of fashion and been forgotten. And in Karl Podlaha's cellar there was none of the placidity with which my great-aunt Rosina had recommended and sold her goods. The village store at Henndorf was as modest as could be, with its wooden shelves and wooden drawers, catering as it did to only a few dozen faithful village customers, whereas the cellar shop on the Scherz-hauserfeld Project had to supply nearly a thousand customers—and there was naturally no comparison between Podlaha, who was after all a quick-witted city-dweller, and my rather ponderous, good-natured great-aunt Rosina. The only point I wish to make is that there was a long commercial tradition in our family. Great-aunt Rosina's father, my great-grandfather, had actually been a *wholesaler*, as one can read on his gravestone at Henndorf. He used to supply the Naschmarkt in Vienna with butter and dripping produced by the peasants of the Flachgau. This occupation made him famous throughout the Flachgau, where he was known as *Joe Dripping* and became very prosperous. Even today many people in the Flachgau have heard about *Joe Dripping*, and if I am asked who I am and where I come from, all I have to do is to mention my ancestor *Joe Dripping* in order to make my provenance clear and command instant respect. In the cellar I was at nobody's mercy—I was *safe*. By committing myself utterly and completely to the Scherzhauserfeld Project as the opposite pole to all my previous experience and upbringing, I had found protection. In this totally different world I was suddenly at home. Each of the hundreds and thousands of tasks I had to perform in the cellar was for me a means to an end, and

the end was to ensure my own survival. Reason had told me that I would
be lost as a consequence of my decision, but what happened was the precise
opposite. Being convinced of the utter futility of my existence as a grammar
school pupil, the utter futility of what the grammar school produces and
cannot help producing in its pupils, I was free to venture into the unknown.
The possibility of survival depends on total conviction. But the cellar was
not altogether a place of joy. I often took refuge in the storeroom, repelled
by the appalling conditions in the cellar, by the people and objects I
encountered there, because I felt that I had failed and that my failure was
due both to myself and to the others. Whether or not I was to blame, I
was after all still a sensitive teenager, and as such I was at a disadvantage
vis-à-vis the general coarseness and brutality of the customers and even, at
times, of Podlaha himself. I was often closer to tears than to curses as I
lugged the crates and sacks and stuck my head in the flour bin. A carelessly
filled Maggi bottle was liable to rouse Podlaha to fury and plunge me
headlong into desperation and fear. The customers were as capable of
coarseness as they were of kindness. Podlaha often overlooked big mistakes
only to become inordinately enraged by minor errors. He was a quick-
tempered man, liable to sudden bouts of fury. He hated sloppiness and
would not tolerate dishonesty. He was vain with regard to his dress, though
I seldom saw him out of uniform, as it were—that is, without his shop
coat. But as far as I know he was modest in the demands he made on life.
He would have had no reason to pretend. Like all Viennese, he loved
parties and outings in the country, but I know this only from what I have
been told. Basically he was too intelligent to be a grocer, which is probably
the reason why he gave up the cellar-shop prematurely, when he was only
in his fifties. He loved Bruckner and Brahms and was a keen concert-goer.
Music was a subject we often discussed. And perhaps it was *because of
Podlaha, the frustrated musician and admirer of the classics*, that I myself, after
a few months as an apprentice in the cellar, once more began to think of
music as a possible career. During the festival he would turn up in the
afternoon wearing a black suit so that he could go straight to a concert
after the shop closed, without first going home, and he was always armed
with the scores of the works that were to be played. After an evening at
the concert hall he was a changed man, as they say, and for days he would
be full of the music he had heard. I realize now that he knew a great deal
about music, more than many an expert I know. Even in the cellar I could
not exist without variety, without contrast, and I began to think again

about music and about my career on the violin, which had come to such
an ignominious end. Meantime I had been experimenting with a new
instrument—my own voice. My voice having broken, I was now a bass-
baritone. When I was alone I practised singing tunes from the operas and
others invented by myself. What I had tried out on my fiddle I now tried
to sing in the almost total darkness of the storeroom or in the side office
or on the Mönchsberg. I had no intention of spending my whole life in
the cellar, even though I had no idea of what my future might be; I had
no intention of condemning myself to a life-sentence in the cellar. Yet if
I did have to spend my whole life in this cellar or any other—and it was
impossible to foresee whether I would—it was all the more necessary for
me to have some other activity which would provide a complete contrast.
Music was the one best suited to my character, talents, and inclinations.
My grandfather—whether on his own initiative or at my request I no
longer remember—had put an advertisement in the newspaper seeking a
singing teacher for me. He already saw me as some sort of Salzburg
Chaliapin, and I clearly recall that the advertisement requested replies to
be marked *Chaliapin*. My grandfather had often told me that Chaliapin
was the greatest bass of his time. He hated opera and everything to do
with it, but the sudden prospect of his beloved grandson becoming a
famous singer struck him all the same as a piece of great good fortune.
He was especially fond of Bruckner, more because of an affinity he felt
with Bruckner's peasant nature than because of any enthusiasm for Bruckner's music. All in all his musical knowledge was of the superficial kind
one finds in the casual music-lover. Like all my family, he was musical,
but music was not particularly important to him. However, he probably
felt now that my earlier violin playing would provide a useful grounding
for my training as a singer, and no sooner had the idea cropped up than
he championed it enthusiastically. He felt that if I did not have some
contrasting activity my life was bound to become atrophied in the cellar
(even though that was a matter of no great concern to me and perhaps
even suited me), and so suddenly all his plans for my future were now
concentrated on the idea of my training to be a singer. He had noted that
I had a reasonable singing voice which was capable of development, and
from that moment on he no longer regarded me, as he naturally had done,
as totally lost, a victim of sheer detestable materialism. The last target he
had set for me was that of becoming a *businessman*; he was now able to
raise his sights to my becoming a *singer*, which meant that I suddenly had

the prospect of becoming an *artist*. In no time the businessman was knocked off his pedestal and replaced by the singer. Though what is fundamentally wrong with a good businessman? And what is so special about a singer? But he was happier at the prospect of my becoming a singer, even an opera singer, than at the thought of my being only a businessman. He suddenly took to saying *only a businessman* whenever he spoke of that profession, whereas he spoke of the singer's calling with the greatest respect. He now spoke of my becoming a singer with the same conviction and enthusiasm he had previously talked of my becoming a businessman, and he delved into the history of music in order to learn whatever he could about singers, especially the remarkable facts about them. He tried to impress me with accounts of the world of Chaliapin, Caruso, Tauber, and Gigli—a world which he found fundamentally distasteful—and to talk me into taking up a singing career. This was quite unnecessary, however, since I myself had suddenly become convinced that I had a future as a singer. I became utterly convinced of this after being taken on as a pupil by Marie Keldorfer, who had sung in the first performance of Richard Strauss's *Der Rosenkavalier* in Dresden. Frau Keldorfer, who lived in the Pfeifergasse, more or less promised me a career as a singer. The old lady had been impressed by my grandfather's advertisement with the code-name Chaliapin and had written to him at once. I went to the Pfeifergasse and sang for her, and she took me, so to speak, under her musical protection. The outcome of this was that one Monday or Thursday I started taking singing lessons in the evening after the shop closed. It was agreed that I should pay for them out of my earnings as an apprentice, which at the time amounted to thirty-five schillings a month. My grandfather provided the additional allowance I needed. On the one hand Podlaha was not best pleased that from now on my mind would be partly taken up with music, especially singing; but on the other hand I discovered that he was interested in talking to me about music, and my music lessons made this possible. Now that I had started singing lessons—in which I at once made rapid progress—it seemed to me that my existence had moved into its proper course. The cellar was suddenly underpinned, as it were, by a musical trick. I now enjoyed going to work there even more than before. My love of music, which has always been the great love of my life, was now firmly anchored in the regular study of music. It was not long before Marie Keldorfer's husband, the famous Professor Theodor W. Werner from Hanover, also took me under his wing. He taught me musical theory after every lesson I had with his wife, without

charging a fee, and later we went on almost exclusively to the aesthetics
of music, the subject he taught at the Mozarteum. It is to him that I owe
my excellent musical knowledge, even though I later had many other
teachers, many well-known music teachers, at our various academies. What
I had always found impossible at the grammar school now came quite
naturally to me: I was able to engage in a precise, scientific study of music.
I no longer was carried away in transports of ecstasy but explored the
foundations of the art and pursued my musical education by building on
these foundations. I approached the study of music as a form of higher
mathematics and achieved excellent results thanks to my eagerness
to learn. I had all the prerequisites for the study of music: on the one hand
an absolute determination both to make music *and* to study music, on the
other the quite remarkable and extraordinary personalities of my new teachers in the Pfeifergasse. They lived in the house in which the Biedermeier
painter Stief had painted the oil paintings which hung in numerous Salzburg
churches, palaces, and patrician houses. He had been Marie Keldorfer's
grandfather. In this three-storeyed house with its many-angled halls and
rooms I saw some of the simplest and noblest arches and some of the finest
plasterwork. It was furnished from top to bottom with the most costly
Empire and Biedermeier furniture, and in the drawing room stood a Steinway grand which was, so to speak, the heart of the house. I visited this
house for years, and it was at this Steinway that I became acquainted with
the beauties—and the horrors—of the study of singing. I realize now that
I would have made a good oratorio singer. My life might easily have been
built around Purcell, Handel, Bach, and Mozart. I not only had the good
fortune to be trained as a singer—in other words, as a performer on the
most important of all instruments—by Marie Keldorfer, who was unquestionably one of the most cultured teachers as well as one of the subtlest;
I had the inestimable advantage of being trained at the same time in the
discipline of musicology. These were two advantages; the third and probably decisive component in my good fortune was the fact that while studying singing and musicology, I was also serving an apprenticeship. The
combination of singing, musicology, and a commercial apprenticeship had
suddenly turned me into a person who constantly lived life at a high pitch
and was constantly occupied, all of which produced an ideal state of both
mind and body. The circumstances were suddenly and unexpectedly right.
On the one hand I had the Scherzhauserfeld Project and my home, on the
other the Pfeifergasse. The contrast between limbo or hell on the one hand

and the Pfeifergasse on the other was bound to be the saving of me; but it was not only that—it was the pre-condition for everything that came later. I think I had been going to the Scherzhauserfeld Project for about a year when my grandfather put his Chaliapin advertisement in the paper. I loved contrasts more than anything else, and still do, and the contrast between these disparate elements of my Salzburg youth was what ultimately saved me: to this contrast I owe everything I have. Now, of my own free will, I was *learning* commerce, and at the same time, also of my own free will, I was *studying* music. I was *learning* the one and *studying* the other with equal thoroughness and assiduity. The important thing was that I was doing all this of my own free will. I did not go easy on myself, and this is what saved me and, up to a point, made me happy. It was a happy time of my life, during which I made no concessions to myself. Learning to be a businessman and studying music were both serious activities, and I did not play the one off against the other. If I became a singer, that would be all right by me; if I became a businessman, that would also be all right. I did not slacken in my interest and enthusiasm for either possibility: both were crucial to my whole life at that time. I could not afford to slacken off, unless I wanted to be once more a prisoner of my misery. My study of music was of benefit to me in my existence as an apprentice and vice versa. I had found my equilibrium. My grandfather could breathe again. I had found a new self-confidence: nature had come to my aid. I had suddenly been granted a gift which others only dream of all their lives: all at once I was bold enough to believe that I had received a gift bestowed by nature, something I had never believed even remotely possible, let alone happening to *me*. If I chose, I could now show the world that I was an artist. I was already singing the most exacting coloratura passages in the most difficult passions and oratorios—Simon in *The Seasons*, Raphael in *The Creation*, Caleb in Handel's *Joshua*. Thanks to the strict discipline imposed by my teacher, who understood my personal situation, I was able to make rapid progress. I was able to sustain the notes so that they no longer fell back into my throat one after the other because it was held too wide. I produced the notes with growing refinement and facility, with increasing artistry and yet with increasing naturalness. I recall the Dettingen Te Deum and the *Messiah*; I had loved Handel since my earliest childhood. I revered Bach, though I could not entirely take him to my heart. Mozart was the composer with whom I felt the greatest affinity. My singing teacher was an intelligent representative of her profession and

gradually got my larynx and my throat and the rest of the singer's vital
organs into excellent shape, while her husband the musicologist worked
on my musical brain. I entered into this training spontaneously and naturally, without the least reluctance. The amazing discovery that learning,
studying, and educating oneself can be pure enjoyment made me happy.
The main advantage I had was that I was immediately able to put into
practice in one lesson the immense theoretical gain acquired in the other
and thus compound my profit. What I learned from Professor Werner was
of immediate use in the lessons I had with his wife, and vice versa. On
every other teaching day, several of my fellow pupils gathered at the house
in the Pfeifergasse. The one I remember best was the son of Petschko the
coachbuilder from the Glockengasse, a baritone with whom I sang duets
for years. Then there was the daughter of a highly respected and inter-
nationally famous freight-forwarding contractor in the city, who joined in
at the weekends with her delicate soprano, and a contralto from Bavaria.
We sang all the well-known duets and trios and quartets, and we often
performed at house concerts held in the drawing rooms of the parents of
my fellow pupils, much to our own enjoyment and the delight of relatives
and friends. At these concerts, our teacher told us, we had to put away
any embarrassment we might feel at appearing before an audience and
present ourselves as naturally as possible. Professor Werner had lost all his
possessions during the war but none of his kindness and charm, and after
each of these concerts he would write a notice in his own neat hand; then
he would take it from the Pfeifergasse, across the Mozartplatz, along the
Judengasse and over the Staatsbrücke to the Paris-Lodron-Strasse and the
office of the *Demokratisches Volksblatt*. The newspaper would then publish
his thoughts, which were always quite remarkable; indeed, I now realize
that each of his notices was a minor masterpiece. He was nothing less than
a musicologist *and* philosopher combined, a fact which the editorial staff
and the readers of the *Demokratisches Volksblatt*, the only socialist daily in
the city, never grasped, though they esteemed him highly. Werner was
always immaculately dressed in a tailor-made three-piece suit. He set great
store by having his shoes highly polished, and in his waistcoat pocket he
wore a watch with a remarkably long chain. Toward evening he used to
drink a glass of red wine in the conservatory next to the kitchen, which
was a pleasant place to sit both in summer and in winter; then he would
disappear to his study to compose. He and his wife had the happiest
relationship—or so it seemed to me, and I knew nothing to the contrary.

It was a marriage of two quite different partners. They were among the people whom the universal misery of the Second World War had not left entirely without compensation. On the walls of their house, which had belonged to Marie Keldorfer's father, I was able to study the period through which they had lived, a period that had long since come to an end. I loved the oil paintings and the prints. Everything in the house was intact—at a time when nothing was intact any longer. It made no sense. When I went to the Pfeifergasse, it was as though I was going through a world that was utterly chaotic and detestable into one that was intact, untouched by the chaos surrounding it. But I was probably mistaken. As I went up the steps inside the bare, cold loggia, I felt as though I was being cleansed, as though my whole being was undergoing a process of cleansing. I would ring the doorbell and be admitted. Usually Frau Werner, née Keldorfer, would greet me with her right index finger pressed to her lips, indicating that I must talk quietly since the musicologist was composing. We would tiptoe into the drawing room and up to the Steinway. All her instructions were whispered—everything took place in what they call a deathly silence. After a while there would be a knock at the door. The musicologist had finished whatever he was doing—perhaps a review of the latest concert. The piano score was opened and we began work. I had a strong voice, and it occurred to me that I could probably use it, if I chose, to shatter everything in the drawing room. My voice was in complete contrast with my long, lanky body, which was nearly always covered with a rash: a symptom of both madness *and* puberty. I loved the Pfeifergasse and I loved the people in it. My teacher had a quite remarkable career behind her, and I do not think she needed to teach because she was short of money. She gave lessons out of the kindness of her heart. It was not long before she got me engagements at several city churches, where I sang at a number of Sunday masses. Provided I had the requisite toughness, discipline, and tenacity, she said, there was no reason why I should not have a great career as a singer. Of course it would take a few years yet, but, as I knew, the time would pass quickly. There were plenty of good voices, plenty of fine voices; but personalities were rare. Was I going to be one of these rare personalities? She did not say so. She was relentless and precise, and she never missed the slightest mistake. Until this mistake was eliminated the lesson was not allowed to proceed. Sometimes she threatened to discontinue my lessons, to stop teaching me altogether, because she was tired of my indolence and laziness. But these were only passing threats. At home my rediscovery of music, the fact that I had discovered it for the second time, met with disapproval; all but one of my family regarded my efforts as a waste of time and money, and they were not convinced by my grandfather, who gave me one-hundred-percent support whenever he could and in whatever way he could. No sooner had I set out on a proper course, a decent course (as they for some time had believed I had done, a decent course being one which they could understand and appreciate), than I branched off into some bit of nonsense, as they put it, and ruined it all. Their suspicions, which sprang from short-sightedness and ignorance, were present all the time, whatever I did and whatever I attempted. By now, however, I had gained enough strength not to have my resolve undermined and let myself be thrown off balance. I had summoned all my energy and will-power and was determined from now on not to let myself be needled. They had all tweaked me and pulled me and placed every kind of obstacle in my way, but now I was impervious to it all. I earned my pay as an apprentice in the cellar and used it to pay for my musical studies; I made no demands whatever. I simply wanted to get out and get on. I no longer asked myself what I wanted to get out of or where I wanted to go, and I did not allow myself to look back. I had to go to the Scherzhauserfeld Project and the cellar in order to be able to go to the Pfeifergasse to sing arias and be happy. In the evenings I went up onto the Mönchsberg, where I would sit under a tree, thinking of nothing, simply observing what I saw and feeling happy. I had a favourite spot above the Riding School from which I could listen to the operas that were being performed there. One was *The Magic Flute*, the first opera I ever saw performed and one in which at one time or another I played no fewer than three parts: Sarastro, the Speaker, and Papageno. In this opera, which throughout my life I have made a point of hearing and seeing as often as possible, all my musical desires were realized to perfection. I sat there under the tree, listening to the music, and there was nothing in the whole world that I would have taken in exchange for what I felt as I sat there listening. Then there was Gluck's *Orpheus and Eurydice*, for which I would have given my soul. For years I went up onto the Mönchsberg in order to listen to rehearsals of operas that were to be performed in the Riding School. In this way I was for years able to enrich, intensify, and perfect my musical experience. Later I took part in rehearsals myself and sang in several masses and oratorios at the festival. But suddenly, before that could happen, another period intervened. One day in October during my third year as an apprentice, when I was seventeen years old, nearly eighteen, I had to unload a truck which was filled with several tons of potatoes. It was snowing all the time and I caught a chill, resulting in a severe attack of influenza. For several weeks I stayed in bed at home, until I became tired of this state of emergency. Despite the fact that I still had a fever, I got up and went back to work in the shop. I had to pay for this piece of monumental folly. It plunged me back into an illness which kept me tied to hospitals and sanatoria for more than four years, during which time I hovered, as they say, between life and death, my condition giving cause for alarm, now more, now less. From my grandfather I had acquired the habit of rising early, almost always before five. It is a ritual I still preserve. Despite the unremitting force of inertia and in full consciousness of the pointlessness of everything we do, the seasons are met with the same unchanging discipline every day. For long periods I live in isolation, isolated both in mind and in body. I am able to cope with myself by subjecting myself completely and unswervingly to my needs. Periods of absolute productivity alternate with others in which I am utterly unproductive. Subject to every vagary of my own nature and of the universe—whatever it is—I can get through life only with the help of a precise daily routine. I am able to exist only by dint of standing up to myself—in fact, of consistently opposing myself. When I am writing I read nothing, and when I am reading I write nothing. For long periods I read and write nothing, finding both equally repugnant. There are long periods when I detest both reading and writing, and then I fall prey to inactivity, which means brooding obsessively on my extremely personal plight, both as an object of curiosity and as a confirmation of everything I am today, of what I have become over the years in circumstances which are as routine as they are unnatural, artificial, and indeed perverse. The tricks of fortune that make me stumble and despair and drive me to distraction every day, cease to have any effect on me when I can get a clear view of them; nothing distresses and mortifies me any longer when I can get a clear view of it. Getting a clear view of existence—not just seeing through it but throwing the brightest possible light on it every day—is the only possible way to cope with it. At one time I did not have this possibility of intervening in the deadly game of existence which is played every day; I lacked both the intellectual capacity and the strength. But today the mechanism switches on automatically. It is a daily process of making order. I make order in my mind, putting things in their proper places every day and discarding whatever is of no

further use, simply *throwing it out* of my mind. Such ruthlessness is another
sign of age. If one is to survive the fashions, one's only salvation lies in
isolation and steadfastness of mind. How many intellectual fashions I have
seen come and go! The dealers in remaindered goods are at work non-stop.
But those who control the market with their bargain offers are easy to
spot, and given time, they always trample themselves in their own dirt
quite automatically. The survivor has to create a favourable corner for
himself to one side, where he can make his conquests. The air is thin, but
I am used to it. For some time now the either/or has been in equilibrium.
What is to be esteemed more highly: the cliché or the elemental insight?
It is impossible to progress beyond *nonsense*. I have listened to everything
and conformed with nothing. I still go on experimenting: what fascinates
the solitary person I have once more become is not knowing how something
will turn out. I have long ceased to wonder about the meaning of words,
which only ever make things more incomprehensible. Life as such, existence
as such—nothing but commonplaces. When we recall the past, as I am
doing now, everything gradually falls into place. We spend all our lives
with people who do not know the least thing about us yet constantly claim
to know everything about us. Our closest relatives and friends know nothing, because we ourselves know very little. We spend our whole lives
trying to discover ourselves, and having reached the limit of our mental
capacity, we give up. Our efforts end in total frustration and in fatal and
unfailingly deadly depression. What we ourselves never dare to assert
because we are not qualified to do so, others have no compunction in using
as a reproach, intentionally or unintentionally ignoring everything about
us and within us. We are continually being discarded by others, and every
day we have to find ourselves again, piece ourselves together, reconstitute
ourselves. We ourselves, as we grow older, pass increasingly harsh judgments and have to put up with judgments twice as harsh in return.
Ignorance vitiates all relations with others and in due course, quite naturally, breeds indifference. After so many years of sensitivity and vulnerability we have become virtually insensitive and invulnerable. We still
notice the wounds but are no longer hypersensitive as we once were. We
deal harder blows and endure harder blows. Life speaks a conciser, more
devastating language, which we have taken to speaking ourselves. We are
no longer so sentimental as to have hopes. Lack of hope has brought clarity
to our view of people, objects, relations, the past, the future, and so forth.
We have reached the age at which we are the living proof of everything

that has befallen us in our lifetime. For my part, I have had three experiences: that of my grandfather; that of all the others, who were of lesser importance to me; and my own. All three, in combination, have spared me the continual susceptibility to matters of minor consequence. I must not deny that I have always had two existences: one very closely approximating the truth, which I may justly call my real existence, and another which was merely an act. The combination of the two has come to provide me with a mode of existence which has kept me alive. At different times the one or the other has predominated, but I must emphasize that both have always been present. Up to now. Had I not actually been through everything which makes up my present existence, I should probably have invented it all for myself and ended up with the same result. The situation I was forced into brought fresh progress every day that dawned, every moment that passed. The illnesses I suffered and, much later, the deadly diseases I contracted brought me down to earth, down to the firm ground of security and indifference. Today I am fairly certain (even though I know everything to be highly uncertain) that I have nothing to show, that everything is mere fascination—repeated and enduring, admittedly, but simply a residue of existence. I am now more or less indifferent to everything, and to this extent at any rate I have won the latest round in the game one always loses. I never had my grandfather's illusions and never fell for the same errors. The world is not as important as he believed it to be, and nothing in the world has the awful value he always ascribed to it. I have always taken the big words and grandiloquent phrases for what they are—pleas that have to be ruled out of order. The poverty to which he fell victim and which embittered his life carried as little conviction with me as the wealth of which he dreamed. The paths I trod he had trodden before me; this was an advantage to me and still is. I had the chance of more intensive study. To the cliché about the rich being the real poor and vice versa I added another cliché of my own—about the intellectual being the true idiot. Shattered as he was by the treatment he had received, he could have ended the whole farce, of which he had been a victim all his life, by smashing all the props and by annihilating the prop men and all the actors, but he never had the strength to do it. My grandfather hated opera and admired the theatre, but opera is no more to be hated than the theatre is to be admired, just as there is no reason for hating some people and admiring others. Nearly everyone destroys himself in between hatred and admiration, and my grandfather, in the course of his sixty-eight years, let himself be ground down by them. For anyone but me he might have paved a way, but I was never one for paved ways. I have never followed any path, no doubt because I have always been afraid of following some endless, futile path, though I have always told myself that I could if I wanted. But I never have—at least not so far. Things have happened, I have become older, I have not stood still; but I have not followed a path. The language I speak is one which I alone understand, no one else, just as everyone speaks a language which he alone understands. Those who think they understand are either fools or charlatans. If I am serious, my seriousness is not understood, or at any rate it is misunderstood. It seems there are no recipes for the higher form of wit. And so everyone, whatever he is and quite irrespective of what he does, is repeatedly thrown back upon his own resources, like a nightmare forced to rely on itself. Were I to believe others, I should no longer exist; yet every day that arrives and becomes reality proves that I do. I feel as though I were a diviner in my own mind. I wonder whether I am a part or a victim of the machine of existence which goes round with increasing rapidity, continually grinding down everything inside it. The question must remain unanswered. My character is made up of all characters put together; my desires consist of all desires put together; and the same is true of my hopes and fears and desperations. There are times when only dissembling can rescue me and others when openness is called for. Whenever we seek refuge we meet with incompetence. When someone flees, the course he takes is the one which corresponds to his state of mind. We see him continually fleeing and do not know from what, though he appears to be fleeing from everything. Man flees from life from the moment he is born. He has known what life is from this very first moment; he flees from it because he knows it and seeks refuge in death which he does not know. Throughout our lives we continually flee in the one direction. The theatre of my life, which I opened between the ages of four and six, is already peopled by hundreds and thousands of figures that have fascinated me. The performances have improved since the first night, the props have been changed, and the actors who did not understand the play have been dropped. This is how it has always been. I am each of these characters, and I am the props and the theatre manager too. And the audience? The stage can be stretched to infinity, or it can be allowed to contract until it is simply a peep-show in one's own mind. What a good thing it is that we have always adopted an ironic view of everything, however seriously we have taken it. (When I say "we" I mean myself.) We have dismantled all our prejudices in order to rebuild them on a larger scale. This is a luxury we have allowed ourselves. We know what people mean when they talk of pride, of being arrogant and overweening. What they say is right, because everything is right and there is no need for recantations. We settle our debts and overcome our shame. Nothing that we heard predicted has occurred. Whatever we were asked to believe has long since turned out to be deception. Possessed by ideas, we succumbed to insanity and madness, and it proved profitable. Where would we be now if we had paid attention to so-called neighbourly advice? The development we have undergone is perhaps ridiculous, but it is obviously viable and has always produced results that were the opposite of what was predicted. And even if it was nothing but a nightmare, it was worth going through it. Sometimes we say it is a tragedy, sometimes we say it is a comedy; and we cannot say that at one moment it is a tragedy and at another a comedy. The actors, it is true, are convinced of the senselessness of both my tragedy and my comedy. And the actors are always right. When we gave directions that the entrance should be from stage left, it was from stage right, and vice versa; but they did not see this and missed the essential point of our play. They do not understand what is being played because I myself do not understand it. What is to be gained from looking at the cards held by a madman—even if he does not deny that he is mad? A child is always a theatre manager. At first I put on a hundred-percent tragedy, then a hundred-percent comedy, then another tragedy. Then the genres became mixed, and it is no longer possible to tell whether it is a tragedy or a comedy that is being performed. This confuses the audience. They applauded me and now they regret it. They received me in silence, making me look contemptible, and now they regret it. We are always a step ahead of ourselves and do not know whether to applaud or not. Our state of mind is unpredictable. We are everything and nothing. Sooner or later we shall undoubtedly perish, exactly halfway between the two. To say anything else is to make a mindless assertion. We started out from the theatre, in the truest sense of the word. Nature is the true theatre. And the human beings in this true theatre are the actors, from whom nothing much is to be expected any longer.

Once, three or four years ago, I was walking past the so-called head of the Staatsbrücke in front of the town hall arch, where to this day there is a famous umbrella shop and next to it a no less famous jeweller's, when I heard a man's voice call out my name. I turned and saw that it came from a man who was leaning on a pneumatic drill, which at the moment he was not operating—a man of about fifty, naked from the waist upwards, his belly hanging over his workman's trousers. He was sweating and completely toothless, with little hair on his head and with piercing eyes—an alcoholic's eyes, as I saw at once. His workmate, who was of roughly the same age though, by contrast, tall and thin and wearing a greasy canvas cap, went on working with his shovel, piling up the bits of stone which his fat colleague had obviously dislodged and broken up with his drill. They were searching for gas and water pipes in the course of alterations being made to the Staatsbrücke. I looked at the fat man's face. He had obviously recognized me, though I did not recognize him. I stopped in the middle of the mid-morning rush but could not remember seeing the man before. He remembered me, but I could not recall where I had seen him. On the other hand I knew I had seen the face before, but that, I thought, must have been a long time ago. The man could not have made a mistake, I thought. Then he came to my aid. He said he had known me in the Scherzhauserfeld Project. I had often filled his mother's rum bottle at Karl Podlaha's shop. He was the one, he said, for whom I had once got a bandage and bandaged his head in the side office when he had hurt it coming down the steps of the shop. I could not recall the incident, but I at once recalled the youth he had been twenty-five years before. He said that at that time I was so little that I could scarcely see over the shop counter. This was an exaggeration, but essentially his observations were correct. It seemed to give him pleasure to recall this time, the time when he was young, just as on this occasion it gave me pleasure too. And for a few moments we stood in silence, not saying a word, thinking back to this period of our youth. He knew nothing about me and I knew nothing about him. Standing among the rush of people at the end of the bridge, we both realized that we had a shared youth in the Scherzhauserfeld Project and had both survived in our different ways. We realized that we had gone through the extremely laborious process of aging and were now twenty-five years older. The man with the pneumatic drill had suddenly brought the Scherzhauserfeld Project back to me after I had forgotten it for years, that blot on the Salzburg landscape from which people were only ever brought into the centre of the city, only ever allowed in, to do the lowliest jobs. Even today, I thought, people from the Scherzhauserfeld Project only do the city's lowliest jobs, and the passersby never give the matter a moment's thought. He asked me what had happened to Podlaha. Did I know what had become of him? But I did not know. He asked about Herbert the assistant and Karl the apprentice; I told him that Herbert had started his own business, a coffee-roasting establishment in the Ernest-Thun-Strasse, and that Karl had joined the Foreign Legion but returned years ago and served several terms in prison, as I had learned from a woman who had a flat above the shop. He was the one, the man told me, who used to go barefoot even in winter—all year round, summer and winter. I could not remember this. He said he had sometimes helped me unload potatoes when times were hard. I did remember this. He said he often went to the sportsground by himself, with his uncle's dog, and would spend hours throwing sticks to the middle of the ground for the dog to fetch, just to pass the time. He mentioned several names, all of which I knew, having heard them spoken or called out every day, names of customers which I had not heard for twenty-five years. Some had died, he said, of natural or unnatural causes. He had had a sister who went to America with an American, to New York, where she had died miserably. Did I remember his sister, an extremely beautiful girl? He said he had been afraid of Podlaha, who had once caught him stealing a few apples. It was not just apples he stole, he added. Young people today had no idea how hard life was in those days. If you mentioned the war and the time after the war and the Nazis and the Americans—all of which had been nothing short of hell—they did not understand. For years he used to come to the cellar-shop to get rum for his mother and take it to her as she lay in her bed, where she finally came to a miserable end. She had such a strong heart that she hung on for a whole year in spite of her cancer, though she was just a skeleton, existing simply on rum and rolls dipped in rum. She was a *religious woman*, he said, though she never went to church. *She believed in God, but she wasn't a Catholic.* Then he asked me what I did. I told him I wrote, but he did not know how to respond to that. He had no idea what a writer did, and so he did not pursue the matter. He asked me whether I had a cigarette. I said no. He had always been impressed by Podlaha, he said; he was such a good businessman. The Viennese were always smarter than the others. He too, like all provincials, despised the Viennese. In a way, he said, without saying what way he meant (and if fact he did not mean anything), he was satisfied with his situation, however lousy it was. At his age it was all the same: one clung

to life, but it was all the same when it was over. Nothing mattered—that
was the truth of it. It was a question of age. Nothing mattered. At that
moment I also felt that nothing mattered. It was a nice, clear, concise,
handy phrase: "nothing mattered." We understood each other. He suggested having lunch together, and so I went a little out of my way and
had lunch with him at the Sternbräugarten—a beer, a sausage and a roll.
He had always imagined his life differently from the way it had turned
out, he said—not in so many words, but this was the sense. I felt the
same. The Scherzhauserfeld Project, with Podlaha at its centre, had been
resurrected. We exchanged any number of memories. Then, when we had
ended our conversation, he said So long! and Nothing matters, just as if I
had said it myself. What characterizes me today is my indifference, aware
as I am that there are no differences in value among the things that have
been or are now or will be in the future. There is no scale of values—that
is all done with. Human beings are as they are and cannot be changed,
any more than the objects they have made in the past or make now or will
make in the future. Nature knows no scale of values. It knows only human
beings, with all their weaknesses, all their physical and spiritual dirt, every
day that dawns. It is a matter of indifference whether one of them despairs
as he stands over his pneumatic drill or another as he sits at his typewriter.
Only theories can cripple us—that is obvious—all the philosophies and
systems of thought which block the way to clarity with their unusable
insights. We have seen through almost everything, and what is still to
come will bring no surprises, because every eventuality has been taken
into account. A person who has done so many things wrong, who has
caued so much irritation and disturbance and destruction, who has toiled
and studied and often worn himself out and half-killed himself, who has
been embarrassed and then again refused to be embarrassed, will go on
doing things wrong, causing irritation and disturbance and destruction,
toiling and studying and wearing himself out and half-killing himself.
And he will go on until he drops. But in the end nothing matters. The
cards come down, one after the other. At one time we had the idea of
tracking down existence, our own and others'. We recognize ourselves in
every human being, no matter who it is, and we are condemned to be
each of these human beings for as long as we continue to exist. We are
the sum of all these existences, all these human beings who exist, and we
go on searching for ourselves and never find ourselves, however frantically
we search. We used to dream of candour and clarity, but we never got

beyond dreaming. We often gave up and started again, and we shall go on giving up and starting again. But *nothing matters*. The man from the Scherzhauserfeld Project with the pneumatic drill gave me my motto when he said that nothing mattered. *So long!* and *Nothing matters*. I keep hearing his words—*his* words, though they are mine too, and I have often used them. We are condemned to a certain life, to a life sentence, for one crime or for many—who knows?—which we did not commit or which we will commit again, for others who come after us. We did not call ourselves into being; we were suddenly there, and at that moment we had responsibility foisted on us. We have developed a capacity for resistance and can no longer be knocked off balance. We no longer cling to life, but we don't throw it away too cheaply either. That was what I wanted to say, but I did not say it. There are times when we all raise our heads and believe ourselves called upon to tell the truth, or what seems to be the truth, and then we lower them again. That is all.

BREATH
A Decision

Being unable to overcome death, misery, and uncertainty, men have agreed, in order to be happy, not to think about them.

PASCAL

4

I T WAS ENTIRELY LOGICAL that I should be taken ill after my grandfather had suddenly become ill and had to go into the hospital, which was situated only a few hundred yards from where we lived. This much became clear to me, a boy of not quite eighteen at the time, shortly after the events and occurrences which I shall endeavour to record here as clearly and truthfully as I can. I remember it all precisely: I can still see him now, in his grey-black winter overcoat, a present from a Canadian officer in the occupation forces, striding out purposefully as though he were setting out on one of his normal walks, and tapping the ground rhythmically with his stick as he passed the window of his room, behind which I was watching him, the only person I really loved, not knowing where his walk was to take him, but quite certainly feeling sad and dejected after saying good-bye to him. I have no more vivid picture in my mind than that of my grandfather disappearing from view one Saturday afternoon behind the garden wall of the greengrocer's house next door. He had been summoned to the local hospital by a respected Salzburg specialist in internal medicine on account of what was vaguely called an *unusual condition* requiring clinical investigation and possibly (these were the exact words) a minor surgical intervention. It must have been clear to me that this moment was a decisive turning point in our lives. My own illness, which had not cleared up properly because of my continued refusal to recognize its existence, erupted once more, this time with quite alarming intensity. The very day after my grandfather entered the hospital I developed a fever, accompanied by a painful state of anxiety, and was unable to get up for work. For lack of space, as well as for various family reasons which I need not go into and in any case did not fully understand, I had been sleeping in the hall; but now—no doubt because I looked so ill that it seemed a necessary and obvious measure to take—I was allowed to move into my grandfather's room. Now, lying stretched out in my grandfather's bed, I was able to look long and carefully at every detail of his room and submit all the objects which were so vitally important to him and so preciously familiar to me to a prolonged and uninterrupted scrutiny. The pain grew worse and my anxiety more intense, causing me to call out from time to time alternately for my mother and for my grandmother, whom I could hear in the passage. The two women had any number of household tasks to attend to and had been plunged into a state of uncertainty and anxiety by the fact that my grandfather had entered the hospital, and so it must have tried their already frayed nerves to have me calling them to

my bedside in my grandfather's room, possibly more often than was really
necessary. Suddenly, therefore, they told me to stop calling to them all
the time, and in their state of growing uncertainty and anxiety they accused
me of *malingering*, of quite deliberately and wickedly tormenting them. I
may on previous occasions have given them grounds for such an accusation,
but in my present serious condition, which was very soon to prove critical,
I could not fail to be deeply hurt by it. Two days later I woke up from a
coma in the same hospital where my grandfather had now been for several
days. My mother and grandmother, finding me unconscious in my grandfather's room, had become gravely alarmed and called the doctor, who had
me admitted to the hospital at about one in the morning—not without
reproaching them for their negligence, as I later learned from my mother.
The chill I had caught while unloading potatoes in the driving snow, but
had quite simply ignored, now had developed into a severe case of so-
called *wet pleurisy*, which from now on, for a period of several weeks,
produced three litres of yellowish-grey fluid every few hours. Naturally
this seriously affected my heart and lungs, and within a very short time
my whole body became dangerously debilitated. Soon after being hospitalized, while still unconscious, I was given a thoracic puncture, as an
initial life-saving measure, and had three litres of the yellowish-grey fluid
drained from my chest. But more of these punctures later. I woke up—
or, rather, regained consciousness—in one of those huge hospital wards
with a vaulted ceiling, accommodating twenty to thirty beds which had
once been painted white but were now all chipped and rusted and pushed
so close together that it required great skill as well as brute force to move
between them. In the ward where I awoke there were twenty-six such
beds, twelve of them pushed up against two opposite walls to form a
gangway which accommodated two more. These two were fitted with bars
between four and five feet high. After waking up I was able to observe
only two things: that I had been given a bed by the window and that the
vaulting above it was chalk-white. During the first few hours after regaining
consciousness my gaze was fixed on this vaulting, or at least on the part
of it directly above my bed. From all parts of the ward I could hear the
voices of old men, though I could not see where they came from, being
too weak even to move my head. The first time I was taken away for a
puncture after regaining consciousness I was naturally not aware of the size
and ugliness of the ward: all I could make out were shadows of people and
walls, of objects on these people and walls, and of noises connected with

these people and walls and objects. On this first journey through the ward, during which I was attended by several nursing sisters and orderlies in white uniforms, my powers of perception were reduced to a minimum by the numerous penicillin and camphor injections I had been given, and I found this condition not only tolerable but agreeable by comparison with my earlier pain. On all sides I was aware of countless hands lifting me out of the bed and onto the stretcher, then pulling me and pushing me and wrapping me in thick blankets, though I could not see the hands or the people they belonged to. Then I was finally taken out of the ward, which seemed to be filled with hundreds of sounds of suffering, though everything was blurred and indistinct, then down the long corridor—by which stage I was completely disoriented—past an endless succession of rooms, some open, some closed, occupied by hundreds if not thousands of patients, and into what appeared to be a narrow outpatients' department, bare and grey, in which several doctors and sisters were working. I could not understand what they said to one another, not even the isolated words that were spoken or called out, but they never stopped talking and calling out to one another. I can remember that after my stretcher had been put down by the door, next to another on which an old man was lying, his head completely swathed in bandages, several medical instruments suddenly fell to the ground. I can also remember the frightful clanking of tin buckets being knocked together, then laughter, screams, doors slamming, and all at once, behind me, an enamel bucket being filled from a tap, then the tap being abruptly turned off. Just at that moment, it seemed to me, the doctors uttered a succession of incomprehensible Latin words, specifically medical terms meant only for themselves, after which further orders and instructions were to be heard, accompanied by the sound of glass containers, tubes, scissors, and footsteps. I had meanwhile probably reached the lowest level of perception and consequently felt no more pain. It was not clear to me what part of the hospital I was now in, and in any case I had no idea where the ward was situated. I must have been quite close to the ground, because I could hear and see so many legs going past, and to all appearances the doctors and sisters had many other patients to attend to apart from myself. But for a very long time I had the impression that I had been deposited in an outpatient ward and forgotten; I thought no one was concerned about me, since everybody walked past. On the one hand I had a sense of being crushed and on the point of suffocating, on the other of being light and weightless. I had been told I was going to have

a puncture, but I still did not know what this meant, as I had been
unconscious when the first one had been done; yet whatever was in store
for me, I had resigned myself to everything—they could have done whatever
they liked with me. As a result of the medication I had been given I no
longer had any will-power, only patience and no anxiety of any kind.
Whatever was about to happen to me, I did not feel the slightest appre-
hension: from the moment the pain ceased I was suddenly no longer anxious
but utterly calm and apathetic. Hence I offered no resistance at all when
I was finally lifted off the stretcher and seated on a table covered by a
white sheet. Opposite me was a large, dull, opaque window, on which I
tried to fix my gaze for as long as possible. Who held me up I do not
know, but had I not been held up I should have immediately fallen
forwards. I felt several hands holding me, and I saw a five-litre pickle-jar
at my side. We had pickle-jars like this in the shop. I heard a doctor
behind me telling me that what he was going to do was necessary and
would be over in a few minutes. Then he made the puncture. I cannot
say that it was painful having my chest punctured, but I suddenly felt
sick at the sight of the pickle-jar beside me, with one end of a red rubber
tube inserted in its neck, the other end attached to the puncture needle,
which was stuck in my chest. The tube was exactly like the one we used
in the shop for siphoning vinegar; and through it, in spurts which were
accompanied by rhythmic pumping and sucking sounds, the yellowish-
grey fluid I have mentioned was gradually drained off into the pickle-jar
and went on being drained off until the jar was over half-full. Immediately
after the onset of the nausea I lost consciousness again and did not come
round until I was back in my bed in the corner of the ward. I had lost all
sense of time. I did not know when or how I had come into the hospital
or how long I had been unconscious before I first awoke in the ward. I
had seen people's shadows, but I had not understood what was said to me.
At first I did not even know why I was there, but I felt that I must have
been taken seriously ill. Little by little I recalled how my illness had started
and how I had lain for several days in my grandfather's bed, then all at
once my contemplation of my grandfather's room had come to an end.
After that I remembered nothing, not even the slightest detail. Now,
however, I realized that it was the *chill* I had caught, the chill I had ignored
for half the winter, that had brought me into the hospital. I had followed
my grandfather into the hospital. I tried to reconstruct the events and
occurrences of the last few days, but I failed. Each time I tried to use my

brain I was overcome by weariness and fatigue and could not go on. I did not see a single familiar face, a single person who could enlighten me. At progressively shorter intervals my bed-covers were removed and I was given an injection. I tried to get my bearings from the shadows I saw and the noises I heard, but all remained confused. At times I had the impression that someone was saying something to me, but by then it was too late— I would not have understood. The objects around me became indistinct and finally unrecognizable, and the voices vanished. It was night, it was day, but nothing changed. My grandfather's face, perhaps my grand-mother's or my mother's. Now and then I was artificially fed. No more movement, nothing. My bed is lifted on to a trolley and pushed through the ward, out into the corridor and through a doorway, until it runs into another and comes to a halt. I am in the bathroom. I know what that means. Every half-hour a sister comes and lifts my hand, then drops it again. She probably does the same with a hand in the bed in front of mine, which has been in the bathroom longer. The intervals between her visits get shorter. At some stage men in grey enter the bathroom carrying a closed zinc coffin. They remove the lid and put a naked body inside, then replace the lid. I realize that the person they are carrying past me out of the bathroom in the closed zinc coffin is the man from the bed in front of mine. Now the sister comes only to lift my hand, to see whether she can still detect a pulse. Suddenly the heavy wet washing hanging on a line stretched across the bathroom and right over my head falls on top of me. A few more inches and it would have fallen on my face and smothered me. The sister comes in, grabs the washing, and throws it onto a chair beside the bath. Then she lifts my hand. All night she calls at various rooms, lifting people's hands and feeling their pulses. She starts stripping the bed, the bed in which someone has just died. She throws the covers on the floor and then lifts my hand again, as though waiting for me to die. Then she bends down, gathers up the covers, and goes out with them. *Now* I want to live. Once or twice more the sister returns and lifts my hand. Then, toward morning, orderlies appear, lift my bed onto a trolley, and wheel it back into the ward. It occurs to me that the man in front of me had stopped breathing quite suddenly. I don't want to die—not *now*. The man's breathing had suddenly stopped. No sooner had it stopped than the men in grey from the pathology department came in and put him in the zinc coffin. The sister couldn't wait for him to stop breathing, I thought. I might have stopped breathing too. I now know that I was brought back to the ward at about five in the morning. But the sisters, and possibly the doctors, were not sure about me. Had they been sure, the sisters would not have sent for the hospital chaplain to give me extreme unction at about six. I was hardly aware of the ceremony. Later I was able to observe and to study how it was performed on numerous other patients. I wanted to *live*—nothing else mattered. To *live*, to live *my life, the way I chose and for as long as I chose.* It was not an oath—it was a decision made by a patient *who had been given up*, a decision which he had made when the other patient in front of him had stopped breathing. That night two options were open to me, and at the crucial moment I opted for life. There is no point in asking whether the decision was right or wrong. It was because the heavy wet washing did not fall on my face that I did not want to stop breathing. Unlike the man in front of me I did not want to stop— I wanted to go on, to go on breathing and go on living. The sister was certainly prepared for me to die. I had to force her to have me taken out of the bathroom and back into the ward, and to do this I had to *go on breathing*. Had I slackened in my resolve for one moment I should not have lived another hour. It was up to me whether or not I went on breathing. It was not the grey-overalled porters from pathology who came to remove me from the bathroom but the white-uniformed orderlies. They took me back to the ward, as I had decided they should. It was I who decided which of the two possibilities to choose. To opt for death would have been easy. To opt for life had the advantage that I remained in charge. I did not lose everything—I kept hold of everything. This is what I think of whenever I want to go on. Towards evening I saw someone I recognized for the first time. It was my grandfather, sitting on a chair by my bed and holding my hand. Now I knew things could only get better. He said a few words, and then I was exhausted. My grandmother and my mother had promised to come too. He had a bed in the surgical department of the hospital, only a few hundred yards away. He promised to come and see me every day from now on. I was lucky enough to know that the person I loved most was close at hand. I had been given a large quantity of drugs in addition to the penicillin and camphor, and these had brought an improvement in my condition, at least as far as my powers of perception were concerned. The shadows of people and walls and objects slowly transformed themselves into real people, real walls, and real objects. It seemed as though everything gradually came into focus on the following morning. The voices were now sufficiently distinct for me to hear them properly, and suddenly I could understand them. The hands that touched me were suddenly the hands of sisters, who until then had appeared only as big white shapes in front of my eyes. I could see a face—two faces—quite clearly. From the other beds I no longer heard just indistinct voices and sounds but actual words, even whole sentences, which I could understand perfectly. Two patients seemed to be having a conversation about me, in which I caught clear allusions to my bed and to myself. Now I had the impression that a number of sisters and orderlies, together with a doctor, were occupied over someone who had died—everything I heard indicated that they were talking about a patient who had died—but I could not see the patient. A name was mentioned, but after that the conversation between the sisters and the orderlies, in which a doctor kept joining in, became inaudible. Then, a little while later, I was once more able to hear their words distinctly, as well as to understand them and reflect on what they meant. The sisters, the orderlies, and the doctor had obviously moved away from the dead patient, and the sisters had started on the task of washing the other patients. There must have been a water tap on the wall, possibly even a washbasin, from which the sisters fetched water. The ward was only dimly lit by a single spherical bulb on the vaulted ceiling. The nights were long, with daylight coming only around eight o'clock. It was now only half past five or six o'clock, yet for hours there had been commotion in the ward and in the corridor. I had seen many dead bodies in my life, but I had not yet seen anybody *dying*. The man in front of me in the bathroom had suddenly stopped breathing, but I had only *heard* him die, not *seen* him die. And now, in the ward, somebody else had died: once again I had *heard* somebody die but not *seen* it. As I lay in my bed, still quite unable to move, I reflected that, until the sisters, the orderlies, and the doctor had had a dead patient to deal with, all the strange sounds I had heard had been the sounds which accompany the process of dying; they had been connected, as I knew, with someone on the point of death. But the man in question had died in a quite different manner from the man in the bathroom, who had suddenly stopped breathing without warning and died. The patient who was now lying dead in the ward—I could not see precisely where, though I knew roughly from the noises going on around him—had died quite differently. I had distinctly heard him throw himself violently about in his bed several times, as if he were repeatedly trying to fend death off and finally pitting his whole physical strength against it. At first I had not been aware that these loud and violent movements I heard were those made by a dying man. This man had finally thrown himself about in one last paroxysm and then died—unlike the man in the bathroom, who had simply stopped breathing *without the slightest warning*. Everyone is different: everyone has his own way of living and his own way of dying. If I had only had the strength to raise my head, I should have seen what I was often to see later: a patient lying dead in the ward, left in his bed for the regulation period of three hours before being taken away. Until now I had not been able to see it for myself, though I did know that this ward was used only for patients who were expected to die. Only very few of those admitted to it left it alive. I later learned that it was the *geriatric ward*, into which old men were brought to die. The majority of them spent only hours, at most days, in this *geriatric ward*, for which I invented my own private designation: the *death ward*. Those whose death was judged imminent were taken out of the ward and along the corridor to the bathroom—if there was room for them there, though there seldom was. Most deaths took place between three and six in the morning, and the bathroom was full by one or two, since it could accommodate only two or three beds. It also depended on the mood and conscientiousness of the sisters, as well as the availability of the orderlies, whether or not a dying patient was moved in time from the ward to the bathroom. In most cases they avoided the tiresome business of transporting the dying patient from the death ward, as I called it—jacking up his bed onto the trolley, pulling it out from the wall, and laboriously pushing it out into the corridor. The sisters had a trained eye for the *death candidates*. Long before the patient himself had the least inkling, they could see that it would be all up with him in no time. They had been working on the ward for years, for decades even, and seen hundreds and thousands of human lives come to an end, and so naturally they were able to carry out their duties with the greatest skill as well as the greatest equanimity. The reason why I had been admitted to the death ward and allotted a bed in which (as I later learned) a man had died only a few hours before was not just that the hospital was full up: the reason was obviously that the doctor on duty at the time of my admission had judged me a hopeless case. He must have been more impressed by the gravity of my condition than by the callousness involved in putting an eighteen-year-old like myself into the death ward, which was peopled by old men in their seventies and eighties. The toughness I had invariably practised against myself ever since childhood, my habitual refusal to acknowledge pain, proved for once not just to have impaired my health, not just to have been positively irresponsible and hazardous to my life, it had put my life in the gravest jeopardy and come within a hair's breadth of extinguishing it completely. For the truth is that throughout the autumn and half the winter I had tried to suppress my illness, which was probably a slight inflammation of the lungs, and finally decided to return to work. This illness, after being suppressed and ignored, quite naturally erupted once more, as it was bound to do, its eruption coinciding with the onset of my grandfather's illness. I recall that for a few days, perhaps even weeks, I had managed to conceal from my family and Podlaha the fact that I had a fever—finally a high fever in fact. I did not want any disturbance in the satisfactory progress of my career. I had discovered a rhythm of existence which answered my requirements and afforded me personal satisfaction. I had constructed for myself an ideal triangle which linked up the three most important points of my development: my commercial apprenticeship, my study of music, and my grandfather and family. I could not afford any disturbance, any sickness. But my calculations did not work out, and with hindsight it is clear that no such calculations can ever work out. Hardly had I left the grammar school and tried my luck in Podlaha's shop—which afforded me a real chance to lead a satisfying existence, emboldening me to take my life into my own hands and, what was most important, into my own head, despite all the opposition I encountered—than I was wrenched out of this ideal existence. It seems to me quite possible that I should not have become ill at all had my grandfather not had to go into the hospital. Of course this is an absurd idea, however natural and well grounded it may seem. Clearly what was crucial was the time of year. The beginning of the year is always the most dangerous time, and most people find January an extremely difficult month to survive. It is this time of the year that *breaks* the elderly, to say nothing of the old. Illnesses that have been long suppressed always erupt at the beginning of the year, usually about the middle of January. Our physical constitution may have held up under the enormous strain of one or more illnesses for the whole of autumn and half the winter, but by mid-January it finally breaks down. At this time of year the hospitals are full to overflowing, the doctors overworked, and the death business in top gear. I was quite simply unable to bear the thought of my grandfather's going into the hospital. For months I had done everything in my power to suppress my own illness, but now, with my grandfather hospitalized, the system I had hitherto operated for suppressing and ignoring it finally broke down. The fact that I could not get up no doubt struck my family as an unpardonable bit of perversity on the part of his precious grandson: they probably concluded that I simply chose not to get up. They probably found it intolerable that the mutual affection between grandson and grandfather should be carried to such lengths that the grandson followed the grandfather *even in the matter of illness*. Nevertheless, my actual condition soon convinced them that my illness was genuine. Yet even so they must have had their doubts, for from their behaviour towards me it was clear that inwardly they were reluctant to take my illness seriously or even to acknowledge its existence. They were opposed to my illness because they were opposed to my love for my grandfather. As they saw it, this illness of mine, which had erupted so violently and so suddenly after my grandfather had gone into the hospital, was a trump card which I had brought out quite ruthlessly to get the better of them and which I had no business to be holding in the first place. But whatever they may have thought and however they may have behaved in consequence, all this was very soon overtaken by a tide of events which took us all by surprise and, I believe, put everything firmly in perspective. Naturally this troublesome grandson, under his grandfather's protection, had at an early age become mentally and temperamentally independent of them, adopting towards them a critical attitude which was in keeping with his age and character but which they always found insufferable. It was after all my grandfather, not they, who had brought me up; it was to him, not them, that I owed everything that made my life liveable and even afforded me periods of real happiness. This is not to say that I felt no affection for them: naturally I was indebted to them all my life, even if I could not feel as much love and affection for them as I felt for my grandfather. He had accepted me when none of them had accepted me, not even my own mother. He had outdone them all in the love and affection he had shown me. For a long time it was impossible for me to imagine life without him. It was a logical consequence of all this that I even followed him into the hospital. As I lay in my bed in the corner of the ward, suddenly fully aware of my situation, I could not help being struck by this thought: that there had been no other choice for me than to weaken and give up the moment my grandfather went into the hospital and deserted me, which is what I had felt he had done as I watched him from behind his window. I knew nothing about his illness, and when he paid his first visit to my hospital bed he did not mention it. He probably knew nothing about it either. Presumably the necessary tests had not yet been carried out, and in any case he would certainly not have talked about it the first time he saw me again, if only to avoid upsetting me and aggravating my obvious physical weakness. However, I was naturally affected by the uncertainty surrounding his illness, and now that I was once more—if only for short spells—capable of logical thought, I was more worried about his illness than I was about my own. During the short periods in which I was able to think, my mind was occupied exclusively by my grandfather's illness; but I could learn nothing about it either from my grandfather or from my mother. I was forced to the conclusion that everybody was concealing its true nature from me: whenever I asked about it, they avoided answering my question and began talking about something else. But the most important thing was not denied me: my grandfather, as he had promised, came to visit me every afternoon as I lay in bed. He was the first person to make me aware of how dangerously ill I was and to tell me about my period of unconsciousness. However, he refrained from talking too much about sickness and misfortune and in this way prevented us from adding to each other's physical weakness. While he was at my bedside, holding my hand in his, I felt supremely happy. As a youth of nearly eighteen, I now had a much more intense relationship with my grandfather than I had had as a boy: it was no longer merely an emotional relationship but above all an intellectual one. We did not need to exchange many words in order to understand each other and the rest of the world. We resolved to do all in our power to get out of the hospital. We had to prepare ourselves for a new start, the start of a new life. My grandfather talked about the future, his future and mine, which would be better and more meaningful than the past had been. It was only a matter of will, and we both had the will to *take possession* of this future, to take absolute possession of it. The body obeyed the mind, he said, not vice versa. The daily routine of the death ward was one that had been fully rehearsed, down to the minutest detail, for decades, and to those who were regularly involved in it even the most appalling events and occurrences were mere workaday experiences. But to the young person who had only recently been caught up in this mechanism of sickness and death, his first confrontation with the process of dying was bound to be profoundly shocking. Until now he had only heard how terrible this process was, but he had never witnessed it, let alone been exposed to the sight of so many human beings who had arrived at the final stage of their lives in such an extremity of pain and distress. What he now saw was a death factory, relentlessly working at full capacity, constantly receiving and processing fresh supplies of raw material. I became increasingly familiar with the procedures in the death ward, and by degrees I was able to observe not only these procedures but the indifference with which they were regarded by the patients, who were entirely preoccupied with their own suffering. Not only was I able to observe what I saw; I was able to examine and analyse it with the help of my intellectual faculty, which was now largely restored. Once I could raise my head, I was able, little by little, to build up a picture of those with whom I had been sharing the ward for days, and I soon realized how appropriate my designation of it as the *death ward* in fact was. There were as many patients as there were beds, and I soon discovered that the patients were replaced not just daily but by the hour. Yet the staff did not find this in the least shocking, for at this time of year patients died at progressively shorter intervals, though it struck me that these intervals were not short enough to make their beds available for their successors. Three or four hours after a patient had died, been lifted out of his bed, and taken away to pathology, his successor had already begun his final death-struggle in the selfsame bed. Up to this time I could not have known that dying was such an everyday affair. All those admitted to the death ward had one thing in common: the knowledge that they would *not come out of it alive*. During the whole time I spent in this ward no one left it alive. I was the exception. And this I believed to be my right, because I was only eighteen and thus still young enough to escape. Gradually I succeeded in doing what I had wanted to do from the moment I woke up in the ward: I was able to study the faces of my fellow sufferers. I could by now raise my head slightly and focus my attention on the man opposite me. Up to now I had been able to see only the blackboards which were fixed over the bedheads, giving the names and ages of the patients. Suddenly I was able to take a brief look at the face of the patient who occupied the barred bed in front of mine. He had a completely bald head and a sunken face, and he was connected to a reddish-coloured respirator by a rubber tube inserted into his open mouth. I now realised why the sister repeatedly went to this bed: it was to replace the tube, which was continually slipping out of his mouth, thus rendering the respirator useless. I now knew the source of the sucking noise that came from this bed and went on day and night, though with diminishing force. On this bald man's temples, which were as sunken as his cheeks, were tiny white hairs which moved in rhythm with the movement of the air caused by his respirator. Since his bed was at right angles to mine, I could not discover his personal details from the board that was fixed over it. His age was impossible to determine, since he was well beyond the stage at which it is still possible to assess a person's age. It must have been during the afternoon visiting hours that the man on the respirator died. I remember it distinctly. My mother had just sat down on a chair by my bed and had just peeled an orange and divided it into sectors for me. She was carefully placing the sectors on a serviette on my sheet so that they would be within easy reach for her to feed them to me, for I was not strong enough even to raise my hand. While she was occupied with feeding me the pieces of orange one after another, the man in the barred bed suddenly stopped drawing on his respirator, after which he exhaled longer than I had ever heard anyone exhale before. I told my mother not to turn round, wanting to spare her the sight of the man who had just that moment died. She went on feeding me pieces of orange without turning round and did not see the sister cover up the body. Those who died were always covered up in the same manner: the sister would stand at the foot of the bed and simply pull the sheet from under the body, then use the sheet to cover it. Then she would take from her pocket a bundle of small numbered labels with short strings attached to them and tie one of them to the corpse's big toe. This was the first time I had observed this procedure of covering up the dead and numbering them for the pathology department. Every patient who died was covered up and numbered in this way. The regulations required that the body should be left in the bed for three hours and only then taken away by the men from pathology. During my time, however, two hours were regarded as sufficient, as every bed was needed. The dead had to lie in the ward for two hours with their numbers attached to their big toes for the pathology department—unless, of course, they were expected to die very soon and did so in the bathroom. When a patient died in the ward, the event caused no more than a few minutes' disquiet among those who had witnessed it. Sometimes a death would take place in our midst without being noticed and without causing any disquiet. I soon grew accustomed even to the sight of the men from the pathology department who came clumping into the death ward every moment, strong, coarse-looking men in their twenties and thirties who made enough of a din in the corridor, let alone in the ward itself. If a patient stole a march on the sisters by dying sooner than was expected—as the man in the barred bed had done—they would, as a matter of course, fetch the hospital chaplain to administer extreme unction, if only to a corpse. The chaplain, who was always out of breath when summoned to the death ward, being bloated with excessive food and drink, brought with him a little black case with silver mountings. This case he at once deposited on the deceased's bedside table, which the sisters had cleared with incredible speed. The chaplain had only to press the buttons at the sides of the case and the lid shot up, automatically bringing a crucifix and two candlesticks, complete with candles, into an upright position. The candles were then lit by the sisters, after which the chaplain could begin the ceremony. No dead patient was ever allowed to leave the death ward without this spiritual solace: the sisters, who belonged to the order of St. Vincent, were stricter in this regard than in any other. But such irregular anointings in the death ward were uncommon. It was part of the daily routine for the chaplain to appear with his sacrament case at about five o'clock in the morning and eight o'clock in the evening in order to ask the sisters about the patients who had reached the stage of requiring the last rites. The sisters would point to this or that patient, and the chaplain would then, as they say, perform the duties of his office. There were days when as many as four or five of my fellow patients were given extreme unction. They all *departed this life* not long afterwards. But again and again it happened that the sisters miscalculated and someone died on them without having received extreme unction. In such cases remedial action was taken as soon as possible on their mortal remains. In fact the sisters invariably paid more attention to the administration of the last rites than to anything else. This is not to criticize in any way their daily performance of their duties, which they carried out unremittingly and almost without exception to the point of extreme self-sacrifice; but it is the truth. Right from the beginning I was so revolted by the chaplain's behaviour—and even more so by the activity he engaged in—that I could scarcely endure his little act, which seemed to me a piece of perverse Catholic theatricality. Yet even this little act of his soon became a familiar part of the daily routine, and like all the other revolting and appalling things that were enacted in the death ward it soon ceased to arouse my indignation or even to irritate me. The routine of the ward, as observed by me from my bed in the corner, pursued the following course. At about half past three in the morning the night sister switched on the light and then went round with a jar full of thermometers, taking the temperature of each patient, conscious or unconscious. After the thermometers had been collected, the night sister went off duty and the day sister came in with washbowls and towels. The patients were washed one after another, only one or two of them being able to get up and wash themselves at the washbasin. Because of the severe January cold the only window in the ward was kept shut throughout the night and until late in the morning, being opened only just before the ward-round. As a result most of the oxygen in the air had long since been used up during the night, leaving the atmosphere foul and oppressive. The window was covered with a thick film, and the smell of all the bodies in the ward, together with the smells emanating from the walls or given off by the medicaments, made it torture to breathe in and out in the morning. Each patient had his individual smell, and the combination of all these individual smells with those of the medicaments produced an atmosphere in the ward which brought on fits of coughing and choking. The consequence was that when the day staff came on duty, the death ward was nothing but a great compound of stench and misery. All the suffering that had been covered up and suppressed during the night was suddenly uncovered and exposed to view in all its unmitigated ugliness and horror. This alone would have sufficed to plunge me back into the depths of despair every morning, had I not resolved to endure whatever had to be endured in the death ward—whatever lay in store for me, in other words—in order to get out of it in the end. With this in mind I gradually perfected a private mechanism for observing what went on in the ward, and in due course this observation mechanism not only did me no harm but actually proved enlightening. I knew that I must not allow myself to be harmed in any way by the things I observed. It was vital that my observations and reflections should all start from the premise that everything here, no matter how shocking it was, no matter how appalling, revolting, or ugly, was in no way exceptional. In this way I was able to bear the conditions to which I was subjected. I had to recognize everything I saw as part of a wholly natural process, a wholly natural state of affairs. Although the events and occurrences I witnessed were more atrocious than anything I had ever experienced before, they were merely a logical consequence of the familiar baseness, callousness, and hypocrisy which the human mind employs in its attempt to repress and suppress nature. I knew that I must not yield to despair but quite simply submit myself to the power of nature, which was laid bare in the death ward more brutally, perhaps, than anywhere else. Having regained my powers of reasoning after a lapse of a few days, I was once more able to make use of them and so minimize any harm my observations might do me. I had been accustomed to living with others day and night, having been a pupil at the grammar school and a boarder in the Schrannengasse, which must have been just about the harshest training one could have; but all my previous experiences were as nothing beside what I witnessed in the death ward. As a boy of eighteen I was pitched straight into this scene of horror by my illness and what had led up to it. My adventure had ended in failure: I had been cast down and had finished up in the local hospital, in a bed in the corner of the death ward, conscious of the fact that by overestimating my own powers I had plunged headlong to the lowest depths of human existence. I had thought to use these powers to secure an existence for myself which would satisfy my needs and even bring me happiness; but now, once again, I had lost everything I had previously possessed. I was over the worst, however: I had managed to get back from the bathroom and had survived the last rites. Everything pointed in an optimistic direction. I was back at my observation post. I was once more making plans, once more thinking of music. As I lay in my corner bed I could once more hear the music of Mozart and Schubert. I was again able, in my imagination, to hear whole movements of musical works, and this imagined music which I listened to in my corner bed became one of the most important elements, if not *the* most important, in my progress towards recovery. Everything within me had been almost deadened, but now I had the joy of discovering that it was not completely dead, that it could be brought back to life and developed. All I had to do in order to bring it back to life and set it in motion once more was to start using my mind. And because I was now able to use my mind, to work out possibilities for my future, to hear music, to rehearse poems and to interpret sayings I had heard from my grandfather, I found it possible to contemplate the death ward and what went on in it without sustaining any harm. Moreover, my *critical faculty* was once again in play, restoring the balance between all the things which had meantime become disconnected and out of control. The result was that I could observe the day-to-day routine of the death ward with the necessary equanimity and draw the proper conclusions from what I observed. Physically I was still weighed down by sickness, and my general debility remained, so that I was capable of hardly any movement, though I could now raise my head and turn it a little to one side. This enabled me to take in the size of the death ward, at least to some extent. I had never managed to do this before, when I was taken away for punctures, for whenever I had been transported from the ward to the outpatients' department I had been so exhausted by the effort it involved that I had been unable to see anything, and in any case I had usually kept my eyes firmly closed to avoid seeing anything. My sickness, then, still afflicted my body, but it no longer afflicted my mind or—what was perhaps still more important—my spirit. After the patients had been washed—a process that took over two hours—the chaplain would turn up at some stage with his sacrament case, between five and six in the morning, to administer extreme unction. He came to the death ward every day, and I cannot recall an occasion when he did not administer the sacrament. Even before the last patients were washed he would be praying and crossing himself beside one of the beds and anointing its occupant, assisted by one of the nursing sisters. When the washing period was over there was always a noticeable relaxation of tension. The washing procedure left all the patients somewhat exhausted. They just lay there in their beds, waiting for breakfast. Only a few of them were capable of eating breakfast themselves; the rest had to be fed by the sisters. When the sister fed me my breakfast no time was wasted. During the first few days I was fed artificially like most of the others, by means of a glucose drip, but now I could be given a normal breakfast consisting of coffee and rolls. All the patients were on drips of some sort, and from a distance the tubes looked like strings. I had the constant impression that the patients lying in their beds were marionettes on strings—though left lying in their beds and only rarely, if ever, manipulated. But in most cases these strings to which they were attached were their only remaining link with life. I often reflected that if somebody were to come along and cut the strings, the people attached to them would be dead in no time. The whole scenario was much more theatrical than I was ready to admit. The ward was indeed a theatre, however conducive to pity and fear, a marionette theatre in which the strings were worked by the doctors and sisters—on the one hand according to a highly sophisticated system yet on the other, it seemed, quite arbitrarily. In this theatre behind the Mönchsberg the curtain was of course always up. The marionettes I saw in the death ward were of course old, for the most part exceedingly old, quite outmoded and of no possible value; moreover, they were so impossibly worn out that they were only ever manipulated with reluctance, after which they were very soon thrown on the rubbish heap to be buried or burnt. It was perfectly natural for me to think of them as marionettes and not as human beings—to think that sooner or later everyone must become a marionette, to be thrown on the rubbish heap and

buried or burnt, no matter where they had once performed, no matter
when or for how long, in this marionette theatre we call the world. These
figures attached to their tubes no longer had anything whatever to do with
humanity. There they lay, of no value to anyone, however well or however
badly they had been made to play their parts—of no use even as props.
Between breakfast and the ward-round I usually had leisure to pursue my
observations undisturbed. When the men from pathology came in with
their zinc coffin I could not help thinking that they had come to clear the
set. During the ward-round the doctors were really concerned only with
me, the other patients being of no interest and hence never discussed. The
doctors and the sisters who attended them seemed to me to be quite
uninterested in anything as they proceeded through the ward until they
halted at my bed. It may be that for some reason my presence in the death
ward annoyed them, but they did nothing about it. Force of circumstances
had brought me here, and I had not died—I had been left behind. There
I lay, a rare case that could not fail to attract their attention. From the
very beginning I had had the impression that it annoyed them, especially
the doctors, to find me lying there far longer than normal, a young person
in a ward that had probably always been reserved not only for the old and
the very old but for the dying. Had I died on the first or second day, as
seemed likely to happen, no one would have given the matter another
thought: it would have been quite proper for me to be there—that was
where the dying were meant to be, in the death ward—and my age would
not have mattered. But now I was over the worst, even from the doctors'
point of view; yet here I was in the death ward. It must have worried
them, but they did not move me. What they did was to double their
efforts to speed my recovery: they kept me on drips day and night (what
the object of this was I no longer recall) and finally gave me double and
triple doses of drugs, with hundreds of injections in my arms and legs,
which became completely insensitive to being jabbed. From the doctors I
could learn virtually nothing, and the sisters were incorruptibly taciturn.
Regularly at about ten o'clock I was taken off to have my puncture. Even
the corridor was lined with beds along its whole length, because an influenza
epidemic had broken out at the beginning of January, reaching its peak
around the middle of the month and forcing the hospital authorities, as I
learned from my grandfather, to cram this and all the other corridors with
beds and stretchers. I was actually lucky to have a bed in a ward and not
in one of the corridors—in fact, I was lucky to have a bed at all. Large

numbers of people were refused admission to the hospital, which could accommodate hundreds but was now too small for the city's population, which had doubled in recent years. It had finally become necessary to erect temporary huts to house the surgical and gynecological departments. My grandfather told me that he was in one of these huts. He had now been in the hospital for more than a week, and the results of his tests were still not available. Possibly, he said, the whole thing was a false alarm and he would be able to go home very soon. He did not feel at all ill. The doctor's suspicions would probably prove groundless. He was counting on spending only a few more days in the hospital. It had struck him that his going into the hospital could have been the reason for the renewed attack of my own illness, which according to him had long since been forgotten. This, he said, was a possibility that could not be ruled out. At all events, he said, his illness and mine were connected, though the sad thing was that this unfortunate connection between our illnesses had had disastrous results in my case rather than his. Now that he knew it could do me no harm, he confided to me that he had been worried about whether I would survive. He had heard about the sisters shunting me off into the bathroom because they thought I was finished, but he had not really doubted for a moment that I should recover. He was horrified at my being given the last rites by the chaplain, whom he had found revolting from the first moment, as I had. He had a profound loathing for priests of the type represented by the chaplain, who were nothing but base exploiters of the Church and its victims, travelling salesmen for Catholicism who decided to settle down when they were getting on in years, especially in large hospitals (because these seemed to offer them more variety and better pickings), and went on hawking their wares. I just had to accept the fact that I was in the death ward, he said, but it was an experience which would be of incomparable value for my future development, above all for my mental and spiritual outlook. He liked my designation of the ward as the *death ward*. In his opinion, however, it was a finely proportioned room and of a piece with the whole building, which was designed by Fischer von Erlach and according to my grandfather a superb piece of architecture. During his visits he showed a sensitive appreciation of my character by shunning all pretence and humanitarian claptrap and by managing to divert me from my troubles without once resorting to lies. The chief physician, in his opinion, was an excellent man, intelligent and well educated—not just superficially—with whom he had had quite a useful conversation about me and my situation and who believed that my illness would subside in a few weeks—he did not say in two or three weeks, but *a few*. After each puncture there was a fresh and disturbingly rapid build-up of the yellowish-grey fluid, which would have to be drained every day for some time to come, but this was also easing off. However, apart from what my grand-father called my mental and psychological resurgence, I should have to be prepared to suffer even greater physical weakness than at present, and for a time my physical condition would continue to deteriorate. On the one hand I was over the worst—not least because of my robustly positive attitude to the calamity that had befallen me—and so to that extent things could be seen to be improving; on the other hand my physical decline had not yet reached its lowest point. Yet the mind and the spirit controlled the body, he said, and even the most debilitated body could be saved by a strong mind or a strong spirit, or a combination of the two. Only now was I prepared to acknowledge that it had been stupid of me to ignore the illness that had erupted in the autumn, despite the nature of this illness and the course it had taken. Illnesses have legitimate claims to make on us, and to ignore them and refuse to acknowledge their claims is to flout nature, and this can lead only to disaster. I told my grandfather what it had meant to me to lie in his room and contemplate all the objects in it. He told me he would take me home and read to me from some of the books in his room, the ones I liked best. This was agreed. He also promised to spend more time going for walks with me on the Mönchsberg, and also on the Kapuzinerberg, which I loved. We would also make excursions to Hellbrunn and the meadows by the Salzach. He said he was thinking of raising the allowance he made me for music lessons with the Werners. He told me himself that music would be the saving of me, and he promised to buy me the scores of one or two Schubert symphonies. But the first thing, he said, was to get out of this hell. These surroundings could drag even a healthy person down, to say nothing of one who was sick. He told me he was sharing a room in one of the surgical huts with a council official two years his junior who had apparently had a successful (though unspec-ified) operation. This man was not in the least irritating. Naturally, he said, he had been shocked to hear that I was in the hospital too, and the first few days, during which I had, as he put it, almost crossed the border of life, had been the worst days of his life, although he had never for a moment thought I might die, as he had already told me. He had been able to get up and leave his room all the time and go into the fresh air whenever he wished. He had gradually familiarized himself with the whole lay-out of the hospital and visited all the departments one after another. He had also been inside the hospital church, which he had passed so often in recent years when out walking. When I could manage it he would take me there and show me the paintings by Rottmayr, which he said had impressed him. On one of his first afternoons in the hospital he had heard the organ being played by an excellent organist, and as he was listening to the music he had thought about my future. This stay in the hospital had suddenly struck him as an unavoidable necessity, not in any medical sense but in an existential sense. Since he had been in the hospital, he said, in an atmosphere of suffering which positively forced one to think hard about the important questions of life and existence, he had given a great deal of thought to his own situation and mine. From time to time such illnesses—whether they were real or not—were necessary in order to make the people think about things they would otherwise not think about. Unless we are naturally compelled—that is, compelled by nature— to spend time in surroundings which encourage such thought, surround- ings such as one finds in this kind of hospital or in fact in any hospital, we must contrive a way of getting ourselves into a hospital, he said, even if we have to discover or invent an illness which will force us into one— or even produce such an illness artificially. Otherwise, we are never in a position to think about the important questions of life and existence. It doesn't have to be a hospital, he said, a prison will do just as well, perhaps even a monastery. Prisons and monasteries are not really any different from hospitals. He had no doubt that his present spell in the hospital had brought him into the kind of atmosphere that seemed to him vitally necessary for this kind of thinking. At no other time in his life had a spell in a hospital been so effective. Now that I was over the worst, I too had an opportunity to see my spell in the hospital as a time spent in an atmosphere conducive to thinking. He was sure, however, that this idea had occurred to me long ago and that I had already begun to take advantage of the opportunity that was now afforded me. The sick, he said, are the ones who have real clarity of vision; no one else sees the world so clearly. When he got out of this *hell*, he said (and from now on he always referred to the hospital as hell), all the difficulties which had recently blocked his work would be removed. The artist, he said, and in particular the writer, is under an obligation to go into a hospital periodically, no matter whether it is a real hospital or a prison or a

monastery. This was an absolute prerequisite for the artistic life. Any
artist, and above all any writer, who did not go into a hospital from time
to time—who, in other words, did not spend some of his time in surroundings where he could think about the crucial questions of life and
existence—was destined in time to fall victim to futility by getting caught
up in the superficial. The hospital he goes into may be created artificially,
and the illness or illnesses that take him there may be equally artificial,
but they must exist, or if they do not exist, they must somehow be
generated, they must be generated at definite intervals, no matter what
the circumstances. Any artist or writer who tried to get round this fact
for whatever reason was condemned to utter futility from the start. If we
became ill in the natural course of events and had to go into a hospital
like this, he said, we could count ourselves lucky. But we do not
know, he continued, whether or not we are in the hospital as a result
of the natural course of events. We may think we are, while in reality we
may be there as a result of an artificial course of events, possibly one that
is completely artificial. But that is neither here nor there. What matters
is having the necessary authorization to spend a period of time in surroundings which are conducive to thought. In such surroundings we are
able to reach a degree of awareness unattainable elsewhere, to achieve
something we can never achieve in the world outside: an awareness of
ourselves and of all existence. It was possible, my grandfather said, that
he had invented his illness just to enter this sphere of awareness, as he
called it. Possibly I too had invented mine for the selfsame purpose. It
was immaterial whether the illness was real or invented, provided that the
effect was the same. Ultimately all invented illnesses were real illnesses.
Either we have an illness or we invent one, he said, for any number of
reasons. And whenever we have an invented illness we become really ill,
because the illnesses we invent are real illnesses. It is by no means impossible, my grandfather said, that all illnesses are invented illnesses,
though they may appear to be real illnesses because they have the same
effects. The real question is whether there is such a thing as a real illness,
or whether it would not be true to say that all illnesses are invented, illness
itself being an invention. We might just as well say, he continued, that
we had both invented our illnesses for our own ends, possibly—even
probably—for the same ends. It did not really matter whether he had first
invented his and then I mine or vice versa. What was not just probable
but altogether certain was that by being in the hospital we had chanced

upon surroundings which were conducive to thought and hence to the saving of our lives. My grandfather admitted that this was all speculation, but it was a speculation which I had no trouble in following. I was now well on the way to recovery and had proof of this. The ward-round had always struck me as little more than a preliminary inspection of the dead. It took place daily at about half past ten or eleven, more or less in silence. The doctors no longer used any of their medical skills on the patients, because from their point of view they were virtually dead already and clearly of no further interest to them. Everything about the doctors betokened a total passivity in the face of all-prevailing death, a passivity which had become engrained and was little more than a cold routine parading through the ward every day in a posse of white coats. My impression was that they no longer had anything to do with these lost human beings in their iron beds, who as far as they were concerned were already dead but for me still existed—and existed, moreover, in the most pitiful manner, in the most distressing and degrading circumstances. The doctors were obliged to go through this irksome procedure every day, and as I observed them during the ward-round I used to reflect that these old people must on no account be allowed to return to life: they had been written off, struck off the rolls of human society. They had no one left to rely on but the doctors, yet it seemed as though these doctors were under an obligation not to interfere at any price and to use all their endeavours—or, rather, all their inertia and cold unconcern—to deprive these pathetic denizens of the death-ward of whatever life still remained to them. The medication prescribed for them was not intended to heal them but to facilitate their dying, to accelerate their death. The containers which fed the drips were simply glass devices for the acceleration of death. They were supposed, of course, to testify to the doctors' effort to heal, and they did this in the theatrical manner I have described, but in fact they were nothing more than glass markers signalling the end of the road. The ward-round was a makeshift device, no doubt justified by prevailing social attitudes, designed to solve the difficulties posed by an embarrassing situation, and requiring the doctors to go on a daily progress to the death ward, a progress which on Fridays was led by the chief physician. During this progress the sisters probably had nothing on their minds but the problems of space. It seemed as though they were simply waiting for beds to be vacated. Their faces were as hardened as their hands, betraying not the least trace of feeling. They had been working on the ward for decades and had become highly efficient nursing robots dressed in the habit of the order of St. Vincent. They were clearly embittered by their lot and hence all the more inaccessible to whatever is meant by the soul. Any contact with the patients' souls had become impossible, since they were constantly required to regard the saving of souls as their paramount task, a task which had to be performed in concert with the Church (in this case in collaboration with the hospital chaplain) and had degenerated into a perfunctory routine. Everything about the sisters was mechanical: they functioned like machines, carrying out their duties in response to a built-in mechanism and with no regard to anything else. The ward-round unfailingly demonstrated to me the white-coated impotence of the medical profession. It invariably brought an icy chill with it; and all it left behind, apart from this icy chill, were doubts about the art of medicine and its pretensions. It was only when they reached my bed that the doctors became disconcerted, because here they were repeatedly confronted by somebody who was alive in the death ward. Only here did they become talkative and prepared to engage in discussion, though only with one another—to me they remained inscrutable. I was never able to make any real contact with them, any attempt in this direction being immediately rebuffed. One had the impression that they were not prepared to lay themselves open to outsiders at any price— not even at the price of a brief, simple conversation, involving perhaps a very slight hint of presumption on the patient's part. Every day they appeared in front of my bed, a white wall of unconcern in which no trace of humanity was discernible. To the youth I then was, the doctors always seemed agents of doom, into whose authority he had been inexorably delivered by his illness. Never for a moment did they inspire confidence in him. All the people he knew and loved, once they had become sick, had been abandoned by the doctors at the crucial moment, nearly always (as he was later forced to acknowledge to himself) as a result of gross and irresponsible negligence. Again and again he was confronted with the inhumanity of the medical profession and rebuffed by its overweening self-importance, its positively perverted need to impress. Possibly the only doctors he had dealings with during his childhood and youth were of the repellent and dangerous kind, for the truth is, as I was to learn later, that not all doctors are repellent and dangerous. It was to his own natural resilience that he owed his repeated recoveries, despite the seemingly casual manner in which all these doctors went about their so-called *sacred calling.* Perhaps his repeated survival was due to the large number of illnesses he had had during his childhood and youth. At any rate it was largely his own will-power, rather than the skill of the doctors, that made it possible for him to get over these illnesses and emerge relatively unscathed. Among a hundred so-called doctors there is seldom one genuine doctor, and so to this extent the sick are inevitably condemned to protracted illness and eventual death. Doctors are victims of either megalomania or helplessness; in either case they can only harm the patient unless he himself takes the initiative. My grandfather may have been able to talk to the chief physician, even to have a useful conversation with him, as he told me he had; but the chief physician was quite incapable of talking to me. He did not address one word to me, though there was no lack of attempts on my part, once I was in a condition to talk. I constantly wished to talk to the doctors who attended me, but they constantly refused to be drawn into even a minimal exchange of words. It was in my nature to want an explanation, to want to be enlightened about my condition, and I should have been grateful to the doctors for any explanation or enlightenment they had vouchsafed me. But it was impossible to speak to them. They refused to subject themselves to the embarrassment of having to talk to me, and I could not help feeling that they were afraid of having to give any kind of explanation or enlightenment. And indeed it is a fact that in a hospital, where the patients are entirely at the mercy of the doctors, they are never able to establish the least contact with them, let alone elicit from them any explanation or enlightenment. The doctors protect themselves by putting up an artificial wall of uncertainty between themselves and the patients and entrenching themselves behind it. In fact they operate with uncertainty all the time, being no doubt aware of their own incompetence and impotence, and knowing that the patient alone can take the initiative if he wants to halt the progress of his illness or emerge from it. But very few of them are prepared to start from the premise that they know practically nothing and can achieve practically nothing. The doctors on the ward-round never did anything to enlighten their patients in the death ward, and in consequence all these patients were effectively abandoned, both medically and morally. Medically, of course, the doctors were powerless, and it would have been too much to expect any moral commitment from them. Here I am recording simply what went on in the mind of the youth I was at the time. Later, it is true, everything appeared in a different light, but not then. These are the feelings I had then, the thoughts I had then, the existence I had then, not my present feelings, my present thoughts, my present existence. During the ward-round, which took only a few minutes, the patients made some attempt, pathetic though it was, to sit up in their beds, only to sink back again when it was over. I did so too. On each occasion I would ask myself: What have I just witnessed, what have I just seen? And the answer I gave myself was always the same: the helplessness and mindlessness of doctors, whose view of medicine degrades it to the level of business, yet without causing them to feel the slightest shame. At the end of the ward-round, having reached the door of the ward, they all turned round, doctors and sisters alike, and looked at the bed facing the door. In it was a former innkeeper from Hofgastein, utterly crippled by chronic rheumatism which affected every part of his body, especially his hands and feet. He was said to have occupied this bed for more than a year, during which time he had continually been expected to die. Every day, when the ward-round was over and the doctors and sisters had reached the door, the innkeeper, sitting upright and supported by three or four pillows, would tap his forehead with the index finger of his right hand, indicating that he was smarter than they were. This gesture would send the doctors and sisters into peals of laughter, the reason for which I did not understand for some time. At the end of every ward-round they could not help laughing out loud at the innkeeper's morbid joke. When they had stopped laughing the ward-round was at an end. The innkeeper from Hofgastein was little more than a skeleton, uttering emaciated and hence apparently grotesquely elongated, to which the yellow skin clung in a manner equally grotesque. He was in the hospital not because of his rheumatism but because of a chronic kidney inflammation. For over a year he had been put on a kidney machine twice a week, always on the days when I had my punctures. He must have had a strong heart, and as long as his joke remained alive, so did he. He just would not die but went on living longer than the doctors and sisters found convenient. But if they were not relieved of his presence in the ward and the daily inconvenience it caused, they could at least appreciate his repeated gesture with his index finger, and during the time I spent in the ward there was not a single day when the joke failed to produce its effect. I shall have more to say presently about the innkeeper from Hofgastein. The ward-round was the climax of every day, but it always brought an anticlimax. Soon afterwards came dinner. The sisters had only three or four meals to distribute, since only three or four patients were capable of eating. The rest were soon dealt with, being given hot tea or a hot fruit drink. One man was never given anything to eat but a large bowl of apples. In the first few days after I regained consciousness he had struck me as a big fat man who never said a word, but in the meantime he had lost a great deal of weight and was reduced to skin and bone like the other patients. I can still remember clearly how he would sit almost motionless, working his way through all the apples in the bowl in order to lose water. Soon after regaining consciousness I caught sight of the word GENERAL written in large letters under his name (a Hungarian name, as I recall) on the board attached to his bed. For a long time my attention was fixed on this one word GENERAL, and all the time I wondered whether I had read it correctly. But I was not mistaken: the man actually was a Hungarian general, a refugee like hundreds of millions of others whom the tide of war had washed up in Salzburg. It was hard to believe that I was in the same ward as a real general, who on closer inspection even looked like a general. He never had any visitors, which led me to conclude that he was quite alone in the world. Then one afternoon, when a sudden snowstorm had plunged the death ward into almost total darkness, he died. The hospital chaplain administered the last rites to him after he had died. It was a completely emaciated body that the men from pathology lifted out of the bed and dropped into the zinc coffin, and the impact of his bones on the metal made such a loud noise that it even woke up those patients who were sleeping. It was hardly credible that this was the same man who had been so fat two or three weeks earlier. The men from pathology treated the general's body no differently from those of all the others, who had been workers, peasants, officials, and in one case, as I have said, an innkeeper, all of them doubtless what are called simple people. Insofar as the patients were aware of this death, it must have given them all pause to think that a real general had died in their midst. The most striking thing about this man, who had made it up to the rank of general (who knows in what circumstances), had been his utter silence—not just his taciturnity but his absolute silence. No one ever heard him say a word, and he was never spoken to by the other patients. If the sisters or the doctors addressed him, he did not reply. Possibly he no longer understood what was said to him. No sooner had he died and been taken away than the word GENERAL was wiped off the board above the bed, and a few hours later this bed I had observed so often and so intently was occupied by his successor. The word GENERAL was replaced by the word FARMER, which had for some time been current in Austria as a replacement for the word peasant. The bed next to it was occupied for one night by a so-called market-trader from Mattighofen. Unlike anyone else during my time in the hospital, this man came into the death ward on foot and was shown to his bed by the night sister, who had just come on duty. He carried his clothes in a bundle under his arm and looked anything but ill. He had obviously just come from reception and been through his first hospital examination. The innkeeper from Hofgastein, two beds away, immediately took an interest in him and instructed the inexperienced newcomer in the way patients were expected to conduct themselves. The two men understood each other at once, being similar types and having the same way of talking. The market-trader had arrived at the hospital and been admitted to the death ward so late that he got no supper, though he would have liked some. Hardly had he got into bed than the sister turned out the light, and the newcomer was probably overcome by exhaustion all at once, just after remarking that he had no idea why he was here, because from that moment on I heard no further sound from him. In the morning he could not bear to stay in bed, and so, before being told to do so, he got up and went out into the corridor, for no reason at all as far as I could see. Taking advantage of the market-trader's momentary absence in order to find out about his complaint, the innkeeper from Hofgastein picked up the temperature chart that had been left on the market-trader's bedside table and pretended to study it. Heaving a deep sigh which betokened not only horror but also not a little malicious glee, the innkeeper replaced the temperature chart, on which there was a brief note of the market-trader's condition. When he returned to the death ward, probably on instructions from the day sister who was now on duty, he was received by the innkeeper from Hofgastein with a silence which was at once gleeful and malevolent, as though he now knew all about him. The innkeeper asked him with feigned concern whether he had had a good night. It had in fact been one of the few peaceful nights I had spent in the ward, without any notable incidents, and the market-trader replied that he had. He then proceeded to tell the innkeeper about a dream he had had in the night. I could make nothing of it. Announcing that he was going to have a wash, he slipped off his night-shirt and went across to the washbasin. For a while I observed how thoroughly the market-trader washed, but then I must have lost interest and looked in another direction. Suddenly I heard a terrible noise and immediately looked in the direction of the washbasin. The market-trader had died while standing at the washbasin and struck his head against the edge of it as he fell. As I turned to look in his direction, I saw his head being pulled out of the basin by the weight of his body and then hit the ground with a loud thud. He had suffered a stroke while washing. The innkeeper from Hofgastein was triumphant, announcing that he had foreseen the death of the market-trader from Mattighofen after one glance at his temperature chart. When they came to pick up the market-trader from Mattighofen and carry him off, the innkeeper sat with his head held high, his arms stretched far apart on his sheet, and his fingers spread as wide as possible. I was shocked by the scene I had just witnessed and often relive it. It was the first time I had heard somebody talking—and talking in the most relaxed way—at one moment and then seen him suddenly lying dead in front of me. This was the only person I ever saw in the death ward who did not have the slightest inkling of his imminent death. The innkeeper from Hofgastein must have been envious when he saw the market-trader from Mattighofen give such a vivid impromptu demonstration of how to die. All those who saw the market-trader from Mattighofen lying there in front of them moments after his death must have envied him. Those who were awake were certainly envious; the others were not aware of what had happened. The market-trader from Mattighofen had given the sisters and doctors the slip before they could get him into their torture machine. The sisters no doubt thought it had not been worth their while to prepare his bed and his temperature chart. There is nothing the dying envy so much, when they know they are dying, as such a happy death, *a death without dying*. As they carried the market-trader from Mattighofen away, I reflected that it had been in his nature to die as he did—he could not have died in any other way. I even found myself envying him his death, because I could not be sure of being able to escape so suddenly and painlessly into the past, of ceasing to exist from one moment to the next. We begin to die the moment we are born, but we only say we are dying when we have reached the last stage of the process, a stage which may be appallingly protracted. What we call dying is only the last phase of a life-long process. To want to evade this last phase is to refuse to pay the bill. When the bill is presented and staring us in the face, we think of suicide; and as we do so, we seek refuge in thoughts which are utterly base and ignoble. We forget that the whole business is a game of chance, and so we finally become embittered. Nothing remains to us in the end but hopelessness. The last stop is the death ward, where there is no reprieve. It was all deception. When we come to consider the matter, we realize that our whole life is nothing but a grubby calendar of events and that by the end of it all the pages have been torn out. Of course the market-trader from Mattighofen was quite unaware of this, but the innkeeper from Hofgastein may have been. But this is an absurd idea. Another death I witnessed was that of a money postman from Upper Austria. This little man, who had a shock of white hair, lay completely curled up in one of the barred beds in front of mine which were reserved for refractory patients. He occupied the one nearer the window. He never uttered a word. I do not know whether he was not capable of speaking, or rather no longer capable, or whether he simply did not want to speak. After being put in his bed, he turned onto his left side, facing in my direction. When I looked at him, I saw a little, boyish face in which only the mouth still moved. The money postman no longer reacted to anything, and when he was being washed—a procedure which was in his case perfunctory and took hardly any time at all—he remained completely passive. I recall too that he was never given any food. When he had visitors, they were told to make their visits as brief as possible. They spoke to him but got no response. I had no doubt that he was going to die at any moment. Sometimes I had the impression that he already was dead and that I had missed his last breath, but when I looked at his mouth, through which he breathed, I could see that he was still alive. These barred beds were used only for men who were expected to die very soon—in a few hours or at most a few days. The money postman (of whose profession we learned from the crippled innkeeper from Hofgastein, always the best informed among us) was no bigger than a young boy, and although he was very old, everything about him was boyish. His shock of hair was undoubtedly the same shock of hair he had had when he was seventeen or eighteen, except that it was now white—it had probably turned white sometime in middle life, possibly quite suddenly, perhaps even overnight. I believe he was well over eighty, yet he was boyish in every way. Watching him, I had the impression that he no longer wanted to be in this world, that he did not want to see it any longer, for he kept his eyes closed, and the way he lay tightly curled up all the time seemed to indicate that he was trying to curl up completely at the end of his life in order not to have to return to this world. Had there been room for him in the bathroom, the sisters would have wheeled him out of the death ward long ago; but the bathroom was full, and so the money postman stayed in the death ward. During the ward-round the doctors cast only a brief glance at him as he lay in his barred bed. Basically they had nothing more to do with him, just as they had nothing more to do with most of the others. I could observe their irritation as they came into the death ward and found the money postman still there. The light from the window fell directly onto his shock of hair and onto his face. Watching his head and his face, I was reminded of the way a fish breathes. Year after year this man had hurried about the surface of the earth, day in, day out, never pausing to rest and probably always in a good humour. This was my impression as I watched him. I had the feeling that the money postman had been what is called a happy man. He had led a normal, happy life, as I could tell from the visitors who appeared one after another at his bedside, among them, I believe, his wife, his children, and other relatives, all of them country people from Upper Austria. Then suddenly, after there had been no change for days, I was woken up in the middle of the night. The money postman, who until now had not made a sound, suddenly began to let out screams and, abandoning his previous posture, jumped over the bars of his bed in one leap like a wild animal and, flailing about like a wild animal, hurled himself against the door. Though I could not see the door, I could tell from the noise which was caused by this whole incident that he collapsed and died there in the arms of the night sister. They did not put the money postman back in his bed but carried him off straight away. Sometimes the dying summon up all their strength in their last moments in order to wrest death to themselves after it has tormented them too long by failing to come of its own accord. The money postman was one of these. Doctors and medical experts in general (a term which subsumes many people beside doctors) will no doubt shake their heads in disagreement with what is recorded here, but no account will be taken of their head-shaking, no matter what persuasion they belong to or how highly they rate their own competence. A record like the present one must naturally always be made in the knowledge that it is likely to be attacked or denounced, or quite simply dismissed as the product of a deranged mind. The writer must guard against letting himself be irritated by such a reaction or by the prospect of it, however ridiculous it may be. After all, he is used to having everything he says or writes attacked and denounced and dismissed as madness—everything he has ever written throughout his life in order to express what he thinks and feels, everything he has been impelled to write for whatever reason. When he is dealing with facts he has no interest in opinion, from whatever quarter it comes. He is not for one moment prepared to alter his conduct or his way of thinking and feeling and thus become untrue to his own nature, even though he is of course aware that nothing can ever be more than an approximation of the truth. He may be convicted of certain shortcomings—and so may what is recorded here—but not of falsehood or falsification, for he has no reason whatever to permit himself so much as *one single* falsehood or falsification. Relying on his memory and his powers of ratiocination, which may reasonably be taken to provide a sound foundation, he is attempting to approach a subject of the utmost complexity. Nor does he see any reason to give up this attempt because of any errors or shortcomings involved in it. Such errors and shortcomings are just as much part and parcel of the present record as the facts contained in it. Perfection is nowhere attainable, certainly not in anything that is written, and least of all in a record like the present one, which is assembled from hundreds and thousands of scraps of remembered experience. All that is being offered here is a collection of fragments which may readily be put together to form a whole, if the reader chooses to do so—that is all. Fragments of my childhood and youth—nothing more. The question that most exercised my mind was whether I should ever be able to resume my singing lessons with my teacher in the Pfeifergasse, for I believed that without singing I should no longer have any future. Twice a week I could not help thinking to myself: Now I should be at my singing lesson, or Now I should be having my lesson with Professor Werner. I lacked the courage to ask any of the doctors whether my illness had put an end to my future as a singer. My grandfather was convinced that it would cause no more than a temporary interruption, though it might be a matter of months. I doubted this when I considered my real physical condition, and especially when I became conscious of the damage suffered by my chest, which was of course my principal musical instrument. My chest had been all but destroyed, so that I was hardly capable of breathing, and it was still only with the utmost difficulty that I could turn over in bed. Even after I had been in the hospital for two weeks, after what my grandfather called my *special treatment*, the yellowish-grey fluid was still being produced with alarming rapidity between the diaphragm and the lungs after each puncture. Sometimes I had the impression that my physical condition had not improved at all. No matter what progress I had made mentally and spiritually, my body was lagging behind and constantly trying to drag my mind and spirit down. I had this impression all the time, though I resisted it with all the energy I could command. I had to repeat to myself constantly what my grandfather had told me: that the mind rules the body. Sometimes I lay in bed repeating it to myself half-aloud, repeating it mechanically for hours, in order to pull myself back to health. But all my mental efforts were frustrated by the sight of the pickle-jar in the outpatients' department. Being taken away to outpatients' invariably meant my total collapse. Even before being taken away for a puncture I could foresee this mental and spiritual collapse and became scared. I was entirely reliant on self-help, though of course I was supported by the knowledge that my grandfather was close at hand. Yet this system of self-help proved ineffective every time I was taken off to have my puncture, as soon as I found myself being wheeled down the long corridor. Again and again the pickle-jar would gradually fill to the halfway mark, making my true situation abundantly clear to me. Admittedly I no longer fainted when I saw it, having long since grown accustomed to the sight, but I still felt utterly destroyed by the brutal procedure I was subjected to. After each puncture I would lie in bed for hours with my eyes closed, incapable of the slightest movement. There was no question of thinking, every image in my head having been obliterated. All I could see at such times was a world in ruins, and I had no capacity to withstand the harm which this condition inflicted on my inmost self. When I came round from this pitiful state of near-annihilation, I often pictured myself running into the city, either from my home or from the shop in the Scherzhauserfeld Project, my music under my arm—running through the Neutor or across Lehen bridge and along the Salzach to the house occupied by Marie Keldorfer and Professor Werner—running for all I was worth to save my musical future. But such visions and the thoughts that accompanied them served only to produce a state of depression and hopelessness from which I thought I should never emerge. Everything to do with my music and my future was now utterly hopeless and pointless. Only my grandfather still found it possible to view things in a different, optimistic light: he still had faith in my musical future, and as long as he was sitting at my bedside his optimism had the intended effect on my whole frame of mind; but when he had gone the effect evaporated, leaving me once more alone with a feeling of helplessness and futility. He had heard of a number of singers, even Wagnerian singers, who had had lung trouble, even serious lung trouble, and this sustained him in his optimism. But my own body told me a different story. It seemed to me that I was breathing with lungs that were completely ruined. Every time I breathed in or out I had clear

evidence of the terrible damage they had suffered. I had only to breathe
in and out, quite deliberately and without any attempt at self-deception,
to convince myself that the truth was quite contrary to what my grandfather
tried to persuade me of whenever he visited my bedside. I was done for.
Between twelve and three the events and occurrences taking place in the
ward were reduced to a minimum. This was usually a period of calm,
everything being concentrated on the approaching visiting time, when the
death ward was thrown open to public inspection. The visitors entered the
death ward cautiously. What greeted their eyes was a species of human
existence which I have no hesitation in calling the most pitiful in the
world—human beings lying unconscious or asleep, panting loudly or drawing breath with enormous effort. As far as possible the ugliness and
wretchedness that prevailed in the death ward were covered up at visiting
times, but it was impossible to hide all the horrors, and the very fact that
these were still visible here and there could not fail to shock the visitors
even more profoundly. On entering the ward they were all confronted by
a picture of misery and wretchedness of which they had previously had no
conception, not even the vaguest notion. They could not help feeling that
their visits to the death ward were experiences which called for the highest
degree of endurance and stretched their devotion to their sick relative or
friend to the very limit. Most of them ventured into the death ward only
once, never to return, not even if the person they came to see lingered on
for some considerable time. Having paid him one visit, they had done
their duty, they had made their sacrifice. I feel sure that the effect the
death ward had on the visitor remained with him for the rest of his life,
yet what he saw during visiting hours was only a fraction of the horror he
would have seen outside them. Nearly all the visitors were country people
who had made long, laborious journeys to get there, unlike the city-
dwellers, who in any case hardly came at all. The city-dweller shows a
greater degree of callousness in the way he shunts off old and sick relatives
when they are condemned to die. He no longer shows his face at all,
considering himself well rid of the person who has been a burden to him
for so long, for so many months or years. He may have a crisis of conscience,
but this is not enough to make him put in an appearance. The person who
has been taken off his hands by being admitted to hospital can complete
the last short stage of his journey into death alone, however terrible it
may be. There they stood, all these peasants and working people who came
during visiting hours, depositing their flowers, their soft drinks, and their

home-made pastries on the various bedside tables. It was all quite pointless, as they must have realized at once, since the recipients of their gifts had no possible use for them, being no longer able to see the flowers or drink the drinks or eat the pastries. Many could no longer see who was visiting them. The visitors tried to talk to the patients, but they were not heard, and the questions they asked remained unanswered. Prompted by decency, or by shock at what they saw, or simply by natural embarrassment, they would linger by the beds for a while in silence, eying each other, before they finally turned and left the death ward. As they went out, they probably all had the same thought in their minds—that this would be their last visit—and so it almost always proved to be. As he had promised, my grandfather came to see me every day. One day he missed coming, and my mother, who now took turns with my grandmother in visiting me, told me that he was having to have more intensive tests and could no longer leave his bed. She told me he sent me his love and said it would be only a few days before he came to see me again. In fact he did come two or three days later. He described how he was getting along with the council official and hardly said a word about his illness. Then, as he got up to leave, he told me the doctors had found out *what* the trouble was. It would involve a minor operation, he said—nothing worth speaking of. The chief physician was a good man. He himself, he said, was anxious to get back to work. His ideas about his work had suddenly got into gear as never before, probably as a result of his illness and enforced hospitalization. In a few days or weeks he would be out, and so would I. One day the yellowish-grey fluid in my chest was drawn off for the last time, and no more formed. I was already able to sit up and was planning to get out of bed. I had decided upon my birthday as the occasion for my first attempt to get up and perhaps even walk. My grandfather encouraged me, saying that there could be no better day to get up and try to walk than my birthday. With his help my plan was bound to succeed. During the three and a half weeks I had spent in the hospital I had lost forty-nine pounds, and all my muscles had wasted away. I was nothing but skin and bone. During the third week Podlaha came to see me and was so shocked by my appearance that he could not bear to spend more than two minutes at my bedside. He brought me an extra-large bottle of orange juice. Later he admitted that he did not think I would survive. It so happened that on the morning of my birthday I had an unexpected relapse, which lasted for several days. My vision became blurred and my hearing impaired; I could

hardly see things that I had seen quite clearly before, and I was quite
unable to raise my hand. My mother, my grandmother, my brother, and
my sister came and stood in front of my bed. They kept saying something
to me that I could not understand. After a while they left. That day they
thought I was lost. I asked after my grandfather but got no reply. Or
perhaps they did tell me why he had not kept his promise to come and
see me on my birthday. There must have been a very serious reason. I was
visited by my guardian too and by my uncle Farald. Even today I can see
them all standing in front of me, trying to keep from me something they
found unbearable but utterly failing to do so. Then suddenly they were
all gone and I was once more alone. It took me a few days to get over this
crisis. They visited me every day, their demeanour becoming increasingly
strange, quite different from before. Naturally I was at a loss to explain
it to myself. For a few days my mother stayed away, and my grandmother
explained that it was because she had a cold. My grandmother and my
guardian took turns in visiting me. They always stayed for only a short
time and became increasingly uneasy when I asked after my grandfather.
One morning, ten to twelve days after my grandfather's last visit, the
sister gave me a newspaper which the innkeeper from Hofgastein had passed
on to me, as he had taken to doing recently. I opened it, and after reading
and leafing through a few pages I suddenly came upon a picture of my
grandfather. It clearly accompanied a full-page obituary. He had died five
or six days earlier, but my family had been advised by the doctors not to
tell me of his death. With hindsight I could not help feeling that this
advice would have been better ignored. Now I was alone with the memory
of what he had said and how he had looked when I last saw him. He had
told me that he had made a note of the piano scores I had asked for—*The
Magic Flute* and *Zaïde*, which I loved, and Bruckner's Ninth Symphony.
The first thing he was going to do when he left the hospital, he said, was
to go to his favourite bookshop in the city, Höllrigl's in the Sigmund-
Haffner-Gasse, and get me these scores as a present to celebrate my return
to health. There could be nothing finer, he said, than to be at one and
the same time an able businessman and an able singer—indeed a famous,
a world-famous, singer who was also schooled in the philosophy of music.
He had not the slightest doubt that when I got out of the hospital—out
of this horrible machine which inhibited recovery and was designed for
the annihilation of human beings—I would achieve the goal which I had
set myself and he so dearly wanted me to achieve. On more than one

occasion he used the word *energetic*, underlining it as he did so by tapping the floor smartly with his stick. Then when we're both well again, he said, we'll have a few weeks' holiday at Gastein and enjoy ourselves with the waterfall roaring in the background. Then he got up and left. On reaching the door he turned round, raised his stick, and called out something I did not understand. I could not have known that this was the last of the thousands and hundreds of thousands of images I was to retain of my relationship with my grandfather. After lying in bed for a few days without saying a word, utterly unresponsive to anything that was said to me, I gradually learned from my family the circumstances of my grandfather's death. They had naturally been so shattered themselves by his quite unexpected death, as well as by the events and occurrences involving myself, that at first they were quite unable to tell me how it had all happened. At first all their concern and anxiety had been concentrated on my grandfather; then suddenly it was all directed towards me; and then once more it was concentrated on my grandfather. For several weeks they had never emerged from this continual state of anxiety over my grandfather and myself. At one point they had thought that my grandfather was dying, then that I was dying; and so it had gone on, backwards and forwards, until my grandfather's death finally took them by surprise just when the doctors had warned them to be prepared for the worst in my case. These weeks must have been spent in an unimaginable state of anxiety, and the result was that they were all too exhausted to be able to take in what had happened, at least for a time. Helpless and defenceless as they were, they could do no more than absorb the terrible shock of the events and occurrences they had just gone through. But it did not take them very long to grasp what had happened. My mother was deeply affected. For days no one could talk to her, and during this time she stopped visiting me, unable to bring herself to do so. From my guardian I learned something concrete about my grandfather's death, if only fragmentarily. By the time the doctors had established the nature of his illness, it was too late to cure it. The specialist who had taken him into the hospital had been confirmed in his surmise by the results of the investigations my grandfather had undergone after being admitted. He ought to have had an operation six months earlier. By the time he was hospitalized his whole system had been poisoned, despite his assurances that there was nothing wrong with him. For several days I believed that he had died as a result of an emergency operation, but the truth was that he had died within a few days of a sudden and massive toxaemia. My guardian told me that he had remained conscious until the end and had been in pain for only a short time. He had died at six o'clock in the morning. My grandmother had been alone with him at the time, the council official having been discharged in good health some days earlier. He had told my guardian several times that he was going to have to die without achieving his goal—the completion of his life's work, which had occupied him for the last fifteen years. In the last night he had asked after me. Throughout this last night his wife and son had been with him, though at the end only my grandmother was present. At about half past five the hospital chaplain, whom he loathed so much, had suddenly appeared at the door of his room, carrying his sacrament case. The chaplain's intention must have been clear to my grandfather, and, according to my grandmother, as soon as the chaplain made to approach the bed to administer extreme unction, my grandfather forestalled him by uttering one word: *Out!* The chaplain duly left the room without delay. Shortly after this my grandfather died, his last utterance being the word *Out!* And so for days my family came to see me, knowing that my grandfather, whom I was so eager to see, had died long before. They may have succeeded in concealing his *death* from me but not the fact that there had been some calamity connected with him. Yet I never dared to ask them directly, perhaps because their behaviour at my bedside had already prepared me for the worst. Of course I ought to have known long before that their strange behaviour could be connected with only one thing, the worst possible thing—namely, the death of my grandfather. They later confided to me that when my brother and sister expressed a wish to visit me on my birthday they had sworn them to secrecy. I had intended to get up on my birthday and make my first attempt at walking, aided by my grandfather. I had not been convinced by the explanations my family gave for my grandfather's not visiting me on my birthday, the very day on which he had wanted to help me get up and possibly take my first steps. I had not been convinced, but I had had no choice but to believe the lies they told me. I now realize how brave my mother was, who loved her father more than anyone else in the world, and what my grandmother and my brother and sister must have gone through. On the other hand, they had all been schooled in the harshest suffering for so long that they were able to survive this latest ordeal relatively unharmed—except for my mother. I followed my grandfather in his sickness, but not any further. Now that I was finally alone, with no one but myself to rely on—a fact which became abundantly clear after my grandfather's death—I staked everything on getting out of the hospital and back to health. I was not prepared to settle for anything less, and every hour of every day I told myself that it was now time for me to get up and leave. The decision had been made long before; all I needed was the means, some trick which would make it possible for me to get steadily nearer the goal I had set myself. Suddenly realizing, after my grandfather's death, that I was on my own, I was able to concentrate all my vital energies on regaining my health. I suddenly saw that it was possible to be alone and to make one's way forward with one's own unaided resources: I discovered not only that it was possible but that there was an incredible existential impulse to do so, of which I had until now been quite unaware. My grandfather's death, though it was a terrible shock and affected me deeply, was in a sense a liberation. For the first time in my life I was free, and I began to take advantage of my new-found freedom in a way which, as I now realize, was to save my life. From the moment when this realization dawned on me I had won the battle against my illness. As soon as I recognized and laid hold of the possibilities inherent in complete isolation, I had an unmistakable sense of deliverance. First I had to make my decision; then I had to apply the lessons I had learnt; and finally I had to bring my reason to bear upon my situation. A second existence was beckoning to me, a new life of total self-reliance. It is possible—it is even probable—that I knew I owed this new opportunity solely to my grandfather's death. I will not elaborate on such speculations. The schooling my grandfather had given me, which can be said to have started when I was born, came to an end with his death. By suddenly dying he had brought my schooling to an end. It had started as elementary instruction, and by the time it ended it had become a form of higher education. It seemed to me that I now had a foundation on which to build my future, a better foundation than any other I might have had. I still spent days lying under the covers in a constant state of deep natural depression and despair because of my grandfather's absence and the reason for it. Meanwhile my family had to come to terms with his death and face the practical problem of how he was to be buried. All the arrangements for his burial were attended to by my guardian, who was the most practical member of the family. My grandfather had expressed a wish to be buried in the cementary at Maxglan, which at that time, in 1949, was still a small village cemetery some way from the city; we had often walked round this cemetery together. I have described elsewhere the difficulties raised by the Church authorities over his burial. My grandfather's obituary was written by Josef Kaut, the editor-in-chief of the socialist *Demokratisches Volksblatt* and a man who was later to play an important role in my life. I have often wondered whether it was necessary for me to learn of my grandfather's death from a newspaper. Had the newspaper not been passed on to me by the innkeeper from Hofgastein, I might never have seen his obituary at all. My first existence had come to an end and my second had begun. When the catastrophe was over, my family retired to their previous positions and addressed themselves to the problems which still faced them. They now concentrated less on improving my lot and were able to allow themselves a degree of relaxation. They no longer needed to be anxious on my account. The doctors were optimistic, and my family could see for themselves that this optimism was amply justified: I was making astonishing progress towards recovery. For far too long they had been forced to neglect themselves and concentrate their concern on the two sick members of the family, and now they discovered the extent to which they had neglected themselves. Suddenly they too felt that they were alone, that they had been left behind, as my mother frequently put it, and at first they found it impossible to envisage their own future. As for mine, it must have seemed completely hopeless. The outlook could not have been worse, especially when they considered that the one member of the family who was going to be in poor health for the rest of his life was the unhappy grandson, who had just lost his grandfather, his teacher and saviour. They found themselves saddled all at once with more responsibility than they could bear. Yet they still did not feel themselves responsible for me: after all, I was eighteen and had been brought up solely by my grandfather. From the moment of my birth my grandfather had withdrawn me from their educational sphere of influence, as it were, and taken me under his intellectual tutelage. For eighteen years they had had no influence over me. My grandfather had excluded them from my upbringing and denied them any right they might have had in it because of their attitude toward me; yet now I was their responsibility, both legally and morally. What's going to happen when he comes out of the hospital? they must often have asked. That time was not far away, or at least it was foreseeable, and they were scared. My release from the hospital drew nearer every day and would probably not be long delayed; yet behind the joy they felt at this happy prospect there lurked a dread of the actual moment of my release which they were unable to conceal. On the one hand, they looked forward to my being discharged as much as I myself did; on the other hand, they dreaded it. For it was clear to them that after my discharge I should inevitably remain a burden on them for a considerable time. there was clearly no question of my having sufficiently recovered, by the time I left the hospital, to go back to working in the shop. There was no chance of my working, hence no chance of my being provided for. And my career as a singer—which they had never believed in for a moment— was finished too. They had at least some small measure of consolation in the fact that they had made arrangements with the Chamber of Commerce for me to take the commercial assistants' examination as soon as I had recovered: it would thus be possible for me to bring my commercial apprenticeship to a proper conclusion. I did in fact take this examination, though a year later than had been envisaged, and I actually passed it, thus bringing my apprenticeship to a proper conclusion. My family was now preoccupied with the question of my grandfather's estate. They suddenly had access to my grandfather's study, which had always been off limits during his lifetime, and were able to enter a domain that previously had been closed to them. I am not just referring to the few clothes and other effects he had left, which they divided among themselves in accordance with their personal needs and preferences unless an item was expressly mentioned in his will. Among the objects he bequeathed to me was his typewriter, bought at an auction in the Dorotheum in Vienna in the early 1920s, on which he made what he called the fair copies of all his works. I still use this typewriter, an American L. C. Smith which is probably over sixty years old, for typing my own works. In addition to the typewriter he left me a suit, two jackets, two pairs of trousers, and a so-called Schladminger, a winter overcoat lined with green baize. Nor must I fail to mention what he called his hiking bag, in which he used to carry his pencil, his note-pad, and other small articles he might need during his long walks. He did not have much else in the way of possessions apart from his bed, his desk, and his bookcase, which went to his son, to whom he also bequeathed his literary estate. However, I was naturally not involved in all these details, being still in the hospital. The greater part of my attention continued to be occupied by the proceedings in the death ward. One day the chief physician suggested to me that I should move out of the death ward into what he called *a friendlier room*. He must have suddenly realized how appalling—and at the same time how foolish—it had been to put me in the death ward in the first place. He now wanted to make

up for this error by telling me repeatedly during ward-rounds that I ought
to move out of the death ward into *a different, friendlier room*. I can still
hear him saying these words, and I can still see his face as he kept on
repeating the words *a different, friendlier room*, without for one moment
being aware of how outrageous and shocking they were. He kept on saying
a different, friendlier room, but he was too stupid and insensitive by nature
to be aware of what he was saying. I no longer wished to move and insisted
on staying in the death ward, having grown accustomed to it over the past
weeks and months. The chief physician could have forced me to move out,
but in the end he shook his head and gave up. For a long time I could
not help reflecting not only on the mindlessness but on the effrontery of
the chief physician, which had led him to talk of my moving into *a friendlier
room*. The fact that he should use such a phrase set me thinking for hours
about the callousness people display and the brainlessness in which they
wrap it up. I was now free from pain, though I was still subject to the
various medical and non-medical inconveniences that are inescapable in a
place like the death ward, and I was by now a past master at living with
the horrors surrounding me and treating them as part of an easily assimilable
routine. I could now observe everything with increasing acuity and was
mentally equipped to reflect on what I observed. It afforded me a welcome
relief to examine the views I had formed and the incidents I had witnessed
as an object of study from which I could derive profit. At a certain point,
when the healing process was well advanced, I rediscovered the pleasure
of thinking, of dissecting and analysing what I saw around me. I now had
time to pursue this occupation and was left undisturbed. My analytical
faculty once more gained the upper hand. One day the chief physician
announced to me, not that I was going to be discharged, but that I was
going to be transferred from the hospital to a so-called convalescent home
at Grossgmain, a village at the foot of the Untersberg quite close to the
Bavarian border. This convalescent home, an annexe of the hospital, had
been a hotel before the war, and it is now a hotel again. It would be
another two or three weeks, however, before this happened. By now I had
started getting up and learning to walk again with the help of the sisters
and (during visiting hours) my mother. Naturally, my first attempts were
dismal failures; then all at once I was able to let go of the bed, to which
I had at first had to cling, and walk a few paces. Every day the number
of the paces increased. My mother would count them—on Monday *eight
steps*, on Tuesday *eleven steps*, on Wednesday *fourteen steps*, and so on. Of

course there were also setbacks. One day I was able to go and meet my mother at the door of the death ward, and we were both overjoyed. After a while she began to bring me newspapers and magazines, then finally books—Novalis, Kleist, Hebel, Eichendorff, and Christian Wagner, who were my favourite authors at the time. Sometimes she would sit by my bed reading a book while I read another. These were the most enjoyable of my mother's visits. She told me about her childhood and youth, which had been no less difficult than mine, and she talked about her parents, my grandparents, telling me many things I did not know, about the happy relationship they had had all their lives, about their journeys and adventures and about the way they had grown old. Here, in the death ward, I suddenly found the close, loving relationship with my mother which had so painfully eluded me for eighteen long years. Sickness had the power to bring us together and form a bond between us after so many years of estrangement. When my mother was telling me stories or reading to me from a book which I knew to have been one of my grandfather's favourites, Laurence Sterne's *A Sentimental Journey*, I could listen for the whole two hours of her visit without once interrupting, praying that she would not stop. But these readings were always brought to an abrupt end by the sister, whose appearance in the death ward, carrying her thermometers, signalled the end of visiting time. We did not speak too much about my grandfather so soon after his death, which still overshadowed everything, though it became more bearable if it was not mentioned. She told me that he had been buried in a grave by the wall outside the cemetery, the only grave in an area that was otherwise unoccupied, where an extension of the cemetery was planned. She told me she visited the grave every day, stood by it for a few minutes, and then went home. She found it hard to enter his room, which was still pervaded by the characteristic smell it had always had. She wanted to leave it unaired as long as possible, to keep the windows closed so that the smell would remain. She now had a constant feeling that there was no longer any point to her life, which had been closely bound up with her father's in a manner which she described by the word *bondage*. She said she was not sleeping. Her sole anxiety concerned my future, about which she was utterly at a loss. The discussions she had had with my guardian, her husband, whom I always called *Father*, had got her nowhere, and in any case they were only the briefest conversations and simply plunged her into even greater perplexity and despair. The younger children, my brother and sister, did not understand anything, she said;

but they had been greatly harmed by all these terrible events and occurrences at an age when they were most in need of care and protection, and
this made her very frightened. The causes of my grandfather's illness and
finally of his death, which had come at an age when under different
circumstances he need not have died—the age of sixty-seven—as well as
the causes of my own illness, could be traced back to the war, she said,
which had for so long starved and humiliated us, physically, mentally,
and psychologically. All my life my relations with my mother had been
tinged with reserve and distrust, even with suspicion, and at times with
enmity. The reasons for this might be worth examining one day, but it
would be too much of a digression at present, and in any case it would
be premature. I now believed, however, that I had found her again, that
I had rediscovered her. I suddenly realized that by nature she had been
closer to my grandfather than his son had been. I recall how quickly visiting
time passed as she sat by my bed telling me stories. In everything she said
she was the acme of charm, sensitivity, and consideration. She had been
a loving daughter, and now for the first time she became a loving mother,
with whom I could spend hours without any misunderstandings. Gone
was all the asperity which had always been a feature of our extremely
difficult relationship. My mother was *musical*—this was an appropriate
word in her case: she had a beautiful voice and had once played the guitar.
My own musicality could only have been inherited from her. What is
called *serious* or *great* music, however, remained a closed book to her. As
a young girl she had been obliged to part company with my grandfather
in order to save herself from his ruthless discipline and the implacable
tyranny he exercised over her and had had to make her own way—one
which, as I know, brought her more than once to the brink of disaster.
Her father, prompted by his life-long *artistic aspirations*, had sent her as a
child not to an ordinary school but to the Vienna ballet school, where she
was to be trained as a dancer at the court opera and pursue the career of
a ballerina. It was thanks only to a sudden and severe illness that the child
was able to escape from this martyrdom imposed upon her by her ambitious
father. Later, for her father's sake, she often put her own helpless and
precarious existence at risk by taking every possible kind of gainful employment simply to support her parents. But she could never escape from
the influence of her father, whom she respected more than any other person.
She was, as she put it, in *bondage* to him, and her love for him was never
returned with equal intensity. This caused her life-long suffering. My

grandfather was not a good father to his children: it was impossible for him to have a serious relationship with his family, and he never had a real home. Home for him was the realm of thought: his family consisted of the great thinkers, among whom he felt safe and secure, as he once put it. One bright, icy winter's day in early March I was transported to Grossgmain in a white ambulance belonging to the hospital. I was carried on a stretcher and covered by three warm blankets. I was driven through the open gate of the hospital into the Müllner Hauptstrasse, across the Aiglhof and through Maxglan, passing our apartment on the way (or so I guessed, for I could not see the route), then up to Wartberg and past Marzoll in the direction of the Untersberg. This journey marked the close of a period which had seen the end of my first life, my old life, the existence I had led hitherto, and the start of my new life, my new existence, which sprang from what was probably the most important decision I had ever made. To this day this decision still determines my whole life. I had not yet been released into the world but had been transferred to another *institution for the sick*, where the air was healthy and there were woods all around. I recall that this journey of only ten miles completely exhausted me, so that when I arrived I was unable to get up off the stretcher by myself but had to be supported by two orderlies who were assigned to me as I walked the few paces from the ambulance to the Hotel Vötterl. An elevator took us up to the third floor. I was put in a room facing onto the road; I had a view of the church and of the churchyard below it. The room had two beds and was already occupied by a young man—a student of architecture, as I soon learned. Hardly had the orderlies seated me on the bed than they disappeared, whereupon a nurse entered carrying towels and various papers as well as a thermometer, which I immediately had to stick under my arm. She asked me where my things were, but apart from my sponge-bag I had none. Although I told her I had not brought any clothes, she insisted on opening one of the two wardrobes in the room and showing me where my clothes were to be hung. I told her that there would be no question, at least for the next few days, of my getting up and walking, let alone of my going out of doors, and so there would be plenty of time for my family to bring me my clothes. Lying in bed with the nurse standing beside me, I had to answer several questions about myself. My fellow patient listened attentively to the replies I gave to the nurse's questions. It worried her that I could not say for certain whether I was born on the ninth or the tenth of February. As always on such occasions, I said *on the ninth or the tenth*, but she would not accept this, and so in the end *she* decided in favour of the tenth—I do not know why—and entered that date on one of the forms. She said it was her duty to acquaint me with what she called one or two essential points in the house rules. As she was doing this I noticed that she emphasized several times that I was forbidden—she always said that *I* was forbidden, not that *the patients* were forbidden—that *I* was forbidden to buy goods in the village shops, visit public houses, or talk to children. I had to be back in the building before eight o'clock in the evening—and this despite the fact that I could hardly walk and she had just been told that I did not even have any clothes. I had to turn up punctually for meals, which would be served in the room. Visitors were allowed only during visiting hours. From nine o'clock in the evening there must be no noise. This introduction to life in the hotel at once reminded me of the schoolhouse in the Schrannengasse. I very soon became tired and drowsy and had no desire to reflect on the nurse's inanities. After I had answered her questions and she had at last declared herself satisfied, she left the room and I was able to turn my attention to my room-mate; but we did not get round to having a conversation, as I went to sleep immediately. Only minutes later it was dinner-time, the food being pushed on a wooden trolley straight from the elevator and into our room, where it was served. Now, during the meal, which I could eat only with great effort, sitting up in bed, I had an opportunity to talk to my fellow patient for the first time. It was his third week in this room, and he thought he would be able to go home after another three weeks. Like me, he had been in the hospital; unlike me, he had been a private patient, and in the hospital he had not been put into a ward with twenty-six beds but into a private room with only two. In this respect alone what he related to me about the hospital was quite different from what I had to relate—indeed, in many respects it was quite the opposite. His experiences had been different from mine, and so had the events he had witnessed, for he had been shielded nearly all the time from events and occurrences such as I had witnessed because, being a private patient, he had been in a room with only two beds, a privilege which ensured that from the start he did not come into contact with any of the daily horrors which took place in such a large hospital. The private patient, lying by himself, has only his own sufferings to put up with and only his own pain to endure. His observations are confined to himself, his own sickness, and his own surroundings, whereas the non-paying patient has to relate what he observes

of his own sufferings and his own pain to what he observes of the sufferings
and pain of all the patients who share the ward with him. In my room-
mate's case there had been only one other person, while in mine there had
been twenty-five, and this accounted for the considerable difference between
what I described to him and what he described to me. This is not to say
that the experiences of my fellow patient, with whom I quickly made
friends, had affected him any less profoundly than mine had affected me,
or that the psychological damage he had suffered was any less grievous
than mine. However, the private patient is bound to have a different
perspective from that of the so-called ordinary patient, who is in no position
to make demands and is ultimately spared nothing. The ordinary patient
is not protected or shielded in the least, while the private patient is seldom
obliged to contemplate scenes of extreme ugliness and horror. For him
everything is mitigated and attenuated; he is not ruthlessly compelled to
put up with everything as a matter of course. All the same, there have
been many changes since those days, even in Austria. The class division
among patients has not yet been abolished, but we must insist on its
abolition as soon as possible, for it is quite inhuman that there should be
class distinction in hospitals of all places—a state of affairs which is nothing
short of a socio-political perversion. Quite suddenly, by being transferred
from the hospital to the hotel at Grossgmain—somewhat abruptly, though
not without warning—I was removed from the disaster machine of hospital
life and lodged amid woods and mountains at a time of the year when the
mountains cast their gloom over the greater part of every day. I found
myself in an atmosphere of calm which affected me day and night, at first
irritating me and then tormenting me, and never allowing me to find
repose. The change from the hospital to the woods and mountains imposed
a burden on me which I found hard to bear and which plunged me
unexpectedly into a state of perpetual self-torment, from which it took
me days to emerge. For the first time I was able to get a clear view, once
I had been removed from it, of the full horror of the hospital and of all
the events and occurrences which were connected with my own illness and
with the illness and death of my grandfather. I was not yet capable of
analysing these events and occurrences; yet the fresh impressions that
greeted me at the Hotel Vötterl—a building which I still had not seen
and of which, in the first few days, I had only vague imaginings—threw
at least some light on the incidents, events, and occurrences I had lived
through during my stay in the Salzburg hospital. I now began to assimilate

what I had experienced there. The daily routine of the Vötterl, which was minimal when compared with that of the hospital, afforded a suitable background. The architecture student did not disturb me as I engaged in this mental exercise, which in due course became an integral part of my new life. I had learnt that there was a proper time for analysing every extraordinary event or occurrence, and by using my factual knowledge I was soon able to discover and determine just what the appropriate time—or, rather, the most appropriate time—might be. I was now in a position to ask myself: What is it that I have escaped from and on no account want to go back to? The method worked: the necessary connections were made, the chronology fell into place, and I had all the linking threads in my head. In my most lucid moments I saw it all as a logical development, one that conformed with not just a superficial but an inherent logic and had reached its conclusion in the bathroom, into which I had been wheeled at probably the most perilous moment of my illness. At this moment I had resolved upon a second life, a second existence, and by my decision not to give up I had extended this logical development to embrace the whole of my future. This decision was mine alone, and it had to be reached in the briefest possible time—in a split second. Seldom before or since have I made such extensive and profitable use of the opportunity to spend days and weeks, completely undisturbed, reflecting on the past and the future and translating these reflections into a genuine intellectual speculation. The events and occurrences I experienced at Grossgmain were suddenly not those I was living through in the present, which were essentially insignificant, but those I had already lived through in the hospital in Salzburg. My present experiences were relatively unimportant, at least in the first few days and weeks, during which I never left my room. Only after I had been at Grossgmain for two weeks and become accustomed to the change of air was I able to get up and take in my new surroundings. The village was situated right on the Austro-Bavarian border, which coincided at a number of places with a rushing mountain stream. Most of the time it was a gloomy place and anything but friendly, and it must be one of the coldest mountain villages imaginable. Round the church, which I could see from my window, and round the churchyard, of which I also had a good view, there were a few peasant dwellings set in the dips of the foothills, and a few inns, all of them dominated by the Hotel Vötterl, which probably had been built about the turn of the century. Otherwise there was nothing. All in all it was a place for the sick, especially for those with lung disease or respiratory complaints of any kind, and this was doubtless the reason behind the decision to turn the hotel into what was officially designated a *Convalescent Home for Patients with Respiratory Complaints*. The war and its aftermath had made the Vötterl useless as an hotel, and so the provincial government had converted it into an annexe of the local hospital. It was only gradually, however, that I learned that the Hotel Vötterl was not only a convalescent home in which patients actually convalesced but also the final destination for many of those who were sent there. My room-mate soon drew my attention to the fact that it also took in so-called *serious* cases, mainly those who were still alive after a fairly lengthy stay in the city hospital and were then transferred to Grossgmain for no other purpose than that they should die there. These were *the hopeless cases* for whom medicine could do nothing more. As I subsequently came to see for myself, some of the patients at the Vötterl were hopeless cases, while others—chiefly younger people—had actually been sent there to convalesce. For a long time, however, I saw nothing of the hopeless cases. Obviously, most of them were no longer able to leave their rooms, at least not alive, and so I never set eyes on them. One day my friend the architecture student pointed out to me from our window—no doubt thinking that the proper time had come to do so—that there were several mounds of earth at the rear end of the churchyard, some of them new and others not so new. The appropriate background for this scene was provided, as he may have judged, by a snow flurry. These mounds, he told me, were the graves of people who had recently died at the Hotel Vötterl. I could make out eleven or twelve of them, but probably several more were hidden by the wall of the church. Every spring, my room-mate told me, there were a few more mounds. Since he had been at the Vötterl he had watched four funerals from the window. These serious cases were concealed from the less serious, and one got to know about them only by looking down from the window at the churchyard. One day, quite by chance, he had discovered the connection between the serious cases in the convalescent home and the growing number of mounds in the churchyard below. Only three weeks ago, he said, he had played cards with an actress, formerly a *famous* actress, in her room. He now pointed to the last mound but one, under which, he said, his partner at cards had lain buried for over a week. March and April were the months which saw the greatest number of deaths from lung disease: proof of this could be found in cemeteries the world over. Since he always spoke of lung disease, I finally concluded that only patients suffering from lung disease were accommodated at the Vötterl. The very words *lung disease* had always filled me with horror. Now I heard them so often that I became accustomed to them. It was actually true that nearly everyone in the Vötterl was suffering from lung disease. To avoid causing alarm the responsible authorities had designated it a *Convalescent Home for Patients with Respiratory Complaints*, and on all the official documents the words *respiratory organs* were used—there was never any mention of lungs. Nevertheless, the fact was that the Vötterl was reserved almost exclusively for patients with lung disease, most of whom had been given up as incurable. In my ignorance I had never classified my own illness as lung disease—perhaps this was to afford myself the necessary self-protection—though naturally it had been a disease of the lungs right from the start. However, I had always thought of lung disease as something different, and people who had it were indeed different. In the strict medical sense I was not suffering from lung disease: although I did in fact have a disease of the lungs, that was not what it was called. All the same I was afraid of contracting lung disease at the Vötterl, which was full of patients suffering from it, some of them serious cases, as I have mentioned. Most of them had open tuberculosis of the lung, which was dangerously infectious and for which at that time, in 1949, there was virtually no treatment. Anyone who contracted it had only a slim chance of being cured. From the very beginning, from the moment I knew for certain that the Vötterl was full of people suffering from *open tuberculosis of the lung*, I found it incredible that I should have been moved there. I now understood, of course, why the nurse who acquainted me with the house rules on my first day had told me that I must not enter any shop or public house in the village and must not talk to children. In introducing me to the home she had treated me as someone with lung disease. I had a lung complaint but not lung disease, and the doctors had had no business to move me to the Vötterl. My family had been told simply that I was being transferred to a convalescent home, but now they too were faced with the fact that I was in an institution full of patients suffering from lung disease and was thus exposed to tubercular infection. For, naturally, everyone in the Vötterl came into direct or indirect contact with everyone else; the danger of infection was of course greatest in the X-ray unit, the washrooms, and the bathrooms, where one was constantly meeting others who might or might not be infectious. It seems probable to me now that it was at the Vötterl in Grossgmain that I contracted tuberculosis, which led to the serious lung disease I suffered from later, for in the extremely debilitated condition I was in on my arrival I naturally could have had no immunity. Indeed, I am inclined to believe that I went to Grossgmain in order to contract the severe lung disease which developed later and has remained with me all my life—not, as the doctors promised me, in order to complete my cure and regain my health. For the first few days and weeks at the Vötterl I was *not suffering from lung disease*. However, from the moment when I discovered that almost everyone here had lung disease I lived in the utmost fear of becoming one of them. I was forced to live with this constant fear: I woke in fear and went to sleep in fear. On the one hand, I went on clinging to a belief in the competence of the doctors, of which I had not yet had a complete *reductio ad absurdum*, because I could not believe that they would knowingly expose me to the danger of contracting lung disease at the Vötterl. Hence the question I repeatedly asked myself was whether or not the doctors who had sent me there really were as brainless, base, and irresponsible as I had often been forced to conclude. As was subsequently shown, they were every bit as brainless, base, and irresponsible as that, in that they had sent a young person who was fighting to regain his health not to a place where he would be cured but virtually to his death. My trust in myself was greater than my distrust of the doctors, and so I continually thought about getting out of the Vötterl one day unharmed and being able to return home in good health. The fresh mountain air which blew in through the open windows day and night was beneficial to me. My family came to see me soon after I arrived and brought me the things I needed for my stay, including a few clothes, some of which had belonged to my grandfather but also fitted me. I was still weak on my legs and inclined to nausea, and I was still unable to think clearly; and so, after trying on these clothes in my mother's presence, I got back into bed. After my mother had left, I was able to lie in bed and gaze through the open door of the wardrobe at the clothes I had inherited from my grandfather. I had loved them when he wore them; now they belonged to me, and for hours I tried to prolong the pleasure of looking at them. The days dragged at the Vötterl, unlike those spent in the hospital, where time passed quickly. The time I spent in my room was almost entirely uneventful, filled with at first hesitant, then more extensive, conversations with my fellow patient, from whom I gradually and somewhat inconsiderately elicited the whole story of his life and finally of his illness. At first I had nothing to read, but after a few days I began to have reading matter brought to me from Salzburg, and I recall that it was at Grossgmain that I began to acquaint myself with so-called world literature, of which I knew nothing. The decision to do so matured virtually overnight. I did not proceed according to a set plan but simply asked my family to bring me those books from my grandfather's shelves which I knew to have been supremely important to him and which I assumed I should now be able to understand. It was in this way that I first got to know the principal works of Shakespeare and Stifter, of Lenau and Cervantes, though I cannot claim that I understood them in all their rich complexity. Nevertheless, I was grateful to have them and eager to understand them, and I profited from reading them. I read Montaigne, Pascal, and Péguy, the philosophers who were to be my constant companions in later life and have always been very important to me—and of course Schopenhauer, to whose world and way of thought my grandfather had introduced me, though naturally he had not introduced me to his actual writings. I often read far into the night, and the books I read provided topics for long conversations with my fellow patient, who, in his own way and considering his background, had had a good grounding in literature and philosophy, though naturally he was more inclined to philosophizing. I was lucky to have such a room-mate. I also rediscovered an urge to read the newspapers, and though I at once found myself repelled by them, this did not prevent me from reading them daily: even at that time I had developed an addiction (a life-long addiction, as it turned out) to the mechanical routine of getting hold of newspapers and reading them—only to be unfailingly repelled by them. Like my grandfather, who had a life-long loathing for newspapers just as intense as mine, I fell prey to this incurable newspaper disease. The days at Grossgmain were thus spent reading books and newspapers, philoso-phizing, or simply chatting with my room-mate, though naturally most of our conversation was about sickness and death. Of course there were repeated diversions due to sudden unforeseen incidents at the Vötterl—arrivals, departures, deaths—and the regular question-and-answer sessions connected with the weekly examinations and X-ray tests, as well as to the official regulations and *rules of conduct*. Though my misgivings about the true nature of my illness could not be dispelled for one moment, and though I was still afraid to look into the future, I nevertheless had a degree of security at the Vötterl: after all, I had escaped—in the best possible way, it seemed—from my recent hospitalization in a city to which I had as yet no wish to return. During the day I was able to repress the nightmare;

but at night the images were all the more terrifying and could not be blotted out, for at night there was no escape. My room-mate told me that I sometimes woke up screaming. He already had the prospect of being allowed home soon and was preparing himself, with the aid of a number of prescribed books, for the resumption of his studies at the Vienna Polytechnic. He had been wrenched from his studies the previous autumn and had been treated first in Vienna, then in Linz, and finally in Salzburg, after which he had been moved to Grossgmain at the end of February. His parents visited him regularly. They owned what from his account must have been a beautifully situated house on the southern side of the Mönchsberg. His father was a senior *railway engineer*—though even now I cannot imagine what that means. He had something I had never had: a so-called settled family life to which all else was subordinated. Sometimes I had the impression of being at a decided disadvantage through not having a family life of this kind and never having known one, though on reflection I realized that this kind of life had always repelled me and that I did not want it. His illness was not precisely specified, any more than mine was, and in his case too the doctors talked round the subject instead of stating the facts and enlightening him. He had not had pleurisy and had never been taken acutely ill, but he did have what he called *some suspicious shadows on the lower right lung* which had shown up distinctly on the X-ray picture and then disappeared. All in all, his visits in various hospitals had been what may be called preventive measures, on which his parents had been more insistent than the doctors. Even now, when he was looking forward to an early discharge from Grossgmain, he came up one day from the X-ray unit with the news that the shadows were back, then on another occasion with the news that they were gone again. The doctors made him feel insecure, but in the end he—and finally his parents—did everything possible to ensure that he could return to his life and his studies. When I observed him, and especially when I heard him talking about his chosen subject, architecture, I had no doubt about his aptitude for it. However, we repeatedly came up against the limits to our mutual understanding. When this happened we simply broke off our conversation and took refuge in our diametrically opposed reading. For a long time I had been so unaccustomed to talking to anyone young that it took me a few days to gear my mind to the fact that I was suddenly once more in the company of a young person, a boy of about my own age; but once I got over this initial difficulty the game was won. I came to feel that my fellow patient was the ideal room-mate; I could have been landed with somebody quite different. One day my mother brought me the piano score of *The Magic Flute*, which my grandfather had promised to buy me. Only he could have told her that I wanted it, for I had told nobody else. My mother told me that he had intended to give it to me on my birthday, but now she had been to Höllrigl's bookshop and bought it for me herself—*a little late*, she said as she pulled the score out of the small rucksack with which she had travelled on the bus to Grossgmain. *The Magic Flute* was my favourite opera—partly, no doubt, because it was the first one I ever heard—and it is still my favourite opera. I was now holding the very object which at one time would have made me supremely happy, but now it could only plunge me into a state of despair, because I had meanwhile lost all hope of being able to sing again. I did not experiment to see whether I still had a singing voice. Holding the piano score of *The Magic Flute* in my hands was thus anything but the joy she had hoped it would be. Once more my limitations were made horrifyingly clear to me, but I gave way to sentimentality for only a very short time. I hid the piano score in my wardrobe, at the same time telling myself that I must refrain from getting it out for as long as possible. My mother, I recall, came out regularly every Sunday with my guardian and my brother and sister. She repeatedly came out on other occasions too, walking the ten miles on foot to save the fare, which was far too great an exertion for her, since the road was still unpaved and the gradient would rapidly have exhausted anyone. She never missed coming, however, because she knew I was waiting for her. My mother was now the person closest to me. After she left I did basically nothing but wait for her next visit. The week passed slowly, and in time it became increasingly difficult to find diversions. Meanwhile, I had for some time been getting up and exploring the interior of the hotel, the corridors of which were kept unlit all day, presumably for reasons of economy, which made them somewhat dangerous to negotiate; and in the public rooms there was naturally nothing left to remind one that this had once been a popular hotel. It was fully equipped for the function it performed—as a place of treatment or a final destination for victims of lung disease—and all the rooms, even the walls, were permeated by the smell of sickness. One day my fellow patient unexpectedly asked me to accompany him to the village. At first I was nervous about undertaking such an adventure, but it proved a success. First we walked round the outside of the church and then, our curiosity aroused, ventured inside. We then walked a little further, in the direction of the border, and back. A start had been made. In the days that followed I went for longer walks, always in the company of my room-mate, and in this way we got to know how beautiful and tranquil the village and its surroundings were. It was now early April, and the careful observation of nature brought a new element of variety into the monotony of life at Grossgmain. Finally my room-mate was discharged and I had to go exploring alone. It was only a few days to Easter. I plucked up the courage to cross the border into Bavaria by simply jumping across the stream a few hundred yards up from the bridge, which was guarded. I walked along the German bank for a while and then returned the way I had come. The very next day, having discovered by experiment how easy it was to cross what was known as the Green Frontier, I went across the border again at the same spot and walked on and on until I reached Reichenhall, which was two to three miles away. In this way I paid my first visit to the town where my grandmother was born. These excursions across the border naturally reminded me of those I had made a few years earlier when my family had lived in Traunstein and I was attending the grammar school in Salzburg. This time I was not afraid of being caught; it would not have caused me the least concern. I crossed the border nearly every day, since I found these Bavarian walks, as I called them, more interesting, and I was never caught once. I recall that on one occasion I even had the courage to cross the border at about nine at night, after supper, because I had discovered that a concert was to be held at half past nine in the Kurpark. I actually stayed to hear the whole concert, arriving back at the Vötterl around midnight without being noticed. This enterprise was possible only because I now had my room to myself and had discovered various tricks which enabled me to leave the Vötterl around nine without being discovered and get back into the building around midnight, likewise undetected. There is no better demonstration of the extent of my recovery than these long walks and trips across the border, which after all were still not without excitement. Gradually I was taken off drugs. The tests showed a daily improvement in my general health. Naturally, the radiographer directed his attention to my lungs, but he told me that there were no visible indications of disease. My doubts remained, however, and my fear of contracting lung disease was increased by what I knew about my immediate surroundings at the Vötterl. This fear was always present among the members of my family and myself, though none of us expressed it, and they grew increasingly apprehensive, especially my mother. There was no remedy against the fear of tuberculosis. On the one hand, they were thankful that I had been given the chance of recuperating at the Vötterl at public expense—of *breathing myself back to health*, as my mother put it. On the other, they could not ignore their own anxiety lest my stay at Grossgmain should prove to have been a big mistake and put my life at risk. Ultimately the most sensible course for all concerned was to avoid talking about it, even though we could not avoid thinking about it. I was living in idyllic surroundings, though unfortunately not as a healthy person but as an invalid, unable to enjoy all the benefits that were afforded by this region protected all round by hills or to take full advantage of the utterly unspoilt nature that was still to be found there. Yet these idyllic surroundings had a *hell-hole* at their centre, just as every idyll has its dark side. This hell-hole was of course hidden from public view by every possible means. Whoever peered into it had to be on his guard not to lose his balance. For my part I was no longer exposed to such mortal danger here at the Vötterl, since I had already gone through the hell of the local hospital in Salzburg. I was quite simply over the worst, and I had a number of things that helped me. The initiative had begun long ago in my own head. The library I had in my room had expanded to several dozen volumes. I had read Hamsun's *Hunger*, Dostoyevsky's *Raw Youth*, and Goethe's *Elective Affinities*, and I had made notes on what I had read, a practice my grandfather had observed throughout his life. I tried keeping a diary but immediately gave up. I could have had contacts with all kinds of people at the Vötterl, but I did not want any, being satisfied with the company of my books and with the long expeditions I made into the vast, undiscovered continents of the imagination. Hardly had I woken up and conscientiously taken my temperature in accordance with the rules, as I had done every morning for months, than I turned to my books, my closest and most intimate friends. It was in Grossgmain that I first discovered reading. This was a sudden discovery which proved decisive for my subsequent life. This discovery—that literature can at any moment provide the mathematical solution to life and one's own existence provided that it is put into gear and operated as though it were mathematics, so that in time it becomes a form of higher mathematics and ultimately the supreme mathematical art, which can be called reading only when we have mastered it completely—this discovery was one which I could not have made until my grandfather had died: this idea, this insight, I owed to his death. I had put my time to good and instructive use, and this had made it pass more quickly. Through reading I was able to bridge the gulf which yawned beneath me even here and was thus able to rescue myself from moods which could have led only to destruction. On Sundays I was visited by my family, who were looking forward to my returning home yet were at the same time apprehensive about it. They were naturally bound to think that my return would inevitably lead to a fresh catastrophe in their existence, which had been devastated by the events and occurrences of recent months. It seemed obvious to them that I should now turn my whole attention to becoming a businessman and forget about becoming a singer, that I should concentrate on a career in commerce and not in music. Whenever they visited me at Grossgmain they tried everything they could, directly and indirectly, to steer me *towards* commerce and *away from* singing. Naturally it must have been obvious to them that a career as a singer was ruled out by the condition of my lungs, and so they staked everything on my aptitude for commerce and what they believed to be the greater and more lucrative prospects of business. They kept on telling me that as soon as possible, as soon as I got back from Grossgmain, I should take the commercial assistants' examination, for which I had long been qualified. Once he's completed his apprenticeship, they no doubt thought, the burden will be off our shoulders. Nor could one blame them for constantly trying to push me into a career in commerce. Yet I was no longer interested in such a career. I was willing to take the examination but not to go beyond that. I was willing to go back to working for Podlaha, but I had not the slightest intention of going into business. I never really had. I had never been serious about the idea, for the fact that I had run away from the grammar school and spent two years as Podlaha's apprentice had never for one moment been prompted by the idea of becoming a businessman. Had I wanted to become one, I should have had to go about it very differently. My family had utterly misunderstood my actions and my motive for rebelling. It was natural that they should now cling to the fact that I had been apprenticed to Podlaha. I was horrified to discover that they were not only sticking to their misunderstanding but apparently still prepared to exploit it quite shamelessly. As I saw it, the problem of what was to become of me, what ought to become of me, when I was well again, was not *their* problem at all but *mine* alone. I did not want to be anything, and naturally I did not want to turn myself into a mere profession: all I ever wanted was to be *myself*. But this was at once too simple and too brutal for them to understand. At Easter my mother came to visit me, bringing my brother and sister with her. This was during my last few days at Grossgmain. I can remember standing with them on a first-floor balcony of the Vötterl, watching several bands march past below. I had always found such processions insufferable, and the music played by the bands had always seemed to me to be irritating—not to say painful—rather than attractive. All my life I have disliked parades and processions. To please my brother and sister—probably because we just could not refuse their wish to see the march-past of the bands—we had gone out onto the balcony and were looking down. Seeing these bands, with their hundreds of players wearing uniforms which purported to be local costumes, all of them brainlessly beating or blowing their instruments like savages, I was at once reminded of the last war. I had always hated anything military, and so I was naturally revolted by this Easter parade, as I always have been by such ostentatious processions which take place in country areas. However, they are exceedingly popular and attract large crowds. The populace has always been attracted by the military and by military brutality. It is a species of perversion which is particularly rife in Alpine regions, where brainlessness has always passed for entertainment, even for art. Hardly had the last band marched past and the curiosity of my brother and sister been satisfied than my mother took me aside and told me that she was going to have an operation *in the next few days*. She had to go into the hospital *the very next day*. It could not be delayed. *She herself* told me that she had *cancer*. Easter had come to an abrupt end. My mother and the children went back to Salzburg soon after the parade was over, leaving me in a state of profound dismay. When I came home, as I recall, it was to an apartment which was cold and empty and utterly neglected. Everywhere I looked I saw evidence of the disaster that had engulfed us all. My mother had long since had her operation. She had been told about her condition two weeks before she broke the news to me—in other words, she had visited me at Grossgmain on several occasions without having had the courage to tell me the truth. I came home by bus and found that my family was at the hospital with my mother. I myself had brought more bad news with me from Grossgmain, but I did not want to confront my family with it there and then: my lungs had been damaged after all. The radiologist had discovered a so-called infiltration in the lower right lung, and his discovery had been confirmed by the specialist for internal medicine. Our fears had been justified: I had suddenly contracted lung disease at Grossgmain. On the day I was discharged I went to see my mother at the local hospital. She had come through the operation satisfactorily, but the doctor held out no hope for her. I spent days sitting in my grandfather's room, then wandering about the city, as may be imagined. I did not want to see anyone, and so I did not visit anyone. Two weeks after being released from Grossgmain the local health authority sent me a so-called *certificate of admission to Grafenhof Sanatorium*. Attached to it was a ticket for the rail journey.

IN THE COLD

Every sickness can be called a sickness of the mind.

NOVALIS

5

WITH THE SHADOW on my lung yet another shadow had fallen on my existence. Grafenhof was a word to strike terror to the heart: a sanatorium where absolute authority was wielded, in total immunity, by the chief physician, his assistant, and the assistant's assistant, under conditions which could only fill a young person like myself with horror. Having gone there seeking help, I was confronted only with helplessness. This was borne in upon me in the first few moments and hours I spent there, and it became even more appallingly clear during my first few days. The situation of the patients did not improve with time but only deteriorated, and so did mine. I was afraid I should go the same way as those who had been admitted to Grafenhof before me, in whose looks I could discern only utter dejection and disintegration. On my first walk to the chapel, where mass was celebrated daily, I read a dozen obituary notices on the walls, laconic memorials to those who had died in recent weeks and who, it occurred to me, had trodden these tall, chill corridors that I was treading now. In their worn-out felt slippers and shabby post-war dressing gowns, with the grubby collars of their night-shirts showing above them, they walked past me, one behind the other, the boards with their temperature charts wedged under their arms, staring suspiciously at me as they passed on their way to the sun-room, a broken-down wooden veranda abutting onto the main building, with a view across to the Heukareck, a six-thousand-foot mountain which for four months of the year cast its half-mile-long shadow over the Schwarzach Valley below the sanatorium, a valley in which for four months the sun never rose. What an infamous invention of the Creator's mind, I reflected—what an appalling scene of human misery! The people here were permanent outcasts from human society, wretched and revolting as they filed past me with their air of martyred pride, unscrewing the tops of their brown sputum bottles and spitting into them. There was a kind of shameless solemnity in the way they would try, wherever they were, to cough up sputum from their eroded lungs—a skill in which they had developed a unique mastery—and spit it out into their bottles. The corridors were filled with the sound of this solemn straining at scores of diseased lungs and with the shuffling of felt slippers on the carbolic-soaked linoleum. The procession I was watching ended in the sun-room and was attended by all the solemnity I had previously witnessed only at Catholic burials. Each person taking part in it carried his own private monstrance in front of him in the form of his brown sputum bottle. When the last person had taken up his place in the long row of rusty beds, all of them fitted with bars—when all these disease-racked bodies with their long noses and oversized ears, their long arms and bent legs, all of them exuding a pungent stench, had wrapped themselves in their musty blankets, which were not unlike horse-blankets and too threadbare to afford any warmth, quiet descended on the scene. I was still standing there in a corner where I had a clear view of everything but could hardly be seen myself, *the observer* of a spectacle which was quite new to me, a spectacle of the most monstrous human degradation, hideous and revolting in every particular, a product of the most atrocious cruelty. Yet already I was part of the spectacle myself. I too held my sputum bottle and gripped my temperature chart under my arm. I too was on my way to the sun-room. Locked in a state of shock, I went to my own bed, which was the third from the end, between two old men who would lie lifeless in their beds for hours until one or the other suddenly sat up and spat into his bottle. Almost all the patients produced sputum non-stop, mostly in large quantities, and many of them had more than one bottle with them, as though they had no more important mission in life than to produce sputum and urge one another on to ever-greater sputum production. Every day they took part in a competition, or so it seemed, in which the winner was the one who had expectorated with the greatest concentration and finished up with the greatest quantity of sputum in his bottle. The doctors expected me to participate in this competition too, but my exertions were in vain: I produced no sputum, and although I spat indefatigably my bottle remained empty. I laboured for days, but without success. My throat was red-raw from my desperate efforts to expectorate. I felt as though I were suffering from a mammoth cold, yet I was unable to produce even the smallest quantity of sputum. But had I not received orders to produce sputum? The lab was waiting for it—it seemed as though the whole of Grafenhof were waiting for it—but I had none to give them. I had the will to produce sputum—there was nothing I wanted to do more—and I practised the art of expectoration, studying how it was performed by those around me and trying to evaluate them; but the only result was an ever-increasing soreness in my throat. It felt as though my whole chest were inflamed. As I contemplated my empty bottle, I had the depressing sense of being a hopeless failure, and my determination to cough something up from my chest became more and more frantic until it amounted to a kind of hysteria. My pathetic efforts did not go unobserved; on the contrary, I had the impression that they were the focus of everyone's attention. The more hysterical I became, the more severely I was punished by the other patients observing me. They punished me ceaselessly with their stares and with their superior mastery in the art of expectoration, constantly demonstrating to me *how* one must expectorate, *how* the lungs must be stimulated into yielding their sputum. It was as though their lungs were an instrument which they had been playing for years and of which, in the course of years, they had attained complete mastery. They played on their lungs as though on a stringed instrument, with matchless virtuosity. I didn't have a chance. The members of this orchestra shamed me by playing perfectly in tune with one another; they played with such consummate artistry that it was futile for me to imagine I could ever become one of them. However much I racked my lungs, the baleful glances of the others, their malevolent suspicion and malicious laughter, only served to underline my amateurish incompetence, my pathetic lack of artistry. The adepts had three or four bottles of sputum beside them, while my one remained empty. I kept on desperately unscrewing it, then disconsolately screwing it up again. *But I must spit.* Everyone demanded that I should. In the end I resorted to violent means, inducing lengthy fits of severe coughing. I finally became a past master at bringing on artificial fits of coughing and at last succeeded in coughing something up. I spat it out into the bottle and rushed to the lab with it. But it was unusable. However, after another three or four days I had racked my lungs to such an extent that I was actually able to cough up something usable. I was still an amateur, but I was beginning to show some promise. The contents of my bottle were accepted, though regarded with misgiving and held up to the light. I had lung disease, and so I had to cough something up! But the result was not *positive*—I could not count myself a full member of this conspiratorial fellowship. I was deeply hurt by the contempt in which the others held me. They were infective—in other words, *positive*—but I was not. Further supplies of sputum were demanded from me, and the demand was repeated every other day. I had got into a routine, and my lungs had grown accustomed to being tortured. I was now definitely capable of producing sputum—half a bottle in the morning and another half-bottle in the afternoon. The lab was satisfied. But my result was always *negative*. At first it seemed as though only the doctors were disappointed, but in the end I was too. There was something wrong. Didn't I have to be like the others and produce a positive result? After five weeks I made it at last: my result was positive. I really was a full member of the community. My open

tuberculosis of the lung was confirmed. Satisfaction spread among my
fellow patients, and I too was satisfied. It did not strike me how perverse
this was. Everyone's face registered satisfaction, and the doctors were re-
assured. The necessary measures could now be taken: not surgery, naturally,
but treatment with drugs. Perhaps they would immediately perform a
pneumothorax. Or they might use cautery. All the possibilities were considered. My condition was not such as to require surgery, and so I had no
need to fear that all the ribs on the right side of my chest would be sawn
through and a whole lung removed. First they'll do a pneumothorax, I
thought. If that doesn't work they'll try cautery, and after cautery comes
surgery. I was now quite well up in the science of lung disease and knew
what was what. The first stage of treatment was always a pneumothorax.
It was a routine matter, as I could see. Everyone here was continually
being connected up to tubes and having his chest punctured—it was an
everyday occurrence. They'll begin with streptomycin, I thought. My
fellow patients were actually gratified by my positive result. They had
achieved what they wanted: they no longer had an outsider in their midst.
I was now worthy to belong to their fellowship; even though still only in
minor orders, I had some claim to parity. Suddenly I too began to look like
them, with sunken cheeks, a long nose, oversized ears, and a distended
belly. I belonged to the emaciated, not the bloated, category of patient.
Sufferers from lung disease first become emaciated, then bloated, then
emaciated again. The course of the disease proceeds from emaciation through
tumidity to renewed emaciation. When death comes, the patient is utterly
emaciated. I already knew the correct way to wear the institutional gar-
ments, shuffling along the corridors in my felt slippers just like the others,
and I suddenly began to cough in all directions without any compunction,
whether there were others around or not. I found myself indulging in all
the inconsiderate and outrageous behaviour which I had previously thought
absolutely unforgivable and disgusting in the other patients. Now that I
had *arrived*, I was determined to be part of this society, even if it was the
most loathsome and revolting society imaginable. Had I any other option?
Wasn't it quite logical for me to have ended up here? Hadn't all my
previous life been leading inevitably to Grafenhof? I too was a victim of
the war! I was going underground. I was doing everything to be able to
go underground. The only thing people do here is die, I thought. I adjusted
myself to the thought—I was no exception. I had managed to do what
three or four weeks earlier I would have considered impossible: I had become

like the others. But was I really like them? I refused to admit this question and adapted myself to the society of the dying. To be here was all I had left. I had no choice but to submit myself to the only duty that counted here—to devote myself completely to my lung disease and all that it entailed, with no chance of going back. I had a bed in the dormitory, a locker in the corridor, a bed in the sun-room, and a place in the refectory. I had nothing else, apart from my memories. I cast about anxiously for some fellow sufferer I could confide in, but I did not find one, at least not in the first few weeks. It was quite futile to resist the course of nature: I simply had to melt into the background of the prevailing grey in order to endure the conditions here; I had to make myself like the rest. When a new patient arrived, I observed his progress with the same suspicion with which my predecessors had observed mine, with the same cold and ruthless intensity of one who is a victim and will not tolerate special treatment for anyone. I would watch the patient start off as a human being and end up as a worthless creature whose humanity was no longer recognizable. It struck me that I now had an opportunity to infect the healthy, this being a power with which all sufferers from lung disease, all carriers of infections, have always been endowed—the very power I had previously found so abominable in those who for weeks had pursued and persecuted me with their stares and their gleeful malice. Now I could cough to my heart's content, secure in the presumption that I was destroying someone else's existence. Weren't my thoughts just like theirs? I suddenly conceived a hatred of everything healthy. My hatred was all at once directed against everything outside Grafenhof, everything in the world, including my own family. But it soon subsided, having nothing to feed on: everyone here was sick, cut off from life, shut out, oriented towards dissolution, geared to death. Fifty years earlier they would all have said, without hesitation, that they were *doomed to die*. The world outside had receded from them long ago and was now out of sight. Whatever news percolated through these walls was so meagre as to seem unreal and irrelevant, so scant as to have no effect on those within them. Whole continents might have been blown to pieces for all the interest such an occurrence would have aroused here, where everything was dominated by the spittoon. Everything was geared to sputum production, to the torture of artificially drawing and expelling breath, to the daily dread of the therapies, the operations, and death—and to putting oneself in good standing with the doctors, especially the chief physician. On this score I hadn't a chance, being just a skinny,

spotty-faced commercial apprentice, an eighteen-year-old nonentity, sent
here by the local health authority, with no reputation whatever and no
one to speak up for me. I had turned up here with luggage that aroused
utter contempt—an old wartime suitcase made of cardboard, two pairs of
cheap, threadbare American trousers, two washed-out army shirts and
heavily darned socks, and wearing a pair of tattered rubber shoes. My pride
and joy was a woollen jacket that had belonged to my grandfather—and
of course my piano scores of *The Magic Flute* and Haydn's *Creation*. One
look at me was enough to ensure that I was put in the poorest room, the
largest on the north side of the building, which contained twelve beds and
accommodated people who even today would rate as underprivileged—
unskilled labourers and apprentices. However, we also had a doctor of law
in our dormitory, though he was regarded as having gone to seed. Only
gradually did it become clear to me why he was there. Everyone had a
locker in the corridor, at the end of which there were two toilets and one
washroom for eighty inmates. One may imagine what a crush there was
every morning when all eighty rushed to the toilets and the washroom
more or less simultaneously: there was complete chaos, but one soon gets
used to such conditions when they recur daily. Three or four days are
enough for one to become accustomed to the way things work. One has
no choice but to accept things as they are; one behaves like the others and
avoids drawing attention to oneself. The individualist is spotted straight-
away and dealt with appropriately. The patients would force their way to
the taps in the washroom like pigs to the trough, the stronger among
them pushing the weaker out of the way. Every morning the taps were
monopolized by the same people, who were able to clear a way for themselves by kicks and kidney punches. Those suffering from lung disease can
summon up tremendous physical strength when they need to. Fear of dying
makes them strong and turns ruthlessness into a guiding principle: the
outcast, the death candidate, has nothing to lose. They were keener on
freshening themselves up than on bodily hygiene. Many of them visited
the washroom only once a week, others more rarely still—before medical
examinations, of course, when they had to be clean—but cleanliness is a
relative concept, like any other. The smell in the rooms was not for the
squeamish, corresponding as it did to the prevalent grey, which threw the
behaviour of the white-coated doctors into striking relief. The ward-round
took place at nine o'clock. The medical triumvirate would appear at the
entrance to the sun-room, whereupon those patients who had their heads

raised would lower them at once, and the doctors would pass through a motionless guard of honour. The chief physician would go from bed to bed, arms akimbo, determining the appropriate therapies and deciding which drugs were to be administered. Sometimes he leant forward and tapped a patient's chest, and he would often glance at a patient's temperature chart, then burst into loud laughter which filled the whole valley. His consultations with his colleagues were conducted in a murmur. Well over sixty, thick-set and running to fat, he had a military bearing and looked upon the patients as private soldiers whom he could treat as roughly as he pleased. He had been the chief physician here during the war, and although he was a Nazi he was not removed from his post after the war, probably because there was no one to replace him. I've nothing to hope for from this man, I thought the very first moment I saw him, and my first impression was subsequently borne out more and more. For years I was at the mercy of this stupid and truly vicious character. His assistants gave him unquestioning obedience; he could not have had better henchmen. They simply took orders from this unsavoury individual, who regarded the sanatorium as a penal institution and ran it like one. I didn't trust him, even though I was naturally in no position, in the first few weeks, to make any assessment of his medical competence, let alone an informed judgment. But it was not long before I was able to assess the chief physician's character and medical skill, as will become clear in the course of this account. From the start I tried to engage him in conversation, but all my desperate efforts to this end were nipped in the bud. He simply told me I must cough up sputum and was angry when for weeks I could not oblige. He was by nature an unhappy person who had found his way into the wrong profession, whom circumstances had placed in a bleak, cold, and inhospitable area where he could not help going to pieces and finally being destroyed. These doctors made me *uneasy*, like the doctors I had known earlier. I had a profound distrust of them—and rightly so, I believe. I observed everything about them with extreme care and attention. They could not elude my watchful eye. I realised from the start that I was dealing with utterly primitive representatives of the medical profession, but I had as yet no proof of this. This medical triumvirate was lacking in more or less all the qualities one expects in a doctor. I didn't simply have nothing to hope for from them—I decided that I must be constantly on my guard against them. Of course I didn't know how much they had on their consciences already, but I told myself that I must be exceedingly vigilant, attentive, and cautious. Despite my youth I was well schooled in scepticism, always prepared for anything—but above all for the worst. I still regard this scepticism as my chief virtue. The patient has to put all his trust in himself: this I knew. He naturally cannot hope for help from others, and it is all-important for him to be well versed in fending off threats and forestalling attacks from outside. My grandfather, my personal philosopher, had given me the necessary grounding. I distrusted others, and that, I may say, was why I recovered. But it was a long haul. The patient has to take hold of his suffering with his own hands—and above all with his own head—and work *against the doctors*. This was my experience, and although I was not yet *conscious* of doing so, I acted according to this precept. I had confidence in myself but in no one else. The greater my distrust of the doctors, the greater my trust in myself. There is no other way to survive a grave and deadly illness and return to health. But is that what I wanted during those weeks? Hadn't I joined the conspiracy of the dying at Grafenhof? Hadn't I let myself be engulfed by it? It would not be at all fanciful to say that during these weeks I fell in love, perhaps deliriously in love, with my own hopelessness and that of all the others. I not only embraced this condition of hopelessness but clung to it with absolute tenacity, like hundreds of millions of others at that time. I clung to the post-war hopelessness, the post-war terror. Here, faced with the prospect of dissolution, under conditions imposed on me by my imminent and palpable end, I felt that I was like hundreds and thousands and millions of others: I was logically prepared for the end, and, as I was now forced to acknowledge, I no longer existed as an individual. What right did I have to escape, when millions of others had perished in the war or its aftermath? I'd thought I'd escaped through what are called fortunate circumstances, but death had tracked me down to my corner, to our corner. It had caught up with me, run me to ground, swallowed me up. I accepted this fact and conducted myself accordingly. I suddenly stopped resisting, stopped rebelling. It did not occur to me to try to hoodwink my new misfortune. There was an amazing logic about it, and so I acted in accordance with this logic—I gave up and surrendered. This place was where I belonged, a place where—as I was forced to conclude—people had to give up and cease to exist after the wartime horrors that had been designed for them. Rebellion and protest were not for me. I was a member of a dying society, a society that was on the way out. I pondered this idea, which no longer seemed in any way absurd, and reached the conclusion that this was where I wanted to be—where else?—and I resigned myself to my step-by-step descent into hell. I had embraced the wretchedness of humanity and did not wish to be deprived of it by anyone or anything. I put away the hatred and loathing I had felt for Grafenhof and the conditions that prevailed there, my hatred of disease and death and what I had regarded as the injustice of it all. It was no longer this place that I hated but all the others beyond and outside it, everything else in the world. But this hatred was soon dissipated, since it was not worth the effort. This *absurd hatred* suddenly became impossible. What lay in store for me, in accordance with laws which had been created jointly by society and by nature herself, was too obvious and too just to allow of any appeal. What right had I of all people—the most futile, worthless, and expendable person in the whole of history—to maintain for one moment that I was an exception to the rule, that I ought to escape when millions had not? I had to go straight through hell to my death. I was resigned to this. For ages I had rebelled, but my rebellion was over. I submitted. What had happened to me? I had been taken in by a logic which I could not help seeing as the only logic that applied to my case, the only one I could follow. Yet immediately I rejected it in favour of a contrary logic. I now realized that everything I had formerly acquiesced in was one hundred percent wrong. My attitude swung right round, and I rebelled more violently than ever against Grafenhof and its laws, against the inevitability of its laws. Once again my stance was radically changed. Once again I was one hundred percent *alive*—I wanted to be. I wanted to hang on to my life, whatever the cost. I could no longer understand the person I had been twelve hours before, the person who had thought the very opposite of what I thought now. How could I have been so far gone as to give up, to submit, to surrender myself to death? Once more, I thought, I've drawn absolutely the wrong conclusions, but I've acted according to *my* lights. That's always been my nature and always will be. Suddenly everything I saw around me, as I observed and scrutinized it with even greater intensity than before, reverted to its previous aspect, and once more it horrified and revolted me. These people around me—I wasn't one of them. I wasn't the least bit like them. And the conditions I was living under—they weren't the right conditions for me; they just couldn't be. All at once it struck me that all my thoughts of the last few days, and all the actions that had resulted from them, had been ridiculous, preposterous, absurd. How could I have believed that I belonged in a place where disintegration and despair strangled the soul and deadened the brain? Perhaps it had been the easier course, just to let go rather than rebel and put up a fight. The truth was as simple as that. We often give in and give up to make things easier for ourselves, but only at the price of our life, of our *whole* existence—and of course I could not know what my existence was worth or might be worth again someday, though I know now that speculations on this score are pointless, because in the end it is futility that carries the day. But that is another matter. What counts is not the individual experience but the totality of existence. I had chosen the easy way and adopted the unworthy course of conforming and yielding instead of resisting and fighting back. Prompted by convenience and cowardice, I had taken my lead from all the millions who had died, for whatever reason; I had not even stopped short of shamelessly exploiting the victims of the last war in my unworthy speculations. I had not recoiled from imagining that my end, my dissolution and death, could be compared with theirs. I had exploited the deaths of millions of human beings by wanting to associate myself with them. I could have pursued this mad idea to the point of utter absurdity, but I took care not to do so. My reflections had been histrionic; I had dramatized my suffering. I felt no shame, however—there was no time for that. What I needed was a clear head devoid of sentiment, and that called for all the energy I could muster. The fact of the matter is that on that very same day I was sent for by the lab to be told that the sputum which I had handed in three or four days earlier and which had been found to contain tubercula was not mine: there had been a mix-up, a thing that had never before happened in the lab. My sputum was still free from infection. I wasn't positive after all. I now behaved as though I myself was to blame for what had happened. I did not make a fuss about it, but being suspicious by nature, I now insisted on having my sputum analysed several times in succession, but the result remained the same. So the lab *had* made a mistake. I was now in a position to resume the fight. Though I was not positive, I still had a shadow on my lung, and this was being treated with injections of streptomycin. The doses, unfortunately, were far too small, allegedly because of the high cost of the drug. Each patient received only a small quantity of the precious substance, so little (I learned later) as to be quite useless. One could be injected with larger doses only if one had it sent from Switzerland or America or if one was well in with the doctors—especially, of course, with the director of the institution, the all-powerful chief physician. When I learned that I was getting too little streptomycin—

a ridiculously small quantity in fact, virtually none at all—I made an approach to the triumvirate but was at once rebuffed. They called my demand to be given an increased dose of streptomycin a piece of outrageous impudence. I knew nothing, they said; they knew everything. By this stage, however, I was not a complete dunce where lung therapy was concerned; my very existence was at stake, and I knew perfectly well that my treatment required larger doses of streptomycin. Yet I didn't get them, because socially I was a nobody. Others got what they needed thanks to influence and position, through having a profession that carried weight. Streptomycin was allocated to patients not according to their needs but according to the most squalid social criteria. I was not the only one who suffered: half the patients got special treatment and half were at a permanent disadvantage. I belonged to the latter category. Naturally, I would not have wished to join the former by making use of *certain* circumstances and exploiting the *appropriate* means: I lacked both the *low cunning* and the will. Yet, although I lacked the means to secure special treatment, I was determined to fight my way out of this hell—for this is what the institution and everything in it seemed like to me. I had been alerted to the defective characters of the doctors, to their baseness and depravity, and to the baseness and depravity of the other patients. My understanding of my position benefited as a result, and I educated myself further by observing the nursing sisters, who were Sisters of the Cross. I began to pay less attention to myself and more to my surroundings: I was no longer positive, no longer in danger of dying, and so I could afford to embark on such a study. What kind of people are they, I wondered, and what kind of relations do they have with one another? I set out to find the answer. This was not my first encounter with a fairly large community. I knew what the masses were like from my experience in the boarding house and the hospitals I had been in. I knew their smell, the noise they made, their aims and aspirations. But here I learned for the first time that in fact they were outcasts, people who had been deprived of their rights. There was nothing to be achieved here by grandiloquent phrases and ear-catching slogans. All one saw here were hundreds of people who had sought refuge by slipping into their dreadful dressing gowns, which would soon be exchanged for the shrouds which were manufactured by a smart firm of morticians down in Schwarzach. No, I did not belong here any longer. That error was now cleared up, and I was back at my observation post. Those who were carried out of here and driven off in the hearse belonged to a different category of

humanity and had nothing to do with me. *They* had been struck down—
I hadn't. *They* were doomed—I wasn't. I suddenly became convinced that
I had a right to draw this distinction. I was playing an enigmatic role
here, shunning the limelight as far as possible, but when the play was
over I wasn't going to end up like them. Most of them had been carried
here by the tide of war and brutally dashed against this cliff by events
beyond their control. Now they were living out their final weeks and
months. Where were they from? What had their circumstances been? It
took time to discover their origins: dilapidated districts of Vienna; dark,
dank streets in Salzburg (the so-called Mozart city, where minor ailments
could rapidly become deadly diseases); small provincial towns where the
less well-off, if they were not careful, were in danger of ruin even before
they were grown up. Lung disease flourished in the post-war period as
never before. Years of hunger and despair had prepared all these people
for lung disease, for the hospital, and finally for Grafenhof. They came
from all ranks of society and all walks of life, and they belonged to both
sexes. Once they had been identified as sufferers from lung disease, they
were shunted off here into isolation, because the idea of lung disease or
tuberculosis—to say nothing of open tuberculosis of the lung—caused
panic among the inhabitants of the so-called healthy world, and still does.
Nothing aroused greater fear. It was only later that I learned at first hand
what it meant to have lung disease oneself, to be *positive*. Whether I believed
it or not, the result was in every case atrocious and degrading. Before I
went to Grafenhof—from the moment I knew I had to go there—I didn't
divulge the fact to anyone. Had I told anyone in Salzburg that I was going
to Grafenhof, I should have been finished. I'm not sure that my family
knew what Grafenhof really meant. They didn't ask themselves the question; they hadn't time, being wholly taken up with my mother's illness,
which had been diagnosed as fatal. Although I couldn't explain it, the
name Grafenhof had struck terror into my heart from my earliest childhood.
To go to Grafenhof was worse than going to the notorious prisons at Stein,
Suben, or Garsten. One didn't have anything to do with a person suffering
from lung disease—one shunned him. Anybody who contracted lung disease was well advised to keep quiet about it. Even within families the sick
were isolated, indeed outlawed; and my family was no exception. But in
their case it wasn't possible to concentrate on my lung disease, since they
were naturally more concerned about my mother's cancer of the womb,
which had already entered its most dangerous and painful phase. She had

been confined to bed for months, and the pain was now so severe that it could no longer be suppressed or even relieved by the morphine injections which were administered at least once an hour. I had told her I was going to Grafenhof, but she probably no longer knew what that meant. When I said good-bye to her, she knew she was going to die shortly. It was not certain whether she would live for another six months or a year. Her heart remained strong, even when she had become thoroughly emaciated and no more than skin and bone. Her mind was not impaired by this most terrible of all diseases, and she remained lucid to the end. The end was slow to come, though we all longed for it, because we could not bear to see her suffering. When I took my leave of her before going to Grafenhof, where a new phase of uncertainty was about to begin, I read her a few of my poems. She wept—we both wept. I embraced her, then packed my case and vanished. Would I ever see her again? She was *forced* to listen to my poems—I gave her no choice. I was sure they were good. They were the compositions of a desperate eighteen-year-old to whom they seemed to be all he had left in the world. I had already taken refuge in writing. I wrote and wrote, hundreds and hundreds of poems—I don't know how many. I existed only through writing. My grandfather had been a writer, and he was now dead. Now *I* was entitled to write; now I myself had the chance. This was my goal, and I now had the means to attain it. I threw all my energies into writing, exploiting the whole world by transforming it into poetry. My poems may have been worthless, but to me they meant everything. There was nothing more important in the entire world. I no longer possessed anything but the possibility of writing poetry. Hence it was the most natural thing in the world for me to recite my poems to my mother before saying good-bye to her. She was being cared for at home, since we knew what it would mean to put her at the hospital's mercy. We didn't have the strength to say anything: we just wept and pressed our temples together. The journey to Grafenhof, along the gloomy Schwarzach Valley, was the most depressing of my life. In my luggage was a bundle of papers containing my latest poems. Soon, I reflected, I'll have nothing in the world that means anything to me, nothing to cling to, but this bundle of poems. Tuberculosis! Grafenhof! And a mother who's incurably sick and given up by the doctors! Once more, so soon after my grandfather's death, my guardian and my grandmother were being put to the test. And I was on my way to a place with the terrifying name of *Grafenhof*. I hardly dared to ask the way. Two hundred yards from the building there were any number of notices with the words HALT! SANATORIUM. PROHIBITED ROAD. This was a prohibition that no healthy person would willingly ignore. The sanatorium itself displayed a notice which read HALT. NO ENTRY! I was entering a realm of despair, having left another behind me. Death reigned over both. It is difficult today to indicate what it felt like, and to do so I have to overcome the greatest psychological resistance. I can no longer describe the state of mind I was in, and I will refrain from going beyond the essential facts because I find it unbearably distressing to cross the border into truth or any part of the truth. When I entered Grafenhof I was entering hell, though at first I thought this was what I had escaped from. I thought I had left hell and all its unbearable horrors behind me and was suddenly surrounded by order and calm. I thought I had escaped from an inhuman, though divinely ordained, chaos: I even had a bad conscience at having left my family and my terminally sick mother behind with all their appalling suffering and wretchedness. I felt ashamed at coming here, to a place where I would be *properly cared for*. I had left the *chaos* of a helpless family, a family that had been almost totally destroyed, and sought *care* for myself. Here I suddenly found myself getting regular meals. I was generally left in peace and could actually sleep properly, something I had not been able to do at home for weeks: none of us had been able to sleep, since we were all preoccupied with my dying mother, who needed constant medical care. Her husband and my grandmother sacrificed themselves for her in the truest sense of the word. With utter selflessness they took the whole burden upon themselves, performing all the tasks that could otherwise have been performed only in a clinic. For months they gave her injections, in the end at hourly intervals, both day and night, and carried out all the other duties which one can understand and appreciate only if one has had to do them oneself or has seen them done with one's own eyes. What casual judgments are made by those who have never found themselves in such a situation! They do not know what it is to *suffer*. After all, it was not long since I had lost my grandfather, the person dearest to me. Six months later I knew for certain that I was going to lose my mother, the person who was closest to me after my grandfather. It was with this knowledge that I had set off for Grafenhof, carrying the cardboard suitcase which my mother and I had used during the war to collect potatoes from the peasants and take them home. You're going to recuperate, my mother had said. See that you get well. I can still hear her saying these words, I can hear them today just as clearly as I heard them then—so sincere, yet so devastating! At the end of the war we all thought we had escaped, and so we felt safe. The fact that we had survived in 1945 made us secretly happy, despite the horrors we had to endure, which were trifling by comparison with what others had endured. We had been through a great deal of suffering but had been spared the worst. We had had much to endure but not the unendurable. We had undergone many ordeals but not the most terrible. Yet now, a few years after the war, we found that we had not escaped at all. Now at last the blow came. It had caught up with us. It was as though we were being called to account. And we too were not going to be allowed to survive. I had left my mother's death room and travelled to Grafenhof, only to move into a death house, a building where death will be domiciled as long as it remains standing. This building was full of death rooms, and it accommodated many death candidates, though not only death candidates. People were constantly dying here, though naturally I was less concerned about them than I was about my mother. I looked into these death rooms, but I was not shattered by the experience. The sight of them did not destroy me, nor did the sight of the dead. Grafenhof was at first reassuring rather than shocking. But this feeling of reassurance was born of self-deception. For a day or two I was not afraid to breathe, but then I was obliged to admit to myself that I had been mistaken. Life is nothing but a penal sentence, I told myself. You have to endure this sentence, this life-sentence. The world is a penitentiary where there is little freedom of movement. My hopes have turned out to be a delusion. As soon as you are discharged you will be re-entering the same penitentiary. You are just a convict, nothing more. If people tell you that this is not true, just listen and keep quiet. Remember that when you were born you were sentenced to life imprisonment and that your parents are to blame. But don't indulge in any facile reproaches. Whether you like it or not, you must obey the prison regulations to the letter. If you don't obey, things will be made harder for you. Share your imprisonment with your fellow convicts, but never ally yourself with the warders. These precepts came to me automatically at the time, rather like a prayer. I still remember them today and often repeat them to myself. They have lost none of their validity. Despite the clumsiness of their formulation they embody an essential truth. But we are not always prepared to accept these precepts; we often forget them, perhaps for years on end. But then they come back to us and make everything clear again. Having the Salzburg hospital and Grossgmain behind me, I was basically prepared for Grafenhof.

I had been through the elementary school of sickness, and also the middle school. I had mastered the multiplication tables of sickness and death, and now I was attending classes on the higher mathematics. It was admittedly a science that had always attracted me, and now I found myself studying it obsessively. For a long time I had subordinated everything else to this discipline. I had chanced upon it automatically, though circumstances were bound to lead me to it sooner or later. It is the discipline which embraces all others. I had become absorbed in it and had progressed quite naturally from being a defenceless victim to being an observer of the victim, namely myself, and at the same time of all the other victims. It was vital to preserve the distance between the observer and the victim, since this afforded me the only chance I had to save my existence. I observed my own despair and the despair of others, though I could not control it, let alone switch it off. The strictest rules were in force here, similar to those I knew from other institutions. Anyone who ignored them was punished, in extreme cases by immediate discharge, which was not in any patient's interest. Again and again people were summarily discharged—whether rightly or wrongly I cannot say—but those who were discharged usually perished in a very short time, because they were no longer under supervision: unacquainted with the dangerous and deadly nature of their disease, they were bound to perish in the brutal world outside, the so-called healthy world, which had no real understanding of their condition. Having been discharged from the sanatorium, they naturally surrendered briefly to their hunger for life and existence, only to come to grief amid the incomprehension, ignorance, and ruthlessness of healthy society. I know of countless examples of sick patients who were summarily discharged or released at their own risk—who discharged themselves, in other words—and survived for only a short time. But I was not concerned with such people here. We rose at six, had breakfast at seven, and at eight we were all lying in the sun-room, where the ward-round took place at nine. For years the performance remained unchanged, and so did the cast—and not only the medical cast, for some of the patients remained there for years. Most patients had to spend years in Grafenhof, not just weeks or months, as they may have fondly believed when they were admitted. Being admitted to Grafenhof meant in most cases spending years in isolation, being kept waiting—being remanded in custody, as it were. It was a blessing for the new arrival not to know how long he was going to spend here, for had he known he would have refused to co-operate. A small number were allowed out after three months, though very few of them stayed out. Most returned for a second spell, usually a long spell lasting for years. Even if one had only a ludicrous shadow on the lung, as I had, a three-month stay at Grafenhof was the minimum one could expect: the victim was told this straight away, after being deceived by the health authority. Three months was the shortest term, which could then be extended to six or nine months, and so on. Some patients had been at Grafenhof for three or more years; these were the so-called old lags, who could be recognized at once by their bearing, by their ruthless and cold-blooded treatment of other patients, and by their attitude to the doctors. There was no pretending where they were concerned; they never left anyone in any doubt about what they knew. They were always on top—sicker and more helpless than all the rest, but on top—closer to death than all the rest, but on top. Inwardly and outwardly repulsive, they were feared as much by the doctors as by the other patients. With time they had acquired rights which others were denied and no one could dispute, not even the doctors and the sisters. The fact that they were closest to death gave them certain prerogatives. They were the real rulers and tormentors of their fellow patients. A newcomer did not have an easy time: being at the bottom of the heap, he had to see to it that he worked his way up from a totally unprivileged position to one near the top. This was a laborious process lasting not just months but years. Most patients, however, did not have this amount of time—they died too soon. They would appear and be seen for a time, observing all the rules, and then they would vanish, first into the smaller rooms of the institution and finally into the ambulance, which took them to the general hospital in Schwarzach, where shortly afterwards they died. For in principle the authorities at Grafenhof were reluctant to have people dying on the premises; and if a patient's death was imminent, they got rid of him and removed him from sight by dispatching him to Schwarzach, whence the reassuring message reached them that he had died in the hospital. However, not every death could be predicted; and if the unforeseen happened, the hearse would do a circuit of the yard, eyed suspiciously from all sides. Even today I can hear the slamming of its rear doors—sometimes I hear it quite suddenly in the middle of the day. After the ward-round the patients set about spitting all the more eagerly. They would converse with one another, even though all talk was strictly forbidden during periods in the sun-room. Opinions were exchanged about medical matters, and the doctors came in for criticism, though not invariably. In general the patients

were too lethargic to move: they all lay under their blankets, stiff and
exhausted, staring straight ahead, at the six-thousand-foot Heukareck, the
grey, unscalable rock-face which to me became a symbol of fate. At first
they had to conform, and then they had to find a way of living in the
institution, though the possibilities were limited. I don't know how many
patients there were—possibly two hundred at a rough estimate. Half of
them were women; they were accommodated on the first floor and strictly
segregated from the men, who occupied the second floor. On the ground
floor there were several so-called loggias for special patients—special because of the nature of their illness or because of the privileges they enjoyed
by virtue of their reputation or social status. These included both men and
women. I saw them only at a distance, from the staircase. At the beginning
of my stay I was in a room for twelve patients. I had no prospect of leaving
it—and why should I? I gradually got to know the names and characters
of my fellow patients. Despite the fact that my grandfather had brought
me up to be entirely self-sufficient and had used every means at his disposal
to develop my individuality, I had in recent years learnt the art of mixing
with others and had in fact mastered it better than most people. I was
used to communal living, having imbibed the rudiments at the boarding
house and then perfected my knowledge in the hospital. I had no difficulties
here, since I was accustomed to living with a large number of other people
and sharing the same opportunities and restrictions, the same difficult
conditions. When I arrived at Grafenhof, therefore, it was easy for me to
fit into the community, once more a community of suffering. With the
exception of the doctor of law, all the inmates of the room were apprentices
and unskilled labourers of roughly my own age, from seventeen to twenty-
two. Here too life was subject to all the unpleasant conditions which arise
when people are thrown together and forced to rely on one another. Here
too suspicion, envy, and vindictiveness prevailed, but there was also a
good deal of humour and high spirits, though naturally somewhat muted
in view of the suffering these young people had to endure. The predominant
mood was one of equanimity but not of indifference. They indulged in
the kind of jokes that are commonly exchanged in such a community, but
the usual coarseness and brutality were mitigated; so too was the mirth.
The patients here guessed more than they knew, though they also knew
a good deal, having already seen a good deal. However, the young are
extremely skilful and imaginative when it comes to playing down the
unavoidable horrors which they can see quite clearly. They see them but

are unwilling to analyse them. Most people here were not confined to their beds like the patients in the hospital. They could get up and move about so long as they obeyed the rules. Within the limits imposed by the regulations they had full freedom of movement. They could leave the building and go as far as the perimeter, which was marked by fences and notices, and take walks either alone or in company with others. I attached myself to a young man about ten years older than myself—despite this difference in age he was still very youthful—whom I first saw sitting alone at the harmonium in the chapel, improvising on a theme by Bach. He was a conductor by profession and had been singled out by the sisters to accompany the daily mass. His playing struck me as remarkable and attracted me at once. I had first heard him playing on my way to the sun-room, and I had stopped and entered the chapel. At first I was too nervous to speak to him, but then I plucked up courage and introduced myself. This was the start of a friendship that has lasted until today, a friendship born of shared suffering if ever there was one. Music had led me to another human being and formed a bond between us—music, which had meant everything to me for so many years and which I had not heard for such a long time. Music had suddenly come back into my life, and in an exceptionally artistic form. I now had someone to talk to on my walks, someone who could explain things to me, who could enlighten me. He was a young man with considerable experience, who had travelled widely and seen much of the world. He had studied at the Mozarteum and then taken up an appointment in Switzerland since there was no place for him in Austria. Austria has never had room for her artists and has constantly driven them abroad quite ruthlessly, to every possible country. Here was yet another example of a phenomenon that preoccupies me continually: the artist who is despised and rejected in his own country and compelled to go into exile. Austria produces the most superb artists, in all the arts, only to drive them abroad. The most gifted are forced into exile: the artists who remain behind are those who are capable of conforming, the mediocrities and nonentities who command attention and whose narrow, petty bourgeois ambitions guide the country's artistic fortunes. The really gifted artists, the artists of genius, return to Austria sick and despairing—but always too late—when they are old or half-dead. This is an old, old story to which I never tire of drawing attention when the opportunity presents itself. At the time I did not know many artists, at least not personally, and I was quite ignorant about their careers, about what was the rule and what the exception. My friend was an extraordinarily gifted musician who seemed to have a clear head and a sharp intellect, and this is what made my conversations with him so enjoyable. Having no means, he took summer jobs as a bar pianist at Arosa, far away from the musical centres of Zurich and Lucerne, and this was the reason for his illness. He had now been at Grafenhof for many months, almost a whole year. We often sat on a bench above the women's sun-room; he would talk while I listened. I had a companion from whom I could learn much. I had long needed such a companion, one who was as able as he was. It struck me that since my grandfather's death I had had no one whom I could listen to without getting desperate, no one whom I could trust. He was a Liechtensteiner by nationality, his father having come from Liechtenstein, but he had been brought up in Salzburg. From the beginning we had many things to talk about—art, music, Austria, Salzburg, and sickness, though we did not talk much about sickness, unlike the others, who talked about little else. We did not find it necessary, for the observation of sickness and the course it followed was an obvious occupation, and we had better and more prof-itable topics of conversation: counterpoint, for instance, Bach's fugues, *The Magic Flute*, *Orpheus and Eurydice*, Richard Wagner, Debussy. Since my friend knew Italian, as well as English, French, and Russian, I asked him to teach me Italian, believing that it would be useful to me as a singer. I had not yet given up my ambition to become a singer—indeed, I pursued it with the greatest intensity, having learned about a number of singers, some of them famous, who had suffered from lung disease in youth but had recovered from it and gone on to practise their art for decades. Having a great cavity in the lung had not prevented one singer, years later, from singing Wotan at Bayreuth. And so almost every day we sat on the seat above the women's sun-room and had our Italian lessons—in between the compulsory rest-periods, of course—instead of walking in the grounds. After a long period of unhappiness I was happy again. I was now able to enjoy the company of someone who could join up the frayed ends of the threads which had once linked my existence with a more agreeable world. What an age it had been since I had heard words like *harmony*, *dissonance*, *romanticism*, etc.! Or the word *creative*—even the word *music* itself! All these concepts, together with thousands of others, had vanished from my mind. And now they suddenly became reference points which were quite simply essential to my existence. But these moods of elation which I experienced did nothing to change the uniform gloom which darkened every aspect of our lives and cast a pall over everything from morning till night, from the first to the last hour of every day. Everyone was acclimatized to this dreariness and gloom. At one moment I would think to myself, I'll get out of here and go back to my studies and become a singer. I would picture myself having an increasingly successful career, singing in all the world's most important concert halls and all the biggest opera houses. Then again I would think, I'll never be healthy again, I'll never get out of here, I'll give up and go to pieces and finally suffocate at Grafenhof like all the others. At one moment I would think, I'll soon be discharged from Grafenhof and be healthy again; and at another I would think, My sickness can't be halted, it'll develop quite logically until all my hopes are dashed, like those of most of the other patients. Such thoughts and feelings were by no means exceptional. No doubt they were shared by everyone else to some extent: one person's hopes might be higher than another's, one might be choked by utter hopelessness, while another's hopelessness was less extreme. And then I would look into the grey or greyish blue faces of the terminal cases as they withdrew by degrees into their private corners; I would watch them groping their way along the walls, hardly able to keep their emaciated bodies upright, taking their places at the refectory tables in their trailing dressing gowns, slumping onto their chairs with their knees bent double, unable to hold the coffee pot and pour out their coffee, having to put it down again, or not picking it up at all and waiting for someone else to serve them. And I would watch them on their way to chapel, walking slowly, close to the wall, their eyeballs bulging in blackened sockets. At such times any thought of having a future of my own would vanish into thin air. At such times I was bound to think I no longer had one. It was shameless and absurd to entertain such dreams. How many of these patients had started like me by having a shadow . . . and then an infiltration and then a cavity in the lung? By which time they were finished. To be able to say *I've only got a shadow* gave one no right to optimism; it was more like the first stage in a straight run to the grave. How often I made light of it all, remarking, *I've only got a shadow!* I was alarmed at the shamelessness and enormity of such light-hearted observations: even as I was making them I felt ashamed of myself for daring to be light-hearted. Each time I returned from the X-ray unit I allowed myself to speculate about the future: if the shadow had become smaller or stayed the same size, I had a future; if it had grown, I had none. The doctors played their cards close to the chest. It was a pure game of chance, and there was no way in which one could cheat. I'll be a singer, I would say at one moment. Then an hour later I would say, I'll never be a singer. I'll soon be discharged with a clean bill of health, I would say. Then a moment later: I'll never be discharged. I was perpetually being pulled this way and that by these terrible speculations. We were all in the same dreadful boat, trying to theorize and phantasize ourselves out of it yet convinced that we should all go down with it and perish without exception. As I sat on the seat overlooking the women's sun-room I would wonder whether I was perhaps being punished for my audacity in having done my sudden about-turn and taken an apprenticeship instead of continuing on my way to the grammar school. It was while unloading potatoes at the shop that I had first caught my illness—or, as my grandfather had said, taken delivery of it. I had not been brave; I had simply got above myself. But what good did such thoughts do me now? I've survived the hospital, I told myself; I've survived Grossgmain; I've even survived the last rites— and so I'll survive Grafenhof. When my mother dies (for I had no doubt that her death was imminent), I'll be completely alone, I thought. I'll have no relative left who matters at all, except my grandmother. I waited for it to happen. Every day I went to the porter's lodge to ask whether there was any mail for me, but there never was. No sign of life reached me from Salzburg. My people had always been lazy about letter-writing. There was a deathly silence between here and Salzburg, between me and my family. If only they had written to me once a week! But they did not write. All the time I was at Grafenhof I did not receive a single letter from them. "Lazy about letter-writing" was a phrase I detested when I was the one affected. The period I spent at home on returning from Grossgmain, the so-called convalescent home, the death hotel from whose balconies one had a view of the grave-mounds in the churchyard—this interim period before I left for Grafenhof had been depressing. It had been a period of leave-taking, for during this period I had to take leave of everything. I could now count up all the things I had taken leave of. I had wandered through the streets of Salzburg, gone up onto the hills in the city, and repeatedly visited my grandfather's grave. Wherever I went it was to take leave of something. And when I returned home, hungry and exhausted, weary of life in the truest sense, it was to take leave yet again of my mother. The whole flat was filled with the odour of putrefaction emanating from her and permeating everything. She knew she was soon going to die, and she knew of what. No one spoke about it, but she was too intelligent, too perceptive, for anything to escape her. She bore her illness without making reproaches—to those around her, to the world, or to God. She stared at the walls, but she felt no hatred. For six whole months she had suffered *unimaginable* pain, which drugs could no longer eliminate and scarcely relieve. She was given increasing doses of methadone and morphine, and she was tended night and day by her husband and my grandmother until they were utterly exhausted. Her children—my brother and sister and myself—were anxious but uncomprehending onlookers, and naturally we were just a nuisance most of the time. We saw everything but understood nothing. We were incapable of understanding. My mother's illness too was the work of a *negligent* doctor, just as my grandfather's had been. The doctor had acted too late and too irresponsibly. Yet he did not blench when my guardian called him to book and reproached him with this fatal negligence. Doctors shrug off such reproaches and proceed to the next business. The surgeon murdered my grandfather, and the gynecologist has killed my mother, I told myself. But what I told myself was ridiculous: it was silly and naïve, and there was a tinge of megalomania about it. I sat on the tree-stump between two beeches and watched the men taking their walks below. They always took walks at the regulation times, when the women were in the sun-room. The rules stated that the men had to be in the sun-room when the women were taking their walks and that the women had to go for walks when the men were in the sun-room. In this way the authorities prevented men and women from walking together, and so the two sexes never met. If they wanted to meet, they had to flout the regulations and run the risk of being immediately discharged. I sat on the tree-stump and reflected on the time I had spent in Salzburg between Grossgmain and Grafenhof. It had been a terrible time, filled with grief and humiliation: I had walked round the city, following the routes I had taken with my grandfather and walking through the streets that had led me to my music lessons. I had even ventured, hesitantly and without drawing attention to myself, into the Scherzhauserfeld Project, though I did not visit Podlaha's shop. I kept at a safe distance from it and observed the customers. I knew them, but I would not have dared to enter the shop under any circumstances. I did not even dare to speak to the customers I knew, who passed within fifty to a hundred yards of me. Whenever there was a risk of meeting one of them, of being confronted by one of them, I hid. I was a failure, I had been a failure before: I had caught a ridiculous chill while unloading potatoes in a snow-storm and been taken ill. I had left the community of the Scherzhauserfeld Project—I had been expelled and in all probability forgotten. How I would have loved to talk to these people, to make myself known! But the instinct for self-preservation inhibited me, with the result that I was once again isolated and even more depressed, thrown back into a double isolation. I had been a failure from the start, at home, as a child, as a youth, as an apprentice—I had failed everywhere and all the time. This thought depressed me; it was as though I were running the gauntlet wherever I went in the city—in all these streets and among all these people I had been a failure. I could not help being a failure, I had to tell myself; it was my nature. I had had music lessons from Frau Keldorfer and Professor Werner in the Pfeifergasse and I had been a failure. I had been a failure at the main school, at the boarding house, at the grammar school. Wherever I had been I had left under a cloud—expelled, humiliated, excluded, thrown out. I still have these feelings when I walk around Salzburg. I feel as though I were still running the gauntlet thirty years later. As I sat on the tree-stump I could see myself knocking on all those doors and not one being opened to me; I could see myself being constantly turned away, never accepted or taken in. My demands had never been accepted. My claims were the megalomaniac claims of a young person who goes on pitching them higher and higher, so that they quite simply cannot be accepted—megalomaniac claims on life, society, everything. And so, arrogant and demanding though I was, I had nevertheless been forced to exist with my head down. How did all this happen, I asked, chronologically? And I proceeded to unpack everything bit by bit, all the things that had been packed up and firmly tied. I now had the quiet I needed. And when I had unpacked it all—the war and its aftermath, my grandfather's sickness and death, my own illness, my mother's illness, my family's despair, the depressing conditions under which they lived, the hopelessness of their existence—I packed it all together again and tied it up. But I could not leave this firmly tied packet lying around: I had to pick it up and take it with me. I still carry it around with me, and sometimes I unpack the contents, then repack them and tie the packet up again. It does not make me any the wiser. I shall never be any the wiser, and that is what is so depressing. And when I unpack it all in the presence of witnesses, as I am doing now, by bringing out all these crude and brutal sentences, banal and sentimental as they often are, without any of the compunction I might have over different sentences, I do not feel the slightest shame. The writer is always devoid

of shame. Only a person who has no shame is qualified to take hold of
sentences and bring them out and throw them down. Only the most
shameless writer is authentic. But that too is a delusion, like everything
else. I sat on the tree-stump and stared at my existence, an existence I
loved fervently yet could not help hating. During the interval between
Grossgmain and Grafenhof I had taken the commercial assistants' examination at the Chamber of Commerce. I wanted to bring my apprenticeship
to a proper conclusion. I was entitled to take the examination, and I passed
it. I had to identify seventy-two kinds of tea which were laid out in front
of me, and I did not make any mistakes. I was asked whether it was
permissible to fill a GRAF bottle with Maggi at a customer's request, and
I said no, which was the right answer: bottles with brand names may be
filled only with the appropriately branded product. This was something I
had learnt, and it helped me to pass the examination. But what good was
my commercial diploma to me now? The fact was that with my diseased
lungs I could not be employed in the food trade. I was condemned to be
a burden on my family in the Radetzkystrasse, with a small social security
pension. I was condemned to idleness, entirely cut off from everything.
My only hope was to wait for the ticket to Grafenhof, to go into an
institution—moreover, into an institution which was universally dreaded
and reputed to be the most terrible of all. To tell the truth, I could hardly
wait to board the train for Grafenhof. When I received the ticket I could
not help feeling happy. Whether or not I wanted to be, I actually was
happy—I was happy to have the chance to go to this dreadful institution.
That is the truth of the matter, however nonsensical it may seem. Once
I'm at Grafenhof, I thought—which is perhaps not as bad as it's made out
to be—I'll have lots of time and fresh air, time to think about what comes
next. In Salzburg, with my family around, I had no time and no fresh
air. As long as I was in Salzburg I was close to suffocation, and during
all this time I had only one thought in my head: suicide. But I was too
much of a coward to commit suicide, and I was also too full of curiosity
about everything. Throughout my life I have been consumed with a shameless curiosity which has repeatedly put a stop to thoughts of suicide. I
should have killed myself on innumerable occasions had I not been held
back on the surface of the earth by my shameless curiosity. All my life I
have had the utmost admiration for suicides. I have always considered them
superior to me in every way. I am a good-for-nothing who clings to life,
no matter how dreadful and valueless it is, no matter how drab and

disgusting, no matter how cheap and contemptible. Instead of killing myself I go in for all kinds of unworthy compromises, debasing myself before all and sundry and surviving ignominiously, taking refuge in my own feebleness of character as in a foul-smelling fur that can still keep me warm. Sitting on the tree-stump, I could see the utter absurdity of my existence. I could see myself walking to the cemetery and back to visit my grandfather. All that remained of our travel plans was a mound of earth, an empty room at one end of the flat, my grandfather's clothes still hanging untouched on the door and in the wardrobe. And slips of paper still on his desk, with notes on his work, but also notes about quite trivial matters he had to attend to: "Don't forget to sew on shirt buttons"—"Shoe repairs"—"Paint wardrobe door"—"Remind Herta about firewood" (Herta being my mother). What did all these slips of paper amount to now? Should I now sit down at his desk? I had no right, I thought, to take any books from his shelves—*not yet*, at any rate—for instance, Works of Goethe, volume 4, or Shakespeare's *King Lear*, the poems of Dauthendey, Christian Wagner, or Hölderlin, or Schopenhauer's *Parerga and Paralipomena*. I dare not touch anything. It was as though the owner of the room and its highly personal contents might appear at any moment and demand to know what I was doing. This was where the unsuccessful, neglected writer had sat down every day at three o'clock in the morning and started work. I could not fail to see how *senseless* it had all been. He had seen this too, though he had never admitted it, not in so many words, but he had been conscious of it all the time. Within the framework of a senseless situation he had imposed the utmost discipline on himself and established a working routine which was uniquely his and became increasingly idiosyncratic. It is a system which I recognize as my own, consisting of getting up in the morning to face a pointless task, then setting to work and thinking oneself into bitter pointlessness. Was I now entitled to take up where he had left off, to adopt his system and make it my own? Yet it was not only his; it had been mine too right from the beginning. It meant waking up, setting to work, and carrying on to the point of exhaustion, till one's eyes could no longer see anything or no longer wanted to see anything, then stopping, switching off the light, and giving oneself over to nightmares, surrendering to nightmares as though they were part and parcel of a uniquely solemn ritual. Then repeating the performance next day, with the greatest precision and urgency, *pretending that it was all significant*. Sitting on the tree-stump, facing the Heukareck, I reflected on

the infamous world I had left behind, from which I had detached myself
provisionally and with many reservations in order to view it from my own
angle and through my own personal viewfinder. This world now appeared
to me exactly as my grandfather had described it to me when I was still
incredulous and unwilling to endorse his description. I had listened to
him but been unwilling to believe him, at least in the early years. Later,
however, I had evidence that his assertions were correct: for the most part
the world is nauseating, and when we look into it we are looking into a
cesspit. Or was he mistaken? I now had an opportunity to examine my
grandfather's assertions. I had an obsessive desire to gather the evidence
in my head, and so I began a strenuous search for the evidence, tracking
it down in every direction, in every corner of the city of my youth and its
surroundings. My grandfather had been right in his judgment of the world:
it was indeed a cesspit, but one which engendered the most intricate and
beautiful forms if one looked into it long enough, if one's eye was prepared
for such strenuous and microscopic observation. It was a cesspit which
yielded up its own natural beauties to the sharp revolutionary gaze. Yet
whoever contemplates it for long, whoever spends decades gazing into it,
eventually becomes exhausted and dies, or plunges headlong into it. My
grandfather had described nature as cruel—and it was. He had described
human beings as desperate and vicious—and they were. I was always on
the look-out for counter-evidence, thinking to prove him wrong in this
or that particular, but I failed: all the evidence I assembled in my head
confirmed his views. He had indicated to me where the truth lay, and I
unearthed it, thus confirming his indication. Sitting on the tree-stump, I
rehearsed the evidence as I recalled it. This was my way of relaxing—
recapitulating my investigations and recalling them to mind. I was already
a past master at investigations of this kind. Whenever I chose I could call
up my memories and subject them to repeated scrutiny. My own history
was by now a universal history, with thousands upon thousands—if not
millions—of dates stored up in my brain and retrievable at a moment's
notice. My grandfather had made me aware of the truth, not just his truth
but mine too—universal truth; but at the same time he had made me
aware of all the errors this truth contained. Truth is always wrong, even
if it is one hundred percent truth. Every error is pure truth. With this
knowledge I could make progress and carry on without having to abandon
my plans. This is the mechanism that keeps me alive and makes my
existence viable. My grandfather had always told the truth *and* been totally

wrong, just as I am wrong, just as everybody is wrong. We are mistaken if we believe we are in possession of the truth, just as we are mistaken if we believe we are in error. Absurdity is the only way forward. It was a way I knew, the only one that led anywhere. Sitting on the tree-stump, I took pleasure in going over the sum that my grandfather had set me, adding up the columns of figures with the same precision I had employed as an apprentice in the shop—and with the same lack of concern for the customer. We go into the shop of life and buy goods, and these goods have to be paid for. The shopkeeper does not miscalculate. All the figures add up correctly, and there is only one correct price. Sitting on the tree-stump, I pondered my origins, asking myself whether I really ought to be interested in knowing where I came from, whether or not I should risk unearthing the facts, whether or not I had the courage to submit myself to a full investigation. It was something I had never done before: it had always been forbidden, and I had always recoiled from it myself, from removing one layer after another and *getting to the bottom*. I had never felt up to it; I had felt too weak and at the same time inadequately equipped for the task. And what material did I have in my hands or in my head with which to embark upon such an expedition, save a few blurred and indistinct facts, a few hints vouchsafed by ill-humoured informants? Was I now in the mood to surrender myself, with only myself as a witness? To do what I had never dared to do under the eyes of my family, let alone my mother: to reconstruct my father's origins at least? To this day I know nothing about my father except that he was a fellow pupil of my mother's in the bottom class at the elementary school and that he died a violent death at the age of forty-three at Frankfurt-on-the-Oder, having fathered another five children in Germany. He died in 1943, but the way he died is not known to *me*. Some say he was beaten to death, others that he was shot—by whom or by which side I do not know. I have meanwhile grown accustomed to living with this uncertainty, never having had the courage to penetrate the human and political fog surrounding his death. My mother refused to say a word about my father—I do not know why, and so I have to rely on guesswork. Everything connected with my father has always been guesswork. Since he *was* my father, I have often asked myself the question *Who was this man?* But it is a question I have never been able to answer. How big a crime or crimes must my natural father have committed for me to be forbidden to mention his name in front of the family, even in front of my grandfather? I was forbidden to utter the name *Alois*. Eight

years ago I traced a woman who had been a friend of his at school. She
had been a class-mate of my mother's and it transpired that she had known
my father as well. I went so far as to arrange a time for us to meet, and
she for her part agreed to tell me about my father. However, on the day
before we were due to meet I came across a horrific picture in the newspaper—a picture of two decapitated bodies on the Salzburg exit from the
Autobahn. My mother's school friend, the only person who could have
told me anything about my father, had been killed in an accident. This
horror picture made one thing quite clear to me: I must not ask any more
questions about my father. He was a farmer's son and had trained as a
carpenter. The letters he wrote my mother were said to be full of lies. He
never acknowledged me and refused to pay a penny towards my keep. I
can see myself at the age of seven or eight going to the town hall at
Traunstein, holding my mother's hand, to have a blood sample taken to
establish the paternity of Alois Zuckerstätter. The blood sample confirmed
paternity, but my father could not be traced, and so he paid no allowance
for me. My mother's revenge often took the form of sending *me* to the
town hall to collect the five marks which the state paid out—monthly!
She did not recoil from sending me, a child, straight to hell with the
words *This'll show you how much you're worth!* Naturally I cannot forget
this—that my own mother, in order to avenge herself on the man who
had deserted her, should punish her own child, who was also his, by
sending it to hell with such diabolical words, the most diabolical words
imaginable. I can still hear her saying them. I know the full extent and
the full depth of despair, having made these journeys to the town hall at
Traunstein, these journeys into hell. Did my mother realize? Was my
father beaten to death or shot? Naturally I am still exercised by this question
today. In 1945, a few months after the end of the war, I succeeded, on
my own initiative, in tracing my father's father. He was living in a cellar
in Itzling, a suburb of Salzburg near the railway, in the cold, damp cellar
of a house which belonged to one of his sons, one of my father's brothers.
I never saw these brothers. I had no interest in meeting them—why should
I have? I knew of their existence but did not want anything to do with
them. This old man, my father's father, was already nearing seventy, and
I recently read in the newspaper that he had just died at the age of a
hundred and four. I imagined at the time, and still do, that he probably
stuck it out all those years in that cold, damp cellar. He spoke of my
father as though he had been an animal. He spoke of all his sons as though

they were animals. My father had been *long gone*, he told me, sitting on a kind of throne amid an immense pile of dirty washing and general squalor. In this basement room stood a huge four-poster bed with heavy velvet drapes; and since both the throne and the bed were carved from the same hard wood and were both equally outlandish, it occurred to me to wonder whether this tasteless furniture had been constructed and carved by my father, who after all had been a carpenter. But I did not ask. My paternal grandfather, whom I saw only on this one occasion, kept on repeating that my father had gone to Germany, where he had fathered five children, but that he had been *long gone*. He kept on saying that his son had married, adding, He got married in Germany and had five children, but he's been long gone. My grandfather then went to a small, rickety table which did not match the other furniture, opened a drawer in it, took out a coloured photograph, and he handed it to me. It was a portrait of my father, and it was so like me that I had a fright. I put the picture in my pocket and raced home. I was quite out of control and described my adventure to my mother—or, rather, I tried to describe it; but she would not let me, for as soon as I started to tell her that I had traced my father's father she began to swear at me and curse me. I had been careless enough to show her the photograph, and the result of my carelessness was that she snatched the photograph out of my hand and threw it into the stove. After this row, which I remember as the worst row of my whole life, I never mentioned my father at home. I never broached the subject again. I had to content myself with speculating on *who* he might have been—what kind of man, what kind of character. This in fact gave me great scope. It is not without significance that it was my mother herself who revealed to me exactly where I had been conceived. What reason could she have had for this disclosure, in view of the fact that she later refused even to be reminded of my father? My mother's school friend, who was the wife of a carter at Henndorf, would undoubtedly have been able to tell me much more, though not everything, and I would have known more than the precious little I know now. With this small amount of knowledge, which becomes more and more pathetic the older I get, it is pointless to institute any enquiry about my father. But do I want to? Is it not a positive advantage to know so little as to amount to virtually nothing about my procreator, to go on guessing about him and turning this guesswork quite simply into an end in itself? Were my family, including my grandfather, right or wrong to eliminate my father from my life? The question remains open; the question of their guilt remains on the files. And my guesses and suspicions continue, amounting all in all to a perpetual and often overwhelming need to impeach my family. But they are all dead, and there is no point in calling them to account. To pass sentence on ghosts is absurd, ludicrous, petty and unworthy. And so I will leave them in peace. However, I go on plucking all the strings of this family instrument in order to hear the sound it makes, no matter how many right or wrong notes I play. They deserve to have their strings plucked, and I freely confess that those which produce the most jarring dissonances are the ones I find most provocative and in any case most pleasing. I would lie in my bed by the door of the dormitory with the covers pulled up to my chin while the others slept and see myself trying to clear the undergrowth from around my origins, but my unremitting efforts were of no avail, since the further I penetrated into the thicket, the deeper the darkness became and the more impenetrable the undergrowth. Helpless as I was and always had been from my earliest childhood, I was increasingly exposing myself to the possibility of being harmed. But I would not be deflected from my futile attempts to force light into the darkness by every possible means, even though I was no stranger to the nightmare it brought on. Where did my grandfather in fact come from? And my grandmother? On both my father's side and my mother's? Where did they all come from, these people who had me on their consciences and from whom I demanded enlightenment? When I called to them they vanished like spectres. I tried to intercept them at every possible turn and cut off their retreat; but they were too quick, too adroit, too cunning in fact, and always eluded me when I thought I had hold of them. They did not answer to their names, they did not understand what I was saying when I addressed them, and they began to speak in a different language, one that I did not understand. I was naïve enough to believe that I could expect each of them to supply a story which I could attach to my own story in my head. I was wrong. I thought that all I needed to do was to call to them wherever I could get hold of them, wherever I could confront them, and that I should then get the information I wanted, the instant truth. I was even naïve enough to imagine that I could put to them the kind of questions that are put in court and get a clear answer every time, without any impertinent contradictions. Though I never stopped putting my questions, I never got answers to them; or if I did get an answer, it turned out to be quite unsatisfactory—a downright bare-faced lie. I fancied I had a right to put my questions and a right to have them answered, and so I went on putting them in my pathetic, ignorant way and was desolated to hear nothing but an echo. Had I put enough questions, I asked myself as I lay in bed—at least to those people I had lived with for some time? The answer was no, I had not. I had repeatedly saved questions up for later, shelved them, delayed asking them, till in the end it was too late. There are so many questions I ought to have asked my grandfather, my grandmother, and my mother, I thought, all kinds of questions; but now it's too late. When we question the dead, we simply display the criminal futility of the survivor who is always intent upon securing his own position. I had had ample time to ask my questions, I reflected, and I had not asked them, not even the important ones. Suddenly it became clear to me what had happened: they had prevented me from asking these questions. They had expected them and, being afraid, had done everything to prevent me from asking them. In the end they had managed to leave the world without having to give me the answers, leaving me with a thicket, a wilderness, a steppe, where I had every prospect of perishing through hunger and thirst, of simply being annihilated. They had had their answers pat but had not given them. They were unwilling to give them, probably because they themselves had been denied answers to their questions and so took revenge by withholding their answers when their turn came. But was I really interested in my origins? Was I really interested in these guardians of secrets who had taken refuge in death, vanishing from the scene at the end of their lives, vanishing into thin air, but leaving their secrets behind for me to speculate on, secrets with which I had nightly intercourse as I lay in bed? I do not know. The questions remained, multiplying as time went on, as my existence became more unmanageable and my craving for enlightenment more intense. How could one put one's present existence to the test while knowing nothing about the foundations on which it rested? My existence was based in large measure upon ignorance, not ineptitude. But where was I to find evidence—legally admissible evidence, so to speak—which would stand up to my own scrutiny? I had never ceased to gather evidence. My whole life had been geared to finding evidence about my existence, and although I had pursued it with varying degrees of intensity, I had always been consistently committed to my search. But even when I did have evidence in my hands and in my head, it was never sound enough; it proved to be unusable and misleading and only took me backwards. Of course I also examined my motives for wanting evidence about my origins. There were times when I despised myself for my single-minded insistence on evidence, because I knew that it was not absolutely essential unless I wanted to sit in judgment and pass sentence, to make pronouncements about what was right when I myself had no rights whatever. But if I persist in my curiosity, I thought, I shall learn something new, something that will explain everything. I spent whole nights watching my sleeping companions and at the same time brooding on my origins. I got used to this practice but had not yet developed it into a method. When for some reason I could not sleep and knew that sleep would not come, I would return to the thicket and try to clear the undergrowth; but it could not be cleared. In the obscurity of the thicket I recognized people by the way they behaved, not by their faces, which were invisible. But these people in my story refused to become involved in my game. They saw through my motives for embarking on my expedition and showed their contempt, wherever they encountered me, by immediately withdrawing. I was cautious in approaching my fellow patients, just as they were cautious in approaching me. Like me, they had an instinct for self-preservation and kept their distance. Though one of their number, I was an observer rather than a member of the company which peopled this stuffy building. On one side of me were the doctors, who matched my distrust by their arrogance and inactivity, simply keeping the medical machine ticking over; on the other side were the patients, who did not—and could not—acknowledge me as one of themselves. They were unable to size me up, and in any case I was probably a bird of passage whom it was not worth getting involved with, too light-weight to be a proper patient who might eventually be a comrade in death. For a time I had tried mixing with them, but it had not been a success, and so I once more had to draw my horns in and resume my reserve. I lacked their wit, their indifference, their viciousness—I had my own brand of wit, my own indifference, my own viciousness. I had my own brand of perversity which cut me off from them from the beginning. My decision had been made long ago: I was going to remain aloof, resist, and get out. Quite simply, I was going to get well, even though for a while I had yielded to superior force on their side. My will to exist was greater than my readiness to die, so by that token I was not one of them. This does not mean that I did not join them formally in the routine life of the institution. I took part in it just as they did, though as unobtrusively as possible; but they could not fail to notice my resistance—nor could the doctors—and this caused me difficulties. I was always the awkward one who refused to conform: the doctors left me

in no doubt about their indifference to me, and the patients left me in no
doubt about their contempt. Having burnt my fingers once, I was wary
of conforming and subordinating myself for the sake of a quiet life. I
listened to the stories they told—stories of suffering like the whole story
of humanity from the very beginning. I took my meals with them; I lined
up with them for X-rays; I forced my way with them to the outpatients'
department; I sat with them at dinner. I lay with them in the sun-room
and joined in when they inveighed against the doctors and the world in
general, and I wore the same clothes. I carried the insignia of the house
around with me: my sputum bottle and temperature chart. On Sundays I
attended chapel, not because I was a Catholic but because I was fond of
music—not just fond of it but crazy about it and still intent upon making
it the supreme justification for my existence, my only true passion, the
essence of my life. And so on Sundays I would stand by the harmonium
and sing my part in a Schubert mass, which was accompanied by my friend
the conductor. Ten to twelve patients would assemble in the chapel at six
in the morning, in their dressing gowns and cheap woollen pullovers, and
sing Schubert's mass with all the fervour of true amateurs to the greater
glory of God. Three or four of the sisters would encourage the singers,
whose pitiful voices issued from trembling, emaciated throats, relentlessly
driving them into the Kyrie and through the whole mass up to the Agnus
Dei, in which their exhaustion reached its peak. Whoever took part in the
singing found favour with the sisters, being given a warmer blanket before
other patients got one, a better bed-sheet, and a better view from the
window. At the end of the service the strains of *Great God, We Praise Thee*
rang out *fortissimo* from all these tattered, croaking throats. I would stand
there singing, screeching and croaking with the rest, my gaze fixed on
their sweating, swaying heads straining up above their grey, scrawny necks
as though clamped in a pillory. On the wall behind me were the obituaries
of the dead, and in front of me stood the living singers. They'll go on
singing until their names appear on the wall behind me, I used to think.
Then there'll be a fresh lot of singers. I would take good care that my
name did not appear on the wall, edged in black. I won't go on singing
as long as they do, I thought. I was beginning to regret volunteering for
singing duties in the chapel. I did not want to attend mass any longer,
but it was too late—the sisters should have told me what was involved.
And so I went on singing, Sunday after Sunday, always the same Schubert
mass, until I could stand it no longer, always fighting back the idea of

having my name stuck on the wall behind me. Had I not sung the Agnus
Dei the previous Sunday with someone whose name was now stuck on the
wall behind me? *Father Ooggl*, with whom I had had a conversation only
a few days before, in the garden behind the annexe, about the way a
gramophone worked, was now resplendent in bold type on the wall, with
two crossed palm-leaves under his name. You'll be singing in the choir
until you drop, I told myself, and then your name will be displayed on
the wall for a while; then one day not too far hence it'll be replaced by
another. They screeched away at *Great God, We Praise Thee* until they were
transformed into a tasteless printed card transfixed by a drawing pin. When
mass was over, the company in the chapel was convulsed by a tremendous
fit of coughing all round, from which the sisters withdrew at top speed.
The singers groped their way along the walls to the stairs and dragged
themselves up by the bannisters, hand over hand, laboriously placing one
foot in front of the other, until they reached the refectory for breakfast.
The whole building was pervaded by the aroma of coffee. After breakfast
the listless column made its way, armed with sputum bottles and temperature charts, to the sun-room in order to rest, completely exhausted
despite the early hour. Cold crept up through the floorboards and cut into
the faces of the patients. Condemned to inactivity, they all surrendered to
mindless boredom, except for my friend the conductor, who always had a
piano score on his lap, busily making notes in it. He was working at his
career, continually preparing himself for the time when he would be free,
for the concert halls and opera houses where he would appear. Sometimes
I would look at him from the side, amused to find him beating time like
a conductor. His fellow sufferers regarded him with suspicion, and the
doctors made tasteless observations when they saw him at his studies in
the sun-room. I clung to the image projected by my friend, to his optimism, to his absolute affirmation of existence. This can be the way for
me, I thought—this is the example I have to follow. There they all lay,
stertorously breathing and coughing up their lungs, victims of the lethargy
that leads to death, but my friend the conductor was putting up a fight,
behaving quite differently, and I tried to emulate him. He expectorated
too, and so did I, but not as much as the others, and neither of us was
positive. Then one day my friend was discharged—*with a clean bill of
health*—and I was once more alone. What a wonderful sound those words
had, *a clean bill of health*, and what a wonderful meaning! I now had to
go my way alone. I now got no response to anything I said—I spoke, but

got no reply. I was once more back at the beginning. The thread which linked me to art—or science—had snapped. *A clean bill of health*—that hardly ever happened, but now I had hopes that it might happen to me. This man was my model, someone who had been determined to escape, who was obsessed by existence, an artist, someone whose sights were set on the future. The shadow on my lung actually diminished and suddenly disappeared. The assistant announced to me that I was cured. I could go; *this* was no longer the place for me. I had drawn a winner! But did I want it? I could not make up my mind. I spent a few more days at the sanatorium and realized that I had been there for nine months. I had grown accustomed to Grafenhof. What awaited me at home? My mother's condition was still the same, and my family more desperate than ever. My return home was not a joyful occasion. Of course that was to be expected. I was far from welcome. My mother's death struggle was nearing its climax, and nobody had time for me. I had remembered the catastrophic state my family was in; but now things were even worse, with everyone on the point of collapse. Language is inadequate when it comes to communicating the truth, and the best the writer can offer is an approximation to the truth, a desperate and hence unreliable approximation. Language can only falsify and distort whatever is authentic. No matter how hard the writer tries, the words he uses drag everything down, misrepresenting it and turning the whole truth, once it is on paper, into a lie. I had made yet another journey into hell, this time by going in the opposite direction. A patient with tuberculosis, even when he is discharged with a clean bill of health, is obliged to present himself for examination by the doctor in charge of his case and provide a sputum sample for the lab. I took my sample along to the lab, and when I went for the result I was told I was infectious. I had *open* tuberculosis and must enter the hospital *at once*. The women at the lab told me that I must be isolated immediately—there was no possibility of a mistake. Two days after being *discharged* from Grafenhof with a *clean bill of health*, I had open tuberculosis—in other words, the dreaded cavity in the lung. I went home and told my grandmother and my guardian that I had open tuberculosis and had to enter the hospital immediately. This announcement did not produce the effect one might have expected, since naturally I constituted only a peripheral problem. It was my mother, not I, who was sick. After a meal with my grandmother and my guardian in the kitchen, the part of the flat where we took refuge, my knife and fork were immediately boiled, and I left for the hospital with only a few necessities

under my arm. We decided not to tell my mother the truth. I walked
to the hospital, which was only a few hundred yards away. The pulmonary
unit was accommodated in a number of huts and could be recognized
even at a distance by the foul smell that emanated from it. In it there
were a number of patients with lung cancer accommodated in a ward with
all the doors and windows open. There was an appalling stench in the air,
but I got used to it. A pneumothorax was performed on me, and after a
few days I was discharged with instructions to return to Grafenhof *at once.*
However, my departure was delayed, and I had to spend several weeks at
home, during which time I had to pay regular visits, at intervals of about
a week, to the best-known lung specialist in the city, who had rooms in
the Paris-Lodron-Strasse, in the second house on the right, to have air re-
injected into my pneumothorax. The patient has to lie on the bed in the
doctor's surgery while air is introduced between the diaphragm and the
diseased lung by means of a thin tube; in this way the tubercular lung
cavity is collapsed so that it can re-seal. I had often witnessed this procedure. It is painful only initially, after which the patient becomes accustomed to it and thinks no more about it. It becomes a routine experience,
and although the patient is always afraid beforehand, by the time it is
over his fear is proved to have been unfounded. However, it is not invariably
unfounded, as I was soon to discover. One day, while this highly respected
doctor (he was in fact a professor) was injecting me with air, he went over
to the telephone, leaving me on the bed with the tube in my chest, and
rang up his cook to give her instructions about his lunch. After a good
deal of to-and-fro about chives and butter and whether there should be
potatoes or not, the professor brought the debate to an end and deigned
to return to his patient on the bed. He injected a further volume of air
and then told me to step behind the X-ray screen. This was the only way
to discover how the air had been distributed. Hardly had I taken the
required position than I was seized with a fit of coughing and passed out.
I just heard the professor say, My God, I've collapsed the other lung!
When I came round, I was lying on a sofa in the corner of the room. I
heard the doctor's assistant sending away the people who were sitting in
the waiting room. When they had all gone away, I was alone with the
professor and his assistant. I was unable to move without bringing on a
fresh bout of coughing, and I could scarcely breathe. I was afraid I was
going to die, and it occurred to me how dreadful it would be to die here,
in this cold, dark, stuffy, and appallingly old-fashioned surgery, with no

one near who meant anything to me, under the horrified gaze and horrifying gestures of my amateurish tormentors. For good measure the professor had gone down on his knees in front of me, clasping his hands together and saying, *What am I to do with you?* This is a true account of what happened. I do not know how long I lay on the sofa in this condition. At all events, I was suddenly able to get up and leave the surgery, and despite the efforts of the doctor and his assistant to restrain me, I ran down the three flights of stairs into the open air. A subsequent reconstructon of events revealed that I boarded a trolleybus and went home. There I must have passed out again. I do not know for certain, but this is what I was told by my family, who took me back to the hospital immediately, to the pulmonary unit where I had been treated a few weeks earlier and which was therefore familiar to me. The professor turned up at the hospital immediately and explained to me that what had happened was *nothing out of the ordinary*. He kept on repeating this emphatically, in an excited manner and with a malignant expression on his face which carried a clear hint of menace. My pneumothorax was now ruined, thanks to the professor's debate over his luncheon menu, and something new had to be devised. It was decided to perform a pneumoperitoneum, which meant injecting air into the middle of the body just above the navel in order to apply upward pressure on both lungs. At the time this treatment was uncommon, a new technique which had hardly been tried out and which I had never heard mentioned, even at Grafenhof. The professor's ludicrous telephone converstation had ruined my pneumothorax and created a dangerous situation. Before a pneumo-peritoneum can be performed, the diaphragm has to be put out of action for some time, for a few years at least, and to this end the so-called phrenic nerve used to be cut. This required an operation, an incision being made above the collar bone with the patient fully conscious, since throughout the operation communication must be maintained between him and the surgeon. I was told that the operation on the phrenic nerve would be carried out in a few days. It would be an operation to crush the nerve, not to sever it: crushing the nerve was the latest technique, which had hardly been tried out before. The phrenic nerve would be crushed and the diaphragm inactivated for a few years, but it would eventually become active again, whereas a completely severed nerve, resulting from what had been standard practice hitherto, would not recover. I was told that this amounted to no more than a minor intervention, not a proper operation but a mere intervention, nothing to speak of from a medical point of view.

Meanwhile I had learnt, to my horror, that the surgeon who was to perform the operation was the selfsame man who had confused my grandfather's blocked and bulging bladder with a tumor and therefore had my grandfather's death on his conscience. Only a few months had elapsed since this last slip-up; however, I had no choice but to acquiesce in everything I was now to undergo, since it was unavoidable. Of course I was not in a position to understand the first thing about lung surgery—how could I be?—and had to agree to everything that was now being planned on my behalf. I reacted to it all with the equanimity of someone in shock. I had been put into one of the huts belonging to the pulmonary unit. Here too I was in a large room with at least a dozen beds, the same kind of iron beds as I had seen in the department of internal medicine on my first visit to the hospital. Everything here was familiar, though I had yet to be familiarized with the atrocious particulars of lung surgery. I could not have been in a better place for this. The huts, which dated from the war, were completely isolated from the rest of the hospital buildings. They had fallen into a state of total neglect; and in the corridors, where one had to hold a cloth to one's nose to protect oneself from the otherwise unbearable stench of the lung cancer patients, it was not uncommon to see rats, though one soon got used to the sight of these sleek, well-fed creatures scurrying across the floor. I can still remember being in a bed next to a young man, fortunately by a large window which was kept permanently open. Until very recently he had been a racing cyclist, but now, at the age of twenty, his lungs were ruined, and he was forced to lie in his bed in the hut, studying the cracks in the roof. He had taken part in several international cycling events, during the last of which he had collapsed and been hospitalized. He could not believe that he had lung disease and was virtually finished, since only a few weeks earlier he had been a top-class sportsman. He had been born at Hallein. When his relatives visited him, they were devastated by the deterioration in his condition. I had no intention of depriving this young man of his illusions and resolutely withheld whatever knowledge I had. He imagined he would soon be out of the hospital, but the horrifying reality is that one morning he was taken to the operating theatre and never returned. I can still see his mother packing up his belongings from his bedside table. My own operation having been postponed for a day or two, I had time to explore the lay-out of the hospital. I had already spent weeks at the hospital without getting to know it. Having been confined to bed in the unchanging surroundings of the big internal ward, I had seen nothing but parts of the internal department. Now I was able to inspect the whole hospital. I naturally visited the unit where my grandfather had been until his death in February. As soon as I entered the surgical wing, the domain of the chief surgeon, I was filled with an intense loathing for the art of medicine and a hatred of all doctors. Here, in this dark, narrow corridor, the chief surgeon had walked up to my grandfather one day and admitted that he had made a mistake: what he had taken to be an abdominal tumor had in fact been a blocked bladder which was on the point of bursting and produced the fatal toxaemia. I left the surgical department and went to the gynecological department, where my mother had had her hysterectomy a year too late. I was too depressed to go on exploring this run-down citadel of medicine, and so I went back to my bed, where I spent my time sleeping, taking very little food, and waiting for the time which had been appointed for the crushing of my phrenic nerve. Until this time I had been tormented by doctors often enough, but they had never operated on me. After being given my pre-med I contemplated what was going on around me with a greater degree of composure. I was lifted out of my bed and onto a trolley, then wheeled out of the hut and into the surgical department. The pre-med transforms the patient in a matter of seconds from an anxious victim into an interested observer of a solemn drama in which he imagines himself to be the principal actor. Everything becomes light and agreeable and takes place in an atmosphere of extreme confidence, extreme *self*-confidence. The noises he hears are like music, and the words that are spoken are reassuring. Everything is serene and uncomplicated. All anxiety is dispelled and he is no longer on the defensive, having exchanged reserve for indifference. The sight of the operating theatre arouses only increased interest in the activities of the doctors and nurses, whom he trusts implicitly. Infinite calm prevails, infinite acquiescence. Even the most personal concerns recede into the farthest distance. The victim, already on the operating table, views everything with the utmost composure, with a feeling of well-being. He tries to look into the faces above him, but they become blurred. Lying on the operating table, he hears voices, the clink of instruments, the sound of water. Now I am being strapped to the table. The surgeon is issuing orders. I sense that two sisters are standing next to me, holding my wrists to keep a check on my pulse. The chief surgeon says *Breathe*, then *Don't breathe*, and again *Breathe*, then *Don't breathe*. I am able to follow his orders. Now I know that he has made the incision. He pulls the flesh apart. The arteries are held apart. His knife scrapes the collar bone and cuts deeper, increasingly deeper. He asks first for one instrument, then for another. He puts one aside and is handed another. There is still infinite calm. Again I hear him say *Breathe in—Don't breathe in—Breath in.* Then he says *Hold your breath—Breathe out slowly—Now breathe normally—Hold your breath—Breathe out—Breathe in—Hold your breath—Now breathe normally.* All I hear is the surgeon. I hear nothing from the nurses. Then again: *Breathe in—Breathe out—Hold your breath—Breathe out—Breathe in.* I am now used to these commands. I want to obey them correctly, and I succeed. Suddenly I begin to feel weak, I grow weaker, and all at once I feel that all the blood is being drained out of my body. At this moment the nurses let go of my wrists and I hear the surgeon say, *Oh, my God!* Instruments fall to the ground and there is a clatter of apparatus. Now I'm dying, I think; it's all over. I feel someone tugging at my shoulder. Everything is dull and painless, brutal but not painful. Once again I can breathe. I now know that I stopped breathing for a while. I am back, no longer sinking; I am saved. *Breathe gently,* I am told, *Breathe in very gently.* Then: *Hold your breath—Breathe out—Breathe in—Breathe out.* The operation is over. The straps on my wrists are undone and I am lifted up, cautiously, very slowly. I hear the surgeon say *Gently, very gently.* My legs are released from the straps and hang down to the ground. I see this only momentarily as I am raised into a sitting position by two nurses. Several pairs of scissors are attached to the open wound in my chest, which I cannot see. The sterilizer is pushed towards me. They lay me down again and put a cloth over my face so that I cannot see the wound being stitched up. I had caught sight of pints of blood and a quantity of blood-soaked gauze and cotton wool on the floor. What had happened? Clearly something had happened, but I'd come through, I told myself. The cloth is removed from my face; I am placed on a trolley and wheeled back to the pulmonary unit in a kind of half-sleep in which I can see nothing but shadows, in which everything is blurred. The operation's over, I tell myself, and I'm in my bed by the window. Now I can go to sleep. Not long after I awoke, the chief surgeon appeared. Half a day had elapsed—it was midday. He told me it had all gone well. Nothing had happened, he said, emphasizing the word *nothing.* But something *did* happen, I thought, and I still think so. All the same I had made it; I had survived my first operation. My phrenic nerve had been crushed, and a week later the pneumoperitoneum could be performed, the wound having healed rapidly. This was unexpected, since my experience was that in my case wounds healed only slowly and with difficulty. Now I was going to have an abdominal puncture, two fingers' width above the navel, to inject as much air as possible into the abdomen so as to compress the lungs and seal off the cavity in the lower right lung. I cannot say that I was properly prepared for this, and suddenly I was scared of having a pneumoperitoneum. I got the head physician to explain it to me, since he was the person who would perform it. He explained that it was as simple as inflating a bicycle tire. He spoke in the normal matter-of-fact tone which head physicians employ when speaking of the horrific and the unspeakable, which to them are all in a day's work. He also told me that up to that time only a few such pneumoperitoneums had been performed in Austria; he had done only three himself but had encountered no difficulties—it was an extremely simple matter. I lay in my bed by the window and observed the rapid healing of the wound by my collar bone. Since they lived so near, my relatives, including my brother and sister, came to see me and told me about my mother's death struggle. She just wouldn't die, though they wanted her to, as they could not bear to see her suffering, and she herself longed for death. I sent her my love and she sent me hers. It never occurred to me how terrible the situation was for my relatives, leaving my dying mother to visit me in the pulmonary unit, then leaving me to go back to her. Only later did I realise that this had almost been the end of them. They brought me a thick book to while away the time—*The Forty Days of Musa Dagh* by Franz Werfel. I tried to read it, but it bored me, and I found myself reading several pages without knowing what they contained. I did not find it at all interesting. Moreover, the book was too heavy for me to hold, and so it gathered dust on my bedside table. Most of my time I spent silent and motionless, becoming more and more engrossed in gazing at the ceiling and trying to exert my imagination. I'll end up at Grafenhof, I thought, but when I go back there it'll be under entirely changed circumstances: *I'll actually be suffering from lung disease—I'll be positive and really belong there.* I tried to get my situation clear in my mind. I knew that they had not had a pneumoperitoneum at Grafenhof before. I'll be going back to the sanatorium with something special, something sensational, I thought. At any rate my second appearance at Grafenhof will be quite unlike my first. I pictured my return— the look on everybody's face, the way they would react to me, doctors and patients alike. They had deceived themselves and hence deceived me by letting me out as though I were cured when in fact I was mortally sick.

How will they look me in the face? What will they say? How should I behave? I wondered. I'll see how it goes. Had not all the doctors failed in my case? I was at their mercy. They kept on seeing something, but not the right thing. They saw something that was not there, or else they failed to see something that was there. When my family came to see me, they held their handkerchiefs to their mouths and noses all the time; it was difficult to have a conversation under these conditions. What did our conversation consist of? *How are you?* they would ask. *How's Mother?* I would ask. It was not permitted to mention my grandfather in his fresh grave in Maxglan Cemetery: whom the Catholic Church had at first refused to bury, but who had then been buried in what was to become one of the city's honoured graves: we did not dare to address ourselves to death, the final and ultimate calamity. After the air had been injected into my body, it forced its way wherever it could, spreading under the skin up into my neck and under my chin. I was sure I was going to die. I felt I had been cheated, used as an object of experiment and deceived yet again. When my family visited me I lay rigid and silent, unable to speak. When they left they were more depressed than when they had arrived. I had listened to their report on my mother's condition without reacting to it, and they had turned and left. Roughly once every two weeks my abdominal wall was punctured and I was re-injected with a carefully calculated volume of air, always in the same unpleasant manner. I was able to walk the short distance for the injection but had to be wheeled back on the trolley. Yet on each of these return journeys through the corridors of the pulmonary unit I counted myself lucky to have *only* a pneumoperitoneum, *only* a cavity in the lung, *only* infective tuberculosis, and not cancer of the lung, like the patients whom I could see lying in the open wards as I was wheeled past. They whimpered quietly to themselves, and when they were out of their misery they were wheeled past in the notorious zinc coffins. It was a daily sight. At least my mother was not going to die in these surroundings, I thought, and I considered myself lucky that she was at home. Whenever possible those with terminal diseases should be nursed at home and die at home—anywhere but in a hospital, anywhere but among others in their situation. There is no greater horror than that. I shall never forget what I owe my guardian, who with the help of my grandmother nursed my mother right up to her death. The huts had been built during the war and were in an utterly neglected state, never having undergone the slightest renovation, but quite suitable, it seemed, for patients with lung disease,

for the outcasts with their deadly expectorations. These huts were dreaded.
No one entered them voluntarily. There was a fence separating the pulmonary unit from the general hospital, and there were notices everywhere
saying ENTRY PROHIBITED. They were well sited, since they stood apart,
to the rear of the hospital complex. Through the open windows the traffic
could be heard in the distance. Less than fifty yards from my hut lay the
road along which I had walked a year earlier as an apprentice on my way
to Podlaha's store in the Scherzhauserfeld Project. At that time I had paid
no attention to the huts hidden behind the bushes that lined the road; I
had never even noticed them. I had always been in a hurry when walking
along this stretch of the road in order not to be late for work. I longed
for the shop and for Podlaha, for the Scherzhauserfeld Project and its
inhabitants. None of them knew what had been happening to me. I had
written Podlaha a postcard to tell him that I had passed the commercial
assistant's examination, signing off with *best wishes*. I had not seen him
again. He must have written me off. He would have had no use for someone
with lung disease: I would have scared off his customers and also brought
him into conflict with the law. What good had it done me to run away
from the grammar school and to put up such resistance against my family
and school, against everything to do with my family and school? What
had been the good of rebelling against normal society and its blind acquiescence in mindlessness? What had been the good of my about-turn in
the Reichenhaller Strasse? I had been cast right back. It was as though
the whole world had conspired against me, against all of us, who had
believed after the war that we could hide ourselves away in the petty
bourgeois world of the Radetzkystrasse. My escape from the grammar
school, my apprenticeship, my musical studies—all of them symptoms of
my disobedience—came to assume in my own eyes all the dimensions of
madness and grotesque megalomania. I had wanted to sing Iago, but now,
at the age of eighteen, I was lying in the pulmonary unit with a pneumoperitoneum. What could this be but a mockery of my pretensions? Yet,
after all, I *had* escaped the fate of the racing cyclist. And I did not have
cancer of the lung like the patients lying only a dozen yards away, who
sometimes cried out at night, in such tremendous pain as to defy any
conception of pain, and polluted the air around me with their stench. I
had one enormous advantage: I was not a death candidate; I did not need
to call myself a hopeless case and say I was finished. In this way I brooded
for days and weeks, alarmed at the change that had come over my body,

which had been made distressingly unsightly by the pneumoperitoneum. When I explored it with my hands I could feel the air under my skin: I was nothing but an air-cushion. As a result of all the medication I had had to take for such a long time, a reddish-grey rash formed all over my body. I had seen nothing like it before, but it failed to impress the doctors. I went on being treated continuously with streptomycin; the hospital could afford to dispense the correct dosage, which was dictated here by medical need, not by the scandalous favouritism that prevailed at Grafenhof. I had to take PAS; every week I swallowed hundreds of the whitish-yellow tablets which were deposited at my bedside by the kilo. They led to an almost complete loss of appetite. I cannot remember all the other things I had to take or have injected into me during these weeks and months. Sometimes during the day, having dozed off to sleep through exhaustion, I would wake up in alarm to see great fat pigeons sitting on my bedcovers. I hated these creatures, which were covered in dirt and exuded a sickly sweet scent and, when they flew up in front of my face, stirred up quantities of dust. They seemed to me like harbingers of death. My grandfather too had detested pigeons and maintained that they carried disease. All my life I have thought of them as ugly, ungainly creatures. They would settle on all the beds and leave droppings everywhere. Having scared them off, I used to feel sick. When I was able to get up and walk a few yards, I ventured to look into the cancer ward, which was adjacent to mine, and was horrified to find the patients smoking. These terminally sick patients, these stinking, putrefying human beings who were little more than skeletons, lay in their beds smoking cigarettes. The mixture of putrefaction and cigarette smoke produces an abominable stench. They're smoking now, I thought, but in a day or two they'll be gone—wheeled out and dumped in the ground. Watching the sisters of the order of St. Vincent undressing patients who had just died, washing them and then replacing their clothes as though it were the most normal activity in the world, I reflected on the degree of insensitivity one would have to attain in order to do such work, or alternatively, the degree of self-abnegation or self-sacrifice. I did not have the courage to admire these heroic women—I was too afraid. When a life has come to an end, the people left behind pick up the jacket and trousers and dirty underclothes and walk away with them over their arms. It was always the same picture, but it never ceased to fascinate me. I was at once repelled and attracted by it. Yet again I was surprised by my capacity for intense observation. A human life, however great its potential and however great the realization of this potential, whether by choice or by destiny, would dissolve under the eyes of those left behind into a mass of putrid flesh held together by skin and bone. Life or existence relegated this mass of putrid flesh to some corner, the last corner left to it, and vanished. The question was where it vanished to. But I will refrain from pursuing this question. Lying on my back with my pneumoperitoneum, a medical curiosity to doctors and patients alike, bloated and utterly unsightly, I had time to think about all the things I had never given a thought to throughout my whole previous life and to venture into areas I had not dared to enter before: the connections between those to whom I owed my existence, my own connections, *my connection with the rest of the world*. But, as I have said, the only outcome of my efforts was to make the thicket more impenetrable, the darkness darker, and the wilderness wilder. If I pursued my father's tracks, I soon came to a halt where they diverged and led off in different directions. I could discern a few shadowy figures in the raging storm or the absolute calm of history, figures which moved towards me but dissolved into nothingness as soon as they came close. What part of me comes from this quarter, I asked myself, and what part from that? From where do I get this or that trait? My unfathomable contradictions, my melancholy, my despair, my musicality, my perversity, my insensitivity, my lapses into sentimentality? What is the source, on the one hand, of my absolute confidence and, on the other, of my alarming helplessness and patent weakness of character? Where do I get my distrustfulness, which has grown more intense than ever? I know that my father decided one day to cast everything to the winds and leave home, to free himself from everything which had been home to him, which he had been talked into regarding as home, which had been forced on him, as it later was on me, like an iron cap intended to crush him. I know that, having made this decision, he carried it to its logical conclusion by setting fire to his parents' house and going off to the railway station with nothing but the clothes he stood up in. He is said to have worked out just how to set fire to the house so that he would see the blaze reach its climax as the train pulled out. His precise calculations were successful, as I know, and he was able to feast his eyes on the spectacle of his parents' house, his own heritage, going up in flames. With this last look at the blazing house he had not only wiped out his home but expunged the very idea of home from his mind. It is said that he never showed any remorse. He lived to be forty-three, and apart from what I have related I know scarcely anything about him. My mother was born in Basel, where my grandfather was enrolled as a student at the university. My grandmother had left her husband and children in Salzburg to follow my grandfather, a student with uncompromising socialist views, to Switzerland. They stayed together for the rest of their lives, but married only after they had lived together for forty years. Before my mother was a year old my grandparents were in Germany, moving from place to place with their baby daughter in the cause of socialism. Rallies and marches were the order of the day, even for my grandfather. My family were all born in different places—which demonstrates better than anything else the restlessness which was always an essential feature of our lives. And when at last they wanted a quiet life and had found one, when they had succeeded in withdrawing into it and taking possession of it, they were visited by sickness and death. Self-deception now took its revenge. There were so many things I had wanted to say to my mother, so many vital questions I had wanted to ask her; but now it was too late. She would no longer be receptive to my questions; she would no longer have an ear for me. We save up our questions simply because we ourselves are afraid of them; then all at once it is too late to ask them. We want to leave the other person in peace and avoid causing him *profound* distress, and so we refrain from putting our questions because we want to leave ourselves in peace and avoid causing ourselves *profound* distress. We put off the vital questions and content ourselves with asking futile, silly, ridiculous questions all the time, and when we do ask the vital questions it is too late. All our lives we put off the big questions until they form a huge mountain which darkens our lives. But by then it is too late. We ought to have enough courage not to be afraid of other people or of ourselves; we ought to torment them with questions, ruthlessly and implacably; we ought not to spare them, to *deceive* them by sparing them. We always regret the questions we have not asked when the person we should have questioned no longer has an ear for them, when he is dead. But even if we had asked all these questions, would we now have a single answer? We are not prepared to accept the answer, any answer. We cannot and we must not—that is the way our minds work, that is our ludicrous mental and emotional system, our existence, our nightmare. I could see my mother's death getting closer and closer; I took it for granted and could foresee its consequences in the most minute detail. I could picture her funeral; I could hear the things that would be said, the things that would be left unsaid. I saw it all before my eyes, but I still refused to believe it was true. She had been crushed by her family, I reflected, with all their post-war ruthlessness, and her father's death had accelerated the progress of her illness. She still sent me her love, and messages about how to conduct my life, thoughtful, tactful suggestions about what I should do later. She let me know that she had decided to spare my brother and sister, who were just seven and nine respectively, the experience of seeing her die. They must not be there to witness her death. My sister was sent to Spain and my brother to Italy. *She* was preparing for her death; *she* was making all the decisions. She had guarded against all the tastelessness connected with terminal sickness and refused to tolerate any sympathy. Her life came to an end with her father's; she said this quite calmly, I was told. I shan't see her again, I thought. Here I am with my pneumoperitoneum, and I shan't see her again. But I did have a last chance to see her. I was discharged from the hospital and allowed to go home. I was to return to Grafenhof two days later; I already had the transfer papers in my pocket. I sat by my mother's bed, but we had no conversation. Her mind was lucid, but everything we said seemed meaningless. I hardly had time to fill my American kitbag with my belongings. My guardian and my grandmother were in the grip of total exhaustion. Although my mother was still alive, still *with us*, the apartment already had *an emptiness* about it, *the emptiness she would leave behind*. We all felt this. We sat in the kitchen, listening for sounds through the open door, but my dying mother made no sound. At Grafenhof I was not put back in the twelve-man room but in one of the so-called loggias between the first and second floors. To my surprise I found that I was sharing it with the seedy doctor of law whom I have already mentioned. Because of the seriousness of his condition he had been moved to the loggia, which was darkened by an enormous fir-tree. I was put there only because my condition was thought to give cause for alarm. My illness had meanwhile wrought further changes in my physical appearance, so that I now melted quite naturally into the background at Grafenhof. I was now in the bloated category. Puffed up by my pneumoperitoneum and by all the drugs that had been pumped into me, I did not appear in the least out of place in these surroundings. I seemed quite *natural*. I looked appropriately ill, and in fact I was anything but healthy. The doctor of law was a socialist, a demagogue, whom the doctors detested and who had earlier pursued me with his socialist ideas when we were in the twelve-man dormitory. He was now no longer in a fit state to ram Marx and Engels down my throat or expatiate on his radical socialist plan

for the world of the future. He had to put up with being confined to bed
and staring ceaselessly at the ceiling. He exuded a smell with which I was
already familiar from the pulmonary unit at the hospital, and at first I was
horrified at having to share a room with him. However, I got used to the
smell and the depressing physical change that had come over him. He no
longer discoursed about soviets and no longer mentioned the names of
Rosa Luxemburg and Karl Liebknecht. He had a habit of first spitting
into his hand and then transferring his spittle to his bottle, a procedure
which inevitably failed. It did not worry him that I was driven mad by
his long, laborious efforts to clear his chest and by the ghastly noises that
accompanied them, especially during the nights, which were dominated
by these attempts to clear his lungs. These nights were the longest I have
ever known. He got up only once a day, to be washed by a nurse. Of
course there was no bathroom in those days, only a washbasin on the wall.
There he would stand, naked and wheezing, this man who was a total
failure, and let himself be cleaned up without raising any objection. This
procedure immediately exhausted him; and, summoning what remained
of his strength, he would let himself be helped back into bed and fall
asleep at once. This gave me a chance to get up and wash. Behind me I
could hear the stertorous breathing that came from his tattered and by
now practically useless lungs. What I was witnessing was the end of an
idealist, a socialist, a revolutionary, for whom the world had chosen a
fitting punishment. I remember the rebukes this man had had to endure
when we were still in the twelve-man dormitory, not just from the doctors
but from the Catholic sisters, the humiliations he was subjected to by the
very people who constantly boasted of being civilized and cultivated. The
way the medical staff treated this man, who was never guilty, as far as I
recall, of any breach of discipline, was beneath contempt, and the contempt—indeed the hatred—that he was constantly made to feel by the so-
called sisters of mercy was vicious in the extreme. Here was an example
of how an honest man can stick consistently and tenaciously to his ideas
while leaving others with different opinions in peace and yet become an
object of scorn and hatred. Such people are dealt with in such a way as to
ensure their annihilation. The incredible decision to put him in the twelve-
man dormitory with its stupid inmates, whose behaviour was as brutal as
it was mindless, amounted to a punishment which was bound to destroy
him. He was not allowed to read a book or a newspaper in peace; he never
had ten minutes in which he could think without being disturbed. De-

liberately or not, malevolently or not, they constantly disturbed him and
systematically destroyed him. It was a foregone conclusion that he would
go to pieces and be moved to one of the loggias reserved for the worst
cases. His tormentors were ignorant juveniles bent upon aimless foolery.
One cannot blame them, since they were all young labourers and apprentices who were understandably out of control and took pleasure in harassing
their victim to the point of destruction. He was already too weak to endure
the incessant torture and gave up. For a brief period he too had been my
teacher, taking me back into a world to which my grandfather had introduced me with such passionate devotion, once more opening the door to
the alternative world that is kept under, the world of the powerless and
the oppressed. These ignorant youths had singled out the doctor of law as
an object of daily mockery and developed their torture technique to a fine
art, giving full rein to their perverted exuberance and making the philosopher into a fool. The philosopher submitted to their insolence and surrendered without resisting. Nevertheless one cannot hold them responsible
for ruining a man's life, for the ignorance they displayed was the crass
ignorance of the immature. The real blame lay with the staff, especially
the chief physician and director: throughout my time in the twelve-man
dormitory I was able to observe the non-stop working of the torture machine
they used on the doctor and the inordinate hatred they felt for this man
whose views were opposed to their own: a socialist who openly and honestly
professed socialism even in *this* environment, this Catholic National Socialist environment, had to be eliminated under any circumstances. They
felt his presence to be an affront and they conceived the monstrous idea
that he was the enemy and must be annihilated. Since, as I know, he had
no one in the world, he submitted to his rulers unconditionally; there was
no possibility of his simply running away. But the truth is that while the
medical staff deliberately and remorselessly drove him into a corner, systematically forcing him into physical and then mental ruin, he himself
took refuge in his own dissolution; and so, with such determination on two
sides, his disintegration was accelerated. It was not difficult for me to
reconstruct the stages in this process. Although I had not witnessed it
directly, I was *now* able to see the development. I tried to start a conversation with him, but I failed: he refused to be drawn. His books lay in a
corner, untouched and covered with dust and dirt. Even if I had wanted
to read them, it would have sickened me to pick them up. I had no desire
to read. Nor did I write anything, not even a postcard. Whom could I

have written to in my situation? The sister fed the doctor his food with a
spoon, as though he were an animal, quite automatically and with evident
distaste. Even she had no conversation with him. When she undressed
him, and when she dressed him again, he tried to stop her, punching her
and hitting her in the face. He became increasingly refractory, but the
sister remained impassive, knowing that in a very short time it would all
be over. I wondered how long it would be before he was taken away, before
they got him off their backs and shunted him off to Schwarzach. His heart
went on beating, and sometimes when I woke up I would immediately
look across at him to see whether he was still alive or whether there was
a dead body in the next bed. But the body was still breathing; its lungs
were still working. I sensed the sister's disappointment at finding the
doctor still alive, still there. Probably the only question on her mind when
she came in every morning was whether the doctor had died, whether the
problem with the doctor had solved itself. She would pull up the curtains
and set to work, getting the towels ready and running the water into the
washbasin, then lifting the doctor out of bed and transporting him to
the washbasin. It occurred to me that *now* I would much rather be in the
twelve-man dormitory on the second floor than here in the loggia with
the doctor. I longed to be back in the dormitory, for I could not help
thinking that I was far worse off in the loggia. Up on the second floor I
had been with people of my own age, while here I was with someone who
seemed ancient and worn out and who became uglier and more antisocial
by the hour. On the other hand, I felt it something of a distinction to be
allowed to be with this ugly, revolting old man, for whom I did not
conceal my admiration, indeed reverence, because he had come to be as
he was through being rejected, hated, and pushed to one side. Everybody
seemed to be waiting for the doctor to disappear; but the time had not
yet come, and they were obliged to contain themselves in patience. The
staff on the medical round regarded him as nothing but a nuisance who
did not suit their plans. Nor were they happy about me, for they could
not be unaware of the fact that I knew they had not acted innocently when
they had made an incorrect diagnosis: they had been guilty of pushing me
to the brink of disaster by discharging me as cured when in fact I had a
great cavity in the lung, and they had been obliged to re-admit me. There
had been two reasons for putting me in the same room as the doctor: in
the first place my condition really did seem to them to be *dangerous and
threatening, a threat to the lives of others*, and in the second, *my reserve, my*

distrust, indeed my hatred of them were no secret; in their eyes I was recalcitrant and rebellious. There were six or seven loggias, half of them occupied by privileged patients whom I hardly ever saw—and in any case I always had the impression that these people were scared stiff of coming into contact with the other patients, with the likes of us. It was obviously embarrassing for them to have to use the communal toilet in the corridor. They were better dressed and affected a superior way of speaking, though they hardly spoke at all to people like me. I constantly heard titles being used, "councillor," "professor," and "countess" among those I recall. Wherever these titles or their owners were to be found, shielded, undisturbed, even cosseted, the sisters would move about almost noiselessly and with a solemnity that seemed to me quite sickening. When the sisters entered our loggia, having just left one which was occupied by a better class of patient, their faces darkened and their tone of voice changed from one which strained after gentility to one which was rough, vulgar, and brutal. The food they took to these rooms was quite different and dished up quite differently, more elaborately. They also knocked on the doors before they entered. They did not knock on our door but walked straight in. One difficulty I had not foreseen: before me there had been no one with a pneumoperitoneum at Grafenhof. It was a concept which was known to them only from the medical literature, but now they were confronted with the real thing. I myself was scared when the time came for me to go to the assistant's consulting room for an injection. He explained that he had never performed a pneumoperitoneum before, though he had now informed himself about how it was done. I had no option but to tell him what to do. He prepared the apparatus under my instructions and pushed it towards me. I waited, but nothing happened. He lacked the nerve. I now had to take the initiative. I literally ordered him to place the needle against my abdomen, then push on it with all his might and puncture the abdominal wall. I told him he must not hesitate for a moment; otherwise the pain would be excruciating and the whole business would become very bloody. The assistant was the son of a Viennese ministry official, very long and lanky, and extremely arrogant, but I knew that he could also be nervous and squeamish. I told him that he must screw up his courage and throw himself on my abdomen with the whole weight of his body, and I explained to him how it had been done by the head physician in Salzburg. Now the assistant was not in the least suited to such an act of violence, unlike his athletic Salzburg colleague, who had only to bring his weight to bear for a second in order to puncture my abdomen. As was to be expected, the first attempt failed. I doubled up with pain, and blood spurted from my useless wound. But it was essential for more air to be injected, and so he made a second attempt, which was so amateurish that I screamed with pain and people gathered outside in the corridor. The amateur succeeded only gradually in piercing my abdominal wall, working by fits and starts and causing me quite unnecessary torment. Then, as if he had scored a triumph, he stood there and noted with satisfaction that the air was flowing into my abdomen and distributing itself. The mechanism was functioning, and this was confirmed by the indicators on the apparatus. There was an audible flow of air, and I saw the arrogant expression, which had been temporarily absent, return to his face. No one was more surprised than he was at the success of the enterprise. I remained lying there for a while, after which I was taken back to the loggia. I had never lost so much blood after an injection, and I had pains in the abdominal wall for days. I was afraid that an inflammation might develop, since I did not trust the instruments used at Grafenhof, where cleanliness was not a top priority. But there was no inflammation, and the pain subsided. Next time it'll be a success, I told myself; and from now on it was. I had been told that a patient might continue with a pneumoperitoneum for five years or more, and I prepared myself for this. After each injection of air, as soon as I could stand up and walk unaided, I was put behind the X-ray screen and checked. After subsequent injections had proved successful the assistant was quite proud of himself: he had added a new discovery to his scientific knowledge. I did everything I could to get myself out of my present room. I even invented a form of gymnastics for myself, and the time came— sooner, in fact, than I had thought possible—when I was allowed out into the fresh air. I made a circular tour round the building, and every day I increased the radius of my tour. I was now able to get as far as the perimeter. What I wanted most was to go into the *village*, but this was strictly prohibited. One day I decided to ignore this prohibition and walked into the village, which was called St. Veit. The inhabitants looked me up and down, immediately recognizing me, of course, as a patient from the sanatorium, but they seemed to find the sight of a patient with lung disease neither sensational nor dangerous. I had only just entered the village when my general weakness compelled me to turn round and go back. Freedom had proved far too taxing. I wanted nothing more than to return to my room and creep under the covers. But I had acquired the taste, and so I made further expeditions to the village. Stealthily, in full knowledge of the fact that I was risking the most draconian punishment at the hands of the authorities, I crossed the perimeter and made a few small purchases in the village—on one occasion a pencil and paper, on another a comb and a new toothbrush. My funds would not run to more, these being limited to my invalidity allowance, which was paid to me by the welfare office—no longer by the health insurance office, since I had exhausted what was due to me from that source. By now the cost of keeping me at the sanatorium had been transferred from the health insurance service to the welfare service. Every afternoon I would go and sit on the bench in the little garden between the main building and the annexe, taking a book with me in a deliberate effort to take my mind off myself and my surroundings. I would sit there reading Verlaine, Trakl, and Baudelaire. A time of calm seemed to have begun. Then one day as I sat on the bench I looked at the deaths column in the newspaper I had taken with me. In it I found the following notice: *Herta Pavian, aged forty-six*. It was my mother. Her name was in fact *Herta Fabjan*, and there was no doubt that the spelling *Pavian* was due to a mishearing of her name on the part of the newspaper, which was informed by telephone of the names of those who had died and printed them in this obscure but avidly read column. *Herta Pavian!* I rushed to my room and told the doctor of law, who was lying half-dead in his bed, that my mother had died and that the wrong name had appeared in the announcement—*Herta Pavian* instead of *Herta Fabjan*. *Herta Pavian, aged forty-six*, I kept repeating to myself. *Herta Pavian, aged forty-six*. I applied for permission to go to Salzburg for the funeral, and it was granted. My mother had wished to be buried at Henndorf where she had spent much of her childhood with her aunt Rosina, and her wish was respected. I went into the empty apartment, as empty as I had imagined it before her death. My family had been so flustered that they had forgotten to let me know she had died. Anyhow I was there, I said, so there was no need for reproaches. My mother's clothes still hung in the hall, and mountains of washing had piled up in all the rooms. Her husband told me that she had died *in front of his eyes, fully conscious*. That morning he had given her some tea and they had talked to each other; then suddenly she had turned white from the forehead downwards. *She just slipped away*, he said. The last drop of hot liquid had ruptured the aorta. I spent the night in the room where my mother had died. They told me she had been wrapped in a white sheet and placed in a simple white wood coffin, like my grandfather. Hundreds gathered for her funeral at the little village cemetery in Henndorf. My mother had been religious all her life, regarding the Church with reserve though also with respect. She had wanted a Catholic burial. When we arrived at Henndorf, the coffin was still in the little whitewashed mortuary chapel. It was carried into the church by farmers' boys who were said to be relatives of hers. After the requiem mass a long funeral cortège was formed by the hundreds of mourners, most of whom were relatives, I was told. Walking behind the coffin with my grandmother and my guardian, I was suddenly seized by a paroxysm of laughter, which I had to fight back throughout the ceremony. I kept hearing the name Pavian from all sides, and I finally had to leave the cemetery before the ceremony was over, with *Pavian! Pavian! Pavian!* screeching in my ears. I almost fled from the village, without waiting for my relatives, and went back to Salzburg. I crept into a corner of the apartment and waited for them to return. Next day I went back to Grafenhof, where I lay in bed for a few days with the covers pulled up over my head, wanting neither to see nor to hear anything. I was brought back to my senses only by the need for another injection of air, which could not be postponed. Now I've lost everything, I thought. Now my life has become entirely pointless. I conformed to the routine, letting everything happen, whatever it was, not refusing to do anything, subordinating myself completely. I let everything come within a certain distance of me, but not close enough for me to see it distinctly. I could bear to see things only if they were indistinct. I remained in this state for several weeks. One day I woke to see the doctor of law being carried out of the room. He had died in the night. I had scarcely got to know his successor when I was moved to the second floor, where I was put in one of the south-facing rooms, each of which always accommodated three patients. I do not know why I was moved. From this room I had a distant view of the upper part of the valley, from the black Heukareck to the snow-capped nine-thousand-foot peaks in the west. Until now I had been unaware of the views the house had to offer. My general condition improved from the moment I was moved to the second floor, just as though I too had emerged from a mortuary chapel. Why had I been moved? I asked; but I was not told. Now I had to go to the sun-room again. The patients in the loggias were exempt from this. I had greater freedom to move about and was once more in the company of others, for during the time I had spent in the loggia I had had no company but my own and had been completely taken up with myself. Now I was once more with other people, a large number of them. There was no doubt that I was on the mend. They all lay there just as I remembered them—apathetic, weary of life, lying in rows, and fulfilling their paramount duty: to spit into their sputum bottles. My bed was now the third from the front, not the third from the back, as it had been before. From my new position I could look down into the village. I decided to transgress the regulations and secretly go into the village every day. It was necessary to break the laws of Grafenhof if I was to improve my condition: I now entertained the supreme ambition of returning to full health. I kept my resolve to myself, guarding it as my greatest secret. I knew that this place was dominated by the urge to die, by readiness to die, by a craving to die, and so I had to conceal my new-found readiness to live, my craving for life. I must not give myself away. Accordingly, I deceived those around me by joining in their dirge while inwardly resisting with all my might. I had to resort to deceit in order to guard my secret. I had to make sure of getting out of this place—and quickly. But to do this I needed the strength to break the laws which were in force here, which prevailed with absolute force, and live according to my own laws. I had to live more and more by my own laws and less and less by those which were imposed on me. I had to follow the advice of the doctors, but only up to a certain point, the point where it could still benefit me, not beyond it. Advice had to be followed only insofar as it was beneficial, and only after I had subjected it to careful scrutiny. I had to take my life into my own hands and, above all, into my own head and ruthlessly eliminate whatever was harmful. The harm came from the medical system prevailing in the establishment. The doctors are the source of all my trouble, I thought. It was inevitable that I should think this. It was time to think for myself if I wanted to make progress. On the one hand it was necessary and unavoidable for me to be at Grafenhof: the medical and clinical facilities it provided were vital to my recovery, and I had to make use of them. Yet on the other hand I must not allow myself to be abused by them. What I required of myself was extreme vigilance; above all I had to pay even sharper attention to the activities of the doctors. Overtly I submitted myself to the regulations and to the authority of the medical staff, but covertly I resisted them whenever it was possible and to my own advantage. I was not inexperienced in this regard, nor did I lack the necessary subtlety and scientific knowledge. The doctors and their subordinates must be controlled by me, not I by them, and this was far from easy to achieve.

I was automatically placing myself outside the laws which were in effect at Grafenhof. In every spare minute I kept a vigilant eye on the medical machinery, aware that if I were to cease or even slightly relax my vigilance, it might turn into a disaster machine because of all the ignorance and lethargy that was built into it. I soon had everything under surveillance, carefully monitoring my repeated examinations and keeping those who performed them under close scrutiny. Nothing escaped my notice—or, at any rate, nothing essential. *I* decided how much streptomycin I needed, not the doctors, though I let them continue in the belief that it was they who made the decisions, for otherwise my calculations would not have worked out. I let my tormentors go on thinking that they decided what was to be done, whereas from now on it was I who decided. Even I was amazed at the uncanny success I had in putting my plan into operation and making sure that my calculations worked out. I became extraordinarily skilful at this sleight of hand. When I concluded that there was no longer any point in swallowing vast quantities of PAS, the doctors decided that I need not take any more; but in fact I had engineered the whole thing— I had done a conjuring trick. I also determined the dosage of all the other medicaments, finally reducing it to a minimum, since I was appalled by the enormous quantities of noxious substances I had already swallowed as a result of what I now saw to be criminal negligence. *I* decided how the wall of my abdomen was to be punctured and how the air was to be injected: the assistant was convinced that *he* was giving *himself* the orders, whereas in fact it was *I* who gave them to him. All contact with home had ceased. I got no news from my family, and as far as I remember I had no interest whatever in how things were at home. They did not write to me, though there was nothing to stop them; they no longer had any excuse after they had buried their dead. They had their reasons. I got no mail and I expected none. I immersed myself in Verlaine and Trakl, and I also read Dostoyevsky's novel *The Demons*. Never in my whole life have I read a more engrossing and elemental work, and at the time I had never read such a long one. It had the effect of a powerful drug, and for a time I was totally absorbed by it. For some time after my return home I refused to read another book, fearing that I might be plunged headlong into the deepest disappointment. For weeks I refused to read anything at all. The monstrous quality of *The Demons* had made me strong; it had shown me a path that I could follow and told me that I was on the right one, *the one that led out*. I had felt the impact of a work that was both wild and great, and I emerged from the experience like a hero. Seldom has literature produced such an overwhelming effect on me. Using slips of paper which I had bought in the village, I tried to keep a record of certain dates which seemed important to me, certain crucial points in my existence, fearing that what was now so clear might blur and suddenly be lost to me, that it might suddenly vanish, and that I might no longer have the strength to save all these decisive occurrences, enormities, and absurdities from the obscurity of oblivion. On these slips of paper I tried to preserve everything that could be preserved, everything without exception which seemed to me to be worth preserving. I had now discovered my method of working, my own brand of infamy, my particular form of brutality, my own idiosyncratic taste, which had virtually nothing in common with anyone else's method of working, anyone else's infamy, anyone else's brutality, or anyone else's taste. What is important? What is significant? I believed that I must save everything from oblivion by transferring it from my brain onto these slips of paper, of which in the end there were hundreds, for I did not trust my brain. I had lost faith in my brain—I had lost faith in everything, hence even in my brain. The shame I felt at writing poetry was greater than I had expected, and so I did not write a single poem. I tried to read my grandfather's books, but found it impossible: I had experienced too much in the meantime, I had seen too much, and so I put them aside. What I needed I had found in *The Demons*. I searched the sanatorium library for other such elemental works, but there were none. It would be superfluous to enumerate the authors whose books I opened and immediately shut again, repelled by their cheapness and triviality. Apart from *The Demons* I had no time for literature, but I felt sure that there must be other books like it. But there was no point in looking for them in the sanatorium library, which was chock-full of tastelessness and banality, of Catholicism and National Socialism. How was I to get hold of other books like *The Demons*? My only chance was to leave Grafenhof as soon as possible and look for my demons in freedom. I now had an additional motive for getting out. When I stepped behind the X-ray screen, I wanted to be told that my condition had improved, and in fact it did improve from one examination to the next. By now I was making excursions beyond the village and getting to know the countryside. What had always seemed to me so dark and repellent suddenly took on a pleasanter aspect and ceased to have such a deadening effect on my mind. The mountains were no longer ugly and menacing, as they had always seemed. The people were no longer the monsters I had thought them to be. I now found it possible to breathe deeply, more and more deeply. I ordered *The Times* once a week (despite the fact that it ate up nearly all my welfare allowance) in order to brush up and extend my knowledge of English, and also to keep abreast of what was going on in the rapidly changing world. I suddenly found the courage to approach the woman who played the organ in the village church and arranged for her to give me a singing lesson in the church. After giving me not just one lesson but three, during which she accompanied me on the organ while I sight-read Bach cantatas and the Note Book of Anna Magdalena, she said she would like me to sing the bass solo in the Haydn mass which was about to be performed the following Sunday. My bulging pneumoperitoneum did not prevent me from following up this solo per-formance by singing the bass parts regularly at morning masses. Of course I also met the organist secretly during the week, behind the backs of the doctors, in order to make music in the church. We studied the great oratorios of Bach and Handel, and it was at this time that I discovered Henry Purcell. I sang Raphael in Haydn's *Creation*. I had not lost my voice: on the contrary, it improved from week to week, and I was able to work at perfecting my technique. I looked forward to these music lessons in the church with intense longing. Despite all the warnings I had been given, I was once more on the right path: I was destined for music. The fact that I was paying secret visits to the village and singing quite openly in church could no longer be concealed. The doctors took me to task and tried to make me see that with my pneumoperitoneum I was putting my life at risk by singing. They threatened to discharge me and strictly forbade me to go into the village. But I no longer had the strength to submit to any prohibition. I could not exist without my singing, and so I wanted to leave Grafenhof as soon as possible, under any circumstances. After all, I had been singing for weeks, and it had not caused any debility: on the contrary, it had improved my general condition to such an extent that I felt justified in believing that music would provide me with the way back to health. The doctors thought this absurd and told me I was crazy. I suddenly saw music as a training for life. However, I dared not go on visiting the village, at least not to make music. I discussed my bad luck with my friend the organist. She was a Viennese, an artist, a graduate of the Music Academy, and a professor. She had been sent to Grafenhof during the war and as a result had become a real victim of lung disease. Afterwards she had stayed on in the village. From now on she was my favourite companion, my new teacher, the one person on whom I could rely. I went to see her whenever I could. But we no longer dared to make music together, having become frightened by our own courage, our readiness to dice with death. And so, because of the doctors' threats, we abandoned the practical study of music in favour of musical theory. Whenever I had the chance I would flee from the sanatorium to what was known as the almshouse, where my new teacher occupied a room with wooden walls just below the roof. It was like a hiding place, and to me it really was a hiding place. It was here that I found my way back to myself, back to the conditions that were essential for my existence. One day I went into the sun-room and could not believe my eyes: my friend the conductor was sitting on my bed. He had arrived that day and wanted to give me a surprise. Ever since he had been discharged—in good health, for all I knew—several months or a year earlier, he had undertaken a veritable odyssey. He had gone on a bathing tour of the Adriatic and been guilty of the stupidest crime a person with lung disease can commit: he had lain in the sun on the beach. He had gone to Italy by motorbike but had to be brought back to Austria by ambulance. He had undergone a complicated operation in a Vienna clinic, where his thorax had been opened up and the whole of his right lung removed. Like most of the patients in Grafenhof, he had the TB trademark on his back: an operation scar which ran from the shoulder to the pelvis. He had not thought he would survive, and he told me that he was surprised to be here now. We told each other our news, none of it very cheerful; but what *he* had to relate was not enough to make *me* waver in my determination to regain my health. On the contrary, *I* was now a model for *him* to emulate. I cannot recall how many months I spent with him at Grafenhof after this; nor can he. Perhaps it was over a year. I could easily work it out, but I do not feel like consulting the calendar. How long did I spend at Grafenhof altogether? When was I finally discharged? I cannot remember. I do not want to remember. One day I demanded to be discharged because I thought the time had come, but the doctors simply refused to let me leave. For a long time, however, despite my pneumoperitoneum, I had been going out sledging at night instead of disconsolately tossing and turning in my bed. I used to sledge down into the Schwarzach Valley, down the ravines and into the empty streets of the town. When the night sister had said good night and turned off the light, I would get up and disappear. I had hired a sledge in the village and kept it hidden behind a tree during the day. At night I would jump onto it and race downhill. I wanted to leave, and so I left. *I decided that I should be discharged*, although the doctors felt that *they* had discharged me. I had to get away to avoid being permanently ground down in this atrocious medical disaster mill. Away from the doctors, away from Grafenhof! One cold winter's day I left, prematurely and *at my own risk*, as I was obliged to tell myself, after saying good-bye to all the people who mattered. I lugged my kitbag to the village and boarded the bus for Schwarzach. From there it took me two hours to get home. I was not expected, and the surprise was a shock for my family. Though no longer infectious, I was far from cured. They took me in and fed me for a while as best they could. I had to look round for a job. This was difficult, as I did not know what work I could do. There was no question of either commerce or singing. So for several weeks I brooded to no purpose, and in this hopeless situation I once more came to hate the city of Salzburg and its inhabitants. I visited numerous firms, but I was no longer capable of starting work with a firm—not because I was still ill, for I would have been capable of working despite my pneumoperitoneum, but quite simply because I had no desire to work. I was revolted by the thought of any work, any job. I was disgusted by the stolidity of the working population, those in employment. I could see how repulsive they were, how utterly futile and lacking in purpose. I was appalled and horrified by the thought of working, of being employed by someone, just to be able to survive. When I saw people I would sometimes approach them only to recoil in horror. My problem was the meagreness of my social security allowance. Whenever I collected it from the social security office in the Mozartplatz, I felt ashamed. I had so many abilities, but the one thing I lacked was the ability to hold down what is called a regular job. Every week or so I had to see a lung specialist who had a surgery (and still has) in the Sankt-Julien-Strasse, to have my pneumoperitoneum refilled. I actually looked forward eagerly to these visits, which were a welcome diversion, for in this specialist I had once more found a person with whom I could have a *useful* conversation, someone with whom I could discuss things. I liked the woman who assisted him too. On one occasion (I do not know why—possibly because I could not be bothered) I missed my appointment for an injection. Instead of going back after ten days, which was the proper interval, I let three or four weeks elapse. I did not remind the specialist that I had overshot the proper date. I simply lay down, and he injected air into me as usual. The result was an embolism. The specialist and his assistant turned me upside down and slapped my face. Their quick reaction saved my life. I was by now well over nineteen. I had ruined my pneumoperitoneum and suddenly put myself once more in the position of having to return to Grafenhof. But I refused and never went back.

Contents

PRIZES

THE GRILLPARZER PRIZE

FOR THE AWARDING OF THE GRILLPARZER PRIZE of the Academy of Sciences in Vienna I had to buy a suit, as I had suddenly realized two hours before the presentation that I couldn't appear at this doubtless extraordinary ceremony in trousers and a pullover, and so I had actually made the decision on the so-called Graben to go to the Kohlmarkt and outfit myself with appropriate formality, to which end, based on previous shopping for socks on several occasions, I picked the best-known gentleman's outfitters with the descriptive name Sir Anthony, if I remember correctly it was nine forty-five when I went into Sir Anthony's salon, the award ceremony for the Grillparzer Prize was at eleven, so I had plenty of time. I intended to buy myself the best pure-wool suit in anthracite, even if it was off the peg, with matching socks, a tie, and an Arrow shirt in fine cloth, striped gray and blue. The difficulty of initially making oneself understood in the so-called finer emporiums is well-known, even if the customer immediately says what he's looking for in the most concise terms, at first he'll be stared at incredulously until he repeats what he wants. But naturally the salesman he's talking to hasn't taken it in yet. So it took longer than it need have that time in Sir Anthony to be led to the relevant racks. In fact the arrangement of this shop was already familiar to me from buying socks there and I myself knew better than the salesman where to find the suit I was looking for. I walked over to the rack with the suits in question and pointed to one particular example, which the salesman took down from the rod to hold up for my inspection. I checked the quality of the material and even tried it on in the dressing room. I bent forward several times and leaned back and found that the trousers fit. I put on the jacket, turned around several times in front of the mirror, raised my arms and lowered them again, the jacket fit like the trousers. I walked around the shop in the suit a little bit, and took the opportunity to find the shirt and the socks. Finally I said I would keep the suit on, and I also wanted to put on the shirt and the socks. I found a tie, put it on, tightened it as much as I could, inspected myself once more in the mirror, paid, and went out. They had packed my old trousers and pullover in a bag with "Sir Anthony" on it, so with this bag in my hand, I crossed the Kohlmarkt to meet my aunt, with whom I was going to rendezvous in the

Gerstner Restaurant on the Kärnterstrasse, up on the second floor. We wanted to eat a sandwich in order to forestall any malaise or even fainting episode during the proceedings. My aunt had already been to Gerstner's, she had already classified my sartorial transformation as acceptable, and uttered her famous *well, all right.* Until this moment I hadn't worn a suit for years, yes until then I had always appeared in nothing but trousers and pullover, even to the theater if I went at all, I only went in trousers and pullover, mainly in gray wool trousers and a bright red, coarse-knit sheep's-wool pullover that a well-disposed American had given me right after the war. In this outfit, I remember, I had traveled to Venice several times and gone to the famous theater at La Fenice, once to a production of Monteverdi's *Tancredi* directed by Vittorio Gui, and I had been with these trousers and pullover in Rome, in Palermo, in Taormina, and in Florence, and in almost all the other capitals of Europe, apart from the fact that I have almost always worn these articles of clothing at home, the shabbier the trousers and pullover, the more I loved them, for years people only saw me in these trousers and this pullover, I've worn these pieces of clothing for more than a quarter of a century. Suddenly, on the Graben as I said and two hours before the awarding of the Grillparzer Prize, I found these pieces of clothing, which had grown in these decades to be a second skin, to be unsuitable for an honor connected with the name Grillparzer which would take place in the Academy of Sciences. Sitting down in the Gerstner I suddenly had the feeling the trousers were too tight for me, I thought it's probably the way all new trousers feel, and the jacket suddenly felt too tight and also as regards the jacket, I thought this is normal. I ordered a sandwich and drank a glass of beer with it. So who had won this so-called Grillparzer Prize before me, asked my aunt, and for the moment the only name that came to me was Gerhart Hauptmann, I'd read that once and that was the occasion I learned of the existence of the Grillparzer Prize for the first time. The prize is not awarded regularly, only on a *case-by-case* basis, I said, and I thought that it was now six or seven years between awards, maybe sometimes only five, I didn't know exactly, I still don't know today. Also this awarding of the prize was naturally making me nervous and I tried to distract myself and my aunt from the fact that there was only half an hour before the ceremony began, I described the outrageousness of my deciding on the Graben to buy a suit for the ceremony and that it had been self-evident that I would find the shop on the Kohlmarkt which stocks English suits by Chester Barry and Burberry. Why, I had asked myself again, shouldn't I buy a top-quality suit, even if it is off the peg, and now the suit I was wearing was a suit made by Barry. My aunt again only focused on the material and was happy with the English quality. Again she said her famous *well, all right*. About the cut, nothing. It was classic. She was very happy about the fact that the Academy of Sciences was awarding me that Grillparzer Prize today, she said, and proud, but more happy than proud, and she got to her feet and I followed her out of the Gerstner and down onto the street. We had only a few steps to walk to the Academy of Sciences. The bag with "Sir Anthony" on it had become deeply repellent to me, but I couldn't change things. I'll hand over the bag before going into the Academy of Sciences, I thought. Some friends who didn't want to miss me being honored were also on their way, we met them in the entrance hall of the Academy. A lot of people were already gathered there and it looked as if the hall was already full. The friends left us in peace and we looked around the hall for some important person to greet us. I walked up and down the entrance hall of the Academy several times with my aunt, but nobody took even the slightest notice of us. So let's go in, I said, and thought, inside the hall some important person will greet me and lead me to the appropriate place with my aunt. Everything in the hall indicated tremendous festiveness and I literally had the sensation that my knees were trembling. My aunt, too, kept looking, as I did, for an important person to greet us. In vain. So we simply stood in the entrance to the hall and waited. But people were pushing past us and kept bumping into us and we had to recognize that we had chosen the least suitable place to wait. Well, is no one going to receive us? we thought. We looked around. The hall was already just about packed and all for the sole purpose of my being awarded the Grillparzer Prize of the Academy of Sciences, I thought. And no one is greeting me and my aunt. At the age of eighty-one she looked wonderful, elegant, intelligent, and in these moments she seemed to be brave as never before. Now various musicians from the Philharmonic had also taken their places at the front of the podium and everything was pointing to the beginning of the ceremony. But not one person had taken any notice of us, who were supposed to be the centerpiece. So I suddenly had an idea: we'll just go in, I said to my aunt, and sit in the middle of the hall where there are still a few free seats, and we'll wait. We went into the hall and found those free seats in the middle of the hall, many people had to stand and complained to us as we forced our way past them. So now we were sitting in the tenth or eleventh row in the middle of the hall of the Academy of Sciences and we waited. All the so-called guests of honor had now taken their places. But of course the ceremony didn't begin. And only I and my aunt knew why. Up front on the podium at ever-decreasing intervals excited gentlemen were running this way and that as if they were looking for something, namely me. The running this way and that by the gentlemen on the podium went on for a while, during which unrest was already breaking out in the hall. In the meantime the Minister for Sciences had arrived and taken her seat in the front row. She was greeted by the President of the Academy, whose name was Hunger, and led to her chair. A whole line of other so-called dignitaries who were unknown to me were greeted and led to the first or second row. Suddenly I saw a gentleman on the podium whisper something into the ear of another gentleman while simultaneously pointing into the tenth or eleventh row with an outstretched hand, I was the only one who knew he was pointing at me. What happened next is as follows: The gentleman who had whispered something into the ear of the other gentleman and pointed at me went down into the hall and right to my row and made his way along to me. Yes, he said, why are you sitting here when you're the most important person in this celebration and not up front in the first row where we, he actually said we, where we have reserved two places for you and your companion? Yes, why? he asked again and it seemed as if all eyes in the hall were on me and the gentleman. The President, said the gentleman, is asking you please to come to the front, so please come to the front, your seat is right next to the Minister, Herr Bernhard. Yes I said if it's that simple, but naturally I will only go into the first row if President Hunger has requested me *personally* to do so, it goes without saying only if President Hunger is inviting me *personally* to do so. My aunt said nothing during this scene and the guests of the ceremony all looked at us and the gentleman went back along the whole row and then toward the front and whispered something from beside the Minister into President Hunger's ear. After this there was much unrest in the hall, only the tuning-up by the players from the Philharmonic stopped it from becoming something really ugly and I saw that President Hunger was laboriously making his way toward me. Now is the time to stand firm, I thought, demonstrate my intransigence, courage, single-mindedness. I'm not going to go and meet them, I thought, just as (in the deepest sense of the word) they didn't meet me. When President Hunger reached me, he said he was sorry, what he was sorry for, he didn't say. Please would I be kind enough to come with my aunt to the front row, my seat and my aunt's were between the Minister and him. So my aunt and I followed President Hunger into the front row. When we had sat down and an indefinable murmur had spread throughout the hall, the ceremony could begin. I think the men from the Philharmonic played a piece by Mozart. Then there were several longer or shorter speeches about Grillparzer. The one time I glanced over at Minister Firnberg, that was her name, she had fallen asleep, which hadn't escaped President Hunger either, for the Minister was snoring, even if very quietly, she was snoring, she was snoring the quiet, world-famous ministerial snore. My aunt was following the so-called ceremony with the greatest attention, when some turn of phrase in one of the speeches sounded too stupid or even too comical, she gave me a complicit glance. The two of us were having our own experience. Finally, after about an hour and a half, President Hunger stood up and went to the podium and announced the awarding of the Grillparzer Prize to me. He read out a few words of praise about my work, not without naming some titles of plays that were supposed to be by me but which I hadn't actually written, and listed a row of European famous names who had been singled out for the prize before me. Herr Bernhard was receiving the prize for his play *A Feast for Boris,* said Hunger (the play that had been appallingly badly acted a year before by the Burgtheater company in the Academy Theater), and then, as if to embrace me, he opened his arms wide. The signal for me to step onto the podium had arrived. I stood up and went to Hunger. He shook my hand and gave me a so-called award certificate of a tastelessness, like every other award certificate I have ever received, that was beyond comparison. I hadn't intended to say anything on the podium, I hadn't been asked to do so at all. So in order to choke off my embarrassment, I said a brief *Thank you!* and went back down into the hall and sat down. Whereupon Herr Hunger also sat down and the musicians from the Philharmonic played a piece by Beethoven. While the musicians from the Philharmonic were playing, I thought over the entire ceremony now ending, whose peculiarity and tastelessness and mindlessness naturally had not yet had the chance to register in my consciousness. The musicians from the Philharmonic had barely finished playing when up stood Minister Firnberg and, immediately, President Hunger and both of them went to the podium. Now everyone in the hall had stood up and was pushing toward the podium, toward the Minister naturally and President Hunger who was talking to the Minister. I stood with my aunt, dumbfounded and increasingly at a loss, and we listened to the rising hubbub of a myriad of voices. After a time the Minister looked around and asked in a voice in which inimitable arrogance competed with stupidity: *So, where is the little poet?* I had been standing right next to her but I didn't dare to make myself known. I took my aunt and we left the hall. Unhindered and without a single person having taken any notice of us, we left the Academy of Sciences at around one o'clock. Outside, friends were waiting for us. With these friends, we went to have lunch in the place called the

Gösser Bierklinik. A philosopher, an architect, their wives, and my brother. All entertaining people. I no longer remember what we ate. When I was asked during the meal how large the prize money was, it was the first time I really took in the fact that the prize had no money attached to it at all. My own humiliation then struck me as common impudence. But it's one of the greatest honors that can be bestowed on an Austrian, to receive the Grillparzer Prize of the Academy of Sciences, said someone at the table, I think it was the architect. It was huge, said the philosopher. My brother, as always on such occasions, said nothing. After the meal I suddenly had the feeling that the newly bought suit was far too tight and went into the shop on the Kohlmarkt, Sir Anthony I mean, and said to them in a fairly brash way but still with perfect politeness that I wished to exchange the suit, I had just bought the suit, as they knew, but it was at least one size too small. It was my firmness that made the salesman I was speaking to go straight to the rack from which my suit had come. Without objection he let me slip into the same suit but one size larger and I immediately felt that this suit fit. How could I have thought only a few hours ago that the one-size-smaller suit fit me? I clutched my head. Now I was wearing the suit that actually fit and I left the shop with the greatest sense of relief. Whoever buys the suit I have just returned, I thought, has no idea that it's been with me at the awarding of the Grillparzer Prize of the Academy of Sciences in Vienna. It was an absurd thought, and at this absurd thought I took heart. I spent a most enjoyable day with my aunt and we kept laughing over the people at Sir Anthony, who had let me exchange my suit without objections, although I had already worn it to the awarding of the Grillparzer Prize in the Academy of Sciences. That they were so obliging is something about the people in Sir Anthony in the Kohlmarkt that I shall never forget.

THE PRIZE OF THE CULTURAL CIRCLE OF THE FEDERAL ASSOCIATION OF GERMAN INDUSTRY

IN THE SUMMER OF NINETEEN SEVENTY-SIX I spent three months in the Lung Disease Hospital that was and is attached to the Steinhof Insane Asylum in Vienna, in the Hermann Pavilion which had seven rooms with either two or three patients, all of which patients died during the time I was there, with the exception of a theology student and me. I have to mention this because it is quite simply essential for what follows. I had, as so often before, hit the limits of my physical existence once again and the doctors had abandoned me. They'd given me no more than another few months, at best no more than a year, and I accepted my fate. I had been cut open below the larynx for the purposes of the removal of a tissue sample and left for six weeks in the certainty that I was going to die of cancer until they discovered that in my case it pointed to a lifelong lung infection causing an illness called Morbus Boeck, although this hasn't yet been proved and I have lived until this day with that assumption, and, I believe, more intensely than ever. Back then, in the Hermann Pavilion, among the hundred-percent-certain candidates for death I made my peace, just as they did, with my rapidly approaching end. The summer, I remember, was particularly hot and the Six-Day War that had already entered history was raging between Israel and Egypt. The patients lay in bed in the shadows in eighty-six-degree heat and in truth, like me, they were all longing for death and they all, as I have already said, got their wish and died one after the other, among them the former policeman Immervoll who was in the room next to mine and who, for as long as he was in a state to do so, came to my room every single day to play Pontoon with me, he won and I lost, for weeks he won and I lost until he died and I didn't. Both of us passionate Pontoon players, we played Pontoon together to kill time until it wasn't time that was killed, it was he. He died only three hours after playing and winning the last game. In the bed next to mine was a theology student whom in the course of a few weeks hanging between life and death I made into a skeptic and thus a good Catholic, forever, or so I think. I undermined him with my theories about bigoted Catholicism using contemporary examples from the hospital, from the daily course of events with the doctors and nurses and patients, and also from the repellent priests and nuns who buzzed around all over the men-

tal hospital on the scrubby, windy Baumgartner Heights, this westerly range
of hills in Vienna, it wasn't hard for me to open the eyes of my pupil. I think
his own parents were grateful for my lessons. I gave them with passion, also
their son, as I know, did not become a theologian, even if he was a very good
Catholic but no theologian, today, I'm sad to say, like everyone else in Central
Europe, he's a rather unsuccessful, sidelined, paralyzed socialist. But it gave
me the greatest pleasure to explicate the God he had clung to so unconditionally, to literally enlighten him, to rouse the sleeping skeptic in his sickbed,
which in turn roused me in my own sickbed and possibly signified my own
survival. I am recounting this because when I remember the price of the prize
of the Cultural Circle of the Federal Association of German Industry, it all,
quite simply, comes back to me, the sweltering hospital in the summer heat,
and the hopelessness. I see the patients and their relatives, both with the
hopelessness steadily tightening around their throats, the perfidious doctors,
the bigoted nurses, all these stunted characters in the stinking, sticky hospital
corridors, meanness and hysteria and self-sacrifice in equal measure, deployed
only for the purposes of human destruction and I hear in the fall the thousands
upon thousands of Russian cranes flying high above the hospital, darkening
and blackening the afternoon sky and shattering the eardrums of all the
patients with their shrieking cries. I see the squirrels picking up the hundreds
of paper handkerchiefs filled with sputum and discarded by the lung patients
and racing like mad with them for the trees. I see the famous Professor Salzer
coming up from the city to the Baumgartner Heights, and going through the
corridors to excise the lobes of the patients' lungs in the operating theater,
with his famous little-Professor-Salzer's elegance, the professor was a specialist
in larynxes and halves of thoraxes, the professor came increasingly frequently
to the Baumgartner Heights and increasing numbers of patients had ever-
decreasing numbers of larynxes and thoraxes. I see them all prostrating themselves before Professor Salzer, although the professor couldn't work any
miracles and could only cut into the patients and mutilate them with the best
of intentions and I see him with his meticulous planning and highly developed skills bringing the victims of his work to an earlier grave than they
would have found of their own accord, although he, the best of the best in his
field, could do nothing about it, quite the opposite, he and his art and his
elegance were totally guided by his high, even the highest, ethics. They all
wanted to be operated on by Professor Salzer, who was an uncle of my friend
Paul Wittgenstein, one of the expert authorities at the University in the city,
and so unapproachable that if they'd been standing in front of him, they'd

have lost their voices. The professor's coming, the word went out, and the entire hospital became a holy place. The Six-Day War between Israel and Egypt was at its height, and my aunt, who came to the Baumgartner Heights every day after a two-hour journey in the streetcar in boiling heat carrying several pounds of newspapers, brought me the first copy of *Gargoyles*. But I was too weak to be able to take pleasure in it, even for a moment. My theology student was amazed that I wasn't happy, that I wasn't proud of the beautifully printed book, I couldn't even lift it. My aunt stayed with me all through visiting hours, how often she held the basin under my chin when I vomited after so-called attacks. I lay there with the same incision below the larynx as the people dying to my right and left, and got the news that I had been selected for the so-called prize of the Cultural Circle of the Federal Association of German Industry. I have sketched this more gloomy than entertaining introduction because I want to establish why this so-called prize was more welcome to me back then than anything could have been. Just to be accepted into the hospital—and I had had to be delivered to the hospital on the Baumgartner Heights!—I had first had to pay over the sum of fifteen thousand schillings, which naturally I didn't have and which my aunt advanced to me. But of course I wanted to pay her back this amount as soon as possible, so I had barely been delivered to the hospital on the Baumgartner Heights before I wrote to my publisher about the amount, more accurately to the editor, with the request that my publisher send me two thousand marks. And promptly a few days after my request two thousand marks arrived for me. Then I wrote to my editor that I would thank my publisher immediately for the two thousand marks, but I had barely sent off the letter to the editor before she sent a telegram *Do not thank the publisher!* Why not, I had no idea. I learned *she* had laid out the two thousand marks from her own private bank account, the publisher had been unwilling. It is depressing to have to get hold of fifteen thousand schillings just to be admitted to a death ward, but that is how things were, those were the circumstances. In brief, this was the situation into which the news arrived that I should expect the prize of the Cultural Circle of the Federal Association of German Industry. The award event would take place in the fall, either September or October, I no longer remember. In any case, I had been out of the hospital for a mere two or three days before traveling to Regensburg, where they planned to stage the award ceremony in the town hall. The poet Elisabeth Borchers was due to share the award with me. I went to Regensburg weak-kneed, with a shoulderbag of my grandfather's. All the way up the Danube, I thought of nothing but the eight thousand marks, the gigantic sum of money I was to receive. I dreamed of the eight thousand marks behind closed eyes and painted the scene that awaited me in Regensburg. I was to be put up at the Hotel Thurn und Taxis, a famous address. My frailty made me keep dozing off at the compartment window the whole way along, the Danube, the Gothic, the German Emperors, I kept thinking, but whenever I woke up from my dozes the first thing I thought about was always the eight thousand marks. I didn't know Herr Rudolf de le Roi, the spokesman of the Cultural Circle of the Federal Association of German Industry, who had given me the award. Probably, I thought, he knows about my illness and because of my illness he has made sure I got the prize. This thought lowered my self-estimation, for I would like to have received the award for *Gargoyles* or for *Frost,* not for *Morbus Boeck.* But I must not brood, I forbade myself to devalue this award even before I'd received it. Doderer and Gütersloh have received this award before you, I thought, writers of major stature, even if I had no access to them, nor could. Three days ago still in your sickbed, now already en route to Regensburg where the Gothic awaits you, I thought. The Danube kept getting narrower, the landscape kept getting more lovely, finally, as it suddenly turned desolate and gray and insipid, there was Regensburg. I got out and went straight to the Hotel Thurn und Taxis. It really was a first-class hotel for a town like Regensburg. I liked it and I truly did immediately feel well in this hotel, and from the very first moment, I wasn't alone, but in the company of Elisabeth Borchers, whom I had already met in Luxembourg at one of the many so-called Poets' Assemblies to which I used to go with my poems when I was around twenty. So there was none of the boredom that always hits me otherwise in every hotel in the entire world where I arrive on my own. I knew that Borchers was an intelligent person and a charming lady and her reputation in my eyes was superb. We wound our way through the town, laughing madly, and used the opportunity to enjoy a casual evening together. Naturally it didn't run late, my illness soon sent me to bed. The next day I met Herr Rudolf de le Roi and the publisher of *Akzente,* Hans Bender, who, I assume, had a say in the awarding of the prize, I still have a photograph of Borchers and Bender in front of a Gothic Regensburg fountain. I didn't like the town. It's cold and repulsive and if I hadn't had Borchers and my thoughts of the eight thousand marks, I would probably have left again after the first hour. How I hate these medium-sized towns with their famous historical buildings by which their inhabitants allow themselves to be perverted their whole lives long. Churches and narrow alleys in which people vegetate, their minds turning more mindless all the time. Salzburg, Augsburg, Regensburg,

Würzburg, I hate them all, because mindlessness has been kept warming over in them for hundreds of years. But I kept going back to the eight thousand marks. During my Morbus Boeck illness so many debts mounted up that I can now pay off, I thought. And at the end there'll still be an amount left over just for me. So I let the morning of the ceremonial awarding of the prize of the Cultural Circle of the Federal Association of German Industry (naturally I want to be sure I always use the full, correct title) creep up on me. Herr de le Roi collected me and Frau Borchers and we went to the town hall, which ranks as one of the precious monuments of German Gothic. It threatened to stifle and choke me as soon as I went in, but I said to myself, Be brave, be brave, just be brave, go along with everything that's going to happen and take the check for eight thousand marks and vanish. The ceremony was fairly short. Herr von Bohlen und Halbach, the Chairman of the Federal Association of German Industry, was to make the presentation to Frau Borchers and myself. We had taken our seats in the front row with Doctor de le Roi. To the left and right of us were the town dignitaries including the mayor wearing his heavy chain of office. I had eaten too much the night before and felt queasy. I can no longer remember whether there was a speech, but probably there was, for such ceremonies always have to include a speech. The guests of honor threatened to cause the main room in the town hall to explode. I could hardly breathe. I was in danger of suffocating in the air of the hall. Everything was all sweat and dignity. But we'd laughed so much the night before, I thought, Frau Borchers and I, that it was all worth it for that alone. And now the eight thousand marks on top of it all! In a moment all the magic rigmarole will be over and we'll have the checks in our hands! I thought. Of course a chamber music ensemble had also taken their seats here too, what they played escapes me. And then, as I recall, the definitive moment arrived without warning. President von Bohlen und Halbach stepped to the podium and read from a piece of paper the following: . . . *and the Federal Association of German Industry herewith bestows the nineteen sixty-seven awards on Frau Bernhard and Herr Borchers!* My neighbor jumped, as I noticed. She was in shock for a second. I squeezed her hand and told her she should just think about the money, whether it was Herr Borchers and Frau Bernhard or Herr Bernhard and Frau Borchers, as was the fact, was irrelevant. Frau Borchers and I got up on the stage of the Regensburg town hall, in which absolutely nobody aside from those affected and perhaps also Herr de le Roi and Herr Bender had noticed Herr von Bohlen und Halbach's mistake, and we each received a check for eight thousand marks. We also spent a beautiful day in the horrible town and

I returned to Vienna where I was welcomed and fussed over by my aunt. A year ago I received a so-called Jubilee Book from the Cultural Circle of the Federal Association of German Industry, the so-called *Jahresring,* which proudly presents all of their prizewinners. My name was the only one missing. Had Doctor de le Roi, the extremely nice (as I recall) gentleman, removed my name from the list of honorees because of the changes in my life meantime, changes I find no fault with myself? In any case, here I have the opportunity to share with you the fact that I too am a winner of the prize of the Cultural Circle of the Federal Association of German Industry. And in Regensburg. And in the town hall in Regensburg to boot.

THE LITERATURE PRIZE OF THE
FREE HANSEATIC CITY OF BREMEN

AFTER FIVE BLANK YEARS, when I wrote *Frost* in Vienna in twelve months (1962), my future was bleaker than it had ever been. I had sent *Frost* to a friend, who was an editor at the Insel publishing house, and the manuscript was accepted within three days. But even as it was accepted, I realized that my work was incomplete and could not be published with its current defects. In a boardinghouse in Frankfurt which was on one of the busiest streets near the Eschenheimer Tower and was one of the cheapest I could consider, I revised the entire book, and all the sections in *Frost* that have a title as a heading, I wrote in that boardinghouse. I got up at five in the morning and sat at the little table in the window and when by midday I had written five or eight or even ten pages, I would take them and run to my editor at Insel to go over with her where these pages had to be slotted into the manuscript. The entire book was transformed during those weeks in Frankfurt, I threw away many pages, probably around a hundred, until it seemed to be acceptable and could go into production. When the galleys came, I was on a trip to Warsaw to visit a girlfriend who was studying at the Academy of Art there. I took a room at the coldest time of year in the so-called Dziekanka, a student residence right near the palace headquarters of the regime, ran around for weeks in the beautiful, exciting, eerie city of Warsaw, and read the galleys. At lunchtime I ate in the so-called Writers' Club and in the evenings with the actors, where the food was even better. I spent one of the happiest times of my life in Warsaw, I had the galleys in the pocket of my coat, my chief interlocutor was Lec the satirist who wrote his famous aphorisms in his wife's kitchen notebook and often invited me home and sometimes also bought me a coffee on the Nowy Âwiat. I was happy with my book, which came out in the spring of sixty-three along with a review by Zuckmayer that ran for pages in *Die Zeit.* But when the general storm of coverage was over, unusually intense and full of controversy, ranging from the most embarrassing effusions to the most vicious attacks, I was suddenly utterly undone, as if I'd fallen into a pit of terrible despair. I thought I would choke on the error of believing that literature was my hope. I didn't want anything more to do with literature. It hadn't brought me happiness, it had trampled me down into that stifling, stinking pit from

which there is no escape, or so I believed. I cursed literature and my prostitut-
ing myself with her, and went to work on building sites and took a job as a
truck driver with the Christophorus Company in the Klosterneuburgerstrasse.
For months I made beer deliveries for the famous Gösser brewery. In the
course of this I not only learned to drive trucks very well but I also got to
know the city of Vienna even better than I'd known it before. I lived with my
aunt and earned my living as a truck driver. I didn't want anything to do with
literature anymore, I had put everything I had into literature and literature
responded by throwing me into the pit. Literature turned my stomach, I
hated all publishers and all publishing houses and all books. It seemed to me
that in writing *Frost* I had fallen victim to an enormous fraud. I was happy to
let my leather jacket drop onto the driver's seat and go thundering through
the streets in the old Steyrer truck. Now it was clear how good it had been to
learn to drive a truck all those years ago in preparation for a job in Africa I had
wanted to take back then, but which, as I know now, very fortunately never
came to anything. But naturally even the good fortune of being able to work
as a driver for the Gösser brewery also came to an end. Suddenly I hated what
I was doing and gave it up from one day to the next and buried myself under
the covers in my little closet at my aunt's. She had understood the state I was
in, for one day she invited me to go with her to the mountains for a few
months. It would do us both good to discard the sheer grisliness and harmful-
ness of the big city for some weeks, and give ourselves over to nature. Her goal
was Sankt Veit in the Salzburg area, the place near the hospital where I had
been a patient for years, twenty-five hundred feet up and an absolutely ideal
place for us to recuperate. Early one morning we began our mountain journey
from the Westbahnhof, my aunt and I, her all-expenses-paid companion. But
I have to say that when the train pulled out of the Westbahnhof I was already
cursing the countryside and longing to be back in the city of Vienna. The
further the train got from Vienna, the sadder I got, I'm making a mistake, I
thought, turning my back on Vienna and going to the countryside with my
aunt, but I can no longer correct this mistake. I'm not a country person, I'm a
city person, I said to myself, and there was no way back. Naturally I'd never
found happiness in the country, the people bored me, I really despised them,
nature bored me and I despised nature, I was starting to hate people and
nature. I had become gloomy and a brooder, who walked through and around
the fields in this direction and that, ran through the woods with my head
down, and finally refused all food. Thus it was that my secret opposition to
life on the land and in the mountains was leading straight to catastrophe, I

was still chained to a truly pitiful caricature of myself and my bottomless existential despair, when the Literature Prize of the Free Hanseatic City of Bremen came. It was not the prize itself that saved me from my emotional, indeed my existential catastrophe, it was the thought that the prize money of ten thousand marks would enable me to get my life under control, give it a radical new direction, make it possible again. The prize was announced, the amount of the prize was known to me already. I had the chance to do the most sensible thing with the money. It had always been my wish to have a house to myself, and even if not a proper house, at least walls around me within which I can do what I want, permit what I want, lock myself in if I want. So I thought, I'll use the prize money to get these walls and I made contact with a real estate agent who immediately came to see me in Sankt Veit and proposed various properties to me. Naturally all these properties were too expensive, if I had the prize money in hand, it would only be a fraction of the sale price. But why not? I thought and I agreed with the real estate agent to meet in January in Upper Austria where he lived and had his range of properties to hand, mainly old farmhouses, some of them already partly derelict, all in the price range of between one hundred thousand and two hundred thousand schillings. But my price was nothing over seventy thousand. Maybe for seventy thousand I'd be able to find the right set of walls I can lock myself up in, I wasn't thinking about a house when I thought about a property for myself, I thought about walls and I thought about walls in which I could lock myself up. I went to Upper Austria and my aunt came with me and we visited the real estate agent. The man impressed me, I immediately took a liking to him, he was capable and seemed to have no character flaws. We came out into a landscape where the snow lay more than three feet deep and stamped our way to the real estate agent's house. He put us into his car and explained by way of a piece of paper where the properties to be visited were situated and what route we should take to get from one property to the next. He had listed about eleven or twelve farms on his paper that were ready to be sold. He slammed the car doors and the tour of inspection had begun. Thick fog already hung over the entire landscape and we saw nothing, we didn't even see the road along which the real estate agent was driving us to the first property. He himself saw nothing ahead of him but fog, but he knew the road and we put ourselves in his hands. My aunt was as curious as I was, we were both silent, I don't know what was going on inside her, she didn't know what was going on inside me, the real estate agent didn't know what was going on inside us both, he didn't say a single word, came to a sudden stop and indicated that we were to get out. And I actually saw a huge wall in front of me in the fog, built of great blocks of stone. The real estate agent moved a large gate that had been torn off its hinges and we went into a big farmyard. There was also more than three feet of snow in the farmyard, it looked as if the owners of the property had departed in a rush, leaving everything lying or standing where it was, I thought: the owners have met with some great misfortune. The property had been standing empty for a year, said the real estate agent, and went ahead of us. In every room we stepped into, he said this was a particularly beautiful room and he kept repeating the two words *exceptional proportions* and it didn't bother him in the slightest that at every moment he was putting a foot through one of the rotted floors and had to rescue himself from the depths of the rot with a well-executed jump. The real estate agent led the way. I followed behind him and my aunt behind me. We went through the rooms as if we were walking along planks that we needed to cross some dull fetid pond, sometimes I looked around for my aunt, who turned out however to be very agile, more agile than me and the real estate agent. There were eleven or twelve rooms to inspect, all of them in totally dilapidated condition and the smell of hundreds if not thousands, I thought, of desiccated ancient mice and rats filled the air. All the floors were rotted through, completely punky and most of the window frames had been torn out by the wind or the weather. Down in the kitchen, where there was a large rusting enameled stove encrusted in dirt, the water had not been turned off and water was running onto the floor and under the floor and the real estate agent said the owners, who'd left the house a year ago, had forgotten to turn off the tap and he went over to the tap and turned it off. He himself, he said, had never inspected the property before this, we were the first he'd shown it to, he was enchanted by the exceptional proportions. My aunt held a handkerchief in front of her mouth to block the stench that pervaded the property, not only the smell of rot, the stalls were full of enormous heaps of manure which the owners had not cleared away. The real estate agent kept saying *exceptional proportions* and the more often he asserted this, the clearer it became to me that he was right, in the end it wasn't *him* saying the property had exceptional proportions, it was *me* saying it, and saying it at every moment. I kept working myself up to say *exceptional proportions* at briefer and briefer intervals until finally I was convinced that the entire property really did have *exceptional proportions*. From one moment to the next, I had been possessed by the entire property and when we were outside the gate again, to drive to the next one and the real estate agent was now hurrying, for we still had ten or twelve properties ahead of us to be inspected, I said that all these properties no longer interested me, I had already found the property for me; it was this one, for it had truly *exceptional proportions,* they were ideal for me and I wished to conclude the requisite contract with the real estate agent immediately. From the start of our inspection to this statement of mine, no more than fifteen minutes had passed. My aunt was shocked, she said I mustn't do anything crazy, she found these walls horrible, naturally, and when we were in the car again, driving back to the real estate agent's house to set up the contract, she kept saying from behind me that I should think the whole thing over carefully, *sleep on it,* she said. But my decision was unbudgeable. I had found my walls. I proposed to the real estate agent that I make a down payment of seventy thousand schillings at the end of January, i.e., after the prize ceremony in Bremen, and settle the remainder of the balance in the course of the year. All the same this remainder amounted to one hundred and fifty thousand schillings, and if I had absolutely no idea yet where this money would come from, I had absolutely no worries about it. *Think it over, sleep on it,* my aunt kept saying while the real estate agent was already drawing up the contract. I liked the real estate agent's manner, the way he wrote, what he said, his surroundings. I myself behaved as if money played no role, it impressed the real estate agent while his wife was making a delicious egg dish for us in the kitchen. Half an hour after I had seen Nathal, that was the name of my walls, for the first time, and not even seen them clearly, for as I've already said they were wrapped in fog, and quite apart from the fact that I had seen absolutely nothing of what surrounded the walls, i.e., the landscape, only made conjectures, I signed the so-called preliminary contract. We ate the egg dish and talked for awhile with the real estate agent and left him. He brought us to the train and we went back to the mountains. During the journey, my aunt didn't miss a single word in expressing her worst premonitions, and I admit I got the willies, now I was suddenly thinking about what had actually just happened, for I had of course got myself into a nightmare. I spent a series of sleepless nights during which I failed naturally to come to grips with what I had really done and what I'd signed and where I would find the so-called balance of one hundred and fifty thousand schillings. But the day of the prize-giving in Bremen will come and then I'll have the first seventy-thousand-schilling installment and I'm saved, I thought. My aunt refrained from any comment whatsoever. For the first time in our lives together I had failed to listen to her advice. So I traveled to Bremen, which I didn't know. Hamburg I knew and loved as I do still today, Bremen I loathed from the very first moment, it's a petit bourgeois, unbelievably sterile city. A room had been reserved for me in a newly built hotel directly opposite the station, I no longer remember its name. I hid in my hotel room so as not to have to see the city of Bremen, waited for morning and the prize-giving. This prize-giving was to take place in Bremen's old town hall and that is where it did. My biggest problem was that I had been instructed to give a speech to the audience and I was already in Bremen and didn't yet have the beginnings of an idea for such a speech, which I'd known about for weeks, and even during the night no idea for such a speech came to me and in the morning I still had none. But now it was getting urgent. During breakfast I remembered that one thing about Bremen is Grimm's "Bremen Town Musicians," and I made up a concept with the Bremen Town Musicians as the centerpiece. I finished my tea and ran to my room and sat down on my bed and did a quick draft. I made a second draft and a third. Then I had to admit to myself that my idea had been a bad one and I needed to come up with another. But time was short. In the meantime there had already been phone calls and questions about how long my speech would be. It's not long, I said into the telephone, not long at all, I said, although I still didn't have even an idea for such a speech. Half an hour before the start of the ceremony in the town hall I sat down on my bed and wrote the sentence "In the cold, clarity increases," I thought: now I have an acceptable idea for my speech to the audience. With this as the center, some further sentences developed, and within ten or fifteen minutes I had written at least half a page. When they collected me from the hotel to take me to the town hall, I had just finished my speech. In the cold, clarity increases, I thought as several gentlemen were escorting me to the town hall, I had the feeling they were taking me away to a trial. They had positioned their prisoner in the middle and had advanced from hotel to city to town hall. The town hall was already full, most of all it was full of schoolchildren. This town hall in Bremen is also a famous town hall, but this town hall also depressed me just as all other famous town halls have also depressed me. Here too medals sparkled and the mayoral chains of office glinted. Then I was led ceremoniously into the first row and had to sit next to the mayor. A man stepped up to the podium and talked about me. He spoke very emphatically and it was full of praise, as far as I recall, but I didn't understand it all. What I was seeing the whole time was my walls in Nathal and what I was thinking was how to pay for these walls. May it all be long-drawn-out enough, I thought, for the money finally to be real liquid cash. When my eulogist had finished and the schoolchildren, or so it seemed, clapped the most enthusiastically of all, I was signaled to go up to the podium. On the podium the prize was then presented to me, and I no longer remember what it looked like, I no longer have it, just as I no longer have any of the other prize documents, they have gotten lost over the years. Now I had the document and the check in my hand and I went to the lectern and read out my notes on the clarity that increases in the cold. Just as the audience was beginning to prepare for my speech, it was already over. That was the shortest speech a Bremen prizewinner has ever given, I thought, and after the ceremony this was confirmed to me. So there I stood and had to shake hands with the mayor again for the photographers. Outside in the corridor my old friend the editor suddenly appeared totally unexpectedly, the one who had accepted *Frost* within three days, and said, knowing himself to be totally alone with me, confidentially so to speak: Please lend me five thousand marks, I need them desperately. Yes of course, I said, without thinking through the consequences, and I said as soon as it's two o'clock and the banks in Bremen are open again, I'll go to a bank with you and cash the check and give you the five thousand marks. How often he's lent me money, I thought, again and again and again and it wasn't long ago that he rescued me out of one of my fatal financial catastrophes. Immediately after the ceremony there was a lunch in a prominent Bremen restaurant, which I left at two o'clock to go with my friend to the bank and cash the check for *Frost.* Anyhow, I thought, I'm going to Giessen after Bremen to give a reading in a so-called evangelical educational institute and I'll be paid two thousand marks. That'll give me seven thousand marks again. This thought immediately made me happy again. The next day I visited another friend in Bremen who lived there in an attic room and with whom I had a terrific conversation about theater over good tea and a view over the pewter-colored river Weser, most of all we talked about Artaud. Right after this conversation I went back to Vienna. And of course I could no longer expect to move into my newly purchased walls in Nathal. How I eventually got control of it and altered and rebuilt it more or less with my own hands and financed it all over the course of the years doesn't belong here. But the Bremen prize was the impetus for my walls, without it everything would probably have taken a different turn for me and unfolded in another way. In any case I made a second trip to Bremen in connection with the so-called Bremen Literature Prize and I don't want to conceal what happened to me on this second trip to Bremen. I was a so-called member of the jury to select the next prizewinner and I had gone to Bremen with my mind already made up that I would vote for Canetti who, I believe, had not until that time received a single literary award. For whatever reason, anyone but Canetti was out of the question for me, I considered any other choice to be risible. There was this

long table, I believe, in a Bremen restaurant where the jury was meeting, and
sitting at it was a whole row of gentlemen who were the so-called voting
jurors, among them the famous Senator Harmsen, with whom I had a very
warm relationship. I think they had all named their own candidates, none of
whom was Canetti, when it came to my turn and I said, *Canetti.* I wanted to
give Canetti the prize for *Auto-da-Fé,* the brilliant work of his youth which
had been reissued a year before this jury met. Several times I said the word
Canetti and each time the faces around the long table grimaced in a self-
pitying sort of way. Many of the people at the table didn't even know who
Canetti was, but among the few who did know about Canetti was one who
suddenly said, after I had said *Canetti* again, but he's *also* a Jew. Then there was
some murmuring, and Canetti landed under the table. I can still hear this
phrase *but he's also a Jew* although I can't remember who at the table said it.
But even today I often hear the phrase, it came from some really sinister quarter, even if I don't know who said it. This phrase nipped any further debate
over my proposal to award Canetti the prize right in the bud. I preferred to
take no further part in the discussions and just sat silently at the table. But
time was passing quickly and although an endless series of appalling names
had been proposed in the meantime, all of which I could only associate with
prattling dilettantism, no prizewinner had surfaced yet. The gentlemen were
looking at the clock and the smell of the evening's roast was already seeping
through the double doors. So the table simply *had* to come to a decision. To
my utter amazement one of the gentlemen, again I no longer remember who,
regardless of a vote, suddenly pulled a book by Hildesheimer out of the
mound of books on the table, and as he was already getting to his feet to leave
the lunch, said in a disconcertingly naïve tone: *So let's take Hildesheimer, let's
take Hildesheimer,* and Hildesheimer was the one name that had not been
uttered in all the hours of discussion. Now suddenly the name Hildesheimer
had been uttered and they all shifted in their chairs and were relieved and
agreed about Hildesheimer and within a matter of minutes Hildesheimer was
voted the new winner of the Bremen prize. Who Hildesheimer really was, not
one of them seemed to know. In a moment the news had been passed to the
press that after a more-than-two-hour meeting, Hildesheimer was the new
prizewinner. The gentlemen stood up and went out into the dining room. The
Jew Hildesheimer had won the prize. For me *that* was the point of the prize.
I've never been able to keep quiet about it.

THE JULIUS CAMPE PRIZE

IN NINETEEN SIXTY-FOUR THE JULIUS CAMPE PRIZE, which the Hamburg publishers Hoffmann und Campe had funded in honor of Heine's publisher Julius Campe, was split three ways and the prize money of fifteen thousand marks went to Gisela Elsner, Hubert Fichte, and me. It was the first time I was singled out for my work as a writer and above all I was enchanted that the distinction came from Hamburg and is indissolubly linked with Heinrich Heine's first publisher, for Julius Campe was the first publisher of *The Harz Journey* and a whole series of the best of all the poems that a German poet has ever written. Julius Campe was not of course unknown to me, I had read Brienitzer's biography of him. In truth the Julius Campe Prize of nineteen sixty-four was not awarded at all because the jury couldn't agree on any one writer and the three equal shares of the prize money were described as so-called Work Stipendiums, but from that moment on, because I had such a stipendium in mind, this didn't hinder me at all from thinking and saying that I'd received the Julius Campe Prize. I was very proud and probably for the only time in my life unequivocally happy to the bottom of my heart about an honor that came in this news from Hamburg and I tried to spread it around as fast as possible. I was living with my aunt in Vienna and I walked through the First District across the Graben and along the Kärtnerstrasse and across the Kohlmarkt and through the Volksgarten and I thought everyone who met me knew of my happiness at having won the Julius Campe Prize. When I sat down at a table differently from before, I held the newspapers in my hand differently from before, and secretly I wondered to myself why everybody in the street hadn't remarked on it to me. And anyone who failed to ask me about it was enlightened by me about my having just won the Julius Campe Prize and I explained who Julius Campe was, which nobody in Vienna knew, and who Heinrich Heine was, for not a lot of people in Vienna knew that either, and what an exceptional honor it was. It's an enormous honor, I said, to receive a prize that's connected with the name of Heinrich Heine and also comes from Hamburg, the city I loved most at that time and has always been one of my favorite cities, even today I know of no other through which I can walk with such uninhibited and happy self-confidence. And in which I could actually live for long intervals, even, who knows, maybe even years. I came to Hamburg very early in my life and maybe it has to do with the fact that I spent the year after I was born on a fishing cutter in Rotterdam harbor that Hamburg was for me what is known in the vernacular as love at first sight. I was often, almost yearly, a guest in a brick house in Wellingsbüttel, not far from the source of the Alster, and I love the people of Hamburg into the bargain. The way the news of my participation in the Julius Campe Prize was announced to me was also, I can say, completely appealing. They wrote two or three sentences that they'd selected me for one of three portions of the prize and I could collect the five thousand marks whenever I wanted, they'd be ready for me in the Hoffmann und Campe offices on the Harvesterhuder Weg. There would be no ceremony, no event. So I actually had a good reason to go to Hamburg again, one day I went to the Westbahnhof and got on a train to Copenhagen and found what seemed the best compartment for me to lean back in and go to sleep. But going to sleep was out of the question because my excitement at being singled out for my work as a writer, for *Frost,* was too great. I got the prize from Hamburg, from Hamburg, from Hamburg, I kept thinking, and I secretly despised the Austrians who had not, until now, extended me even a trace of recognition. The news had come down from the north, from the Binnenalster! Hamburg now was not only the most beautiful of great cities to me but also the pinnacle of clear-sightedness, quite apart from the immense cosmopolitanism that has distinguished Hamburg from time immemorial. In Hamburg the Hoffmann und Campe people had reserved a big room for me in an old villa on the Binnenalster, and I had a taxi take me there. I had hardly reached the room before a newspaper called, wanting to interview me. I leaned back in an armchair and said yes. I unpacked my few things and already the phone rang and the people from the newspaper were there and had pulled out their pencils. It was the first interview I ever gave in my life, it's possible I gave it to the *Hamburger Abendblatt,* who knows. I was so excited that I couldn't finish a single sentence, I immediately had an answer for every question but I wasn't happy with my skill in phrasing things. I thought: people are noticing you come from Austria, the back of beyond. The next day I saw my picture in the paper and instead of being on top of the world, as I'd expected, I was ashamed of the nonsense I'd talked to the people from the newspaper when I was giving it my best shot and I loathed my photograph, if I really look like I do in this photograph, I thought, it would be better for me to retreat into some dark valley deep in the mountains and never set foot in the world again. I sat there spreading a thick layer of marmalade on my breakfast bread and felt deeply wounded. I didn't dare even open the curtains and spent several hours sitting in my armchair as if stricken by some indefinable paralysis in my whole body. I felt worse than I'd ever felt before. But suddenly I thought of my share of the prize, the five thousand marks suddenly dominated my mind, and I slipped into my jacket and ran to the offices of Hoffmann und Campe, it was a beautiful walk in the best air and I felt I was seeing the elegant world for the first time in my life. I looked at each of the comfortable villas on the Binnenalster with the greatest interest and the greatest attention. Finally I reached the offices of Hoffmann und Campe. I announced myself and was immediately welcomed by the head of the house in person. The gentleman shook my hand, invited me to sit down, and took an envelope that was already prepared out of the open desk drawer and handed it to me. The check, he said. Then he asked me if the place I was staying was comfortable. Then there was a pause, during which I kept thinking I should say something clever, something philosophical, or at least something sensible perhaps, but I said nothing, my mouth didn't open. Finally I got the sense that the situation had become embarrassing and right at this point the gentleman said I must come and have lunch with him in the so-called English Club. And I went there for lunch with the gentleman, and ate one of the most outstanding meals I'd ever eaten until then. The meal ended with a generous shot of Fernet Branca and then I was standing in the street on the Alsterufer, and had already said goodbye to the head of Hoffmann und Campe. The main reason for my trip to Hamburg was herewith at an end. I spent another night in the old villa on the Alster and then went to Wellingsbüttel to my friends. I no longer know how long I stayed there. Now I was a famous person, said my friends, and if they went to visit people with me, they said to their hosts, this Austrian we brought with us is now a famous person. These people all made it hard for me to say goodbye to Hamburg. When I arrived in Vienna, I immediately made good on the decision I'd already reached on the journey to Hamburg: I used the entire amount of the prize to buy myself a car. The purchase of the car happened in the following way: In the display room of the car dealer Heller opposite the so-called Heinrichshof, surrounded by other luxury cars, I saw a Triumph Herald. It was brilliant white and upholstered in red leather. Its dashboard was made of wood with black buttons and its price was exactly thirty-five thousand schillings, i.e., five thousand marks. It was the first car I'd seen on my reconnoitering expedition to look for cars and it was the one I immediately bought. I spent around half an hour in total, coming and going in front of the showroom and looking at the car. It was elegant, it was English, which was already almost a given, and it was exactly the size that suited me. Finally I entered the showroom and went up to the car and walked around the car several times and said, I'm going to buy this car. Yes, said the salesman, he would arrange for a similar car to be delivered for me in the next few days. No, I said, not in the next few days, now, I said, right away. I said *right away* the way I've always said it, very firmly. I am not going to wait for a few days, I said, I can't, I didn't give any reason why, but I said I absolutely couldn't and I said this is the only car I will buy, as is, standing right here. I was making as if to go, without closing the deal, when the salesman suddenly said all right you can have the car, this one, it's a beautiful car. He said it with sadness in his voice but he was right, the car was beautiful. Now I myself, as was flashing through my mind at that moment, had never driven a motorcar in my life before, only heavy trucks, for I had originally taken the truck driver's test because I wanted to go to Africa to deliver medicines to the Africans, but this fell through, driving heavy trucks was a requirement for my job in Africa, I was supposed to go to Ghana, but because of the death of the American manager who would have been my boss my job in Africa got postponed and finally made redundant, so, I thought, I don't have any idea how to drive the car out of the showroom. Yes, I said to the salesman, it's a done deal, I will buy the car but it has to be parked out front for me, in front of the showroom, I said, I would pick it up in the course of the day. Of course, said the salesman. I signed a contract and paid the purchase price. The entire Julius Campe Prize went on it. I had a little money left over for gas. For a few hours I crisscrossed the inner city in jubilation over owning a car, the first car in my life, and what a car! I congratulated myself on my taste. That I should have asked even one person for expert advice on whether the car was worth something under the hood never crossed my mind. I have a car! I have a white car! I thought. Finally I turned around and went back to the Heller dealership, which was one of the most elegant car dealers in Vienna, and when I came around the corner my car was already standing in front of the door. I collected my papers inside, got into the car, and drove off. In the event I had no difficulty steering the car, although it would incontrovertibly have been easier to steer heavy trucks than this little Triumph Herald. Now of course I drove to the Obkirchergasse and showed the car to my aunt. She was absolutely amazed that such an elegant car could be bought for five thousand marks. On the other hand, five thousand marks was an awful lot of money! Of course I couldn't rest in peace until I made my first major trip, which took me first to the north across the Danube and then, because I couldn't get enough, by way of Hollabrunn all the way to Retz. In Retz I'd already used up a lot of gas. I filled up the tank and drove back, it was a beautiful day. But when I was back and in the vicinity of the Obkirchergasse, I didn't want to stop and get out and so I now drove east. First I drove through the entire city and then out into the Burgenland. Shortly before Eisenstadt it began to get dark and I thought if I keep driving I'll be in Hungary in half an hour. I drove back. During the night sleep was not even to be thought of, it was a wonderful feeling to own a car, and an English car what's more, white, with red leather seats and a wooden dashboard. And all that for *Frost,* I thought. The next day I took my aunt on an outing to Klosterneuburg and on the way we stopped at the cemetery in Grinzing. Two months later, I'd accustomed myself to being a car owner and trips in my Herald were already becoming normal, I drove to Istria and the coast of Lovran where my aunt had already gone to stay several weeks before. We were living as so often before in the Villa Eugenia, a villa of the gentry built in 1880 with splendid broad balconies and a pebbled path that curved gently directly down to the deep blue water. Gagarin had just completed his first space flight, I still remember. My white Herald was parked downstairs next to the gateway, it was no gate, it was a gateway and upstairs on the third floor, as the sole master of three large rooms with six large windows behind whisper-thin silk curtains that dated from before the war, I wrote *Amras.* When I'd finished *Amras,* I immediately sent it to my editor at Insel. Four or five days after dispatching *Amras* I was already up at three in the morning with a rush of energy, a feeling I had to head out, up and out, for it was a perfectly cloudless, clear, tangy day. Wearing only trousers and gym shoes and a sleeveless shirt, I climbed the rocky slopes of the so-called Monte Maggiore, now named Učka. Halfway up I lay down in the shade and looked at the sea in front of me, far below, crisscrossed by ships. I had never been happier. At midday, when I ran down the mountain again, laughing aloud, exhausted with happiness, I can say I felt once again that I wouldn't change places with anyone in the world. In the Eugenia there was a telegram waiting for me. *Amras outstanding, everything fine,* was the text. I changed clothes and got into my car and drove into Rijeka, the ancient Croatian-Hungarian port town. I walked all around the little streets and I was quite unbothered by how gray all the people were, unbothered by the pollution in the air from hundreds of cars. I absorbed everything with the utmost intensity, I listened to everything, breathed everything in. Around five in the afternoon I drove back to

Eugenia, the coast road, past the shipyards. I think I sang. Before Opatija, where the great rock face catches the harsh light of the evening sun, a car swung into my lane from the left, slamming heavily into the near side of my car and staving it in. It hurled me right out of the car but I just stood there and didn't feel any pain. The car belonging to the Yugoslavian was completely demolished too. The driver had jumped out and run off screaming, pursued by a woman who kept screaming *Idiota! Idiota! Idiota!* after him. There was a pile of metal in front of me in the middle of the road and all the traffic coming out of the shipyards was blocked. The *Idiota! Idiota! Idiota!* faded away and I was standing there alone. Suddenly I saw people running toward me and screaming and I saw that my whole body was covered in blood. I had a head wound, the bleeding was so severe I thought I'd lost my scalp, but I still felt no pain whatever. Then someone who'd leapt out of a little Fiat 500 grabbed hold of me and put me in his car. He gunned the engine and raced me along the coast road to the hospital and he raced so incredibly fast that I thought this was when the real accident would happen. During this whole race I kept holding my head because I thought all the blood would pour right out of it. I also had the feeling I should at least write down my name on a piece of paper, for otherwise no one would know who was involved if I did actually bleed to death. And of course I also didn't want to dirty the man's car with my blood and I tried to keep directing the blood flow just onto me and between my knees. Soon I'm going to lose consciousness, I thought, and then that will be that. Once at the hospital, I was immediately put flat on a gurney by a nurse and taken away. In a washroom the nurse shaved half my skull. Then I immediately found myself in an operating room and I was in luck, for the surgeon spoke German and promptly asked me all the relevant questions in German— vomiting or no vomiting, et cetera. Then they gave me an anesthetic, only a so-called local anesthetic, and worked on me and sewed my head back together again. What I had thought was an enormous wound was only a laceration, after two days I was allowed to go back to Eugenia. Before, I had already been able to see my wreck at the police station right near the hospital. And to my amazement the police had been able to sketch an exact reconstruction of the accident. The Yugoslavian was one hundred percent responsible, and this was also stated in the report. The person who had kept screaming *Idiota!* as he ran away was his wife, who to her misfortune was a nurse at the hospital and, as I learned later, was instantly fired from her job in the nursing service because instead of helping me she had run away with her husband. I was sorry about this, but there was nothing I could do about it. My Herald was a lump of metal, I walked around it several times and I thought about how I'd only driven it for seven hundred and fifty miles. A shame. With a white turban around my head and my aunt and all her considerable luggage I set off on the journey home to Vienna. Not at all depressed, because finally I had by some miracle escaped with my life, but still very disappointed over the end to my automobile happiness. At the Heller car dealership they put me in touch with a Nobel-class lawyer who lived in the Heinrichshof. He would pursue the case with his renowned thoroughness, the lawyer said, while the people whom I told about my accident thought I'd never see so much as a cent from Yugoslavia, it was well known that they never paid a thing in such cases, even when the other party was one hundred percent guilty. I got angry that I'd taken on this, so it seemed to me, very expensive lawyer, I was furious over my own stupidity. Now I've not only lost my Herald, but I'm also paying the lawyer, who was set up like a prince in three or four enormous rooms with a direct view of the Opera. I'm really stupid, I told myself, a completely unrealistic person. *Amras* was typeset and I walked around the city of Vienna rather despondently. Nothing gave me pleasure, I missed my Herald, and I suddenly had a feeling again that I'd reached the end. Unlucky people never escape their bad luck, I said to myself, meaning me. It was unjust, but understandable. Every few days or weeks a letter from the lawyer fluttered in, in which he told me, always in the same words, that he was pursuing my case with the greatest diligence. Every time such a letter arrived, I went wild. But I no longer had the courage to go and see the lawyer and tell him he should give up the case, I was afraid of the enormous costs. In the Wertheimstein Park and the Zögernitz Casino I read the galleys of *Amras*. The book works, it's romantic, something born of a young man who'd been reading Novalis for months. After *Frost* I'd thought I could never write anything again, but then, by the sea, I'd sat down and *Amras* was there. It was always the sea that saved me, I only needed to go to the sea and I was saved. One morning another of those letters from the lawyer fluttered in and I was ready to tear it up. The content of the letter was different. Come to my office, the lawyer wrote to me, I have been able to settle your case with the fullest satisfaction. The Yugoslavian insurance people had actually agreed to all my lawyer's demands, without any restrictions whatever, it should be noted. Not only was my car replaced, but I also received damages. And a so-called compensation amount for my clothing that was unbelievably large. The lawyer had not admitted I was wearing nothing but cheap trousers, a shirt, and sandals, he'd stated I was in an expensive suit and most costly underwear. I left the lawyer's office in the highest order of happiness, naturally. I bought myself a new Herald and drove it very frequently to Yugoslavia, which had shown itself to be so correct and indeed so very generous to me in my misfortune. I've written all this, because, as you can see, it's all tied up with the dividing into thirds of the Julius Campe Prize. In the most self-evident way.

THE AUSTRIAN STATE PRIZE FOR LITERATURE

I RECEIVED THE AUSTRIAN STATE PRIZE FOR LITERATURE in 1967 and I must say right away that it was a question of the so-called Small State Prize, which a writer receives only for a particular piece of work and for which he has to nominate himself, by submitting one of his works to the relevant Ministry of Culture and Art, and which I received at an age in which under normal circumstances one no longer receives it at all, namely in my case the late thirties, because it has become customary to award this prize to twenty-year-olds already, which is quite right—so it was a matter of the so-called Small State Prize and not the so-called Large State Prize, which is given for a so-called life's work. No one was more surprised than I was that I'd been awarded the Small State Prize, for I hadn't submitted a single one of my works, I would never have done that, I had no idea that my brother, as he later admitted to me, had handed in *Frost* at the great entrance to the Ministry of Art and Culture on the Minoritenplatz on the last day submissions were being accepted. I was the opposite of delighted with the news that I was getting the prize, a mass of young people had received this prize before me and, in my eyes, had fully devalued it. But I didn't want to be a spoiler and I also took the prize because I would receive it thirty years to the day after my grandfather received it in 1937. This point was what made me tell the Ministry I would accept the prize with the greatest pleasure. In reality I had a queasy stomach at the idea that as an almost forty-year-old I would have to accept a prize which should be offered to twenty-year-olds, and in particular I had a very strained relationship with my country, as I do today to an even greater degree, and my most strained relationship of all was with our Ministry of Culture and Art, which I despised from close and firsthand knowledge, the first place in my contempt being held by the then-incumbent Minister. In my youth I had been in this Ministry more than once to procure a so-called Foreign Travel Grant, this was in my twenties, for I wanted to travel around a great deal almost all the time and I had no money for it, and the Ministry had given me such a grant two or three times, I know for sure I have them to thank for two trips to Italy. But every time I came out of the Ministry I cursed its officials and the way the Ministry dealt with people like me, and I also had learned to hate it for many other reasons I don't want to broadcast here. I found the officials there self-important and dull-witted, and they didn't know what I was talking about when I talked with them and they had the worst imaginable taste in any and all fields of our art and culture. In short, now I had to come to grips with the fact that one day in the new year I had to collect the State Prize for *Frost* which my brother for whatever absurd reason had handed in at the porter's lodge on the Minoritenplatz. I felt it a humiliation that they were now throwing the so-called Small State Prize at my head, but I didn't want to make a scene and my brother had succeeded in convincing me that the right thing to do was to accept the prize without protest. So now I had to go to this very Ministry and allow these very people to hang a prize on me when I heartily despised both them and it. I had sworn never again to set foot in the Ministry in which only dull-wittedness and hypocrisy reigned, but now I was in this straitjacket my brother had stuck me in. Several newspapers had played up the announcement that I was getting the prize as if it were the Big Prize while it was the to-me-humiliating Small Prize. I choked on this fact and went around for weeks with this choking in my throat. But I didn't want to expose myself by refusing it, for then everyone would have accused me again of being arrogant and mega-lomaniacal, and incapable of real self-judgment. But much as the thought of having to go to the Ministry and collect the Small Prize made me choke, I kept being saved by the fact that even the Small Prize carried a sum of money, twenty-five thousand schillings back then, that, being in debt way over my head, I urgently needed. It was these debts my brother was thinking of when he allowed himself the outrageous liberty of handing in my *Frost* at the por-ter's lodge of the Ministry. So, I admit, because of the prize amount of twenty-five thousand schillings, I came to terms with the prize, with all the horrible, repellent things that necessarily came with the prize, I still despised the prize only as long as I didn't think about the twenty-five thousand schillings, if I thought about the twenty-five thousand schillings, I bowed to my fate. The whole time I thought about having or not having the twenty-five thousand schillings, and moreover my brother was right when he said I should just go and collect the prize without any fuss and refrain from making any comments. Secretly I was thinking that the jury was indulging itself in sheer effrontery in giving me the Small Prize when of course the only thing I felt absolutely prepared to accept, should the question arise, and it had already been raised, was the Big Prize and not the Small, that it must be giving my enemies on this jury a fiendish pleasure to knock me from my pedestal by throwing the Small Prize at my head. Did they, I thought, really think *I* personally would have competed for the Small Prize and offered myself up with open eyes and in full awareness to their aesthetic dilettantism? It was possible they thought I had handed over *Frost* at the porter's lodge of the Ministry myself. That is probably the case, that's how they were and they were incapable of thinking otherwise. The people who spoke to me about the prize all assumed I had naturally been awarded the Big Prize and each time I was faced with the embarrassment of saying to them that the one in question was the Small Prize which every scribbling asshole had won already. And each time I had to explain to people the difference between the Small Prize and the Big Prize, and when I did, I had the impression they simply didn't understand me anymore. The Big Prize, I kept repeating, was for a so-called life's work and one gets it closer to old age and it's awarded by the so-called Cultural Senate which is made up of all those who have previously won this Big State Prize and there wasn't just the Big State Prize for Literature but also for the so-called Fine Arts and for Music, et cetera. When people asked me who had already won this so-called Big State Prize, I always said, All Assholes, and when they asked me the names of these assholes I listed a whole row of assholes for them and they'd never heard of any of them, the only person who knew of them was me. So this Cultural Senate, they said, is made up of nothing but assholes because you say that everyone in the Cultural Senate is an asshole. Yes, I said, the Cultural Senate is full of assholes, what's more they're Catholic and National Socialist assholes plus the occasional Jew for window-dressing. I was repelled by these questions and these answers. And these assholes, people said, elect new assholes to their Senate every year when they give them the Big State Prize. Yes, I said, every year new assholes are selected for the Senate that calls itself a Cultural Senate and is an indestructible evil and a perverse absurdity in our country. It's a collection of the biggest washouts and bastards, I always said. And so what is the Small State Prize? they asked and I replied the Small State Prize is a so-called Nurturing of Talent and so many people have already won it you can no longer count them, and now I'm one of them, I said, for I've been given the Small State Prize as a punishment. Punishment for what? they asked and I couldn't give them an answer. The Small State Prize, I said, is a dirty trick if you're over thirty and as I'm almost forty it's a huge dirty trick. But I said I'd sworn to come to terms with this huge dirty trick and I had no thoughts of declining this huge dirty trick. I'm not willing to give up twenty-five thousand schillings, I said, I'm greedy for money, I have no character, I'm a bastard too. People didn't give up, they drilled down. They knew exactly where to drill to drive me crazy. They met me in the morning

and congratulated me on my prize and said it really was high time for me to
get the State Prize for Literature, and then made a pregnant pause. I then had
to explain that my prize was the Small State Prize, a dirty trick not an honor.
But no prizes are an honor, I then said, the honor is perverse, there is no honor
in the world. People talk about honor and it's all a dirty trick, just like all talk
about any honor, I said. The state showers its working citizens with honors
and showers them in reality with perversities and dirty tricks, I said. My aunt
always had the highest opinion of our state and of states in general, her husband had been a senior state official, and she behaved as if I'd received an
honor when the news was published in the papers that I was to receive the
State Prize. So I had to explain to her too that this was the Small Prize and not
the Big Prize and once again I tried to explain the exact differences between
the two prizes and at the end of my explanation I said neither the Small
nor the Big State Prize was worth anything, both prizes were a dirty trick and
it was a low thing to accept either one of them, but I was sufficiently lacking
in character to accept the prize because what I wanted was the twenty-five
thousand schillings. My aunt was disappointed in me, until then she had had
too high expectations of me. I shouldn't accept the prize, she said, if what I
thought was what I said. Yes, I said, I think what I'm saying and I'm going to
accept the prize all the same. I'm taking the money, because people should
take every penny from the state which throws not just millions but billions
out the window on a yearly basis for absolutely nothing at all, every citizen
has a right to it and I'm not a fool. We had a worthless government that used
every means to play to the gallery and hold on to power even when the state
was going to the dogs, of course I would take twenty-five thousand schillings
from a state like this. Base or not, lacking character or not, I said. My aunt
accused me of inconsistency. She was not to be persuaded of my point of view.
I don't believe, I said, that I'm lacking character if I take the prize amount
from people I bottomlessly loathe and despise, quite the opposite. To compensate for the humiliation of being given the Small State Prize I should be able
to take a trip, so many countries even in Europe were still unknown to me, the
twenty-five thousand schillings would give me the opportunity to go to
Spain, for example, where I'd never been. If I don't take the money for myself
and use it to pay for a trip, I said, it will be thrown to some useless person in
revenge, who causes nothing but damage with his creations and poisons the
air. The closer the day of the prize-giving came, the more almost unbearably
sleepless nights I had. What possibly had really been dreamed up by idiots as
an honor, to me, the more I thought about it, was a despicable act, a behead-

ing would be putting it too strongly but even today I feel the best description of it is a despicable act. All the twenty-year-old and twenty-two-year-old and twenty-five-year-old fashionably dressed writers of radio plays I met on the street were winners of the State Prize. They behaved as if I had just been consecrated by them. It rankled. Moreover their perspective was right. My *Frost* had not received a single positive review anywhere in Austria, on the contrary, it was given a takedown in every single Austrian newspaper as soon as it appeared, not in the appropriate places, the way I'd imagined, but at the bottom, be it left or right, where worthlessness and contempt have made their home forever. I was angry, my anger had the absolute limitlessness born of lack of self-control, but in the end I kept asking myself if all these people might not be right. Perhaps I really wasn't worth any more than the value they put on me! I forbade myself to go on brooding about it. Time is pitiless. It was then too. The morning of the prize-giving had arrived. On this occasion too I was supposed to give a speech, but I'm no speaker and I can't give any speech whatever, I've never given a speech because I'm incapable of giving one. But I had to give a speech, it's a tradition that the writer, who receives this prize at the same time as a painter and a composer et cetera, gives a speech that was characterized in the Ministry's invitation as a speech of thanks. But as always, when I was supposed to give a speech, no speech came to me, in this instance too I had spent weeks thinking about what I would say, what my speech would be, but I had reached no result. What was there to say on such an occasion except the words *Thank you!* which still stick in the throat of the person who has to say them and sit in his stomach for a very long time. I found no theme for a speech. I wondered if perhaps I should go into the world situation, which, as always, was bad enough. Or the underdeveloped countries? Or the neglect of health care? Or the terrible state of our schoolchildren's teeth? Should I say something about the state per se, or art per se or about culture in any way at all? Should I even say anything about me? I found it all repellent and queasy-making. Finally I sat down with my aunt at the breakfast table and said, I can't give a speech, I have no idea what to say in a speech. I haven't thought of a theme, I haven't thought of anything. Maybe after breakfast, said my aunt, and I thought yes, maybe after breakfast and I ate breakfast and ate breakfast but still nothing came to me. Now I had my suit for best occasions on, the anthracite-colored single-breasted one, and I'd tied my tie and was struggling to swallow the last mouthfuls of breakfast and still I didn't have even the trace of an idea for a speech, suddenly I had absolutely nothing in my head except a feeling of fear, I was afraid of what was ahead of

me, if I couldn't know precisely what I was afraid of, I feared something perverse, something unlawful, something unjust, something utterly embarrassing. My aunt was all ready to go, once again she looked very elegant and I
admired her. If only I'd declined, and now didn't have to go to the Ministry, I
said. And then, at the peak of my despair, I sat down at the table in the window of my tiny room and typed a few sentences on my machine. Again it was
no speech, as they were requiring of me, again it was only a few sentences that
I had in my head. Only a few sentences, I said to my aunt, and I was embarrassed to read her these newly minted sentences. I also wouldn't have had time
to, for we had to leave, we caught a taxi on the corner of the Obkirchergasse
and the Grinzinger Allee and drove into the city. This journey was the journey
to the scaffold. The prize ceremony was taking place in the so-called Audience
Chamber of the Culture and Art and Education Ministry. When we arrived,
all the so-called honored guests were already there. Only the Minister was still
missing, Herr Piffl-Perčevič, a former Secretary of the Provincial Agricultural
Department in Steiermark with a walrus moustache, who had been summoned straight from his position in Steiermark to become Minister of the
Ministry of Culture, Art, and Education. By his friend in the party, who'd just
become Chancellor. I had always loathed this Piffl-Perčevič, for he was incapable of uttering a sentence correctly and it may be that he understood something about Steiermarkian calves and cows and Upper Steiermarkian pigs and
Lower Steiermarkian hotbeds, but he understood absolutely nothing about art
and culture although he talked about art and culture everywhere nonstop. But
that's something else. The Minister with his walrus moustache came into the
Audience Chamber and the prize ceremony could begin. The Minister had
taken his seat in the first row where the prize candidates were sitting, five or
six of them excluding me. This prize ceremony also began with a piece of
music, it was a piece for strings and the Minister listened to it with his head
tilted to the left. The musicians weren't in good shape and they stumbled in
a lot of places, but on such occasions there's no expectation ever of accurate
playing. It pained me that the musicians stumbled over all the best passages
in the piece. Finally the piece came to an end and the Minister was handed a
piece of paper by his secretary with what was probably a text the secretary had
written, whereupon the Minister stood up and went to the lectern and gave a
speech. I no longer remember the content of the speech, it introduced all the
prizewinners, some of their biographical details were read out and some of
their works were named. Naturally I couldn't know if what the Minister had
read out about my co-winners was correct, what he said about me was almost

all wrong and crude and manufactured out of thin air. He mentioned, for example, that I had written a novel that takes place on an island in the South Seas, which in that moment when the Minister shared this information was absolute news to me. Everything the Minister said was wrong, and evidently his secretary had confused me with someone else, but it didn't make me more upset, because I'm used to politicians always talking nonsense on such occasions and things that have been conjured out of midair at best, why should it be any different with Herr Piffl-Perčevič. But what did wound me deeply was the announcement by the Minister that I, and I can still hear every word in my ear, *was a foreigner born in Holland,* but who *had already been living among us for some time* (i.e., among the Austrians, of whom Minister Piffl-Perčevič did not consider me one). I was amazed at my calm as I listened to the Minister. One shouldn't hold their provinces against provincials, but when they appear in public with Herr Piffl-Perčevič's unrivaled arrogance, one should try not to let it slide. Now I had the opportunity and I didn't let it slide. A literally indescribable arrogance had displayed itself on the dull-witted, totally insensible, and unmusical face of the Cultural Minister as he proclaimed to the audience who I was. But probably even in this case nobody but my friends had any idea that the Minister was scattering nothing but dull-witted falsifications about me around the room. He felt nothing, he read out his secretary's brainless inanities in his natural monotone, one false statement after the other, one vulgarity after the next. Did I need this? I asked myself while the Minister was speaking if it wouldn't have been better not to come. But this question no longer made any real sense. I sat there and couldn't defend myself, I couldn't just jump up and say to the Minister's face that what he was saying was all nonsense and lies. I was tied to my chair by invisible cords, condemned to immobility. This is the punishment, I thought, now you have your reckoning. Now you've made yourself one of them, the people sitting in this hall listening with their hypocritical ears to his Holiness the Minister. Now you belong to them, now you're one of the pack that's always driven you mad and you've avoided having anything to do with your whole life. You're sitting there in your dark suit taking blow after blow, one brazen lie after another. And you don't move, you don't jump up and box the Minister's ear. I told myself to stay calm, I kept saying to myself, *calm, calm, calm,* I said it over and over again until the Minister was done with his arrogant outrages. He would have deserved having his ears boxed, but what he got was tumultuous applause. The sheep were applauding the God that fed them, the Minister sat down amid the deafening clapping, and now it was my turn to stand up and go to the lectern. I was still shaking with rage. But I hadn't lost my self-control. I took the piece of paper with my text out of my jacket pocket and read it out, possibly in a trembling voice, it could be. My legs were shaking too, not surprisingly. But I hadn't got to the end of my text before the audience became restive, I had no idea why, for my text was being spoken quietly by me and the theme was a philosophical one, profound even, I felt, and I had uttered the word *State* several times. I thought, it's a very calm text, one I can use here to get myself up out of the dirt without causing a ruckus because almost no one will understand it, all about death and its conquering power and the absurdity of all things human, about man's incapacity and man's mortality and the nullity of all states. I hadn't even finished my text when the Minister leapt to his feet, bright red in the face, ran at me, and hurled some incomprehensible curse word at my head. He stood before me in wild agitation and threatened me, yes, he came at me with his hand raised. He took two or three steps, then an abrupt about-turn, and he left the hall. He rushed to the glass door of the Audience Chamber without any of his attendants and slammed it with a loud bang. This all took place in a matter of seconds. Hardly had the Minister single-handedly and above all furiously hurled the door of his Audience Chamber shut behind him than there was chaos in the hall. That is, first, after the Minister had slammed the door, there was a moment when embarrassed silence reigned. Then the chaos broke out. I myself had no idea what had happened. I had had to allow one humiliation after another to be heaped on me and then I had read out what I thought was my harmless text whereupon the Minister had gotten angry and left the hall in a rage and now his vassals were coming for me. The entire mob in the hall, all people who were dependent on the Minister, who had grants or pensions and above all the so-called Cultural Senate, which probably attends every prize ceremony, all of them rushed after the Minister out of the hall and down the broad flight of stairs. But all these people rushing away after the Minister didn't rush away after the Minister without first giving me a dirty look, as I was apparently the cause of this embarrassing scene and the sudden wrecking of this ceremony. They cast their dirty looks at me and rushed after the Minister and many of them didn't stop at dirty looks, they also waved their fists at me, most of all, if I remember correctly, the President of the Cultural Senate, Herr Rudolf Henz, a man then between seventy and eighty, he rushed at me and waved his fist and then chased after the Minister with the others. What have I done? I asked myself, suddenly left standing with my aunt and two or three friends. I wasn't conscious of having done anything wrong. The

Minister hadn't understood my sentences and because I had used the word *State* not in a subservient way but in a highly critical context, he had leapt to his feet and attacked me and had run out of the Audience Chamber and down the broad staircase. And everyone else, with the meager exceptions already mentioned, had rushed off after him. I can still hear the way the Minister slammed the door to the Audience Chamber shut, I have never heard anyone bang a door that loudly. So there I stood and didn't know what to say. My friends, three or four, not more, and my aunt had moved over to me and had no answer either. The whole group turned toward the buffet that was still flanked by two waiters provided by the Sacher or the Bristol, gaping with shock, and wondered what was going to be done with the totally untouched spread. It'll go to an old age home, I thought. The Minister cold-shouldered you, not vice versa, said one of my friends. It was well said. He cold-shouldered everyone, I said. The Minister slammed the door to the Audience Chamber so hard, I thought, the panes must have given way. But when I investigated the door to the Audience Chamber, it turned out that not one pane was broken. It had only sounded as if the panes in the door to the Audience Chamber had broken. The newspapers next day wrote about a scandal that the writer Bernhard had provoked. A Viennese newspaper, which called itself the *Viennese Monday,* wrote on the front page that I was a bug that needed to be exterminated.

THE ANTON WILDGANS PRIZE*

ANTON WILDGANS, LIKE WEINHABER, is a Hölderlin of the Vienna suburbs who fits the soul of the people to a T. The prize that is named for him is funded by an industrial association that has its headquarters on the Schwarzenbergplatz in Vienna in a magnificent palace of the later nineteenth century. A week before I was to receive the Austrian State Prize, the president of the industrial association, Mayer-Gunthof, long since dead, informed me that the relevant jury had decided to give me this year's prize, which is to say the prize for 1976. The president ended his letter with the customary formula that he was extremely pleased to be able to share this news with me. At the given moment, I receive the invitation to the ceremony. The prize is endowed with twenty-five thousand schillings. I didn't give any thought to Wildgans, for I estimated him lower than my writer friends on the jury who, for whatever absurd reason, had hit upon the idea of awarding me the Wildgans Prize for 1976. In Austrian acting schools, it's customary for the students to have a constant diet of Wildgans and above all they're already learning a passage from *Armut* for the entrance exam and they spend their waking minutes reciting Wildgans poems and when it's a question of holding some highly official state occasion, be it in the Burgtheater or in the so-called Josefstadt or even in some ministry, someone is sure to reach for something by Wildgans. The dilettante's conception of Austrian poetry finds its ideal in Wildgans, as in Weinhaber, and practices it wherever there is a ceremony to be held, even today. What people admire in Wildgans is not only what they think of as his exceptionally sincere poetic art but, more importantly, the fact that he was once the director of the Burgtheater. What I myself always admired about Wildgans was his trombone-playing son, who was a musician of absolute genius and was among the most promising composers of his generation. But I don't want to talk about Wildgans here, I want to talk about the prize that bears his name. A few days before the ceremony for the State

---

*Anton Wildgans (1881–1932), poet and playwright, author of dramas of earnest social criticism, became the director of the Burgtheater in 1930. A vocal defender of Austria's independence against the National Socialists' plan to annex Austria to Germany.

Prize took place in the Ministry on the Minoritenplatz, the invitation reached me for the prize-giving in the Industrial Association, on a grandiose piece of letterhead printed by the famous firm of Huber & Lerner on the Kohlmarkt, and on which it was announced that Minister Piffl-Perčevič would be the special guest of honor. If, I thought, I want new storm windows to replace the old ones on my house which are almost totally rotted, I have to accept the prize, and so I had decided to take the Wildgans Prize and take myself off to the Löwenhöle Salon on the Schwarzenbergplatz. I mostly thought that one should take money when it's offered and no one should waste time fussing around over the how and the where, all these reflections are nothing but total hypocrisy and so I ordered the storm windows from my local carpenter, the savings on heating costs will be considerable, I thought. No sensible person says no to twenty-five thousand schillings out of a clear-blue sky, whoever offers money has money and it should be taken from him, I thought. And the Industrial Association should be ashamed of funding a prize for literature with a mere twenty-five-thousand-schilling award, when they could fund it with five million schillings right there without even noticing it, but from their perspective, I thought, they're valuing literature and literary figures quite accurately and I even was surprised at their estimate of literature and the literary figures who created it. I would have taken twenty-five thousand schillings from anyone, even the first person I met on the street. No one reproaches a beggar on the street for taking money from people without asking where they got the money they're giving him. And it would have been utterly absurd to ask the Industrial Association, of all bodies, to actually have thoughts about their Yes or No, it would have been laughable. When I add the Industrial Association's twenty-five thousand to the twenty-five thousand for the State Prize—both shamelessly low amounts for such purposes, I thought, the state should be as embarrassed as the Industrial Association, for they award literary prizes in amounts that would be a poor monthly salary for a middle-ranking municipal employee—that makes fifty thousand and with that I really could do something. The state awards a prize that's no more than a shoddy pay packet and the Industrial Association does the same and both of them thus reveal themselves to the world, which totally fails to notice how vulgar and perverse this is. The Industrial Association with its millions or rather billions uses the giving of a shoddy prize sum of twenty-five thousand schillings to elevate itself to the lofty status of a truly exceptional Maecenas of Art and Culture and is even praised for this in every newspaper, instead of being denounced for their meanness with no regard for the consequences. But my intention wasn't to denounce, merely to report. The Wildgans Prize was to be awarded a week after the State Prize. As per the invitation. But after, as I have reported, the State Prize ceremony exploded and the Minister slammed the door to the Audience Chamber in his Ministry with a huge bang and stormed out, the Industrial Association on the Schwarzenbergplatz suddenly lost their guest of honor for their planned Wildgans Prize award ceremony, for the Minister in his role as guest of honor had abruptly informed the Industrial Association that he did not wish to be the guest of honor at a ceremony whose central focus would be *a certain Herr Bernhard,* he declined and the Industrial Association was left standing. But because the Industrial Association no longer had their chief attraction, namely the Minister, at their disposal, they no longer wanted the writer Bernhard, with whom they had merely tried hypocritically to set themselves up as a Maecenas on a national scale. And what did the Industrial Association do? They canceled the entire ceremony and re-sent the same invitation cards they had had printed by Huber & Lerner on the Kohlmarkt and sent out two weeks before, not as *in*vitations now but as *dis*invitations. The celebration they had announced two weeks before would not take place and was *canceled,* it said on what I called the *disinvitation cards,* still in the same Hispano-Hapsburgian fashion of court announcements from Huber & Lerner, all in black and gold. I was sent this disinvitation minus any further communication about the whys and wherefores, just like the other invitees, and I was sent the prize certificate, also minus comment, in a shabby tube for printed matter that came by regular mail. Luckily they had also sent me, without comment, the twenty-five thousand schillings, a sum which in my view was completely inadequate for this whole tawdry outrage.

Shortly afterward I met Gerhard Fritsch, a member of the jury and my friend until then, in the Museum Café at the very table where Robert Musil used to sit, and asked him if after this disgusting business with the Industrial Association he was going to protest their behavior and step down from the jury and resign his seat. But Fritsch had no intention either of protesting or of stepping down from the jury. He had three wives and a whole bunch of children with these wives to take care of, he said, and could not indulge himself in any such protest even if it was self-evident to me, or any such self-evident resignation (self-evident to me, that is) from the Wildgans Prize jury. As a father of many children and provider for three female money-pits he felt really sorry for me and asked me to show him consideration in a tone that was repellent. The poor man, the malleable, pitiable, wretched man. Not long after this conversation Fritsch hanged himself from the hook on his apartment door, his life, which he'd bungled with no help from anybody, had closed over his head and extinguished him.

THE FRANZ THEODOR CSOKOR PRIZE

FRANZ THEODOR CSOKOR WAS A PHILOSOPHER AND DRAMATIST and the author of a book titled *As a Civilian in the War in the Balkans,* which I had discovered in my grandfather's library, and he was for many years the president of the P.E.N. club and a friend of my grandfather's whom he deeply honored, and for many years he stayed in the tavern on the Wallersee that belonged to relatives of mine and in which I ran around when I was three and four and five and six and even when I was seven and eight, without having the faintest idea who the two gentlemen, Franz Theodor Csokor and Ödön von Horváth, were who were staying below me in the large rooms embellished with their Empire and Biedermeier furniture and a whole series of valuable late-eighteenth-century pieces and magnificent stucco work and their view onto the woods. Csokor and Horváth, the two friends who wrote the majority of their plays and novels in my relatives' tavern, supposedly played with me on the wooden floors downstairs in the lower taproom and took me on walks to the lake, but I myself can no longer recall this. My grandfather often took walks with Csokor and Horváth, as I know. In my relatives' tavern was a large room on the second floor where plays were put on all year round and perhaps this was the right atmosphere for the two playwriting friends, I still remember the mountains of brilliantly colored theatrical costumes under the roof and also a piece that was put on in the room in which a naked man tied to a post was whipped, for what reason I don't know, but I can still see the scene quite clearly, it made a horrible impression on me, it was a political drama. Maybe Csokor and Horváth were inspired by this stage, it's probable. I only met Csokor one time later on, in Salzburg, what the occasion was I no longer recall, but I do remember that he sat with the novelist George Saiko and me on the terrace of the restaurant in the fortress and talked uninterruptedly about my grandfather, all things that had gone on that were unknown to me. He loved my grandfather, for the way he talked about my grandfather is the way one only talks about someone one loves. Because I myself loved my grandfather like no one else on earth, I was happy to listen. For Saiko, a thoroughly self-important and egocentric type, and then a famous man, these descriptions of Csokor's were almost unendurable, sometimes he tried to interrupt Csokor, but Csokor wouldn't allow himself to be interrupted. *This man,* said Csokor, *was once the Director of the Albertina in Vienna,* and this information impressed me enormously. After the end of the meal Csokor, who was already an old gentleman at that time was tired but Saiko wasn't tired and said goodbye to Csokor and said to me that as I was young and therefore naturally not yet tired, I should show the city of Salzburg to him, Herr Saiko, who wasn't tired either. I had no idea at that moment what catastrophe was ahead of me. Csokor had barely taken his leave before Saiko, who had written the novel *The Man in the Reeds,* started to explain to me what a novel is. So we walked through the city in the burning heat and Herr Saiko told me nonstop what a novel is. I led him from one little street to the next, from one church to the next, but all he talked about was the novel, he stuffed me full of his theories about the novel, completely obliviously, he had absolutely no idea that his incessant articulation of his theories was already giving me a headache and I hated literary theories more than anything in my life, but most of all I hated so-called theories about the novel, particularly when promulgated by fanatical theorists like Saiko, who started by extinguishing all feeling for the material in the listener by talking at full volume. Herr Saiko talked and talked and talked for four hours about what a novel is and never stopped citing major or minor novelists and sometimes he said he'd misspoken, it wasn't Joyce who'd said this or that, it was Thomas Mann, not Henry James but Kipling. My admiration that the man had once been the Director of the Albertina shriveled to the barest minimum over the course of this four-hour lecture, yes I suddenly despised this speechifier, I hated him and I kept thinking the whole time how I could get rid of him. But it was five hours, as I remember, before Saiko, having worn himself out, suddenly realized that he had more or less annihilated me with his lecture and said goodbye. I was too tired to catch my breath. I traveled to Venice overnight, as I recall, I woke up there to a beautiful morning and ran to St. Mark's Square. But who suddenly spread his arms wide when he saw me coming, Herr Saiko! Naturally I wasn't shocked by this absurdity, but willed myself to accompany Saiko to a restaurant near the Bridge of Sighs to eat cheese and olives and drink red wine. Herr Saiko had now stopped his perorations and was a pure pleasure-lover. He was going to Ancona that evening with his wife, he said, and pointed to a white ship in the background. But I didn't want to talk about Herr Saiko but about Franz Theodor Csokor whom everyone who knew him had to love. After I returned from Venice I found a letter from Csokor in which he informed me that the P.E.N. club had just elected me a member! Unanimously! By ballot!

Now I had a real mess. As with every other association in the world, I had no desire, naturally, to be a member of the P.E.N. club either. How to say this to the lovable old gentleman who wrote the Austrian national play *3 November 1918* without wounding him? I had nothing against the P.E.N. club fundamentally, even today I don't really know what it is, but on no account did I wish to be a member, I had always hated associations and societies, and of course literary associations most of all. This is the reason I only recently resigned from the so-called Darmstadt Academy which I'd never signed up for and thirty years ago I also resigned from the Socialist Party, which I had actually signed up for not long before, I didn't and don't like parties and societies. So I sat down and wrote Csokor that I was conscious of the enormous honor of being elected to the P.E.N. club by ballot, as he'd told me, but that I couldn't overturn my principle of never becoming a member of another association and it was because of this very principle that I couldn't even be a member of an association of which he, Csokor, was president. I felt dreadful after mailing the letter. I did not receive an answer. Eventually Csokor died, and then so did Herr Saiko, after he'd received the Big Austrian Prize for Literature four or five weeks before his death and had explained to me (three days before his death) on a streetcar ride from Döbling to the First District that when buying shoes you should never buy them before four in the afternoon because it's only around four in the afternoon that the foot takes on the correct and proper consistency for shoe-buying. Whenever I'm reminded of Saiko, who, as I mentioned, was the author of *The Man in the Reeds,* the first thing I think of is his lecture about never buying shoes before four in the afternoon and I have retained something of that lecture even today, and his four-hour lecture on what a novel is comes in second. But I have a real affection for both of these dead men today, whether they wrote the most incredible masterpieces of Austrian literature or not I come back to them, because my encounter with them is intimately connected with the awarding of the Franz Theodor Csokor Prize. When I won the prize which is dedicated to Csokor's memory, the people who gave me the prize assumed that of course I was a member of the P.E.N. club. When I said no, of course I wasn't a member of the P.E.N. club and told them my P.E.N. club story, they were very disappointed, for maybe they would never have given it to me as a nonmember. When I received the prize, in the P.E.N. club palace in the First District near the Minoritenkirche, presented by Piero Rismondo, the only one of the critics in Vienna who had time for my plays, I was in the process of being exposed to a particularly savage wave of personal attacks in the Austrian newspapers.

Why, I don't know. At any rate, it was definitely thumbs down. So the award gave me a real boost. Herr Rismondo, that subtle, cultivated man from Trieste, could not know that his words of approval lifted up a man who had been laid flat, that his prize speech was received greatly like music to the ears of someone who'd almost been broken. It was at this time that my *Shooting Party* and *The President* and Peter Handke's *A Leap in the Dark* were being produced and this, it is thought, caused a deputation of the so-called Cultural Senate of the state, led by their president, the writer Rudolf Henz, to the Minister of Culture in his Ministry, in the form of a resolution demanding that the Minister should kindly intervene with the directors of the Burgtheater to ensure that Bernhard and Handke would no longer be produced, Bernhard and Handke being, as one could read daily in the Vienna papers, bad writers whereas he, Henz, and his fellows in the Cultural Senate were good writers. The scribblers who were all suckling on the bosom of the state were full of themselves! Every newspaper reported this hair-raising event without a single critical comment. This is only one example of the literary mood that prevailed in the country back then against me and Handke. Not for the first time, I wondered around then whether prizes should be accepted or not. After the Julius Campe Prize, the only one I accepted with a sort of leap of joy, I had a constant empty feeling in my stomach whenever there was a question of accepting a prize, and my mind balked every time. But I remained too weak in all the years that prizes came my way to say no. There, I always thought, is a major hole in my character. I despised the people who were giving the prizes but I didn't strictly refuse the prizes themselves. It was all offensive, but I found myself the most offensive of all. I hated ceremonies but I took part in them, I hated the prize-givers but I took their money. Today I can no longer do it. Until you're forty, I think, but after that? That I didn't accept the prize money of eighteen thousand schillings attached to the Franz Theodor Csokor Prize, but had it donated to the care of prisoners in Stein,* was also no way out. Even actions like this, that have a so-called social aspect, are not free of vanity, self-prettying, and hypocrisy. The question simply no longer presents itself, the only answer is to decline all further honors.

---

* Famous Austrian prison.

THE LITERARY PRIZE OF THE
FEDERAL CHAMBER OF COMMERCE

THE LITERARY PRIZE OF THE FEDERAL CHAMBER OF COMMERCE was the last prize I received, together with Okopenko and Ilse Eichinger, for the book *The Cellar* in which I describe my time as an apprentice salesman in the Scherzhauserfeld estate on the edge of Salzburg, and from the beginning I associated this prize not with my activities as a writer but with my activities as an apprentice salesman and during the ceremony, which had no connection whatever to the city of Salzburg but which took place nonetheless in the old Schloss Klessheim on the Saalach, the only thing spoken of by the gentlemen of the Federal Chamber of Commerce who had given me the prize was Bernhard the apprentice salesman and never Bernhard the writer. I felt tremendously well among the worthy gentlemen of the merchant class and the whole time I spent with these gentlemen I had the impression I didn't belong to literature, I belonged with the merchants. In singling me out and inviting me to the Schloss Klessheim they brought back vividly a time when I was an apprentice that had served me well my whole life, supplying the population of Scherzhauserfeld with groceries under the care of my master Karl Podhala. Walking up and down in front of the Schloss before the ceremony, the autumnal mood in the park was extremely conducive to my reconstruction of my life as an apprentice, I was once again the sixteen- or seventeen-year-old in a gray work coat pouring vinegar and oil into the narrowest of necks of bottles from a height of almost two feet without a funnel, like a virtuoso, something that nobody in the shop could imitate. I carried the hundred-and-seventy-five-pound and two-hundred-and-twenty-pound sacks from the storeroom into the shop in the cellar and at midday on Saturdays I knelt on the floor to wash it while my boss did the day's accounts. I opened the concertina barrier in the morning and closed it at night and in between it was my constant wish to serve the people of Scherzhauserfeld and my master. A few weeks ago when I went into one of the hundreds of branches of Austria's largest chain of shoe shops, in one of the neighboring villages, there hanging on the wall were the rules for the conduct of apprentices I'd formulated in *The Cellar*. The management had copied these rules from my book and had them printed up for their apprentices by the hundred. I stood in the shop, where I'd wanted to buy myself some gym shoes, and read my own rules on the walls and for the first time in my literary career I had the feeling that I was a useful writer. I read my rules several times without letting on who I was, and then I bought the pair of gym shoes I wanted and went out of the shop and felt the deepest satisfaction. *The Cellar* describes my about-turn in the Reichenhallerstrasse, the moment one morning when instead of going to high school I went to the employment office to look for a place as an apprentice, and what followed. Now in the park of Klessheim I had the time and the peace before the prize-giving ceremony to yield to the melancholy that had overtaken me here in this park and I gave myself over to it happily. First alone, then with friends, I walked along the familiar walls, these were the walls, I thought, I'd slipped along at the end of the war, to cross the heavily guarded, forbidden border in the twilight. That was thirty-five years ago. Hitler had wanted to create a residence for himself in this Schloss. But where is Hitler? In this Schloss Presidents Nixon and Ford spent the night more than once, as did the Queen of England. Now the Schloss was home to the Federal Chamber of Commerce's hotel school, which is world famous. And the students at this hotel school had cooked an absolutely magnificent meal for all the participants in the ceremony, the prizewinners and everyone else, and laid a beautiful table. The prize-giving took place in the hall, opened by a quartet or a quintet. Merchants are economical with words and the President of the Federal Chamber of Commerce had accordingly kept himself brief. All three prizewinners were treated, one after the other, to a eulogy by a university professor, in which the attempt was made to base the awarding of the prize. I had, according to mine, found a totally new form of autobiography. When the checks were handed over, mine was for fifty thousand schillings. The group of musicians brought the morning celebrations to an end. As was appropriate in such a setting, everyone took their places at a table decorated with little handwritten place cards. And now, to my surprise, I was sitting right next to the President of the Salzburg Chamber of Commerce, Haidenthaller, who told me once I'd sat down that it was he who had tested me at my oral apprentice salesman's exam. He could remember the event of more than thirty years ago exactly. Yes, I said, I remember too. President Haidenthaller had a soft voice and I liked his way of speaking. My aunt was seated opposite me and my Salzburg publisher on my left. While my neighbor on my right, President Haidenthaller, fell silent once for a long moment, my publisher whispered into my ear that Haidenthaller was terminally ill, and had only another two weeks to live, cancer, my publisher whispered into my ear. When Herr Haidenthaller turned back toward me, there was naturally a new dimension to the conversation. Now I was much more careful with the distinguished gentleman who came, as I knew, from one of the oldest families in Salzburg, a dynasty of mill owners, and it turned out later that he was even related to me. He had read *The Cellar,* he said, nothing else. He had asked me about several sorts of Chinese tea in my apprentice salesman's exam and I had given the correct answers. That question was always the hardest, he said. The event was as relaxed as could be, it's the way merchants are. Today the apprentices didn't need to be able to specify so many kinds of tea at their exam, nor so many kinds of coffee, around a hundred kinds of tea and around a hundred kinds of coffee, a hundred kinds of tea and coffee all different in their look and smell, the trickiest question in the exam, said President Haidenthaller. Naturally all through the rest of the conversation with him I was thinking about what my publisher had said to me, about the imminent and inevitable death of my table companion. The whole time I was thinking what I might say to my former examiner in the apprentice salesman's exam to make this lunch as enjoyable for him as possible. We exchanged some experiences we'd had in our common hometown of Salzburg, named a whole series of names we both knew, laughed a few times, and I noticed my table companion even guffawed once. Did he know he was about to die? Or was the whole thing a nasty rumor? Conversation with someone you know is about to die is not the easiest. Deep down I was glad when the table was cleared and all the participants said their goodbyes. The prizegiving had begun so beautifully and ended so sadly. In the days following the ceremony in Klessheim I went daily to my coffeehouse in Gmunden to read the papers, and first of all always the column that contains the death announcements. Two weeks had already gone by and the name Haidenthaller had not appeared in print, neither in the deaths column nor on the obituaries page. But on the fifteenth or sixteenth day Haidenthaller's name was in the paper, in large letters and bordered in black. My publisher had only been off by one or two days, he hadn't been spreading a rumor. I sat in the coffeehouse and observed the seagulls in front of the window as they greedily pecked the old retired women's chunks of bread out of the stormy waters of the lake and screeched off and suddenly I heard everything again that Herr Haidenthaller had said to me at the table in Klessheim, with the greatest reticence and distinction that he owed to his position and his ancient family. Without the Prize of the Federal Chamber of Commerce I would not have seen Herr Haidenthaller again and I wouldn't know as much today as I know about my own forebears as I did after my meeting with him, he knew my people well.

THE GEORG BÜCHNER PRIZE

I RECEIVED THE BÜCHNER PRIZE IN 1970, when the so-called Student Revolution of 1968, having subsided as a merely romantic and thus totally unsuccessful dilettantish revolt, had already entered history as an unfit attempt at a revolution, alas. The frivolousness of this protest had finally led to a result that was the opposite of what was intended and thus an intellectual catastrophe and a sad awakening. The people pushing this movement with one eye on the French did not, as they intended, bring back to Germany the good, the best, the spirit that feared no consequences, they only drove it out for a long time with their dilettantism which had nothing revolutionary about it but was merely a fashion stolen from the French, as we can now see. The general attitudes now reigning in Germany are obviously more depressing than they were before the events of 1968. It was no movement in the sense of Büchner's and his gang's movement, only a perverse game with the intellectual boredom that has been a tradition in Germany for hundreds of years. The Büchner Prize is linked with a name I had conjured only with the deepest respect for decades. For my work in directing, at the end of my studies at the Mozarteum I chose, without needing much reflection, alongside Kleist's *The Broken Pitcher* and Thomas Wolfe's *Mannerhouse,* Büchner's *Leonce and Lena.* But because I've never been able to be very articulate about any of the things I've loved most in my life, I've also almost never said anything about Büchner. The speech that the German Academy required of me for being awarded the Büchner Prize had to go against this inarticulacy and so it never took shape. On the contrary, I was certain that I had no right to express myself in any way about Büchner on the podium in Darmstadt, indeed, I was certain that the name Büchner should not even cross my lips if possible, and in this I was successful, for I only said a few sentences in Darmstadt and these had nothing to do with Büchner. We are not allowed to keep talking endlessly about those we consider great and to hitch our own pitiful existence and inadequacies to these great ones with all our efforts and our clamor. It is customary that people when they get a Kant plaque or a Dürer Prize give long speeches about Kant or Dürer, spinning dull threads that extend from the great ones to themselves and squeezing their brains over the audience. This way of proceeding doesn't appeal to me. And so I only said a few sentences in Darmstadt which had nothing to do with Büchner, though everything to do with me. Finally I had no need to explain Büchner, who needs no explaining, at most I needed to make a short statement about myself and my relationship to my surrounding world, from the center of my own world which is also, of course, for as long as I live, the center of the world itself for me, and must be so, if what I say is going to be true. I'm not reciting a prayer, I thought, I'm taking a standpoint which can only be *my* standpoint, when I speak. In short, I spoke few sentences. The listeners thought that what I said was an introduction to my speech, but it was the whole thing. I gave a short bow and saw that my audience wasn't pleased with me. But I hadn't come to Darmstadt to make people happy, but only to collect the prize, which came with ten thousand marks and with which Büchner had nothing to do, since he knew nothing about it himself, having died so many decades before there was any idea of funding a Büchner Prize. The so-called German Academy of Language and Poetry had everything to do with the Büchner Prize, while Georg Büchner himself had nothing. And I thanked the German Academy of Language and Poetry for the prize, but in truth I was only thanking them for the prize money, for when I went to Darmstadt I no longer had any relationship to the so-called honor that such a prize was supposed to signify, this honor and all other honors had already become suspect to me. But I had no cause to share my views with the Academy, I packed my bag and went to Darmstadt with my aunt because I wanted to spoil myself and my aunt with a beautiful trip through Germany after a long barren period at home in the country. The gentlemen of the Academy couldn't have been friendlier and I had several pleasant conversations with them which contained nothing dangerous, for I didn't want anything to disrupt my trip through Germany. I had to take the prize ceremony upon myself as a curiosity and Werner Heisenberg, who was being honored in the same ceremony with a prize for scientific writing, had also said to me more than once how curious the ceremony was, what the famous critic from the *Süddeutsche Zeitung,* Joachim Kaiser, who was also getting a prize then, thought, I can't say, he was inscrutable. After the distribution of the prizes, when I said to Joachim Kaiser, who was sitting next to me in the front row, that my prize certificate was a third larger and thus also heavier than his, embodying the different relevant weights of the prizes, he made a face. But I have to say that afterward in a nearby cellar restaurant he impressed me with his knowledge of musicology, in the face of such astonishingly concentrated richness I had nothing to contribute. The city of Darmstadt gave me a lunch, to which some of my friends also came, I was allowed to provide names and they were all invited. During lunch when my aunt told her neighbor at the table, Minister Storz, that it wasn't only Büchner who had his birthday that day, it was hers too, she was seventy-six, one of the gentlemen of the city got to his feet and went out. Somewhat later he returned carrying a bouquet of seventy-six roses. Here I have to say that the main reason I went to Darmstadt was to make a beautiful birthday for my aunt, for she was born, like Georg Büchner, on October eighteenth. Of course it wasn't the only reason but it was the main reason. At the end of the meal my aunt and I signed our names in the Golden Book of Darmstadt. The newspapers covered the tripartite prize, albeit from different perspectives and with wildly different resources, in ways that pretty much matched my own opinions. The articles are there to be read. The jury of the German Academy, from which I have since resigned, because they elected me a member without my knowledge, and I couldn't defend this, is answerable for my being voted the winner of the Büchner Prize, not me.

SPEECHES

SPEECH AT THE AWARD CEREMONY
FOR THE LITERATURE PRIZE OF
THE FREE HANSEATIC CITY OF BREMEN

HONORED GUESTS,

I cannot follow the fairy tale of your town musicians; I don't want to tell a story; I don't want to sing; I don't want to preach; but it's true: fairy tales are over, the fairy tales about cities and states and all the scientific fairy tales, and all the philosophical ones; there is no more *world of the spirit;* Europe, the most beautiful, is dead; this is the truth and the reality. Reality, like truth, is no fairy tale and truth has never been a fairy tale.

Fifty years ago Europe was a single fairy tale, the whole world a fairy-tale world. Today there are many who live in this fairy-tale world, but they're living in a dead world and they themselves are dead. He who isn't dead lives, and *he doesn't live in fairy tales; it's no fairy tale.*

I myself am no fairy tale and I do not come from a world of fairy tales; I had to live through a long war and I saw hundreds of thousands die, and others who went on right over them; everyone went on, in reality; everything changed, in truth; in the five decades during which everything turned to revolt and everything changed, during which a thousand-year-old fairy tale gave way to *the* reality and *the* truth, I felt myself getting colder and colder while a new world and a new nature arose from the old.

It is harder to live without fairies tales, that is why it is so hard to live in the twentieth century; it's more that we *exist,* we don't live, no one lives anymore; but it is a fine thing to *exist* in the twentieth century, to *move,* but to *where?* I know I did not emerge from any fairy tale and I will not enter any fairy tale, this is already progress and thus already a difference between then and now.

We are standing on the most frightening territory in all of history. We are in fear, *in fear of this enormous material that is the new humanity,* and of a new knowledge of our nature and the *renewal* of our nature; together we have been only a single mass of pain in the last half century; this pain today is *us;* this pain is now our spiritual condition.

We have a wholly new system, a wholly new way of seeing the world, and a wholly new, truly most outstanding view of the world's own surroundings, and we have a new morality and we have new sciences and new arts. We feel dizzy and we feel cold. We believed that because we are human, we would lose our balance, but we haven't lost our balance; we've also done everything to avoid freezing.

Everything has changed because it is we who have changed it, our external geography has changed as much as our internal one.

We make great demands now, we cannot make enough great demands; no era has made such great demands as ours; we are already megalomaniacal; because we know we *cannot* fall and we *cannot* freeze, we trust ourselves to do what we do.

Life is only science now. The science of the sciences. Now we are suddenly taken up with nature. We have become intimate with the elements. *We* have put reality to the test. Reality has put *us* to the test. We now know the laws of nature, the infinite High Laws of nature, and we can study them in reality and in truth. We no longer have to rely on assumptions. When we look into nature, we no longer see ghosts. We have written the boldest chapter in the book of world history, every one of us has written it *for himself* in fright and deathly fear and none of us of our own free will, nor according to his own taste, but following the laws of nature, and we have written this chapter behind the backs of our blind fathers and our foolish teachers, behind our own backs; after so much that has been endlessly long and dull, the shortest and the most important.

We are frightened by the clarity *out of which our world suddenly is born,* our world of science; we freeze in this clarity; but we wanted this clarity, we evoked it, so we cannot complain now that the cold reigns and we're freezing. The cold increases with the clarity. This clarity and this cold will now rule us. The science of nature will give us a greater clarity and will be far colder than we can imagine.

Everything will be clear, a clarity that increases and deepens unendingly, and everything will be cold, a coldness that intensifies ever more horribly. In the future we will have the impression of a day that is endlessly clear and endlessly cold.

I thank you for your attention. I thank you for the honor you have shown me today.

SPEECH ON THE OCCASION OF THE
AWARDING OF THE AUSTRIAN STATE PRIZE

HONORED MINISTER, HONORED GUESTS,

There is nothing to praise, nothing to damn, nothing to accuse, but much that is absurd, indeed it is all absurd, when one thinks about *death.*

We go through life impressed, unimpressed, we cross the scene, everything is interchangeable, we have been schooled more or less effectively in a state where everything is mere props: but it is all an error! We understand: a clueless people, a beautiful country—there are dead fathers or fathers conscientiously without conscience, straightforwardly despicable in the raw basics of their needs . . . it all makes for a past history that is philosophically significant and unendurable. Our era is feebleminded, the demonic in us a perpetual national prison in which the elements of stupidity and thoughtlessness have become a daily need. The state is a construct eternally on the verge of foundering, the people one that is endlessly condemned to infamy and feeblemindedness, life a state of hopelessness in every philosophy and which will end in universal madness.

We're Austrian, we're apathetic, our lives evince the basest disinterest in life, in the workings of nature we represent the future as megalomania.

We have nothing to report except that we are pitiful, brought down by all the imaginative powers of an amalgam of philosophical, economic, and machine-driven monotony.

Means to an end when that end is destruction, creatures of agony, everything is explained to us and we understand nothing. We populate a trauma, we are frightened, we have the right to be frightened, we can already see in the background the dim shapes of the giants of fear.

What we think is secondhand, what we experience is chaotic, what we are is unclear.

We don't have to be ashamed, but we are nothing, and we earn nothing but chaos.

In my name and in the name of those here who have also been selected by this jury, I thank all of you.

SPEECH AT THE AWARDING OF THE
GEORG BÜCHNER PRIZE

HONORED GUESTS,

What we are speaking of here is unfathomable, we are not properly alive, our existence and suppositions are all hypocritical, we are cut down in our aspirations at the final, fatal conclusion of our lethal misunderstanding with nature, into which science has led us and abandoned us; appearances are deadly and all the hundreds and thousands of hackneyed words we play with in our heads in our loneliness, the words that are recognizable to us in any language and within any context as the monstrous truth revealed in monstrous lies, or better, monstrous lies revealed within a monstrous truth, the words we say and write to one another and the ones we dare to suppress, the words that come from nothing and go to nothing and serve nothing, as we know and keep secret, the words to which we cling because our impotence makes us insane and our insanity makes us despair, these words merely infect and ignore, blur and aggravate, shame and falsify and cloud and darken everything; by mouth and on paper they abuse by means of their abusers; the very character of words and their abusers is an outrage; the spiritual condition of words and their abusers is that of helplessness and catastrophic good cheer.

We say we're putting on a performance in a theater that will last for all eternity . . . but the theater in which we're prepared for everything and competent in nothing is, from the time we're able to think, a theater of ever-increasing speed and lost shorthand . . . it is absolutely a theater of the body—and secondarily of spiritual angst and thus of the fear of death . . . we don't know whether we're dealing with tragedy or comedy, or comedy for the sake of tragedy . . . but all of it deals with the terrible, with misery, with mental imbalance . . . we think we should keep quiet: he who thinks destroys, annuls, metes out disaster, corrodes, demolishes, for thinking is consistent with the dissolution of all ideas . . . we are made up (and this is history and the spiritual condition of history) of anxieties, bodily anxiety, spiritual anxiety, and the anxiety about death that drives creativity . . . what we reveal is not identical with what is, being shattered is something else, existence is something else, we are something else, the unendurable is something else, it isn't illness, it isn't death, those relationships are quite other, as are those circumstances . . .

We say we have a right to what's right and just, but we only have a right to what's not right and what's unjust . . .

The problem is to get work done, which means advancing over all one's inner resistance and evident mindlessness . . . and this means advancing over myself and the bodies of dead philosophers, over all of literature, all of science, all of history, everything . . . it is a question of one's spiritual constitution and one's spiritual concentration, of isolation and distance . . . of monotony . . . of utopia . . . of idiocy . . .

The problem is always to get work done while thinking that work will never get done and nothing will ever get done . . . The question is: to go on, heedless of the consequences, to go on, or to stop, to call it a day . . . it is the question of doubt, of mistrust and impatience.

I thank the Academy, and I thank you for your attention.

ON MY RESIGNATION

THE ELECTION OF SCHEEL, the former President of the Federal Republic, as an honorary member of the Academy for Language and Poetry, was for me the final and definitive reason to separate myself from this Academy for Language and Poetry, which in my view has nothing whatever to do with either language or poetry and the justification for whose existence must self-evidently be denied by every thinking person with a good conscience. For years I have wondered about the point of this so-called Darmstadt Academy and I have always had to tell myself that the only point consists in an association which in final analysis was founded merely for the self-image of its preening members, comes together twice a year to indulge in self-adulation, and there, after traveling in luxury at the expense of the state, eats splendid high-class dinners and drinks high-class wines in good Darmstadt hotels for almost a week while beating around the bush, literarily speaking. If one poet or writer is laughable and hard for human society to bear, how much more laughable and ridiculous is a whole horde of writers and poets and people who think they're writers or poets, all in a heap! At bottom, all these previous prizewinners come together in Darmstadt at the state's expense, after a year of impotence and mutual loathing, to spend another week in Darmstadt boring one another to death. Writers' chitchat in the hotel lobbies of provincial Germany is the most distasteful thing imaginable. The stink is however even stinkier when it's being subsidized by the state. The whole contemporary steaming subvention racket stinks to high heaven! Poets and writers should not be being subsidized, and certainly not by an Academy that is itself subsidized, they should be left to themselves.

The Academy for Language and Poetry (the most absurd title in the world!) gives out an annual *Yearbook,* and maybe this has a point? But every *Yearbook* prints so-called essays which are dust covered before they're even typeset and have nothing to do with either language or poetry, or anything to do with the creative, because they come from the clogged typewriters of thick-witted gasbags, or as we'd say in Austria, heedless busybodies. And what else is in the *Academy Yearbook,* aside from these stale effusions? A long list of all the possible and impossible obscure honors that these intellectual earthworms have received in the preceding year. Whom does this interest, aside from the earthworms themselves? Plus also, not to be forgotten, a hypocritical "list of the deceased," with embarrassing obituaries playing a sort of Academy poker game of the dead, each one raising the stakes of cringe-making stupidity against the others. A shame that this *Yearbook* is printed on such expensive paper that it's no good for heating my stove in Ohlsdorf. Every time the mailman leaves this load with me, I have the greatest difficulty with it.

But, people will say, the Academy for Language and Poetry (the Büchner Prize should be awarded to its inventors for this term alone!) gives out the Büchner Prize, the so-called most-admired literary award in all Germany. I don't see why this obscure Academy has to award the Büchner Prize, for nobody needs an Academy to hand out this award. Certainly not an Academy for Language and Poetry which is a conceptual and linguistic curiosity as its title indicates, nothing more. Seven years ago exactly, when I was elected to the Academy, I didn't think about it further or take it seriously. It was only gradually that the dubiousness of this Darmstadt Academy dawned on me, and I literally took this dubious entity seriously for the first time at the moment when I read that Herr Walter Scheel had been elected to this Academy, and I promptly resigned. If Herr Scheel is entering, I thought, I can exit at the same time.

I wish the Academy for Language and Poetry, which I consider the most dispensable institution in Germany and indeed the entire rest of the world, and which most certainly is more noxious than useful to those poets who are real poets and those writers who are real writers, the very best with Herr Scheel. Whenever one of its members dies, the Darmstadt Academy (for Language and Poetry!) always automatically sends out a black-bordered death-announcement card with an identically worded obituary text (whose language and poetry could furnish cause for argument). Maybe I'll live to experience the day when they send out a card memorializing not the death of some honorable member, but their own.

Printed in the United States
by Baker & Taylor Publisher Services